Come with me through

ISAIAH

Come with me through **ISAIAH**

David Pawson

Terra Nova Publications

Published in Great Britain by
Terra Nova Publications International Ltd.
Orders and enquiries: PO Box 2400 Bradford on Avon BA15 2YN
Registered Office (not for trade): 21 St. Thomas Street, Bristol BS1 6JS

Cover design by Roger Judd

Cover image: 'War Cry'
Original painting by Marc Jones
Used by permission.

ISBN 978 1 901949 68 1

Printed in Great Britain by
CPI Bookmarque, Croydon

Contents

	Preface		9
	INTRODUCTION	*1:1*	11
1	WHITE AS SNOW	*1:2–31*	19
2	SWORDS INTO PLOUGHSHARES	*2–4*	27
3	HERE AM I: SEND ME	*5–6*	41
4	A CHILD IS BORN	*7:1–9:7*	55
5	A REMNANT WILL RETURN	*9:8–10:34*	65
6	A BRANCH OF JESSE	*11–12*	79
7	PLAN FOR THE WHOLE WORLD	*13–23*	91
8	KEPT IN PERFECT PEACE	*24–27*	105
9	PRECIOUS CORNERSTONE	*28–29*	117
10	THIS IS THE WAY	*30–31*	131
11	THE KING IN HIS BEAUTY	*32–33*	141
12	ENTER ZION WITH SINGING	*34–35*	155
13	ROOT BELOW AND FRUIT ABOVE	*36–37*	169
14	POULTICE OF FIGS	*38–39*	181
15	PREPARE THE WAY	*40:1–11*	195
16	WINGS LIKE EAGLES	*40:12–41:29*	211
17	SING A NEW SONG	*42*	223
18	JEHOVAH'S WITNESSES	*43:1–44:23*	235
19	NO OTHER GOD	*44:24–46:13*	247
20	THE FIRST AND THE LAST	*47–48*	259
21	CAN A MOTHER FORGET?	*49–50*	271
22	BEAUTIFUL ARE THE FEET	*51–52:12*	285
23	LAMB TO THE SLAUGHTER	*52:13–53:12*	299
24	WHILE HE MAY BE FOUND	*54–55*	315
25	NO PEACE FOR THE WICKED	*56–57*	329
26	NO-ONE TO INTERCEDE	*58–59*	345
27	ARISE, SHINE!	*60–62*	359
28	TREADING THE WINEPRESS	*63–64*	373
29	NEW HEAVENS AND NEW EARTH	*65*	385
30	UNDYING WORM, UNQUENCHABLE FIRE	*66*	399

This book is based on a series of talks. Originating as it does from the spoken word, its style will be found by many readers to be somewhat different from my usual written style. It is hoped that this will not detract from the substance of the biblical teaching found here.

The outlines at the head of each chapter are intended to help with the reading, and were not necessarily fully followed in the talks.

As always, I ask the reader to compare everything I say or write with what is written in the Bible and, if at any point a conflict is found, always to rely upon the clear teaching of scripture.

David Pawson

PREFACE

The studies on which this book is based were originally preached some years ago at Gold Hill Baptist Church, Chalfont St Peter, Buckinghamshire. The unexpected attendance of a number of Anglican students from the then London College of Divinity was due to Isaiah being the set book for examinations that year!

But God's Word is timeless. Apart from the odd reference to current affairs, the content of Isaiah remains as relevant today as ever, even though it was first spoken two and a half thousand years ago. It is also the most quoted book of the Old Testament in the New. A case could be made out that it was Jesus' favourite scroll in his scriptures. The chapter titles are taken from the portion expounded. Outlines of each study were put up on a large blackboard or, later, on the service sheet. Their purpose was to reveal the shape or structure of each passage. Their only drawback was that the congregation could calculate how much longer they would have to listen!

Alliteration, the rhyming of the headings, is said to be 'the province of fools, poets and Plymouth Brethren'. I am neither the first nor the third category, so must belong to the second. It can be an aid to the memory of the preacher and the attention of the congregation. Actually, much of Isaiah is poetic as well as prophetic. The printing layout of the New International

Version clearly indicates the difference between prose and poetry. (For an analysis and description of Hebrew poetry, see my book *Unlocking the Bible*, chapter 11. There is also a useful overview of Isaiah in chapter 21.)

The Hebrew name of God is written in four consonants: JHVH, but pronounced 'YAHWEH'. Older English versions added vowels and pronounced the letters in national style to produce 'JEHOVAH', familiar from hymns such as 'Guide me, O thou great . . . .' Hence the rather risky title of chapter 18.

I recently stood in the Shrine of the Book in Jerusalem, where the entire scroll of Isaiah recovered from the Dead Sea caves at Qumran is the centrepiece. I thanked God for those who preserved the text so accurately and that it was discovered just when the State of Israel was declared. A providential coincidence. Finally, I hope the reader will have as much joy going through this book with me as I did myself in my study as I prepared this appetising food for people hungry for the truth. So 'read, mark, learn and inwardly digest the same', to quote the Book of Common Prayer. Bon appetit!

INTRODUCTION

Read Isaiah 1:1

(i) Who? (ii) When?

In the eighth century BC many things were happening around the world that have changed the course of history. Rome was being founded, as were Athens and Sparta. In the Holy Land, which is the corridor between Europe, Africa and Asia, at the centre of the then known world, a baby boy was born, to whom his parents gave the name 'Isaiah'. Of all the events of that century, Isaiah's ministry was the most important for the history of mankind. The name his parents gave him means 'salvation of God' or, in other words, 'Jehovah will save us'. They must have been a godly couple, but they could scarcely have imagined that their boy would grow up to be one of the greatest prophets of all time and would say more about salvation than any other prophet of the Hebrew people —and his whole book is a book of salvation.

Isaiah was brought up in the royal court. His parents were related to the king. Indeed, his father was the son of a king and the brother of a king of Judah. Therefore the boy grew up in high society. He was an aristocrat; he was in a wealthy family; he had access all his life to the royal court, and God used this to get his word right to the throne and the very top of the nation. He married, later in life, a prophetess, a woman whom God used to give his word to the people. This godly couple were used of God to bring a nation to listen to what he had to say to it. Isaiah laboured for some sixty years giving the word of God as God gave it to him. For those sixty years kings came and went — four kings altogether were on the throne during this man's life, and to each of them this aristocratic prophet brought the word of the Lord. He died at the age of 120, not of old age or sickness, he was murdered, sawn in pieces by a wooden saw in the days of the wicked king Manasseh. When you read Hebrews 11 and the list of heroes of faith, and come to that phrase 'some were sawn asunder', it is a reference, among others, to the prophet Isaiah. Such is the background of his life; we know very little more than this.

The important thing is not the man but his message. This book which contains the messages he delivered over forty years is a compiled collection of his writing and speaking, so there is no clear outline or order running through it. Each speech, sermon or address to the people needs to be taken by itself and we shall ask when it was given, why it was given and what it has to say to us.

I suppose that if I asked a group of Christians for their favourite passage or text in the Old Testament, many of them would choose one from this prophet, whether they knew it came from there or not. I think of such texts as: *"In the year that King Uzziah died, I saw the Lord"* (6:1). We have heard that read again and again, though when we study it I will show you that most preachers who read it are very naughty and stop reading it at the crucial verse, at the words: *"Here am I. Send me!"* (6:8), and they do not go on to read the last part of that chapter which is the most important. Or I think of 40:21, *Do you not know? Have you not heard?* Or of the theme of Chapter 40, the Creator of the ends of the earth. Or again, 53:5 (NIV),

But he was pierced for our transgressions,
he was crushed for our iniquities;
the punishment that brought us peace was upon him,
and by his wounds we are healed.

Or 55:6–7 (NIV),

Seek the Lord while he may be found;
call on him while he is near.
Let the wicked forsake his way
and the evil man his thoughts.
Let him turn to the Lord, and he will have mercy on him,
and to our God, for he will freely pardon.

One could go on reciting passages, texts from Isaiah, and you would say that you know them because you have heard them. But there are whole sections of this book that many have never read. There are precious promises of God here that some could not recall if they tried. For while some of the passages of Isaiah are the best known in the Old Testament, other parts are the least known and we have missed a great deal because we have just had our favourite passages. If you listen to Handel's *Messiah* you will hear more from the book of Isaiah in that than from any other part of the Old Testament. *He shall feed his flock. Behold a virgin shall conceive. Comfort ye, comfort ye my people. Gross darkness the people* . . . , and all the rest of it.

Isaiah could be described as the whole Bible in miniature. It is as if God took the whole Bible and squeezed it down to one book. Whilst Isaiah is difficult to analyse and break up into parts, it is not *too* difficult. There is one obvious division into two parts which are quite different from each other: chapters 1–39 and chapters 40–66. They differ in subject, content, atmosphere and tone, so some people have even thought they must have been written by different authors, but that is by no means established. I am quite sure myself from studying the evidence that the same man wrote both. There are the same peculiarities of style and phrase. Notice there are thirty-nine chapters in the first part and twenty-seven in the second. Does that strike a chord? In the Bible there are sixty-six books: thirty-nine in the Old Testament and twenty-seven in the New

Testament. The astonishing thing is that the atmosphere of the first section chapters is the atmosphere of the Old Testament and the atmosphere of the second is the atmosphere of the New.

Let me give one or two illustrations. The book of Isaiah begins with the sin of the people — so does the Old Testament. Right from the beginning, in Genesis 3, it is about *sin*. In the book of Isaiah this section ends with a promise of a coming King of righteousness who will redeem Israel — so does the whole Old Testament. The second half begins this way:

A voice of one calling:
"In the desert prepare the way for the LORD"
40:3a

In the New Testament Mark begins with John the Baptist and uses those exact words of him —

". . . a voice of one calling in the desert,
'Prepare the way for the Lord . . . .'"

About half way through this section we have a chapter, Isaiah 53, about the cross; half way through the New Testament we have chapters on the cross. What does the book of Isaiah finish with? A vision of new heavens and a new earth. When we read the New Testament it finishes with a vision of a new heaven and a new earth. I could continue drawing these parallels; I have just given a rough picture to show that Isaiah is the Bible in miniature.

Just as many people find the New Testament easier to read and understand than the Old, I warn you now that you will find the first section of Isaiah heavier going than the second. When we get to chapter 40 we will move into top gear, but in the first part we shall have to labour and struggle. There are some very long chapters, as there are some long books in the Old Testament, and it takes a certain amount of wading through and studying and understanding. But, just as we understand the New Testament best when we have got a knowledge of the Old, we will understand the later chapters when we have gone through the earlier ones.

In a sense, we have in chapters 1–39 the disease, and later we have the cure. If any doctor is going to help you he has got to tell you what is wrong with you first; he has to find out what the symptoms really reveal that is going wrong in your body, and then he will give you a prescription or tell you that you need to go to hospital. In the same way the Bible always begins here, but people don't like this. They love to hear of the cure, they love to hear of the love of God and the mercy of God and the pardon of God, but that is only the cure for the disease that the justice and the wrath of God reveal. So we go through this first to that. When you get to chapters 40–66 you can really preach the gospel from that section, and many preachers do.

Of all the books in the Old Testament, this one says more (and most clearly) about Jesus Christ. His birth is there, his family background is described, his anointing with the Holy Spirit is given in detail. His character, his simplicity and his gentleness are here described. I need not underline how chapter 53 gives us a clearer picture of Christ's sufferings on the cross than anything else in the whole of the Old Testament. His resurrection is here as well as his death. His future reign in glory is described perfectly. So we are studying a Christian book! When Jesus was on earth he taught: search the scriptures for they are about me, they bear witness to me —and the only scriptures they had were the Old Testament. But I meet a lot of people today who think that the New Testament contains all the scriptures about Jesus and that the Old Testament does not contain any. But Jesus taught that the Old Testament is about *him*, and we are going to search Isaiah for what we can find about Jesus, and we will find for example the nativity in 7:14, with the promise, "*. . . The virgin will be with child and will give birth to a son, and will call him Immanuel.*"

We start with a brief historical background before looking at chapter one. You can pretty well draw a graph of Israel's history. They were in slavery in Egypt at the very bottom of their history. They had no land, no name, no government, no king, nothing. Their history then began to climb. Moses brought them out, led them through the wilderness; Joshua brought them into Canaan and got them established and drove out the Canaanites. They had judges to rule over them and fight their battles. Then Samuel the prophet led them, and through him they got their first king, until finally they reached a peak under King David. Never did they have such peace and prosperity as they enjoyed in that reign. To this very day the Jews look back to David as the king of that golden age. That is why they longed for another king like him. But as soon as David died they began to go down. Solomon with his grandiose building schemes, Solomon with his many wives, some of them from other nations, caused such trouble that as soon as Solomon died there was civil war, and from then on the nation became two nations — Israel in the north and Judah in the south. They even fought one another — the people of God divided and fighting one another, and down they went: lower and lower went the two nations — Israel in the north with ten of the tribes in it, Judah in the south with two of the tribes.

Why did things go wrong? The people inside Israel blamed everyone but themselves. They even blamed God. But they blamed the Philistines who kept raiding them from the west. They blamed the Edomites who kept raiding them from the south. They blamed the Moabites who raided them from the east. They blamed the Syrians who raided them from the north. They saw their land increasingly ravaged, and becoming desolate, before their very eyes, but they could not see that the real people to blame were themselves and no-one else. For God had said that provided they remained obedient to him then he would keep them safe in that land from all attack. Situated as it was on that corridor it was open to attack from every direction; it was the focal point of the world; every world conqueror passed through their land. The real difficulty was that they had become disobedient people, and God had allowed these attackers to come and make life difficult and take their land from them. The prophets, from Isaiah to Malachi, were people who were sent to say one thing: the dangers outside are due to disobedience inside. That sums up the message of all the prophets. They came to say: you are to blame for your troubles, no-one else; if you were right with God then things would be right for you.

Israel, in the north, was worse than Judah, in the south. And to Israel God sent two prophets, Amos and Hosea, to tell them what was wrong. Amos came and told them of the judgement of God — of their sharp tricks in the shops, their false weights on their scales in the marketplace, their selling poor people for a pair of shoes. Amos came and told them what was wrong and they did not listen. Hosea came and in the most dramatic way: he married a prostitute. He said: I have done this to show you what you are like to God. God is your husband and he has got a prostitute for a wife and you are turning away from him, you are going after other lovers who will give you money and will make you prosperous, that is what is wrong. But Israel did not listen and in the eighth century BC the ten tribes were attacked by Assyria from the north-east and they were led off with fish-hooks in their flesh; they were taken into slavery and the ten tribes disappeared from history. That left only two tribes in the south, Benjamin and Judah, with Jerusalem the capital in the centre. Unless they saw what was wrong and put it right they would go exactly the same way. To the two tribes in the south God sent two prophets, Isaiah and Micah. That is why it says, *The vision concerning Judah and Jerusalem that Isaiah son of Amoz saw* . . . (1:1). Israel had gone; ten tribes had disappeared because they had got it wrong with God. And even though God had sent prophets to them they laughed at those prophets, they mocked them, they turned them out, they persecuted them, they would not listen. Because naturally a person who says, 'It's your fault' is not a popular preacher. A person who comes and says to them, 'Your troubles are due to you, you are not right with God', is not going to be acceptable except to those who *want* to put their lives right. And the kind of preaching that the prophets gave is never popular preaching. Jesus said to his disciples, *"Blessed are you when people insult you, persecute you and falsely say all kinds of evil against you because of me"* (Matthew 5:11, NIV). That is how they treated prophets, so I will not pretend that this study is going to be popular — at least not chapters 1–39. They are not comfortable, they are not nice, but when you get through to chapter 40 it is as if the thunder clouds clear away and the sun comes out again.

I wish to take out (or renew) a subscription to HEART newspaper for the next six issues.

Please post my papers to ....

....

....

Your email ....

tel no (in case of queries) ....

IF YOUR SUBSCRIPTION IS A GIFT, please add your name and address below:

Giver's name and address: ....

....

PLEASE SEND ME (tick box):

1 copy £14.75 p.a. ☑ **2** copies at £26 p.a. ☐ **3** copies at £34 p.a. ☐

4 copies at £42 p.a. ☐ **5** copies at £48 p.a. ☐ **6** copies at £54 p.a. ☐

If you'd like a copy of an old issue, send £2.50. For multiple copies, please see price list on our website.

Donation towards costs of printing and journalism: £ ....

Total: £ ....

Please send your cheque to Heart Publications, 24 Grafton Road, Worthing, West Sussex, BN11 1QP. Alternatively, email admin@heartpublications.co.uk, or call 01903 209383 to pay by card or online

...n September 2018, he came across ...
which seemed to be written just for him!
...iting for his bypass operation, he encour-
...elf by reading businessman Gary Guillon's
...estimony (Aug/Sept 2018). Appropriately, it
...adline 'Nearly dying showed me there is a

...is seven weeks in hospital, Stuart was able
...EART with the hospital staff and other pa-
...says: "I told them the paper had good news
...ge. I think there should be copies in every
... the country."

...sword

...ruk

...p like ... and wither (7)
... the clouds of Psalm 18:9

...ment (8)
...ospel the Gentiles are ...
... Israel (Ephesians 3:6)

...rd often ending a prayer

...night into ...

...hes of the cremated

... cannot be hidden
... (4)
...od is ... and active
...) (5)
...gns used to enclose (8)
... one to the shore
...)
... (Deuteronomy 14:15)

...e riding gear (7)

... all his ... people
... (8)
... (Isaiah 1:19) (8)

1		2		3		4	■	5		6	
	■		■		■		■		■		■
7			■	8							
	■		■		■		■		■		■
9					■	10			11	■	12
	■		■		■		■	13			
14			15	■	16	■	17	■		■	
	■	18				■	19				
■	20	■		■		■		■		■	
21								■	22		
■		■		■		■		■		■	
23				■	24						

3. To entangle (6)
4. In a business transaction; one to be removed (Ruth 4:7) (7)
5. With no chance (6)
6. To ... cats and dogs (4)
11. The ... anthem (8)
12. God spoke to them through the prophets (Hebrews 1:1) (singular, 8)
15. Type of football (6)
16. Ministering spirits (6)
17. Jehoram: he ... away to no one's regret (2 Chronicles 21:20) (6)
20. Is recognised by its fruit (Mathew 12:33) (4)

Answers on page 22

1

WHITE AS SNOW

Read Isaiah 1:2–31

A. THEIR REBELLION (2-9)
1. INIQUITY IN THE NATION (2-4)
2. RETRIBUTION IN THE PAST (5-9)
a. Ruin b. Residue
B. THEIR RELIGION (10-20)
1. INSINCERITY IN THE TEMPLE (10-15)
2. REPENTANCE IN THE PRESENT (16-20)
a. Judah b. Jehovah
C. THEIR RELATIONSHIPS (21–31)
1. INJUSTICE IN THE CITY (21-23)
2. REFINING IN THE FUTURE (24-31)
a. Purifies b. Punishes

Isaiah chapter 1 introduces the whole book but it may not have been the first thing Isaiah said in the course of his ministry. Looking into the chapter carefully, it was probably said much later in his ministry. But it is put at the beginning as a kind of summary of his message, a condensed version of chapters 1–39. We get the feel of a courtroom scene. Here is the judge sitting behind the bench; here is the dock; here is the jury; here are the witnesses; here is the charge; here is the prosecution; here is the defence; here is the sentence. On the judge's seat is God, in the dock Judah and Jerusalem, in the jury heaven and earth.

Hear, O heavens! Listen, O earth!
For the LORD has spoken . . . .

1:2

There are three basic charges: iniquity in the nation, insincerity in the temple and injustice in the city. To each of these three prosecution charges a defence is given, but God, the judge, answers that defence. One charge has already been dealt with, one is about to be dealt with and one will be dealt with in the future. God is on his throne, judging the nation.

The first charge is that of juvenile delinquency, for the judge on the throne is the Father of the prisoner in the dock. Here we have an extraordinary scene. Imagine a situation in which a magistrate said, 'Next case', and into the dock was brought his own son. What would he do? This is the drama of this chapter: God is the Father of Israel; they are his own sons and daughters, and yet God has to be the judge. He tells the jury that his children have rebelled against him. There are many parents who could echo the cry of the Father's heart here, having showered love upon their children, done everything for them, sacrificed for them, brought them up, cared for them —and when the children have got into their late teens they have rejected their parents. In this case it is even more tragic because here is a *perfect* Father who has done everything for his children, yet they are even worse than dumb brutes.

"The ox knows his master,
the donkey his owner's manger,
but Israel does not know,
my people do not understand."

1:3 (NIV)

This is a charge that could be brought against the whole world. Animals know their owners, but which men know their Creator and realise that their owner and master is the Lord? By the way, the ox and the donkey mentioned here are the origin of the Christmas cards that depict those animals, and it is the mention of the master's crib that did it! But that is quite incidental — just the first little link with Christmas in this book. The point is that those animals know better than God's children. The animals recognise and obey their owner, their master, but his own sons have dealt treacherously with him; they do not know their Father and there is no discipline in the family.

Three words are used of them. They have *forsaken*, they have *despised* and they are *estranged*, and those are progressive steps. That they have forsaken God means they have deliberately decided to have nothing more to do with him. That they have despised him means that they not only leave him but they talk about him with contempt, with laughter. And that they are estranged means that they have got so far away that they cannot come back from their side now; the relationship has been broken utterly, they do not recognise when he comes near. That has happened and is happening this very day to family after family. Children have forsaken their parents then despised them, and are now so estranged from them that the relationship has gone and they might not even recognise their own parents if they passed them in the street. That is the charge.

One of the most awful things said here in v. 2 is this. I give you my own translation: *"My people do not think, do not understand, do not consider."* There are many young people who just do not think what they are doing to their parents, nor about how their parents feel. And God, the Judge, the Father, says, *"I reared children and brought them up, but they have rebelled against me"* (1:2). They have forsaken, they have despised and now they are estranged; they do not recognise him any more. This charge God has dealt with in the past. As a good Father he has chastised his children; he has punished them. And frankly he says that he has got to the point where he cannot punish them any more. In a most awful vision Isaiah sees a man covered from head to toe with bruises, open sores and bleeding wounds. A man who has been beaten from top to bottom, a man on whom there is no flesh left to beat. And in the picture Isaiah realises that God has punished Israel in every way he can and they still go on in this rebellion.

"Why should you be beaten any more?
Why do you persist in rebellion?"

1:5a

There was no part of them that had not been touched. In fact the whole nation had felt these raids from enemies all around their borders. There was not a part of the nation that was not suffering; the whole body was sick. There were bruises that needed softening with oil, there were sores that needed pressing out, there were bleeding wounds that needed binding up from head to toe. They had been punished in every part of the body and still they did not come any nearer to God. Their land was desolate, they were like a besieged city; there were so few inhabitants left throughout little Judah that it was like a hut in a vineyard, like a little shelter in a cucumber field. That was all that was left of the cities. Even the city of Jerusalem was desolate (1:9). If there were any left, it was because God stopped punishing.

You would think that people who rebelled against God and despised him and became estranged from him would not worship, but the peculiar fact of our human race is this: we are incurably religious. We read now that, though they had got away from God, the temple was packed, they had no shortage of sacrifices, they still held their religious feasts; they still burned their incense and they still brought the blood of rams, goats and bulls. Religion was booming! We need to learn this lesson: booming religion does not mean that people are near to God; full churches do not mean that people are near to him. Because we are incurably religious we can rebel against God and be estranged from him and go to church and go through all our ritual and services. You can have a beautiful cathedral and the most moving songs and music, the most eloquent preaching and prayers, and the people in that cathedral may be a million miles from God. We need to know that religion does not mean godliness. Although these people had got away from God they kept up their religion. I find this a very deep challenge and I want to pass it on to your heart too. Because you are in church, because you like the services, because you are regular every Sunday, it does not mean you are godly. You can go through all the outside of it without having the inside of it, and many people do. Why do people do this? For one thing it keeps their conscience quiet. You feel that if you have done your bit in the services that will keep God happy for another week! That is what they thought here. And God speaks through the prophet and says that he is fed up with it. That is the literal Hebrew. It may be translated 'I have had enough' or 'I am filled', but literally, in modern English, God is 'fed up'. He is fed up with people who have the outside of religion and not the inside, people who don't behave as his children during the week, and come on Sunday with their big collection, people who worship with the right ritual but don't have righteousness in their hearts.

This is a strong message but it is the message of most of the prophets. God looks at the heart, and if their hearts are not right he will not listen to their prayers. (See v.15.) So the first question we must ask of every service is this: what has God got out of it? What is it to him? It does not really matter whether we have had a good time or not in church, the important question is has God had a good time? Has God been blessed? Has God been glorified? Have our prayers and our praise reached him and pleased his heart? They may have come away from the temple service saying, 'Great service this morning — packed out. And did you see all those sacrifices? Wonderful service, and the music and the incense, wasn't it great?' And God might say: I didn't have a good time. I was fed up with it because you are not my children. You don't recognise your heavenly Father during the week.

What is God going to do about this? What the Judge now says has been handled badly in the translations. He says two things. He says that what he is really wanting from you when you come to worship him is not incense and sacrifices but, first of all, *repentance*. He wants people who realise that they are in the wrong, and who will wash themselves and clean themselves up, cease to do evil and learn to do good and put right what is wrong. That is the sort of people God wants. That is what repentance is. When they came to John the Baptist and said will you baptise us? John said, *"Produce fruit in keeping with repentance"* (Luke 3:8), and they asked what he meant. He answered, *"The man with two tunics should share with him who has none, and the one who has food should do the same"* (Luke 3:11). He also told the tax collectors that if they were making more money than they ought to by sharp practice, then they were to go and put their books straight. He told soldiers not to extort money from people by accusing them falsely.

Supposing I did that. Supposing I repented of my past and put right what was wrong. Supposing I ceased to do evil and learned to do good. That has not been the whole answer to this charge of hollow religion. The whole answer is this: what do I do about those things I have *already* done wrong? Supposing I turn over a new leaf this morning and cease to do evil and learn to do good from now on — that does not deal with *past* evil, does it? It just stops the bill getting any bigger, but it does not cancel the debt of my sin. What deals with that?

The Judge says, *"Come now, let us reason together"* (1:18). But the best translation here is JB Phillips': "Let's settle the matter now." The Hebrew word does not mean to *discuss* together. It is not as if God is saying, Let's sit down and have a discussion group, you put your point of view, I'll put my point of view and we'll try to come to some agreement! God does not talk to us like that. God says: Come now, let us settle the matter, let's deal with it. You repent and I'll wash your sin away. Let's try and get this case dismissed, let's try and get it dealt with once and for all here in this court right now. You wash yourselves, make yourselves clean and that will mean that you have repented of your sin, and I'll take those sins of which you repent and though they are double dyed I'll get them out. Scarlet was the strongest colour dye in the ancient world. If you got some scarlet on your clothes you would never get it off, a bit like blackcurrant juice today. This scarlet dye was a very deep purple; incidentally, it was the colour of the robe that Jesus wore when they dressed him up with a purple robe (they called it purple then, but it was deep scarlet), and God says that though your soul is as deep-dyed in sin as that, if you repent he, the Judge, will wash you whiter than snow. There is nothing whiter than snow known to man, it sparkles with whiteness. All the soap powders in the world cannot get your clothes like snow — hang your clean clothes out against the snow and you will find out! So on this charge of insincerity in religion, if they would repent, cease to do evil, learn to do good, God would deal with their sins and wash them clean. If they accepted this they would eat of the fat of the land, no more trouble, but if they refused and rebelled they would die by the sword, as some of their fellow countrymen in Israel had already done.

The third charge is that because they had rebelled against God not only did their religion go wrong but their relations with their fellow men went wrong. When people get away from God, justice goes. Everybody is after a bribe, everybody is after money, everybody gets selfish — and is this not what is happening to our nation at the moment? The two groups that suffered most in those days at any rate, because there was no-one to look after them, were widows and orphans. There were no pensions, there were no societies to care for them, and in a day when everybody became selfish they suffered.

Charge number three is that in this city of God which was a byword for justice and fairness, commerce was now the biggest thing. That is why the Judge calls the city a 'harlot'. Instead of honour, profit has now become the main consideration. So we have a city that used to be the place where people went to find justice and fairness, to have their rights vindicated. This was the court of the nation — now injustice. The Judge says: *"I will turn my hand against you"* (v. 25a) In v. 31 we learn that this would result in fire —and within a very few years Jerusalem was burned down. God brought back into the city many years later, after it had been burned down, people who would be fair and honest and just, and that city was once again to be called the city of fairness, the city of righteousness, the city of justice, the city where people think of each other's needs and rights. But the city would have to go through a terrible time before it was cleaned up. History proved that God did clean up the city by fire.

That was the courtroom scene and it is a moving one. History has proved the word of God to be true. Everything that I have written in this chapter is historical fact. You can now read the history books and you can read this as history, not just as prophecy. The mouth of the Lord has spoken.

2

SWORDS INTO PLOUGHSHARES

Read Isaiah 2–4

A. HIGHNESS OF JERUSALEM (2:2-4)
1. INTERNATIONAL PILGRIMAGE (2-3)
2. WORLD PEACE (4)
B. HAUGHTINESS OF JACOB (2:5-4:1)
1. MEN - IDOLATRY (2:5-22)
a. Their folly (5-11) b. Their fall (12-19) c. Their fear (20-22)
2. CHILDREN - INSOLENCE (3:1-15)
a. Their freedom (1-5) b. their frustration (6-7) c. Their fathers (8-15)
3. WOMEN - INDULGENCE (3:16-4:1)
a. Their flamboyance (16-17) b. Their finery (18-24)
c. Their femininity (25-4:1)
C. HOLINESS OF JUDAH (4:2–6)
1. INDIVIDUAL PURITY (2-4)
2. WILDERNESS PROTECTION (5-6)

One of the problems of studying the prophets is that they are constantly changing their viewpoint. Sometimes they are looking at the nation of Israel through a microscope and sometimes through a telescope. In the passage before us, which is one whole prophecy from chapters two to four, we have the interchange between these two instruments. In the first section (2:2–4) Isaiah is looking through a telescope at his nation. Then (in 2:5–4:1) through a microscope. Then he goes back to the telescope. Obviously I am expressing this metaphorically, and what I mean is this: when he looks through the 'telescope' he sees the distant future in the general picture; when he looks through a 'microscope' he sees the details of the present, he sees the wrongs among the people of God. This is the kind of detail that comes out when he uses that viewpoint. Then he switches back to the distant viewpoint of the future of the nation. There is a balance in this. Whenever he looks through the telescope he has a message of good news, hope, comfort — but whenever he looks through the microscope he has a message of bad news, condemnation, judgement. When he looks into the future there is a kind of lift in his words and your voice rises as you read them aloud, but when you look into the present there is a hush that comes on you, as it hits and you begin to realise what awful things are being said about the people of God in the present. So we have a sandwich, and this is the balance of true preaching — to offer at the same time justice and mercy, punishment and pardon; condemnation of the present but hope for the future. A Christian is both an optimist and a pessimist: a pessimist about the present, an optimist about the future, and those two together make him a realist.

We turn first to the vision. Notice that he *saw* (not heard) this prophecy; it came in the form of a vision. And the first picture he saw through his telescope was a remarkable one — of the future of the people of God. It is as relevant as tomorrow morning's newspaper. It concerns the problems of world peace and disarmament, things with which our statesmen are grappling today. Here is the Bible's answer to man's search for world peace, world disarmament and nations living together.

Let me draw the picture for you. Looking through his telescope he sees a range of mountains and recognises them as the hills and mountains of Judea. But as he looks more carefully he notices that a change has taken place in the topography of the land. A mountain that was comparatively low is now the highest, standing out above all the others. I have a photograph taken from the south of the mountains around Jerusalem, surrounded by the hills of Judea (including the Mount of Olives) which are higher than Mount Moriah. If you can imagine a nightlight in a soup bowl you have roughly got the geography of Jerusalem. That little nightlight is Mount Moriah, the holy mountain of God on which the temple was built. It is surrounded by the ring of hills that are higher than Mount Moriah. But now in the vision the middle mountain has risen above the others and become the highest of all, so that the temple can be seen from every direction; so the house of the Lord has been lifted up above and is not hidden in that hollow. You cannot see the house of God, you cannot see the temple area from further than a mile away from any direction in the *present* geography of the Holy Land —but *then* it is high and lifted up. As he looks at this high mountain with the temple of God on top of it, Isaiah sees a stream of people all climbing up to the temple. As he looks more closely, he is astonished. He sees something that he has never seen in his life: people from *all* the nations of the world. Yet that is a thing the Jews never saw — they only saw streams of Jews coming up to the temple. So the remarkable thing here is a picture of Gentiles seeking the God of Jacob, the nations of the world turning to the Jewish faith, the Jewish God. Why? Disillusioned with every other source of help, the nations of the world at last are turning to the God of Jacob for advice. They are bringing their problems to him. The relevance of all this seems so clear. We think of the spectacle of statesmen trying their level best in sincerity to sort out their differences, rushing around from warships in the middle of the Mediterranean to big buildings in New York, and the futility of it strikes you, because there is no one centre to settle all our problems. There is the International Court at the Hague, a fine building which was erected to be a kind of consulting centre where all the nations could bring their differences, that could settle in justice the problems of the world — it has never really worked out, nor will it. A Christian is pessimistic about the United Nations as a Christian was pessimistic about the League of Nations. Why? Because there can never be any just solution to our quarrels and differences until the nations of the world turn to the God of Jacob for his word, for his judgement, his fairness, his advice.

Notice that as soon as the nations turn to God, the God of

Jacob — I do not mean when all the nations become religious I mean when all the nations turn to one God, the Jewish God, the God and Father of our Lord Jesus Christ — when they bring their international disputes to him, they will get such a fair and a just answer that this will satisfy them completely and they will immediately engage in a policy of disarmament. To advocate a policy of disarmament *before* the nations turn to God's will would be utter folly, because the positive justice on which peace is based is still lacking, and only when there is righteousness can there be peace, only when God's will is done can we safely disarm — and how we would love to do so.

Three things are stated here. First, the nations would stop building up armaments, and throw the resources released into food production. Wouldn't it be a wonderful world if we could do that? When God reigns, and he conducts the affairs of the nations and we stop trying to conduct the affairs of the world ourselves, then nations will not build up armaments, we shall beat our spears into pruning hooks and swords into ploughshares to produce food. Here is the divine solution to our problem.

The second thing that is said here is that *Nation will not take up sword against nation* (2:4), meaning that there will be no aggression in the world and therefore no need for defence. All our armament is against aggression. But if there is to be no aggression as well as no armament there is no use for defence.

Thirdly, there will be no armies, no national service. Why? Nations shall not learn war any more. We shall not teach our young people to be soldiers and how to fight and kill. They will not even have military training in the world.

Here is the big question: how and when will all this happen? Some commentators feel that Isaiah is simply painting an ideal picture, and I think some of them would go on to say it is an idle picture as well as an ideal one. They think he is only saying that if the nations would see God then we could disarm. I want to disagree profoundly with that. There is nothing conditional about this prophecy; it is a definite prediction, not an offer.

I am thrilled to be able to tell you that I am convinced as a Christian that this is going to come, that there will be world peace, that there will be disarmament, but it is God who will bring it and not man. Any hope that man can do this is an empty, vain hope. Christ said that we would hear of wars and rumours of wars until the end of history, and we will; it is God who must do this, but one day I can see the nations turning to God as their ruler, turning to the Lord as their King and settling their differences in a proper, reasonable way by *his* justice. Only God knows every factor in a situation. Heads of government do not know everything about each other's countries, only God could tell them what it is absolutely fair and right to do. The UN is not omniscient and one sees the confusion of thought about situations even in the Security Council. Only God knows what is right in any situation, and only when all sides seek the God of Jacob can it be solved.

Some others have felt that this picture is being fulfilled in the church, that from Jerusalem came out the gospel of peace to every part of the earth, and that gospel has brought all nations together into the church. I agree there is an element of truth in this, but you have really got to force the prophecy to fit this kind of interpretation. The church has not been able to bring peace between nations (or disarmament), nor do I believe it ever will.

So how and when will this come? Linking this up with other scriptures, seeking to interpret scripture by scripture, it seems to me that here we have a promise that is linked to the return of our Lord Jesus Christ. You cannot have the kingdom without the King; you cannot have peace without the Prince of Peace. It seems to me that here we are looking forward to that consummation of history, that 'one far-off divine event to which the whole creation moves', that event of our Lord's return when he will come and establish such a reign of righteousness and peace as the world has never known. That is where my hope is placed, in the coming of Christ, the only one who could rule this world safely, the only one whom absolute power would never corrupt, the only one who could handle such authority as world authority and handle it wisely and well, and rule in justice. What a wonderful vision of world peace, when the nations turn to the God of Jacob, and putting his judgements into practice discover that they can disarm, go all out to produce food, abandon their armies and not learn war any more, knowing that no nation will be an aggressor against any other. That is a wonderful picture; it is a wonderful promise; it is a certain prediction.

From the glory of that future we turn to the grim realities of the people of God in that very place, Jerusalem, in the present. We turn from that wonderful picture to a most horrible picture of the house of Jacob as it was seven hundred years before Christ came, the time in which Isaiah lived, and the question is: in view of your glorious future why don't you walk in the light of the Lord now? In view of what your God is going to do, why are you living like this? He paints not a caricature but a dreadful picture of Israel as it was in his day. Quite frankly as I read this picture I discover a picture of the world *today* — men, women and children without God. Let us see what the picture reveals.

In a household there are men, women and children. In the household of Jacob there were these three groups and Isaiah looks at each in turn. What are they doing? How are they behaving? This is the people of God; the one nation to whom the Messiah was to come. The first thing is that the men are given to idolatry. In all the three paragraphs about the men the word *idols* comes every time. But there is more to it than that. Vv. 5–11 quite briefly describe their folly. I approach these verses by asking: in what were those men putting their trust for the future? What were they trusting to see them through? The answer is four things: superstition, money, military power and idols. The world of today is doing very much the same thing, but let us look at the world seven hundred years before Christ.

Firstly, superstition – the land was full of soothsayers, astrologers, horoscope writers, diviners and practitioners of black magic and the occult. It astonishes me that this is here in the twenty-first century too. Right through Europe there is a wave of superstition in this scientific age. There is hardly a popular magazine or paper that would dare to go to print without its horoscope, one of the most popular columns. Many do not realise that by dabbling in these things they are playing with fire. People have been led away from the Lord by such superstition. The people were trusting in their horoscopes, their stars, their 'luck'. And a nation that becomes a gambling nation is a nation that becomes a superstitious nation, because it is a nation putting its trust in luck. A nation that does that is a nation that cannot trust in the Lord.

Secondly, they were putting their trust in money. The land was filled with silver and gold and there was no end to their treasures. They were investing, trying to get as much laid up for their future as possible, like the foolish rich man of whom Jesus spoke. The folly of it, because when you die you have got to leave every penny, and money is not going to keep its value even during your lifetime. If your future is trusting in money and only in money it is folly.

Thirdly, trusting in military might. The land was filled with horses and chariots, the latest military weapon. And God had said: you must never have chariots among my people, I will protect you; you don't need the latest weapons.

Finally, they put their trust in idols. There are two sorts of idolatry. One is to worship something God has made, whether it is a tree, a mountain or a river. The other is to trust something man has made. Here is a man who has taken a block of wood and shaped it and then he bows down before it and says: I trust you to get me out of trouble. The folly, the degradation of it!

Their land is full of idols;
they bow down to the work of their hands,

to what their fingers have made.
So man will be brought low and mankind humbled —
do not forgive them.

2:8–9 (NIV)

There is still idolatry today — and many people idolise human achievements, thinking too highly of what we have made and done. We put our trust in our own power, the power of our hands and our minds, thinking we can get ourselves out of trouble. The result of idolatry was that men were proud of themselves, their money, their armies, their idols. But God can bring everything that is high down to the ground (see vv. 12–19). He can bring the highest tree down — the cedars of Lebanon or the oaks of Bashan. He can bring the highest hills and mountains down to a plain; he can bring the highest walls and fortifications down; he just needs to blow to bring down the ships with the tallest masts, which sail to Tarshish. God is going to bring down the proud who put their trust in money, in luck, in military power, and in things they make.

In 2:20–22, the fear that will come in that day is underlined. In the hills of Judea (which are made of limestone) there are many caves, as there are in the rocks of Cheddar Gorge or Derbyshire, because wherever there is limestone the water wears away the rock. In Judea, whenever men were frightened, whenever they were attacked, they made for the nearest cave as their shelter. When God comes to humble them,

Men will flee to caves in the rocks
and to holes in the ground
from dread of the L*ORD* . . . .

2:19a (NIV)

There is no terror like the terror of a proud man who is going to be brought low. If you are humble then you will not be afraid of being brought low, you need fear no fall. But a proud man is afraid of losing his money, power or position — afraid of being humbled.

From studying the men we turn to the children. First of all, God says they are going to get their freedom, because he is going to remove from the land all those who restrain the young people and guide the nation. He is going to take away the elders, the princes, the rulers, the magistrates, the army. As a matter of fact this is what happened. If you read 2 Kings you will learn how Nebuchadnezzar came and took away all the leaders of the nation. Who was left? Young people without leadership. What happened? They became insolent to the elderly. The base fellow became insolent to the honourable. Boys became their princes, babies ruled over them, people oppressed one another — there was anarchy, chaos. When young people are without leadership and guidance this is the result. They are quite incapable of ruling and leading themselves. We have a picture of a nation ruled by incompetent youths. The people are frustrated as they try to appoint leaders and fail. We are shown a breakdown of society: young people, without the older leaders of experience and wisdom, trying to get leaders from among themselves, who will not take the job on because there is such chaos.

Notice that Isaiah says that the fault is not theirs but their fathers'. The next paragraph tells us that God's people are ruled by women and children because of the men doing what they did. It is all very well saying it's the young people's fault. It was the fathers' bribery, corruption and avarice that led the young people astray. If young people would do anything for money and become violent for money, was it because they saw in their parents people who just wanted more and more money? So Isaiah now castigates the parents for their partiality, their bribery, the fact that they enriched themselves and ground down the faces of the poor. If parents are like that, you cannot blame young people for going astray. So the third paragraph about the children is a kind of woe upon the nation that it was the elders and the princes who lined their own pockets; there was corruption at the top and young people were simply following them. When there can be immorality in a cabinet minister in his forties or fifties, can you say it is entirely the fault of the young people that they are not chaste in their relationships? Isaiah's message is clear: God is your Judge, and he contends with you in his court. You should have been fair, you should have been honest, just and impartial; but you were not, you were too busy taking bribes, and it is because of this that the young people rule you; it is because I have taken you away that they have their way. You were not fit to lead them.

So much for the children. Now we come to the very down-to-earth prophecy about the women who formed the social set of the national capital in this degraded society. The women reflect social standards as much as anyone else. We have here an awful picture of the women of the city. Notice that it was in a day when the poor were being ground down in the countryside. What were the women of the city doing? Lavish, extravagant luxury sums it up. The women were going all out for clothes, luxuries, everything they could get, in a day when the poor were getting poorer, the rich were getting richer, as incidentally has been happening in Britain for some time. Three things are said about the women here. Remember that the hand that rocks the cradle rules the world. Remember that a degenerate womanhood can wreck a nation. Remember that even when men go astray it is the mothers who often hold the moral standards for their families, again and again. Now let us look at what the women were like.

Amos, who was prophesying in the north of Israel just before Isaiah prophesied in the south, said much the same thing about women. He called them the 'cows of Bashan' — not a very pleasant title but it was a realistic one. Isaiah talks about women who instead of being modest deliberately flaunt themselves at other men, walking down the streets with wanton eyes, mincing steps, throwing themselves at the men, deliberately going out of their way to be over-attractive to them. That is the import of the first paragraph. He is talking about married women who want to flirt with other men's husbands, openly, in the streets. God, with a terrible judgement and a poetic justice, says to them: You want people to look at you, do you? I will smite your heads with a disease that will bring unsightly scabs upon your head, and when they look at you they will turn away from you. You are going all out to make the men turn around when you walk down the street, then I'll make them turn away from you in disgust. You are exposing yourselves more than you should, then I will lay bare your secret paths, I'll make you go the whole way. These two things came true in history. Those women did get that disease and when the Assyrians came, we know from historical records, those women were stripped and led away naked as slaves. God said: if you are throwing yourselves at men like that, then this is the punishment that will come. It came because they took no notice of Isaiah the prophet. They laughed at this young man saying such things.

From their attitude, and their flaunting themselves at others, Isaiah turned to their finery, their clothes, and there is such a list of the fashions of Jerusalem. They had their dress designers; they had everything; they had their 'West End'. Some people have said that Isaiah must have been pretty observant of women's clothes. May I remind you that it was God who said this! God listed what they wore. I read a testimony of a girl who said that when she realised that Jesus noticed what she wore and she began to dress to go out with him each day, her habits of dress changed. To every woman of the people of God, Isaiah's words pose the question: who are you dressing for — men or the Lord? That does not mean that Christians will be dowdy, untidy or unattractive, but it does mean that they will remember that the Lord notices what they put on. That is a sobering thought. But they did not listen to Isaiah the prophet, they went on with this dress and God said that instead of their perfume they would smell. Instead of their beautiful robes — the very latest fashions — sackcloth, the poorest covering for the human body; instead of beauty, shame; instead of a sash, a rope of slavery. To women who had ignored God and lived for men rather than the Lord this was the prophet's word.

The third thing he told them was this. We need to remember that in the Middle East it was considered a reproach and disgrace to be unmarried. It is not today because there are now many other callings for women, but in that day there was no other but marriage. Since parents often arranged the marriage, parents were regarded as responsible to see that their child got married, and if they did not it meant that they thought that there was something wrong with their child. Isaiah says that you are so keen on getting men that one day after Jerusalem has been sacked men will be so scarce that seven of you ladies will take hold of one man and you'll say: look, we'll pay for our own keep, we'll earn our own bread, we'll wear our own clothes — even though the law in Exodus said the husband must provide food and clothes for his wife — we'll do all that, just let us be called 'Mrs', just let us be called by your name. You who are so keen to get hold of the men, not content with one husband, seven of you will be trying to get hold of one. Again it came true and it is a sad picture. It is interesting that after both world wars there were letters to the British press advocating polygamy because of the shortage of men after those wars had devastated social life. This was going to happen to Jerusalem. God will humble the proud. Whether men are proud of themselves or women are haughty, God will bring them low, but the humble will be exalted.

So we come to the final picture. We look back into the 'telescope'. We have looked at the glorious future of Jerusalem as a world centre of peace and justice, the nations disarming and producing food and living together without aggression. Then we turn from that to the horrible social degradation of Isaiah's day — and, as I have tried to hint, a picture in miniature of the nations of the world today. But now let us turn our eyes back to the future. The prophecy here ends as it began, with hope, comfort and encouragement, with the divine answer to the wrongs of man. The contrast to human pride and glory is divine pride and glory. There is nothing wrong with pride and glory provided it is in the right things, and it is not to be in ourselves, it is to be in the 'Branch of the Lord'. This is a strange phrase that had never been used in the Bible or in Hebrew history until this point. What is this? The question we should really ask is rather: *who* is this? When you read through the rest of Isaiah, and then you read Jeremiah and Zechariah, you find this phrase again and again: the Branch of the Lord, or the shoot of the Lord, or the sprout of the Lord, the new 'Branch' of Jehovah. We come to the wonderful discovery that the Branch of the Lord is to be the Christ, the Saviour, the Messiah. This was one of his titles. We find it used right through the prophets, and I believe in the New Testament. The branch, the shoot, is to come out of God. He is to be the pride and glory of Israel. We are not to be proud of our own dress, our own achievements, our own money, our own military might; our pride and glory must be in the beautiful and glorious branch of Jehovah. This is the first mention in the prophets and in this prophecy of Isaiah of someone who is to come to bring the glory of God to the people of God, and it is in *him* that we are to find this glory. When he comes, this branch of God, about whom I will say much more later as we continue our study of Isaiah, he will bring two things.

First, he will bring individual purity. The survivors of Israel and Jerusalem shall each be called holy, and those shall survive whose names are written in the book of life. Here we have a picture of *individuals* made holy. This is part of the future Isaiah sees. Not only that, but he sees a return to the days of the wilderness when God protected his people. He sees above Jerusalem and Judah a canopy, a pavilion. He sees a pillar of cloud by day and a pillar of flaming fire by night. This is back to the wilderness where God watched over his people. They had no money in the wilderness, no army, no chariots, no soothsayers, no magic, no idols, except for that one regrettable lapse of the golden calf — but they had God. They had a pillar of fire, and Isaiah sees that returning. He sees God's protection as in the days of the wilderness once again over his people, as it is *not* in the days of Isaiah. When the Assyrians came there was no canopy over Israel, there was no pillar of cloud or fire, there was no protection, the Assyrians took them off. When the Chaldeans came, when one enemy after another came — the Egyptians, the Greeks, the Romans — there was no protection, God was not over them because they had sunk into sin. But Isaiah sees in the future the people of God under the shade of God — shade from the sun and a shelter from the rain and storm. It is a picture, but a picture of protection, God looking after his people. So not only is there international peace with the nations coming to the God of Jacob for their judgements, there is a wonderful picture of individual purity and God's protection as in the days of the wilderness.

We have looked at three sections. Two are about the future. They are hazy but we can see the main outlines. We can see the details of the present much more clearly through the microscope. Every single thing predicted in the middle section (2:5 – 4:1) about the men, the children and the women came true historically. We can read the secular records; we can read the records in the books of Kings and Chronicles. On those grounds, I dare to believe that the first and the third sections will equally come true. When God says he will do a thing he does it. Sometimes he is a long time doing it, but he does it. In the fullness of time God sent his Son born of a woman. Think how many centuries God took to prepare, how long he waited — four hundred years after the last prophecy of Malachi he waited before sending Jesus, but he said he would send him and he did. It may be a long time yet or it may be a short time until we see the international peace for which we long, but I know that God is going to send it. This is God's word, no-one has ever been able to prove, nor will they ever be able to prove, that what God says he will do he has not done.

3

HERE AM I: SEND ME

Read Isaiah 5–6

A. THE VINEYARD OF GOD (5:1-30)
1. SONG OF JEHOVAH (1-7)
a. Real disappointment (1-4) b. Right decision (5-7)
2. SINS OF JUDAH (8-30)
a. Woes - material pursuits (8-12) b. Warnings - exile (13-17)
c. Woes - mental perversions (18-24) d. Warnings - invasion (25-30)
B. THE VISION OF GOD (6:1-13)
1. SIGHT OF JEHOVAH (1-8)
a. Holy light (1-5) b. Healing love (6-8)
2. STUPOR OF JUDAH (9-13)
a. Deadened hearts (9-10) b. Deserted homes (11-13)

Chapters five and six are among the best known in the first half of Isaiah. You have probably heard chapter six read so often that you could almost recite it by heart. *In the year that King Uzziah died, I saw the Lord seated on a throne, high and exalted* . . . (6:1), right through to *"Here am I. Send me!"* (6:8). The difficulty is that whenever I have heard chapters five or six read in church I have noticed that every single time the reader has stopped halfway through the chapter, and this is really not fair, nor is it helpful. Next time you hear this passage read, notice that they stop with the words *"Here am I. Send me!"* This of course tends to obscure the real meaning of the passage; unless you read the second half of each chapter you will not understand the first half, and the big advantage of studying whole chapters in the Bible is that we get the point by seeing how one thing leads to another. Similarly, you cannot understand the matchless song of the vineyard at the beginning of chapter five unless you read the end of that chapter.

We begin, then, with chapter five, the story or song of the vineyard — a song about God. It seems as if by this time the people were getting sick of Isaiah's preaching and he had a job to make them listen. So he tried an unusual way of presenting the message of God. The strange thing is that sometimes people who do not like listening to sermons will listen to a song, Notice that it was a love song Isaiah gave the people. No doubt they gathered to listen. This was something new, a prophet singing a love song, and he began to sing. At first it sounded like an ordinary love song, but as he sang his way through this song, under the inspiration of the Holy Spirit who supplied both words and music, there were four startling things that emerged which must have made the people begin to ask: What sort of a love song is this? What's he really getting at? What's it about?

The first surprising thing about this song is that it was a song that should be sung by a woman, not a man. It is a song about a lover.

I will sing for the one I love
a song about his vineyard . . . .

5:1a

At the very least it was open to considerable misunderstanding, but it would certainly have caused these people to listen carefully. Isaiah spoke of his lover who had a vineyard, and he has looked after it. That would have made them sit up for a start and wonder what on earth he was going to sing about. We will see later the reason for this and why he sang as if he were a girl singing about her lover. He continued the song:

My loved one had a vineyard
on a fertile hillside.
He dug it up and cleared it of stones
and planted it with the choicest vines.
He built a watchtower in it

and cut out a winepress as well.
Then he looked for a crop of good grapes . . . .
5:1b–2a (NIV)

He did everything he could for his vineyard. What happened? He didn't get a single good grape out of it. That is surprise number two, because if you bought a fertile hillside and you planted it with the finest stock, you could at least expect some grapes. Instead he got those horrid little black things called 'wild grapes'. They look like grapes in miniature and they are no use at all for eating or for anything else. They are bitter, they are small, they are full of stones, they have thick skins. That sort of thing may not happen in real life, but in the song it did.

Then comes surprise number three, for in the next verse of the love song Isaiah stops using the word *he* and he starts using the word '*I*'.

What more could have been done for my vineyard
than I have done for it?
When I looked for good grapes,
why did it yield only bad?
5:4 (NIV)

Why? They must have begun to wonder at this point who he was singing about. Is this his own vineyard? He told us he had a lover, and he said 'he', now he's saying 'I'. What's it all about? And this love song gets — as Alice in Wonderland would say — curiouser and curiouser, and they began to listen to what was happening in this story.

At this point Isaiah appealed to their judgement and, as it were, got them on his side. It was brilliant, really using the form of teaching known as parable, which is a teaching device to get people to make a decision and a judgement about something before they realise what it is, to enable them to come onto your side mentally before you have challenged them morally.

So what Isaiah is communicating is this: I want you to judge now; what should I do about my vineyard? Is there anything more than I have done that I could do? We can hear the crowd shouting 'no'. Then what shall I do with my vineyard? Now he moves on to sing the next verse of this strange love song. He says,

"Now I will tell you
what I am going to do to my vineyard:
I will take away its hedge,
and it will be destroyed;
I will break down its wall,
and it will be trampled.
I will make it a wasteland,
neither pruned nor cultivated,
and briers and thorns will grow there."

5:5–6a (NIV)

We can imagine the people in the crowd saying: Well, that's just what I would do. There is nothing more you can do, you will have to try somewhere else. There must be something wrong with that soil. You will never get any grapes from there.

Then they heard him sing, *"I will command the clouds not to rain on it"* (5:6b). Here is point number four that must have surprised them. Who does he think he is to tell the clouds to stop raining? A man can pull down his garden fence but he can't stop it raining on his garden. Who is this?

Look again at those four surprising things. Isaiah talked about his lover as *he*. The vineyard: the choice vines produced wild grapes. Then Isaiah stopped talking about *he* and started saying *I*, as if it were his own vineyard he was singing about. Finally, he was going to tell the clouds not to rain on *my* vineyard. Up to this point he carried the crowd right with him even if they were a bit puzzled, but now he turns the whole thing round on them and says: you are the vineyard and Jehovah is the owner of it. This is brilliant preaching. It has the people making a decision, making a moral judgement first, and then telling them: this is you I am talking about. Nathan the prophet used a similar device with king David.

The prophet now said, I have been singing about you and God. He had sung as though he were a woman because the relationship between God and Judah, his people, was like the relationship between a husband and wife. Again and again the prophets use that relationship. Judah was the wife, the husband was God, and it was his responsibility to provide for and protect the wife. So the vineyard was really the wife and the owner was the husband — the owner was God, the vineyard was the people of Israel. Suddenly they saw it all. What Isaiah has been saying to them is this: What more could God have done for you than he has done? He has brought you into this fertile land of Canaan, a land of milk and honey, protected you against your enemies, sent the law to you, sent prophets to you, priests, kings; he has provided every single thing you needed. He has hedged you about with his own protection; he has got his own watchtower in the middle, his temple, and yet . . . nothing but wild grapes. I apply this to my heart and to your heart now. What more could God have done for each of us than he has done? Answer that! What more could he have done for you than he has done to make you one of his holy people? It means that every one of us is as holy as we want to be, no more, no less. God has done everything he could have done to make us holy, to set us free from sin, to make our lives what they were meant to be. What more could he have done to make us better Christians than we are? When we answer that question we find it profoundly disturbing. What more, I ask you, said Isaiah, could God have done for this vineyard than he has done? What more? They must have been silent, for there was nothing more he could have done.

When we consider the evil in the world, and when we consider the mess that the world is in, I challenge anybody to tell me one thing more that a God who is wholly love could have done or should have done to cure this world of sin. If we look at the wild grapes that he got in Israel we shall also see the wild grapes that he is getting from the world today, so let us now leave the song of God in which his real disappointment with his people is clearly seen.

Let us now look in detail at the wild grapes, the sins of Judah, because Isaiah, having gained the interest and the attention of his audience, now begins to be quite specific, and he tells them what the wild grapes really are. He uses a word for the rest of chapter five — 'woe'. It is a curse. It is the opposite of 'blessed', and if 'blessed' means to have the favour of God upon you, 'woe' means to have the curse of God upon you. Jesus often used this word 'woe' — as often as he used the word 'blessed'.

The first wild grapes mentioned are those people who have given their lives to material pursuits: business, pleasure, sometimes both. There were, first of all, men who lived for business. That is nothing new and it is nothing old either. Men who want to build up bigger and bigger businesses. I have met them, so have you. It is a disease with them. Even after they have got enough to live on comfortably for the rest of their lives they still want to buy another business, they still want to enlarge the company, they still want more and they have got to go on adding. A businessman in London collapsed and he went to the doctor who said, 'Your business is killing you. You must get right away from it and have a complete rest. Go down to Devon.' The man went down to Devon into a hotel to have a complete rest. He unpacked his bags, came down to the hotel foyer, went over to the reception desk and said to the man behind the desk, 'Do you know anyone around here who wants to sell some cattle?' Before he had been there five minutes he was hard at it again! I know the justification often given for this is that unless your business is going forward it will go back. But I am concerned now with the heart of the man in business, not business method. And Isaiah says,

> *Woe to you who add house to house*
> *and join field to field*
> *till no space is left*
> *and you live alone in the land.*
>
> 5:8 (NIV)

Monopolies, big business, crushing out the little man. Here is the picture of Judah and it is strangely up to date.

Some people pursue material things by living not for their business but for their pleasure, and they rise early in the morning to get at the bottle. Of course, drinking is unnatural early in the morning; even those who drink heavily usually leave it until later in the day. (Peter, on the day of Pentecost, said that they were not drunk, it was just nine o' clock in the morning.) Isaiah said, *Woe to those who rise early in the morning to run after their drinks* (5:11). Not only were people getting up early in the morning to drink, they continued late into the night. Woe to these, because says Isaiah (in chapters 13 to 17) it will lead to spiritual famine. The leaders will be hungry, the people will be thirsty. For people who live for business and pleasure do not see what God is doing, says Isaiah. They do not know about God's business or God's pleasure, they are too busy with their own. What a challenging picture! Let me make it quite clear that I am not saying that a Christian ought not to be in business and cannot be a good businessman — he can — though there are moral difficulties and they are growing in our world. But if the business comes *first* in someone's life, then he will not see God's business. Let me say again that I am not of those who think that if you enjoy anything in life it is bound to be wrong — that a Christian should not have any pleasures. Some people think like that, but what I am saying is that if one's own pleasure is the *first* consideration, God's pleasure is unnoticed. Isaiah is saying that they do not see what God is doing, they are not aware of his activity. This is a picture of our society, with so many people bent on either business or pleasure that they have no idea what God's business is about and they have no idea what gives God pleasure. They can only study the stock exchange page in the paper; they do not see in the other headlines God's activity, God's work in history. There is a little picture of the end of that sort of thing in vv. 16 and 17 in which men who have lived for business and pleasure will one day be humbled and God exalted, and animals will graze among the ruins of their business. From their total land area of the large business they will only get a tiny crop, smaller than they got from their original business. From ten acres of vineyard they will only get a few gallons of wine. That is the picture of their humbling. But God will be exalted, and animals, grazing among the ruins of their estates and homes, will be better off than these men.

The other perversion mentioned in vv. 18–30 is mental perversion — people who are twisted in their thinking. Isaiah mentions four kinds of people. First there are those who mock God and say, 'Where is he? Let him come and show himself to us. Let him do something and then we'll take notice of him.' I once stood at Speaker's Corner in Hyde Park, London, when I was a young boy, and I have never forgotten it. There was such a mixture of speakers there — the cheapest entertainment in London, so I am told — but I enjoy listening to a good heckler in the open air. A man stood up and said, 'I defy God to his face. If there is a God in heaven then I blaspheme him and I challenge him to strike me dead at this moment.' Then he waited. 'There,' he said, 'nothing's happened.' I wonder how that man will feel when he faces God in the day that God has appointed. That man wanted to be boss. He wanted to tell God what day the day of judgement should be. What utter impudence for a creature to defy the Creator like that. Oh, it got a laugh from the crowd — in fact it improved his audience, in quantity, though not in quality. But that man challenged God: 'Do something; you show me; you challenge me, I challenge you.' God is not childish, he has appointed a day when he will judge the world, including that man. No man's silly challenge is going to alter God's timetable.

The first group of people mentioned here are those who say, 'Let God prove himself to me. Let God do something then we'll see.' But they are so busy with business and pleasure they would not see it if he did. How many people noticed when God sent his Son to Bethlehem? How many people were aware of what was happening? Yet God had prepared them for nearly two thousand years for that. People say let God do something and we'll notice — but it does not follow.

The second group are those who call evil good and good evil, bitter sweet and sweet bitter, light dark and dark light — those who have got their ideas so mixed up they do not know any longer what is right and wrong. This is the kind of distorted thinking in which we live, this kind of outlook that a thing is good or bad according to our opinion or our pleasure, with no reference to the standards that God has set. This is what Isaiah is talking about.

A third group he mentions is those who think they know everything, who are wise in their own eyes, think themselves shrewd and say, 'I know better than you, I know better than God, I know better than anyone else; my ideas are the best in the world for me.' That is a very common attitude. You argue with some unbelievers and you will find how common this is.

Fourthly, those whose thinking is affected by drinking. It is interesting that Isaiah mentions wine twice in this chapter: first as an example of those who live for pleasure; second, those who drink excessively to the extent that their minds are befuddled and confused, especially when this affects other people. The innocent suffer. A man is over the limit, gets behind his steering wheel, goes on the road, knocks down and kills a pedestrian and it is the innocent person who has suffered and the guilty who has got off. Such can be one of the results of alcohol abuse.

Here is a picture of mental perversions, and now God would 'whistle' for an invader. Did you notice that graphic description of the invasion? Suddenly it comes,

. . . swiftly and speedily!
Not one of them grows tired or stumbles,
not one slumbers or sleeps;
not a belt is loosened at the waist,
not a sandal thong is broken.
Their arrows are sharp,
all their bows are strung;
their horses' hoofs seem like flint,
their chariot wheels like a whirlwind.

5:26b–28 (NIV)

Go to the British Museum and study the reliefs in stone of the Assyrian might — and you have a perfect description here in Isaiah. There is no-one bending down to tie a bootlace; they are perfectly equipped, they are immaculate and their wheels are like whirlwinds as their chariots rush on to that little nation of Israel. You can see Isaiah's words for yourself there in London — the invasion he called on a nation living for material things and mentally twisted. How would you like to preach to a nation like that? What would make a man go on preaching in a situation like that?

We move on to chapter six. When did it happen? In the year that King Uzziah died. Uzziah died of leprosy, a lingering death. He had been a good man, he had been a wise king, and it seemed as if the old era was passing — something like Britain felt at the death of Queen Victoria. When King Uzziah died there was no good king on the horizon to follow him, and people felt there was an era coming to an end, things were going to slip because Uzziah was dying. There was a general atmosphere of depression.

So in the year that King Uzziah died, when everybody was wondering who would be on the throne next, Isaiah said, *I saw the Lord seated on a throne . . .* (see 6:1). Do you see the connection now? God does not waste a word, and I often wondered why it said this in God's word — in the year that king died — and now I can see it. It was when everybody thought, 'This king's going, who will reign after him? Who will keep the nation together?' — Isaiah saw the King, the Lord of hosts, and his kingdom, for the King was on a throne and the train of his robes filled the temple. He saw the power of God and he saw the glory of God; the earth was filled with his glory; the seraphs, the angels, bowed down and worshipped him and called, *"Holy, holy, holy is the LORD Almighty . . . ."*

The thing that struck Isaiah about God when he saw him was that God was *holy*, or in New Testament language that he was *light*. I have heard so many sermons about the love of God and so few about the light of God; so many about healing from God and so few about the holiness of God. But if you really meet God the first thing that you will notice is the holy light of God, God's utter purity, his utter majesty, his utter righteousness, his cleanness. Holy, holy, holy is the Lord God of hosts. If you just think of the love of God you have never really met God, and I do not think you can ever really understand the love of God until you have seen his holiness. If somebody asks me what was the most fundamental, basic thing about God's character that I knew, I would not say 'God is love', I would say 'God is light.' I would say holy, holy, holy is the Lord of hosts. Why would I say that? Because that is the basic Bible teaching. God's holiness is his basic character. When you come up against a holy God your first reaction will not be to run to him but to run from him, not to be drawn to him but to be repelled. It will be to say, 'I'm lost, I'm undone, I'm a filthy person.' You never realise how filthy you are until you meet someone who is clean. There are people who think they are clean, measured by the very much lowered standards of those among whom they live, but when you meet God and see that he is holy you will say 'Woe is me.' Notice again the word *woe*. Isaiah has pronounced the curse of God on his nation. Woe to *you*. Now he is saying woe is *me*, before woe to others. Similarly, no one has a right to preach on hell to anyone else until he has realised that but for the grace of God he was heading for the same place. We notice that Isaiah's sinfulness was realised not in anything he did but in what he had been saying. If we take that seriously we realise that everybody is a sinner. Is there a man or a woman on earth who can say, 'I have always said the right thing; I have always spoken kindly about others? I have always been silent when I should have been silent, and I have always spoken when I should have spoken'? There is not one of us clean in lips. Then, having seen the holiness and the light of God, Isaiah experienced the love. Here is the order: logically you cannot love God until you have been forgiven by God and logically you cannot be forgiven by God until you have realised that you are a sinner —and you cannot realise you are a sinner until you have realised that God is holy. **You cannot love God until you have seen that he is holy. We only experience God's love through forgiveness.**

Isaiah had an awful vision now. He saw one of those angels take a pair of tongs and take a red-hot coal from the altar, the place of sacrifice for sin. Notice that it linked forgiveness with sacrifice in Isaiah's mind indelibly. The angel flew straight for him with a red-hot coal — how would you feel about this frightening vision? Imagine you saw an angel with a red-hot coal coming straight for your face! Isaiah was told that his guilt was taken away, his sin atoned for. Then he heard God say something. God the Father, God the Son and God the Holy Spirit were present (for Jesus said, 'Isaiah saw my glory.') The Father, said, *"Whom shall I send? And who will go for us?"* (6:8). This is an amazing revelation in the Old Testament of God the Holy Trinity. *"And who will go for us?"* (We recall, *"Let us make man in our own image."*) The Father was speaking to the Son and the Spirit. Isaiah, when he had been forgiven and cleansed, could say, *"Here am I. Send me!"*

Now comes the second half of this chapter. God let Isaiah

know quite plainly that when he went, firstly, his ministry would be a failure. The people would listen and listen but not understand, they would look and look but never see the point. This is a preacher's constant frustration and nightmare. It would be very disturbing for many of us preachers (and humbling and healthy) for us to be able to know just how much of what has been said has gone into the minds of the congregation. I know you have listened, but have you understood?

Furthermore, worse news than this, Isaiah was told that his preaching was going to make them worse. It would actually cause them to be hardened and deadened. The more he preached the harder they would be. But God still wanted him to go and preach. I have noticed that when someone has got away from God and settled their mind to be against God and lived for business or pleasure or something else, every time they hear a sermon preached they get harder. You can see it in their face, until sometimes at the end of the sermon they are sitting like granite. The word of God either softens your heart or it hardens it — you cannot stay the same. When you leave a church service you cannot be the same as when you went in. You are either nearer to the Lord or further from him, either softened by his word or hardened by it and resisting. We cannot be neutral. Isaiah had the awful experience of seeing his congregations get harder and harder, and he preached for sixty years. The amazing thing is that though Isaiah died without appreciation, a lone figure after sixty years' work, now his words are precious gold to millions of people the world over. But at the time they got harder and they would not listen. He tried everything he could to make his hearers interested, and we will see some of the devices he used. He even at one stage walked naked through the city to try and draw attention to God's message. Isaiah asked the Lord how long he would have to preach if it was just going to make them harder. It would be until their country was desolate, like the fields of Flanders in World War One, a wasteland with tree stumps. Isaiah preached for sixty years until it was like that, until homes were desolate, until most of the land was a desert. He saw the people get further and further from God but he preached because God said, *"Go and tell this people . . ."* (see 6:9). It is interesting that this hardening effect of the word of God, and these words of Isaiah, are quoted in Matthew, Mark, Luke, John and Acts, and they are quoted in Matthew, Mark and Luke of the parables of Jesus. When Jesus told parables it hardened people, it drove them further from the truth. Parables were not nice stories to get them nearer to God but to harden their hearts if they had set their heart against the truth. Sermons still do this, if there is a determination never to come to God, never to respond to him. We talk about gospel-hardened people —what a task.

My last word is the last sentence in chapter six. Have you ever seen a devastated area with just a few tree stumps remaining? Burned down, chopped down, destroyed, until there does not seem any sign of life anywhere. Come back in a year's time and you will see that from the old tree stumps leaves and shoots are growing — and in a few years' time, it will be woodland again. Even though Isaiah will see that vineyard devastated, just left as stumps, in 6:13 he is told that, *the holy seed will be the stump in the land*.

From that there would come a shoot. This idea gripped Isaiah and later he applied it to Jesus. He said there shall come forth a shoot from the stump of Jesse. The stump of Jesse will seem to have been cut right down and destroyed and yet there will be a little shoot and from it a Saviour — unto us a Son is given, unto us a child is born. And when a baby was born at Bethlehem of Judea it was the shoot from a stump of Jesse, from the ruins of Israel, our Lord Jesus Christ. It is marvellous but in the darkest passage in the Bible you will find hope; in the most awful condemnation of men's sin anywhere in the Bible you will find a glimmer of God's plan for the future to bring something out of that chaos, to bring a remnant, to bring his Son.

4

A CHILD IS BORN

Read Isaiah 7:1 – 9:7

A. JUDAH'S ANXIETY (7:1-8:22)
1. SECRET TALK - 'Shear-Jashub' (7:2-9)
a. Human forecast (2) b. Divine forecast (3-9)
2. SUPERNATURAL TOKEN - 'Immanuel' (7:10-25)
a. Immediate fulfilment b. Ultimate fulfilment
3. SIGNED TABLET - 'Maher-Shalal Hashbaz' (8:1-10)
a. Northern fate (1-4) b. Southern fate (5-10)
4. SEALED TESTIMONY - three children (8:11-22)
a. wong fear (9-15) b. Right fear (16-22)
B. JEHOVAH'S ANSWER (9:1-7)
1. A DESPISED PLACE (1-5)
2. A DIVINE PERSON (6-7)
a. His name (6)
i. Wonderful counsellor - wisdom ii. Mighty God - power
iii. Everlasting father - love iv. Peaceful prince - peace
b. His nation
i. Galilee ii. Gentiles

One of the big problems in the Christian life is the relationship between religion and politics. Sometimes these two things get far too close together and a careful reading of the scripture would seem to suggest that church and state are to be separate and that religion and politics must never become too identified. From time to time some people have dreamed of a Christian political party, and in some continental countries that has come about. In this chapter we have religion and politics getting too close together and beginning to influence one another for ill.

Of course, religion and politics can get too far apart so that one does not affect the other at all. Life cannot be lived in compartments. If you have a faith, it has to affect every part of your life, your public as well as your private life. There are certain things that we would wish to say, in the name of Christ, to politicians. Religion and politics are therefore related; they must not get too far apart so that they have nothing to do with each other, nor must they get so close together that preachers in the pulpits talk of nothing but social and political reform. A healthy balance is needed.

For the people of Israel this problem was acute. It was far more difficult than for us, because in the Old Testament Israel was both a religious people and a political people. She had her own king, her own nation, her own borders, and she had to have relationships with other nations as a state, even though she was the people of God. Therefore we find in the Old Testament prophets a great deal said about the politics of the nation. For the politics of Israel reflected the religion of Israel so closely. Her relationship with other nations reflected her relationship with God. Therefore, the prophets would prove that the relationship with God had gone wrong by pointing to political activities. This is what Isaiah is doing in chapters seven and eight.

There is a key group of words which keep recurring in these two chapters. Did you notice the key word? It is *fear* or dread. In the national life they were going through a period of fear or terror, and this was no way to face the future. The lesson I want to draw is just this: to go into the future with fear, dread or terror is entirely the wrong attitude for the people of God. If we fear other people, disease, loneliness, poverty or death — whatever it is we fear — it reveals that we have got out of touch with God; our terror and our fear betray a broken relationship with our Father. Therefore I want to encourage you from this ancient scripture to live without any fear at all in your heart, except one. And this passage finishes with the *right* fear that cures all others. If you have the one right fear in your heart you will have none of the wrong ones. That was the lesson of Isaiah for the people as they faced an uncertain political future. Today, too, we face an uncertain future. We are in a mess and everybody knows this. Just what is going to happen economically, politically, socially, morally over the coming years only God knows, but the prospect is not very inviting!

You will recall that after the days of Solomon and his rather foolish reign (though he was given wisdom in some things he was very foolish in others) he so sowed the seeds of discontent among his people that, as soon as he died, the nation of Israel split, there was a civil war, and the people of God were fighting each other for the first time in their history. It was a sad chapter that continued right to the days of Isaiah nearly 250 years later. The tribes did not split equally. Most stayed in the north, and remember that they kept the name 'Israel', or alternatively they called themselves 'Ephraim', because that was the name of the largest of the ten northern tribes. Israel/Ephraim rebelled against the royal line, setting up their own king, a rival throne with the capital at Samaria. Left in the south were two tiny tribes who were the real people of God. They kept the capital, Jerusalem, and they kept the royal line, but they were a little remnant. They called them Judah because Judah was the larger tribe and Benjamin was the smaller. So 'Ephraim and Judah', but the people in the north liked to call themselves Israel and claimed to be the true nation. That was the political situation.

Further north was another powerful nation, not belonging to the people of God at all — the nation of Syria with its capital at Damascus. If you know your geography you will remember that there is a fertile crescent running round from the Nile to the Euphrates and the Tigris, and the nations were all around this fertile crescent. So we have Egypt, then a strip of Sinai desert — the Gaza strip — then little Judah with two tribes called after the larger of the two. Then Israel, or Ephraim, called after the largest of the ten tribes. Then Syria that did not belong to the people of Israel at all. And finally, looming up on the north-east was a huge and growing empire called Assyria, with its capital Nineveh. So we see a tiny nation surrounded by nations bigger than itself. The fear which was striking terror into the heart of the people, so that the king's heart and the people's heart shook like trees in the wind, was this. The other half of the people of God, Israel, formed a coalition with Syria, with the object of conquering and wiping out the tiny nation centred on Jerusalem. In other words, Judah was being caught in a huge political pincer movement and they knew that Syria and Israel had set their hearts on wiping out this awkward little remnant. That is a word that Isaiah uses a lot. That was all that was left of the people of God, a remnant, two tribes (some would say one and a half because Benjamin was so small). Just a tiny little remnant with Ahaz on the throne of Jerusalem.

I wonder whether you know how Ahaz thought he could get out of this political situation. He decided to make a pact with Assyria. He thought that if he could do this then, if the other two powers attacked him, he would just need to send a message up to Assyria and they would come charging down from the north and keep him safe. Poor old Ahaz thought that you could trust a political alliance for your security. Isaiah's message in a nutshell was: no wonder you are afraid if you think you can get yourself out of your troubles; you need to fear God and he will protect this tiny nation. In other words, don't try and escape from your enemies by putting your trust in an even bigger enemy. That is exactly what Judah would do under Ahaz.

What was Isaiah going to do about this situation? First of all, God told him to go and have a secret talk with the king. God told him where to find him on his own. He would take a walk from the palace down the Washerman's Field and find the king there. God also told him to take his boy, Shear-Jashub, with him. That is an extraordinary name which we find nowhere else in the Old Testament. I can imagine the king wondering what on earth that meant. The name of the boy was 'a remnant shall return'. As we will see, Isaiah had a habit of giving his children names that were messages, so that whenever anybody asked the baby's name they got a sermon! Isaiah was a walking, living signpost to the message of God. We recall that 'Isaiah', meant *the salvation of Jehovah*, and his son's name meant, in other words, that God will always see that there are some of his people Israel safe. That is a promise that God has kept for more than three thousand years. A remnant shall return. Paul makes a great deal of this in Romans chapters nine to eleven. He said that God always keeps his word. He will always have something of Israel safe in his hand. What a message of comfort to Ahaz —Isaiah called his little boy this because he was absolutely convinced that God will always have a remnant of his people and there will always be an Israel. It is the most astonishing thing to me today that the one nation that has survived from the world of three thousand years ago is the nation that others have repeatedly tried to destroy.

So Isaiah met the king, and we have a contrast in this secret talk between the human forecast for the future and the divine forecast. Isaiah forecast that within sixty-five years Syria and Israel would have gone. He was right to the year! Within sixty-five years those two nations on the northern borders of Judah, Israel herself (the ten tribes) had disappeared and Syria had disappeared. And Ahaz lived to see it! It is obvious from the end of verse nine that sceptical Ahaz did not believe it. And Isaiah finished the secret talk by saying, "*If you do not stand firm in your faith, you will not stand at all*" (7:9).

Then Ahaz was invited to ask the Lord for a sign, and we will see why Isaiah offered that in a moment, but the king would not accept the offer. He said, '*I will not put the LORD to the test.*' That sounds very pious and very fine, but when God tells you to put him to the proof you should do so. Gideon put out the fleece, remember. We should not normally ask God to prove himself, we should take God by faith. But when he tells us to ask for a sign, we should ask, it is disobedience not to. Why did Ahaz not want proof? The answer is really that he was a wicked man, he did not want to put his trust in God, he would rather put his trust in Assyria; he could see Assyria; he knew the strength of its army, and he wanted to put his trust in things he could see. There are those to whom you say, 'Why don't you put your trust in God?' And they say, 'I can't see God.' 'Then prove it. Try it and trust him and see what happens.' But no, they would rather put their trust elsewhere. They say, 'I can see my money, I know how much I've got in the bank.' Or they prefer to put their trust in this or that political party, in the government. They can see them and they believe that they will do things for them. God is invisible, he is intangible. You cannot see his forces. Ahaz did not want to trust the invisible God so he refused the test. Isaiah then told the king that God would give him a sign. It would prove that what he said was right.

Now we come to this controversial verse. It is impossible for Christians to read this next verse without thinking about Jesus, but I want to point out that Ahaz when he first heard this did not think about Jesus at all. This verse 14 is important because Handel's *Messiah* and our preaching at Christmas has so linked this verse forever with the babe at Bethlehem that we must go back and ask what it originally conveyed to Ahaz. "*Therefore the Lord himself will give you a sign: The virgin will be with child and will give birth to a son, and will call him Immanuel*" (7:14, NIV).

The first problem about this is that the word rendered 'virgin', sometimes translated as *young woman,* is an ambiguous word. In Hebrew it can mean any of three different things. It can mean someone who is a virgin, who has never had relations with a man; it can mean someone of marriageable age, a young maiden; it can mean a married woman who keeps her age so well that she still looks as if she was courting.

Next I want you to notice a most surprising thing in this verse. It is the *mother* who will name the child. Yet in Israel it was the father who named a child. Isaiah named all his children.

Then we we notice that the name to be given to the child was *Immanuel* (meaning 'God with us'). That was a name that was never given to Jesus (he was called 'Jesus', not Immanuel) and it was Joseph who gave him the name 'Jesus', not Mary.

But the most surprising thing about this verse which makes

us sit up and think when we recall our normal understanding is this: when we read this verse with the verses immediately after it, it would seem quite clear that this verse refers to someone who was to be born in the days of Ahaz, a son which he would see, and of course our Lord was not born until nearly 750 years after this, when Ahaz had long since been dead and buried. What is the answer to this puzzle? What does this verse mean? Are we wrong in thinking that it refers to the virgin birth of our Lord himself?

One of the puzzling things about prophecy, until you are on to it, is this: predictions in the Old Testament often have a double meaning —they are often fulfilled twice, once in the immediate future and once in the ultimate future, and the promise covers both. We will come across this again in Isaiah. It is as if the prophet, looking through his telescope into the future, saw two events together. This is undoubtedly what has happened here.

Let me take the first fulfilment, in the days of Ahaz. It was not a virgin birth; it was simply a young woman of marriageable age. And undoubtedly the ambiguity of the word means that the first fulfilment was a natural birth of a woman of marriageable age. Who was she? Some have thought that it was Isaiah's wife and that Immanuel was his own son, but the way he talks of him indicates that it is not that. Others have thought that the woman is Abijah and the son was Hezekiah, the good king who came later, but I do not think that is really supported by scripture. I can only give you my guess, for what it is worth. We know that Ahaz had a harem, that he had wives and concubines; he should not have done but he had. In the royal palace in Jerusalem there were a number of young women, not wives but young women of marriageable age who were his concubines, and they were the only women in that ancient society who gave the names to their own sons, as they were not wives. The text clearly implies that it was a woman within the royal palace, a young woman of marriageable age. And the word used is the exact word used of women in a harem. So Isaiah is saying to Ahaz that a young woman in his court would conceive and have a son, and when he asked her what she had called the child she would say 'Immanuel'. Before the child reached the age of moral responsibility, Syria and Damascus would have gone, and that would be the proof of the timetable of sixty-five years. We have no details of that fulfilment. We have lost sight of the girl and the son she bore. But no doubt there came a day when Ahaz would have seen this fulfilled, and Damascus, the capital of Syria, would be ruined; Samaria, the capital of Israel, would be ruined. By 722 BC both of those capital cities had indeed been ruined, so we can almost date the birth of this boy Immanuel. That was the immediate fulfilment of the prediction. It was in the days of Ahaz. It was a natural birth of an unmarried woman, a concubine in the royal household, with a boy whom she called Immanuel and this was the sign because God had led her to call him by that name and Ahaz would have the proof he refused to ask for.

But now let us look at it again. As the years passed following the death of Ahaz, the Jews used to read this passage again and again. Whenever they read this verse they began to see a double meaning in it. If I can just give you two Hebrew words here, the Hebrew word *betulah* means a virgin, but that is not the word used here. The word used here is *almah*, which means either a virgin or a woman of marriageable age or a married woman who looks as if she were still unmarried. It is an ambiguous word, and long after the days of Ahaz the Jews noticed it could have a double meaning: 'virgin' as well as 'young maiden'. They began to realise that God had hidden within this verse a double prediction. Five hundred years after Isaiah, two hundred and fifty years before Jesus Christ was born, seventy Jewish scholars in Egypt set out to take the whole Old Testament and translate it from the Hebrew into the Greek language. When they came to this verse they chose from Greek a word that can only mean *virgin*, for the original fulfilment had come and gone and the second fulfilment was still ahead, so for the second fulfilment they took the other meaning of the word, *virgin*, and they translated it into Greek: a virgin shall conceive. There would be a supernatural birth, the second fulfilment. They saw in the name now not a literal name but the nature of the child. The child was to be God with us, the child was to be God. So the sign was not just to be the child's name but the child's nature. It was that second prediction which was fulfilled in Bethlehem. The first child was a sign that God the Father was with Israel, the second was a sign that God the Son was now with us. Only with this in mind will we understand the differences of translation. When the translators of the Authorised Version translated this text they took the meaning of that ambiguous word that will point to the second fulfilment. So they wrote: 'Behold a virgin shall conceive'. When the translators of another translation came to this verse they translated it in line with its original meaning, what it meant in the days of Ahaz, and so they wrote: 'Behold a young woman shall conceive'. They were both right. If you had read some of the vitriolic discussion over this matter you would be amazed. Some people won't touch the Revised Standard Version because they think it denies the virgin birth. That is utterly ridiculous; you just have to read Matthew and Luke to realise that this version is equally firm on the virginity of Mary — it is stated quite clearly that Mary was a virgin (where Isaiah is quoted).

Returning to the first fulfilment, we read that before the child knows how to refuse the evil and chose the good he would eat curd and whey. The awful significance of that rather nice sounding diet is lost on us. This is the food eaten in a time of famine when normal agriculture has ceased, when the farms have gone, when the fields are no longer cultivated. Judah would be going through a very difficult time.

Note that Ahaz, in disobedience, practised and encouraged spiritualism. Among the people of God there were now wizards and magic (see 8:19).

Syria and Israel were to be wiped out, but Assyria would not stop there — they would come down, and Egypt would come up.

5

A REMNANT WILL RETURN

Read Isaiah 9:8–10:34

A. GOD'S INDIGNATION (9:8-10:4)
1. PRIDE AND PROPERTY (8-12)
2. ATHEISM AND ANARCHY (13-17)
3. WICKEDNESS AND WAR (18-21)
4. INJUSTICE AND INVASION (1-4)
B. GOD'S INSTRUMENT (10:5-19)
1. AMBITION (5-11)
2. ARROGANCE (12-14)
3. ANNIHILATION (15-19)
C. GOD'S INTENTION (10:20–34)
1. REMNANT OF JACOB (20-23)
2. ROD OF JEHOVAH (24-27a)
3. RESCUE OF JERUSALEM (27b-34)

I recall the words of a well-known journalist who spoke of looking out from the breakfast table and seeing a bird after a worm, the cat after the bird, and the dog after the cat. That picture gives you some understanding of the morning's news. It also summarises the political situation behind the passage we are studying. Recall that we have in the south the little kingdom of Judah made up of the two tribes of Judah and Benjamin. You could think of that as the 'worm'. After the 'worm' was the 'bird' and the 'bird' was called Israel, even though they had no right to that title. There were ten of the tribes of Israel that had hived off by themselves, formed their own kingdom and kept the national name. But the capital of the nation was still down in Judah — Jerusalem was still with the two tribes and they were the true people of God. Then, further north, above the 'bird', was the 'cat', and this was the kingdom of Syria which was bigger and stronger still. Then after the 'cat' was the 'dog', a great big kingdom called Assyria in the north.

Assyria was after Syria, Syria was after Israel, Israel was after little Judah, and little Judah was scared stiff and thought that the best way out of this problem was to try to make friends with the 'dog'. The 'worm' thought: If the 'dog' will enter into an alliance with me, I can call on him to attack either the 'cat' or the 'bird' when they come after me or move in my direction. The only thing that the 'worm' had forgotten was that when the 'bird' and the 'cat' are out of the way the 'dog' will get interested in the 'worm' and will probably come on to attack it. Instead of putting her trust in God for her defence, Judah was trying to put her trust in Assyria, that mighty growing empire in the north-east. Some years ago, a series of newspapers was produced, giving the Bible history as headlines. You could buy them in the shops and they were a very interesting way of reading the Bible. They put all this in normal newspaper form with big headlines such as, 'Assyria attacks Syria', just as in modern times there have been headlines such as 'Syria attacks Israel', which happened near the Sea of Galilee, so they were really quite up to date.

Against that background we have three things said about this situation, and all of them are said to the 'worm', the little kingdom of Judah that was so frightened of the others. First of all, Isaiah talks about God's anger, God's indignation, God's wrath. He teaches that this whole political situation has developed because God is angry, and he gives four reasons for this. Then he goes on to tell the people what God is going to do about this situation, what instrument he is going to use to put it right. Thirdly, he reveals something of God's intention for the future as to how far he will go toward putting this situation right.

First of all, then, God's *indignation*. It is possible to learn a great deal about a person's character if you know what makes them angry. If I could get you to take a piece of paper and write down on it the things that really get you worked up I could tell you what sort of a character you have. Perhaps you are sitting a little smugly and thinking, 'Well, I don't get angry.' Frankly, may I suggest that there is something seriously wrong with your character if you never get angry, for our Lord was angry from time to time and it is part of a perfect character that you do get angry *at the right things*, but a lot of our anger is at the wrong things. God gets angry, Jesus got angry and a perfect character will be angry, but look at the things that make a good person angry and you will find that they are quite different from the things that make a bad person angry. For one thing, the things that make a good person angry are things that are happening to someone else. The things that make the bad person angry are things that are being done to them. That is a very broad summary. There are other things that we could say about anger. What makes God angry? What sort of things fill God with indignation and wrath? Of course that wrath and that anger work out in things that happen here on earth. In our daily newspapers we can find item after item which is nothing more nor less than the anger of God working itself out in society. Read Romans chapter one and you will find it is rather like a Sunday scandal paper. It tells you exactly what happens on earth when God is angry.

What makes God angry? First of all, *pride*. I know that God made man as the peak of creation to control it all for his own purposes. I know that God made man last as the high point of his handiwork, but that does not mean we should be proud and self-sufficient. It does not mean that I should be arrogant and strut around saying I am the master of my fate, I am the captain of my soul. But that is what the kingdoms of Israel and Judah were doing. They were proud, they were arrogant and, although God brought them low repeatedly, they kept popping up again. Proud people do this. You can chastise them, you can take things from them but they will come back up with greater ambitions yet. God had taken from these proud people their simple homes of brick and thatched roofs — because they were so proud. They said: That's fine. Instead of brick we'll build with stone. You have just cleared the decks for a finer house, Lord. You may have taken away the sycamore beams of our house but we'll have cedar beams in the next house. You may take our houses away but we'll build mansions in their place. You may rob us of this but we'll have better — you see. Such arrogant pride that popped up again — you may do what you like to us but we'll always get the better of the situation, we'll always come out on top again — this pride and arrogance that never asked, Why have the Syrians taken our homes? Why did God allow the Philistines to come? They never asked why. This is true of people today as it was true then. We suffer, we lose something. We go through difficulties, and instead of questioning why we are so proud and self-sufficient, we say, We'll get ourselves out of this; we'll come out on top; we'll be better off afterwards than we were before. We do not stop to ask why that trouble came into our life. We do not stop to ask God why he allowed that. What were you trying to teach us? What did we need to learn? We simply devote ourselves to picking ourselves up again and finishing up better than we were before.

The next thing was *practical atheism*. They were living as if God did not exist. There are very few intellectual atheists around, very few people who will tell you straight to your face, 'I am absolutely convinced there is no God.' But there are thousands upon thousands of practical atheists. A godless man is not a man who denies the existence of God but a man who ignores the existence of God. An atheist in Bible language is a man who can live from Monday to Saturday, and often right through Sunday, without ever thinking about God at all. Remember that Isaiah is talking about the people of God, and yet the very people of God were living as if God did not exist, and you can do this. In church you can do it. You can come into a service and not realise that God is in the place, and that your worship is to please him, not you. It is in order that he may get a blessing, not you. You can forget this and simply come to church and say: What do I get out of it? Did I enjoy this morning's service, or did I not? We, God's people, can live as if God is not in our lives, as if we can get on without him. This is what the people were doing, and it always leads to anarchy, it means that people mislead one another. It means that those who should be leading a nation can't lead it. It means that those who should be led in the right ways are misled and follow misleading leadership. It means that those who ought to be preaching the truth preach lies. That was the situation described in vv. 13 — 17 and one feels there is something very modern about it. Even the orphans and widows lacked some sense of a need of God, so it is rather sternly said that God found that he had no compassion for the widow and the orphan. This is astonishing. The Bible consistently presents God as interested in such people who have need of him. Yet here he says even the widows and orphans are godless — they don't turn to me in their need and I find no compassion for them in my heart. What a picture!

The third thing that makes God angry is *wickedness*, which is like a fire burning in a man's heart. Another word for the Bible word *wickedness* is simply selfishness — wanting what you have not got. Wickedness leads to war; selfishness leads to strife. James, in his epistle, asks: Where do wars come from? What starts them? The answer is very simple. A nation wants a bit of land that it has not got so it starts an aggressive war. Some people want to force their ideas and their leadership on someone else and it starts a war — they want a bigger following. And in private, within a family, watch three children playing. One of them wants something that the other has and it starts a 'war'! Here we have a picture of civil war. Ephraim is fighting Manasseh, then together they fight Judah. God saw his children, his family, fighting one another, wickedness burning like a fire in their hearts, and he does not like children fighting any more than earthly parents do — but what started it? Some of his children wanted something others had and they were prepared to fight for it.

The fourth thing that makes God angry is *injustice*. The beginning of chapter ten is all about the dreadful way in which widows and orphans who should have been receiving attention and justice and help were being exploited by bribery and corruption, even in the courts themselves. This was happening among the people of God.

I wonder whether you know that Solon was at this very same time writing out the first laws for Athens. He wrote this as his first principle: justice can only be achieved if those people who are not directly affected by a wrong are just as indignant about it as those who are personally hurt. That is an interesting sentence. You will only have justice when the people who are not hurt are as angry about what has been done as the people who are hurt. In other words, you can only have justice when you have *righteous indignation*. Yet we live in a day when it is literally true that if someone is being assaulted in the street people will hurry away so that they do not get involved. They are not angry about a defenceless person being attacked, they are only concerned to keep out of trouble themselves. This happens again and again, and you read it in your papers. Justice was going, and the result of injustice would be that Judah would lose its freedom. God would allow a powerful nation to invade and rule the land for a time. Notice at the ends of 9:12, 9:17, 9:21 and 10:4, the same words occur as a kind of chorus:

Yet for all this, his anger is not turned away,
his hand is still upraised.

God is a Father, that is true, and a father's hand is for two main purposes in relation to children. One is to work for the children, provide for them and do things for them. It is the protective and providing hand. The hand of God is stretched out to his children to provide and to help. Go out into the unknown and put your hand into the hand of God. It is a hand that holds, a hand that guides. But a father's hand is for something else as well. The

Bible teaches about the hand of the heavenly Father not only that it provides but also that it punishes. And his hand is upon his children. If I lay my hands on somebody else's child I'll either have them at my front door or the policeman with them. I must not lay my hand in punishment on someone else's child, but on my own child I could. That is why whom the Lord loves he chastises or chastens. Indeed, says the New Testament, if you never feel the hand of God upon you in punishment you are a bastard, you are not a son of God; you are not his true son. To the people of God, to the children of God, Isaiah says: your Father's hand is stretched out still to chastise. Not to provide but to chastise. Until these four things that have caused God to be angry and indignant have been removed, his hand will still be stretched out, as if he is trying to deal with unruly children and must do it in this way. And the only way he can deal with these people is to allow them to be invaded.

Now comes the surprising turn of events. Judah was afraid of Israel, Israel was afraid of Syria, but Assyria was so far away that Judah was not afraid of it. Aren't we prone to this? We fear the things that are near, we just do not seem able to look ahead, or to look far away and see the danger that looms on the horizon, it is the immediate threat that fills our attention. Little Judah was not afraid of big Assyria at all, and when Assyria marched and conquered Syria, it was as if Judah threw her hat up in the air and shouted hurray, serves them right. And when Assyria went on marching into Israel, Judah felt that served them right too. Still they did not see what was going to happen. Because there was another great big giant of an empire, Egypt. Most of ancient history is the struggle between the seats of two empires, between the Nile and the Tigris and Euphrates. It was like a shuttlecock going backwards and forwards. But to get through to Egypt, Assyria had to pass through Judah. And what Isaiah now communicates is this: the instrument of God's chastising, the way you will feel his hand upon your nation, is when that big empire goes on marching and marches right up to the gates of your capital city of Jerusalem. They never thought this was possible. The 'worm' never considered that the 'dog' would be interested in attacking and killing the 'worm', but that is precisely what happened, for the 'dog' was on its way to meet another 'dog'.

So we come to God's instrument. Once, I had half an hour to spare before an appointment in London so I slipped into the British Museum. I went into the Assyrian Room to see the fantastically threatening monuments of those lions and other figures in stone from the Assyrian empire. I commend this to you. If ever you want to have the Bible come to life take a walk round the British Museum. Go to the Egyptian Room and you will see the mummies of those who lived in the time of Moses. Go through to the Assyrian Room and you see the arrogant statuary of this growing empire. They thought they could tread down every nation. Read the inscriptions on the stones, or the translations hanging beneath the stones, of how they conquered one nation after another. You are looking at the might of Assyria, and the statues make you feel very small as you gaze up at these gigantic stone objects. God says through Isaiah: Assyria is the instrument in my hand. They did not realise it but they were, and he was allowing them to invade the land to bring the people to their senses, to cause them to wake up. It is strange, but invasion or the threat of it seems necessary to make people wake up. Look how our nation turned to God in prayer when the threat of invasion came to our land. How quickly the days of prayer vanished when the threat was removed. It sometimes seems as if the only thing that wakes us up, gets us together — the only thing that makes us real and serious and takes away the flippancy of life — is the threat of losing what is precious to us. The threat of invasion was going to be God's way of bringing Judah to her senses, bringing her back to himself, and Assyria was going to march. Notice that God is able to use anyone in his hand. Assyria was a godless, pagan nation worshipping idols, yet God could use them. God is in charge of all things. His kingdom is in the heavens and he rules over all, and he can use any nation on the earth to chastise another. God can allow anything to happen in history — and then he puts his hand down to restrain.

From vv. 5–19 we see how the empire Assyria felt about itself. As other tyrants have done, Tiglath-pileser was developing a master plan for conquering the world. That is modern, is it not? Again and again, wars start because a nation gets an idea that it is going to establish a kingdom that will knock down and take over other nations: first on its borders, then tackling other big powers, and then ruling the world. Tiglath-pileser was on the march. He had no idea that he was in the centre of God's hand. He had no idea that he could only go as far as God allowed him and not a step further. His ambitions took no account of the fact that there was a God in heaven who could allow him so much rope, and then enough rope to hang himself. He did not realise that any aggressor is a bit like the man who was tied by a long rope to a post and who could walk around that post in ever increasing circles unwinding the rope, but who would come to the point where he would have to come in again, and the rope would wind in again and ultimately strangle him on the post. This is what happens to tyrants who set out upon world conquest. How many times this has happened! The ambition of Assyria was this: I have dealt with Syria, I have dealt with Israel and its capital, Samaria. Little Judah? That'll be nothing to me. I can deal with Judah just like that. But when a 'master race' sets its face against the chosen race it is finished. It is as simple as that. And when Tiglath-pileser set his face against Jerusalem and the people of God he signed his own death warrant and that of his army. His ambition was to destroy Jerusalem and go on to attack Egypt.

Now look at his arrogance. In 10:13–14 in my Bible I have put a little ring round the word *"I"*. Do you notice the recurrent: 'I', 'my'? This is megalomania! We think of Nebuchadnezzar in Babylon many years later, when he said: 'Is this not great

Babylon which I have built for my glory by my great power?' Again: 'I', 'my'. Tyrants, world conquerors, develop this megalomania; they think they are the great 'I am', and they want thousands to shriek their name, but there is only one great 'I am' and that is God himself.

In 10:15–19 we learn that God will allow the invader to come as an instrument in his hand, but only so far, and not a step further, and then the invader would be destroyed. Today you can go and see the ruins of Nineveh. You can go to the British Museum and you will find not the Assyrians, just their ruined monuments. They are gone, they are dead —as ancient Egypt has gone, as Rome has gone, as Greece has gone, as Babylon has gone. All these great empires built up on military might rose, and they got so far and then it seemed as if God said: not a step further, now you are finished. Within a very few years they seem to collapse and fade away.

The Assyrian leader was vaunting himself against God, not realising that he was no more than a tool in God's hands, and we need to remember this. A preacher needs to remember this as does any evangelist or Christian involved in ministry: if ever you get proud you have misunderstood the situation. You are nothing more than God's instrument, and the instrument can do nothing by itself. All Christians need to remember this. 'We have done this', 'We have achieved that'. 'We have built a new church', 'We have given money for this', 'We have established this new work'. And God says: 'No, you haven't.' It is not for the tool to turn round to the hand of the one who wielded it and say, 'I did it.' Pride and arrogance is very unfitting, whether in a believer or an unbeliever, for both are in God's hand. The annihilation of Assyria would be so complete that a child could count the number that would be left in the army. Do you know that that came true literally? You can study the records of secular history and within a few years of these words the Assyrian army was reduced to ten, and a child can count up to ten because a child has ten fingers! The historical records state that a disaster overtook the Assyrian army which people thought nothing could stop, and that the disaster left ten soldiers alive! And God had said through Isaiah years before that God would so reduce the army that a child could number them. Ten men were left of the Assyrian might that you can still see displayed in the British Museum today.

We come now to God's *intention*. At this point I can imagine a number of Isaiah's hearers asking first, 'How much of Judah will they be able to destroy?' And second, 'How long will God leave them in control of our land?' Third, 'How near will they get to Jerusalem?' Isaiah spends the rest of this passage answering these three questions.

How much would be destroyed? Isaiah's answer is: most of you. There will only be a remnant left. We remember that Isaiah's first little boy was called Shear-Jashub, which means 'a remnant will return'. God has promised that from his chosen people there will always be some left, and to me this is one of the most amazing facts of history — inexplicable if you do not believe in God — that, when nations have risen and fallen, where empires have come and gone, there has always been a remnant of Israel, and there always will be! When God sets his love upon a people they are his forever, for his promises are irrevocable.

How long will this go on for? How long will the Assyrians occupy the land? Here God has a very comforting word for his people. He says through Isaiah that it is only for a little while. The empire that looked as if nothing could stop it for a thousand years, and looked as if it would conquer the whole world, reached the gates of Jerusalem and collapsed. Only God could have done this, and in a moment I will tell you how he did it.

Notice in the text the two words *rod* and *staff*. We have seen them used twice: God's rod and staff, Assyria's rod and staff. The rod and staff of God either frighten or comfort you. It depends whether you are in the right relationship to God or not. If it is a wrong relationship his rod and his staff will be used against you. The rod is a kind of cudgel and the staff is a long stick which is used against the sheep. Both can be used to hit the sheep. The rod and the staff in Psalm 23 comfort the man of God. In *this* passage God's rod and staff which are normally used to protect are used to punish. So we could ask: is God's rod your comfort or your challenge today? If you are right with God you will know that his rod will be used for you; if you are wrong with God his rod is used against you. Isaiah teaches that when the rod and the staff of God come against you it is only for a little while and then they will be removed. As God sent the plagues upon Egypt he will also send plagues upon Assyria.

Now let me tell you what happened. There is a dramatic description at the end of chapter ten of the advance of the Assyrians, city by city, spreading terror in their wake. Down they came through Israel, and the names mentioned in verses 28—32 are names of cities on the route. He has gone up from Rimon, he has come to Aiath, he has passed through Migron, at Michmash he stores his baggage. They have crossed over the pass. At Gibeah they lodge for the night. Ramah trembles. Gibeah of Saul has fled. The advance of the army — it is like reading the newspapers during the Second World War when we saw town after town had fallen. Here they were, hearing the news. Town after town had gone. Nothing seemed to stop the Assyrians. The situation was terrifying, until the Assyrian stood and shook his fists at the gates of Jerusalem. There were 186,000 soldiers in the Assyrian army. They surrounded the city of God and they looked like a forest. You could not see the bare hills of Judea around the city for troops. Can you imagine the fear? Can you imagine Isaiah preaching that Sabbath in the city and saying, 'It's alright, the waters of the rivers will reach to the neck and then they will go down again'? As they looked around at the soldiers massed upon the hills they realised the water had reached to the neck. Or, as Isaiah put it using another picture:

'You see this forest around us now, this forest of soldiers? God will wield an axe and God, the mighty woodman, will chop the forest down until a child can count what's left.' It did not seem much like that. It seemed as if they were finished and yet this is what happened. One morning the Jews in Jerusalem got up and looked out, and the soldiers were not standing up around the hills, they were lying down — they were desperately ill. You can see this in the Assyrian monuments, on their records. A plague struck the camp and it went through them like a prairie fire. Soldier after soldier became sick and could not fight. Then they began to die, and the living rushed the dead away, burying them. The soldiers went on dying, and 185,990 died that night, and the people of God had not lifted a finger against them. God can use a natural or a supernatural instrument. He could use the army of Assyria and he could use a disease against that army. That was what he did and what Isaiah had said he would do. Prophecy is history written before it happens! That night, the Assyrians overreached themselves. That night, the Assyrian army was finished. It was most dramatic.

What does this teach us about God? First, it teaches us that God can be angry — with his own people as well as others. Second, that he is a righteous God and that he is angry about things that are unrighteous, unjust and wicked. Third, it teaches us something of the power of God — he is in control of history, in control of the affairs of the nations, and he will allow an aggressor to go so far and then no further. God's restraining hand comes down after his punishing hand, and he stops the instrument that he had wielded to bring people to their senses. It also tells us of the love of God that cannot let his people go, that has to chastise his children and yet brings back a remnant to go on with him within his purposes. God in his great mercy and wisdom holds on to his people, even when they rightly deserve his indignation for what they do.

6

A BRANCH OF JESSE

Read Isaiah 11 – 12

A. SUPERNATURAL RIGHTEOUSNESS (1-5)
1. HIS ANCESTRY
2. HIS ANOINTING
3. HIS ABILITY
B. NATURAL RECONCILIATION (6-9)
1. PRESENT HOSTILITY
a. Animals and animals b. Animals and man
2. FUTURE HARMONY
C. NATIONAL RECOVERY (10-16)
1. GENTILE REUNION
2. JEWISH RETURN (second time)
D. INTERNATIONAL REJOICING (1-6)
1. DIVINE PRAISE
a. God is no longer angry b. Men are no longer afraid
2. HUMAN PROCLAMATION

Isaiah often talks about trees — cedars, oaks, myrtles, briars. He uses these as pictures of people, and he has a remarkably clever way of likening a person to a tree sharing their characteristics. At the end of chapter ten we saw that Isaiah pictured the nation of Assyria as a forest chopped down by the axe of God, and an army of 186,000 men was chopped down in a single day, with only ten soldiers left out of a mighty army. But notice that Isaiah likened the Assyrians to the cedar tree. Lebanon, he said, would be cut down. The Assyrian might was majestic and impressive, yet God chopped it down.

At the same time, Isaiah pictures the nation of Israel, the people of God, as a woodland chopped down — with just a lot of stumps left lying around. This time he does not liken them to cedars but to the oak trees, the deciduous trees of the Holy Land. Looking to the north they looked to the place of the cedars. So when the army came from the north they likened it to cedars. But there is a difference between chopping down a cedar forest and chopping down an oak, beech or elm forest. Chop a deciduous tree down and you will leave the stump, and the likelihood is that if you leave it, and the root from that stump, a shoot will come and then a branch, and ultimately another tree will replace that tree from the root. Perhaps you have seen that happen in a woodland that has been chopped down, and from the old stump there comes another tree, another shoot, another branch. The cleverness of the picture which Isaiah draws is this: Assyria — like the mighty, majestic, impressive forests of the cedars of Lebanon — God would chop down, and it would not rise again. But when Israel was chopped down by the Assyrian, from one stump there was to come a branch, a shoot. It was to come from a particular stump in the chopped-down nation — the stump or the root of Jesse, the same stump from which King David grew, the same family tree. From the 'family tree' of Jesse, which looked as if it had been finished and chopped down, would come a branch, a shoot, a person who would do wonderful things. This word *branch* is very interesting. In Hebrew it has the same root as the word 'Nazareth', and the word *Nazarene* means a branch. Perhaps you have wondered about something in Matthew 2:23 which puzzles many people: *So was fulfilled what was said through the prophets: "He will be called a Nazarene."* But if you search the Old Testament you will never find those words spoken by any prophet. If you take the Revised Standard Version and look at the marginal cross references they will refer you back to Isaiah 11:1: *...from his roots a Branch will bear fruit.* And the word *Branch* is the word *Nazarene*, *Nazareth*. Jesus was called a Nazarene, and this word *Branch* became yet another name for the Messiah, the Saviour, the one who would put all their troubles right. If you study the prophet Zechariah you will find there again this title is given to the coming Saviour, the branch. It all goes back to this picture which Isaiah painted of a woodland chopped down. Unlike the Assyrian nation, Israel would rise again. Indeed, that is the nation of Israel and it always will be. Time and again, people have tried to chop down God's chosen people, and from the stump there just rises another branch. You cannot kill that kind of tree. The root remains there, to grow again. So here is this picture of a nation that is devastated, the people of God chopped down and just left — but the stumps are still there, and from the stump of Jesse comes this wonderful person, the branch, the Nazarene, and Jesus is that branch.

Let us look at the things that are said about him in the rest of the chapter. There are four things he will do for people. If we can understand the picture language and the meaning of it all, this will give us four wonderful truths about the Lord Jesus Christ which help us to know him better, to love him more and to realise how wonderful he is.

The first thing is that when Jesus comes he brings supernatural righteousness into the affairs of men. Jesus is absolutely fair and just and good, right and righteous.

Let us look at how this happens. It happens first of all because he will be given the inward equipping needed by a man who is to be fair to others and for others. If I were to have to go in the dock before a judge I would hope it would be before a judge who is fair and just. He would need understanding, wisdom, counsel, and to have might behind him to enforce his decision. He would need knowledge. He would need the fear of the Lord. These are the perfect attributes of a wise judge. Isaiah 11:2 has been read again and again in English history when judges and magistrates have been appointed. They need the Spirit of the Lord and they need these things from the Spirit of the Lord if they are going to judge fairly. These very words have been said or sung at the coronations of our kings and queens for centuries. In a unique way Jesus was endowed with these gifts of the Spirit. Of this branch from the root of Jesse, this descendant of the line of David, it is said the Spirit of the Lord will remain permanently on him. Therefore he will be absolutely fair, wonderfully wise, understanding everything. So when you go with your problems to the Lord Jesus you go to someone who is wise, you go to someone who understands, you go to someone who will counsel you well, you go to someone who has the might to help you to see something through. You go to someone who has knowledge — he knows you better than you know yourself — and you go to someone who has a reverence for his Heavenly Father. Could you go to a better person for help? Could a better person be on the throne? Could a better person judge the rights and wrongs of any given situation? I notice that when Jesus came to earth all his answers reveal this very verse. How wise he was, how understanding, how right in everything he said. You could never catch him out even with a trick question. He always knew the right thing to say or do. The Spirit of the Lord rested on him. We are told in the Gospel of John that God did not give him the Spirit by measure but filled him full of the Spirit of the Lord.

Because of this, the outward equity follows. He will judge or decide fairly for the meek of the earth. Every decision he will make for people will be right. This needs to be seen against the background of chapter ten, and chapter nine where it is stated that in Israel of that day you could not get justice. The courts were filled with bribery and corruption. The judges judged by what their eyes saw or by hearsay, and that is not justice. So here we have the hope for the future, that God will send someone to judge who will not judge by appearance or by hearsay. How prone we are to judge by those two things: what a person seems to us to be and what we have heard about them. When I was studying science at university we had a lecturer who was very bad-tempered, very short with us, never satisfied with our work. We really did not think much of him at all, and we grumbled and complained about his manner. Then we discovered that he went through years of refined torture in a concentration camp during the war, and we realised we had been judging by appearances. As soon as we had that knowledge we began to think of him more fairly. The Lord does not look at a person's outward appearance as we do, he looks at the heart. It is not what a person seems to be but what they really are that the Lord Jesus knows. Nor does he judge by hearsay. Many people gossip about others and judge them from what is heard.

The next thing this Branch will bring is even more exciting and stretches our imagination to the utmost limit. We now have a most amazing picture painted for us of nature reconciled within itself and to man—the lion and the leopard and the wolf and the kid and the calf and the yearling lying down together, and the bear sitting alongside and a little child in the middle of that lot, its hand on top of a nest of adders and a few more snakes slithering around its feet! Imagine this picture of a child with its hand on an adder's den. It seems so right and so pure that a child should be able to play with any animal that God has created, but we know perfectly well that if you take a child to the zoo you are glad of the bars! Here is a picture of nature with the animals reconciled to each other and to man, including children, and that picture has fascinated people for centuries.

Let us look for a moment at the present hostility between the animals and between the animals and man. Someone who had seen a nature documentary told me that what little faith he had in a good God had vanished because in it he saw that one species preys upon another, and that the whole of nature is 'red in tooth and claw', as the poet puts it, and that it is literally a jungle of killing and cruelty, with animals pouncing on one another and living on one another. It is nice to live in England where there are not many wild beasts — just a few adders here and there and that's about all — but if you lived in most of the other countries of the world where there are dangerous animals, where people do die from snake bites, where a man-eating tiger can bring terror to a village, you would understand this picture much better. In the Holy Land in those days, on either side of the Jordan, there was a thick jungle of thickets and thorns, and in there lived the lions and the bears, and at night they would prowl up the hills of Judea to get the lambs. That is how David came to kill both a lion and a bear with his sling as he watched over his sheep. Man has dealt with that problem now. Every such beast has been exterminated in the region, so now there are no lions in the Holy Land and no bears. That is one way to deal with the problem; God's way to deal with it is to turn the lion into a vegetarian and make him eat straw like the ox! When God made nature he made it good. He did not make it 'red in tooth and claw'. The Bible's account of the present hostility between the animals is very different from the scientific one. The question arises: has nature always been like this and will it always be like this? Science says yes and the scripture says no. But scripture has more ground for saying no than science has for saying yes. For this is how scripture sees it: when God made the world he made it good, but there is something that has gone wrong with the whole of it — not just with man, but with nature itself — and God has linked man and nature so closely together that man's sin affects nature. When man became subject to bondage, God deliberately linked that bondage to nature.

Not only is there hostility between animals at the moment there is hostility between animals and man, and that is an unnatural thing. No less a person than Charles Darwin wrote: 'It deserves notice that at an extremely ancient period when man first entered any country the animals living there would have felt no instinctive or inherited fear of him and would consequently have been tamed far more easily than at present.' That was one of his observations and you can still make it if you can find a place where man has not been and where there are animals. This is just a little indication that God's purpose is that the animals should live together in harmony and that all the animals should be in harmony with man. That indeed is what he gave man to do — to tame all the creatures, subdue and use them all. They were all put there for man to conquer, for man to use, for man to live in harmony with them, and that is the purpose of God which is yet to be fulfilled. There is coming a day when salvation will have its effect on nature. Sin and salvation affect both man and nature. And the symbol or metaphor of this truth is simply that Noah took animals into the ark. Here we have almost a picture of how God's plan of salvation reached through man to nature, and what happened in Noah's day will happen in the days of the coming of the Son of Man to which the days of Noah are such a remarkable parallel in so many ways.

When Jesus came he showed this. There are not many things recorded about Jesus and the animals, but there is one very striking thing: on Palm Sunday Jesus rode on the colt of an ass on which no man had sat before. Does the miracle of that strike you? If it does not then you go out and try and ride on the colt of an ass on which man has never sat! You won't do it for long! Here we have the Branch perfectly in control of nature. Not only could he still the storm, he could still the colt of an ass without ever breaking it in; without trying to tame it, he sat on it and it carried him where he wished, into Jerusalem. Here is a little foretaste of what we are reading about here.

The third thing that he is to bring is national recovery, not just to his own nation but to all the nations. Here the word *ensign* is introduced, meaning a flag or banner. It was normally used to rally the troops for battle. You found a little hill on a battlefield, displayed your ensign, and all your soldiers came running to it and centred on it — this was their gathering point and then they were ready for anything. Mixing his metaphors Isaiah now says that this Branch will be a flag. If you can imagine the stump and then a branch coming out of it, and then someone tying a flag to the branch, you have got the picture in Isaiah's mind — people will gather around, and when they do they will be ready for everything.

The Branch will be an ensign to the Gentile nations. One

commentator said that it seems a little unfair that Isaiah should mention the Gentiles in one verse and then the Jews in seven verses, but in fact there is no unfairness about this because Isaiah in chapter two gave us the whole picture of the Gentile nations coming to Christ, now he is going to give us a fuller picture of the Jews coming to Christ. In Isaiah chapter two all those words about beating their swords into ploughshares, spears into pruning hooks — nation shall not lift up sword against nation, neither shall they learn war — were about Gentile nations gathering around the banner of Christ, coming to him, looking to him to rule the nations. If the nations would do that we would have a United Nations in deed as well as in word — if the nations would allow Jesus to reign, if they would look to him. One day they will: one day he will reign; the kingdoms of this world will become the kingdoms of Christ, and then the kingdoms of our God. What a hope for the world! It is not a hope in men's schemes, it is a hope in God, and we are pessimistic about men's attempts to disarm until the Gentiles gather around the ensign of Christ, then they can beat their spears into pruning hooks, their swords into ploughshares. Nations cannot afford to disarm until they gather around the ensign of Christ — it would be folly. But they can disarm when Christ reigns because he will be fair and just. All that is covered in one verse in Isaiah chapter eleven because it has been dealt with previously.

But the other side of it was not dealt with so fully and so now he deals with it. 'In that day' is the phrase that comes as a refrain. In that day the Gentiles will gather around the flag, the banner of Christ. In that day, also, God will a second time stretch out his hand and bring his own people, the Jews, to this banner. It is a wonderful picture. We must ask now: what does the phrase *a second time* refer to? When was the first time he did this? There are two possible explanations. One is that the first time he brought them to this land was out of Egypt. If that was the first time then the second time would be when they came back from Babylon, back from slavery in the north, about 450 years before Christ. I am not convinced by that explanation, for this reason: it says that for the second time God would bring together the remnant of his people, but when he brought them out of Egypt it was not a remnant, it was the whole lot! When he brought them out must still be in the future. Perhaps we are already living to see it. But for the second time God will get a remnant, what is left of his people, from all over the world, and bring them together. He will restore them to their place, but it will be a place around Jesus Christ. Such a hope for the people of God is wonderful.

God is going to bring his people back and he will even make it easier for them to travel. The western tongue of the Red Sea is to dry up as it did in the days when they came out of Egypt, so that all the Jews in Africa can get home quite easily on foot; it is to be split so that you can ford it. We are given a wonderful picture of national recovery for the Gentiles and for the Jews.

So, finally, there will be international rejoicing, true worship. Do you know that worship springs out of God's mighty acts? You cannot really worship until God has done something for you. That is why the first time the children of Israel sang was when they were on the far side of the Red Sea. I would imagine that the Jews did not sing much in Egypt while they were being whipped. I do not think they had energy to sing but as soon as they got the other side of the Red Sea they sang. We recall that in the New Testament singing is related to the salvation of God. You want to sing songs of praise if you have been redeemed and this is what happens in chapter twelve, the shortest chapter in Isaiah. In that day when you have seen these things you will want to give thanks to God. You will want to say thank you from the bottom of your heart. Why? For two reasons. First, God is no longer angry and therefore, second, men are no longer afraid.

The Jews had a perfect right to be afraid of God at this time. Do you remember chapter nine, when his hand is stretched out still? Do you know that you do not really want to sing to God until you know you are redeemed from his wrath? Until you have found Jesus Christ you can be quite sure of one thing: God is angry with the sins that are spoiling your life. God's wrath rests upon those who do not believe in the Lord Jesus. It is bound to, because they are ruining their own lives and other people's lives. But when you have been redeemed from the wrath of God by the blood of Jesus Christ, the Lord God becomes your strength and song, your salvation. He is no longer the angry judge who must deal with my sin, and therefore I will trust and not be afraid.

A favourite verse for Jews and Christians is v. 3 (NIV) —

With joy you will draw water
from the wells of salvation.

Outside the town of Tiberias on the southern shore of Galilee are some hot mineral springs and you can bathe in them. In fact, in our Lord's days on earth people would come from all over to these springs to get healing. Did you ever wonder why there were so many cripples in Capernaum? Now you know. They had gathered at the springs, as people gathered at Bath and Harrogate when the craze was on for taking the waters at those spas. There is a notice outside the springs today: 'water from the wells of salvation'.

The Jews, in Jerusalem, have a most magnificent annual celebration called the Feast of the Tabernacles, when they remember how God brought them through the wilderness. They commemorated the occasion when water gushed from the rock when Moses' rod struck it. The high priest took a silver jug holding about a pint and a half, which he would fill with the precious water from the spring. He would pour it out on the altar — the crowd would be hushed as he poured out the water from the 'wells of salvation' — and they sang this verse. Just as they did this one year, a voice rang out: *"If any man thirst let him come to me and drink*." The voice was that of Jesus. Jesus came to bring the wells of salvation. To a woman at the well he said, "*. . . but whoever drinks the water I give him will never thirst. Indeed, the water I give him will become in him a spring of water welling up to eternal life*" (John 4:14, NIV). Those who have been filled with the Spirit know the living water that springs up, and they know joy as they draw water from the wells of salvation. Jesus came to fulfil that verse. The tragedy is that the Jews still, whenever they think of it or read it, think of literal water, but the living water of the Holy Spirit is the water that refreshes forever.

When you drink of the well of the Holy Spirit you are in a position to tell the whole world. Notice in v. 6 the word 'shout'. Do you notice the progression there? The deeper you drink, the louder you will shout. Some people just say prayers, other people sing hymns, still others shout for joy. Believe me, it is one thing to *say* God is a wonderful God, it is another to sing and shout! I would love to stand on the housetops and shout that God is a wonderful Saviour! It is when you have drunk deeply of the wells of salvation that you will want to shout. Here are Jews telling Gentiles about the Lord Jesus. What a picture! At the moment it is mostly Gentiles telling Jews. Do not forget, however, that Jesus called twelve men who were Jews. The first people to say this, the first people to sing it, the first people to shout it, were Jews — the first people to whom it was said: "*But you will receive power when the Holy Spirit comes on you; and you will be my witnesses in Jerusalem, and in all Judea and Samaria, and to the ends of the earth*" (Acts 1:8, NIV). We have not really seen all these things happen yet. To a degree in the life of Jesus, to a degree in the life of the church, but we have not really seen complete fulfilment of these two chapters, which must lie in the future, and though this chapter talks of things which are strange and perhaps unimaginable to us, it is part of a Christian's life to be filled with hope as well as faith and love. These chapters are to build up your hope for the future, to look forward to the day when the Branch from the root and stump of Jesse will bring justice, will bring reconciliation to nature, will bring the Jews and the Gentiles gathered together around one banner, one flag, Jesus the ensign to the nations — and we shall all shout and sing praises to our God in all the earth, declaring what wondrous things he has done.

7

PLAN FOR THE WHOLE WORLD

Read Isaiah 13–23

A. INTERNATIONAL PROPHECIES (13-23)
1. BABYLON (13:1-14:23)
2. ASSYRIA (14:24-27)
3. PHILISTIA (14:28-32)
4. MOAB (15:1-16:14)
5. SYRIA (17:1-14)
6. ETHIOPIA (18:1-7)
7. EGYPT (19:1-20:6)
8. BABYLON (21:1-10)
9. EDOM (21:11-12)
10. ARABIA (21:13-17)
11. JERUSALEM (22:1-25)
12. TYRE (23:1-18)

B. UNIVERSAL PRINCIPLES
1. DIVINE SOVEREIGNTY
a. His purpose b. His power
2. HUMAN SINFULNESS
a. Our pride b. Our pugnacity

It has rightly been observed that these eleven chapters are not an easy part of Isaiah's prophecy. Most of this section must be devoted to matters of geography and history, and only then will we be able to draw out the lesson that God has for us. But I thank God that he put his lessons into geography and history, fixing his truth by time and place —so you cannot argue about it, it is there, it is written into history. Our Bible is not a book of philosophy, just thoughts, as most of the world's 'sacred' writings are, it includes history and geography so you can check up on the facts. Our faith is built on facts, it has a solid foundation.

The fertile crescent, as we have already observed, covers most of the green areas of the Middle East. It covers the corridor which links three continents: Africa, Asia and Europe. It stretches from the Persian Gulf in a huge circle away down to Egypt on the further side. That fertile area, surrounded as it is by yellow sand and brown mountains, is the world of the Old Testament. The nations mentioned are nations that lived within that crescent or just on the edge of it. This is particularly true of Isaiah chapters 13 — 23 which deal with some ten nations, all of whom lived in that region. Notice that the area was conditioned by certain natural features, by rivers — which between them supplied the moisture needed for growth, turning the desert into a place that would blossom. Away over in the east lies the Persian Gulf with two gigantic rivers, the Tigris and Euphrates, creating the Mesopotamian basin. At the other end is the gigantic Nile which creates a green gash through the African desert, and Egypt is virtually that green strip. The region is bounded by the Mediterranean, and the Red Sea, and then in the middle there is the Jordan, a much smaller river than the others, running through the Sea of Galilee and to the Dead Sea. Two powerful empires lay at either end of the fertile crescent, and in between them, tossed around as in a game of shuttlecock, you have the people of God, Israel and Judah, with their little river and their little sea. Much of Old Testament history concerns how one after the other of the extreme ends of this fertile crescent became *the* power: how the Jews were down in slavery at one end in Egypt, and how God brought them back; how they were taken as slaves to the other end in Babylon and how God brought them back. They were tossed to and fro, and when any empire, like Assyria or Egypt, wanted to become the 'master race' of the whole world they had to conquer the rest of that crescent and they would march around to meet the other end — and of course they would have to pass through Israel and Judah, right in the middle. As well as the two big centres of power at either end, there were smaller powers:

the Philistines, the Moabites, the Edomites, the Syrians, the Phoenicians of Tyre and Sidon. That is the geography of the Old Testament world, and there is a lot of politics in the Old Testament. We must study what is happening to these nations around if we are to understand these chapters.

In the last chapter we left this political picture, and here we come to the history. Assyria, the growing empire of the period, is getting bigger and more powerful and so is going to press down to conquer Egypt to try to control the world. So the first country she conquered was Syria, then, pressing down, she conquered Israel. At first she bypassed Judah, conquered the Philistines and went on for Egypt, but turning back she came to attack Judah with its capital Jerusalem, and it was there that the mighty Assyrian army was defeated.

Something else had happened which lies behind these chapters. Sargon, the mightiest king of Assyria, had died. With his death the little nations he had overrun saw a chance to regain their freedom, throwing off the Assyrian bondage. So there was a spate of alliances between little nations in the middle, against Assyria. For example, Israel and Syria had made an alliance. We learn that the Philistines, of all people, came to Judah and invited Hezekiah to join with them, and Judah, the people of God, were very much tempted to do this. Isaiah came into that situation and warned against putting trust in alliances with other peoples; the people of God were to put their trust in God. Isaiah was in the court at the time covered by these chapters. He had been brought up in the royal court and was very near to the throne of Hezekiah. So when ambassadors from other countries came to the king and proposed an alliance, Isaiah could warn against trusting in men rather than God. He prophesied or predicted the future of other nations in the region, warning that if God's people put their trust in those nations they were putting their trust in a people who were going to vanish, who would be a broken reed. He mentions Babylon, which was then quite a second rate nation, but Judah was thinking of allying with Babylon against Assyria. He mentions Syria, Tyre and Sidon, the commercial empire of the Phoenicians, Israel, Moab, the Philistine empire, Edom, the Arabs, Egypt, Ethiopia and the Medes. Of these peoples, one after the other, he warns that if you put your trust in them, know that they are on the way out and you will come to nothing. The people of God should look to God.

If I give you a lot of history in this part I hope that this one lesson will come through to you: when you are in trouble, when you are in real need and you are tempted to look around and ask who can help, don't forget to look to God, who can really help you. That is the simple lesson of these chapters.

Now let us look more closely at the key nations of that time. The first one mentioned is the kingdom of Babylon, a rather small nation, south of Assyria, with its capital city, Babylon, on the Euphrates, and it was completely overshadowed by Assyria at this time. Assyria was controlling Babylon. But, when Sargon died, all those other nations thought that, if they could get Babylon with them, Babylon could attack them from one side while they could attack from the other — they had it all worked out. Judah was considering making an alliance with Babylon, and Isaiah was warning against doing so. If they put their trust in Babylon, that would come to nothing. But the most unusual thing about Isaiah's prediction here is that he assumes that Babylon is going to become greater and more powerful than Assyria, and was going to become the most powerful nation that Israel had ever known. This was long before it happened. A trip to any museum will tell you that Isaiah was right and that in fact the real enemy in the future was not to be Assyria but would be Babylon — the worst enemy they had ever had. If Assyria attacked Judah and nearly succeeded in taking Jerusalem, Babylon would actually take Jerusalem and take the Jews back as slaves for seventy years.

The next thing that Isaiah predicts about Babylon is that it would later collapse and completely disappear. Therefore to put your trust in Babylon would be wrong for two reasons. 13:17 predicts the fall of Babylon after it has risen and does so in remarkable detail. There is a graphic picture of the eclipse, the death struggle and the overthrow of Babylon. Is it not astonishing that, when God says something, it is going to happen! The Medes were those who were called by God to deal with Babylon, as Babylon was called by God to deal with Assyria, as Assyria was called by God to deal with Syria. God is in charge of world history.

You may be interested to know how the Medes took Babylon. That city had a wall around it forty-five miles long (if you walked along the top) and two hundred feet high. It was thought that no-one could ever take Babylon. But Cyrus, king of the Medes, dug a canal. Right through the city, with its wall, ran the great river Euphrates, and he diverted the river round the city. The watercourse dried up and he simply marched his army through the dry tunnel into the city of Babylon and it fell in one night. It is a most dramatic story, but God gave the idea.

One even more interesting thing is that when Alexander the Great from Greece, establishing his empire, marched here, he decided that Babylon would be an ideal place for his eastern capital, and gave orders to rebuild it. He died within weeks, at the age of thirty, and Babylon was not rebuilt.

In chapter 14 the significance of all this is put on a much broader scale. From Genesis to Revelation, Babylon is a name for godless human civilisation that seeks, in its own pride and glory, to establish itself where God ought to be. This goes back to Genesis chapter 11, the Tower of Babel, and Babylon and Babel were the same place, when men built a tower to reach to heaven and they left God out of their thinking. God wrecked that scheme!

Babylon was undoubtedly the greatest empire of the Old Testament days. The Hanging Gardens were one of the seven wonders of the world. And Nebuchadnezzar, strutting among those gardens, said: 'Is not this great Babylon which I have built by my might for my glory?' Notice he is saying *mine* is the kingdom, *mine* is the power and *mine* is the glory. And in the next chapter we see Nebuchadnezzar as a madman with nails like an eagle's talons, eating grass in a field. God will not allow man to be as proud as that. God builds up those who say, '*Yours* is the kingdom, the power and the glory', not *mine*. This picture continues right through to the New Testament, where the Roman empire is called 'Babylon' in 1 Peter; and we read in the book of Revelation of Babylon at the end of history, and we think of a gigantic civilisation that is godless, built up on commerce, built up on political intrigue with the nations of the earth. And before God's kingdom comes, Babylon is destroyed. The king of Babylon is regarded in the Bible as a symbol for the god of this world, Satan.

Now look at Isaiah 14:12, words that are said originally about the king of Babylon. Today, man is getting so excited. We have put a man on the moon; there is talk of sending manned flights to Mars. We are going to establish human scientific achievement right through the universe and there is hardly a word about God in it all. As with Babel, godless human civilisation is proud of its own achievements, determined to place itself anywhere in God's universe, determined to control everything in its own name rather than the name of God. This is, of course, Satan's ambition. Satan has the ambition of being like the most high, of setting up a kingdom instead of God's kingdom — a kingdom of darkness instead of the kingdom of light. Therefore these words, which were applied originally by Isaiah to the king of Babylon, have been for Christians a picture of Lucifer, Satan himself. This is exactly what Satan put into the mind of the king of Babylon because it is in Satan's mind. "*. . . I will make myself like the Most High*" (14:14b). But what happened to the king of Babylon is to happen to Satan. As the king of Babylon was cast down from his place, Satan is to be cast down from his place.

The second nation with which Isaiah deals — and he does

so quite briefly — is Assyria. In essence his theme is: why are you worried about Assyria, because Assyria is going to fall too? The days of any such empire are numbered, and in 14:24–27 Isaiah reminds Hezekiah that Assyria will soon be finished. We will return later to that particular prediction.

Now Isaiah speaks of the Philistines, who had been enemies of Israel for many years. They inhabited the Gaza strip of coast from just south of Mount Carmel down towards Egypt. The main road round the fertile crescent ran right through that territory. Now, astonishingly, the Philistine envoys offered Judah an alliance to stand together against Assyria. Isaiah told Hezekiah that the Philistines were finished, their doom as certain as that of Babylon and Assyria. Look at the last verse of chapter fourteen and you find the prophet's answer to the proposition:

What answer shall be given
to the envoys of that nation?
"The LORD has established Zion,
and in her his afflicted people will find refuge."
14:32 (NIV)

In other words: we are going to trust the Lord, we are not going to trust you!

Isaiah now turns his attention from the Philistines to a nation on the other side of Judah, which was making an approach at the same. What a lot of coming and going there was! They were all getting excited about the death of the king of Assyria and thinking if they could just line up with each other they would be able to win the battle.

What had Isaiah to say about Moab? He said that sudden catastrophe would come upon them in a night, and it came. You can read the history of Moab, such as it is. You will have to read stones and their inscriptions to get it, but disaster came. Look at 15:5 concerning Moab. Isaiah found himself weeping for it.

Even though he had to pronounce doom on the nations, Isaiah was one who felt it deeply and he wept, as Jesus would weep over Jerusalem. Isaiah was not hard — he did not take delight in pronouncing doom on other people. No prophet of God took delight in this kind of prediction. They wept for those whom they had to condemn, and that is the right attitude.

Now we turn further north. In chapter 17 we look at Syria, about which an oracle or prediction is now made. But this prediction, interestingly enough, includes Israel, because by this time Israel and Syria were so closely tied together in their own treaty that you could virtually treat them as one. It is predicted that only a tiny fragment of each will be left, and again it came true. Under Tiglath-pileser, the Assyrian conqueror, Syria and Israel were only left a tiny remnant each.

It is interesting to see why God allowed this to happen. Look at 17:1–11, when there were only a few of the Syrians and the Israelites left: in that day men would regard their Maker and their eyes would look to the Holy One of Israel. They would not have regard for the altars, the work of their hands, and they would not look to what their own fingers had made, the Asherah poles and the altars of incense. Then, in v. 10, the reason for their downfall is given:

You have forgotten God your Saviour;
you have not remembered the Rock,
your fortress.

17:10a (NIV)

Notice this: the Syrians, who were pagans, had forgotten their Maker; the Israelites have forgotten the Holy One. God's judgement is for a pagan nation *and* his own people, the Israelites. Only after there were just a few left would they remember. That applies to most people — when they are in real trouble they remember their God. But many forget God when things are going all right — and put their trust in others. So at this present time, when to my mind this nation needs to turn to God more than it ever did, we may be thinking about the European Union for our economic salvation. We are thinking about this alliance and that alliance and this treaty and that treaty. We are negotiating with men, but if ever our nation needed to go back to God and pray that he would have mercy on us as a nation we need to do so now.

When the trouble comes, Syria will remember her Maker and Israel will remember the Holy One of Israel. It takes a war, it takes an invasion, it takes a disaster, it takes a tragedy to remind some people of their Maker and to bring back God's people to the Holy One of Israel. That is the prediction about Syria and it all came true.

Now, in his thinking and preaching, Isaiah roams far to the south. What a big man he was; what a big view of God he had. He did not just think of God as wrapped up in his little part of the world, he thought of God as the God of history, the God of nations, the God over the whole world — this is the picture of God in Isaiah. The nations are just a drop in the bucket, as dust on the scales, to God. He can move nations, and he moved the nations around the fertile crescent. Isaiah now thinks of the south-west, Ethiopia. This is not modern Ethiopia which is away up in the highlands, the plateau further south. But ancient Ethiopia was what we now know as the Sudan, and the people tall and smooth mentioned in chapter 18 are not the modern Ethiopians but certain tribes which you can still find up the Nile. They are very tall, very thin, very lithe and very black, so black that they almost shine purple in the sun and their skin is as smooth as velvet. These are the descendants of the Ethiopians of the Bible and some of them are still there as very small tribes, perhaps you have seen pictures of them. They were a very powerful nation in Isaiah's day and, when he said this, Ethiopia was ruling Egypt. Ethiopia had brought Egypt under her control and that is why chapter 18 begins '. . . *the land of whirring wings. . . .'* If you have ever seen the flies of the Nile you will know what that means.

Go, swift messengers,
to a nation tall and smooth-skinned,
to a people feared far and wide,
an agressive nation of strange speech,
whose land is divided by rivers

What was said about Ethiopia? Quite simply that one day they would bring a gift to God in the temple of Jerusalem and acknowledge that he was the God of all the nations. I do not know if that did happen or if it is yet to happen. The people are still there so it could be in the future.

Now chapters 19 and 20 move down the Nile to Egypt. What is said about Egypt? In 19:1 we learn that their morale would collapse; and v. 2 says that Egypt would have civil war; v. 3 that there would be a great growth in superstition and consulting idols, sorcerers, mediums and wizards; v. 4 that the Egyptians would become slaves. Again I simply have to tell you that every word of this came true. We also learn that five cities in Egypt would speak Hebrew and there would be a temple to Jehovah in the middle of the land and that one of those five cities would be the city of the sun (see 19:18), and the city of the sun was called Heliopolis ('heli': sun; 'polis': city). The interesting thing is that 150 years before Jesus was born in Bethlehem of Judea there were five cities in Egypt that had more Jews than Egyptians and where Hebrew was the official language of the city. One of them was Alexandria, where the Old Testament was first translated into Greek. One of those five cities was Heliopolis. Bear in mind that between Isaiah 19:18 and the events which fulfilled them to the letter there was a period of at least 550 years. How can a man five and a half centuries before a thing happens tell you in detail what will happen? How can a man say there will be in an Egyptian country five Jewish cities including Heliopolis? He can only say it because God has shown it to him, because God knows the end from the beginning and God is in charge of history. Isaiah predicted this and it came true. A temple was erected to Jehovah in the land of Egypt.

Now there is an amazing prediction towards the end of chapter 19 which apparently has not yet come true: that one day the fertile crescent as a whole will all be God's land, there will be one great highway from Assyria through Judah to Egypt. And we learn, in vv. 24–25, that Egypt, Assyria and Israel will be a blessing on the earth. This is the first time God ever says of Egypt and Assyria '*my*', together with his own people Israel. When and how God is going to do that I do not know, but I look forward to the day. Here we have a picture of free communication because there will be no fear of one another, no wars. If it seems incredible then it is no more so than the other predictions which came true to the letter. If you had told the Israelites in those days that Babylon would fall they would not have believed it. And if I tell you now that they will one day all be God's people you may find it difficult to believe. It is much easier to believe the past than the future, but what the word of God tells us will happen is as certain as what has happened.

Chapter 21 reminds the Israelites not to put their trust in Babylon, and in that passage there occurs the phrase: "Go set a watchman to report from the watchtower . . . ." When Babylon falls, when he sees the refugees streaming out, finally the watchman replies *'Babylon has fallen'* —words that are taken up in the book of Revelation: *"Fallen! Fallen is Babylon the Great! . . . ."*

In 21:11–12 we turn briefly to Edom, descendants of Esau, down in the south, in the valley of the Arabah below the Dead Sea, with its capital Dumah ('Silence'). Here we have the watchman on the watchtower again. Isaiah asks the watchman about Edom and says, *"Watchman, what is left of the night?"* And the watchman says,

"Morning is coming, but also the night.
If you would ask, then ask;
and come back yet again."

With such uncertainty Isaiah could not tell Hezekiah at that moment what was going to happen to Edom.

Then he comes to Arabia — the wandering Bedouin, the Arab traders with their camels, the travelling merchants. Here he says this: God has said that at night they will have to hide in the thicket for safety and when they hide in the thicket they will find refugees from all these nations coming through and hiding in the thickets too. The Arabs will be hiding, they will also be afraid.

Then he speaks of Jerusalem. In all this uncertainty the people of Jerusalem are having the wrong reaction. They are saying let us eat and drink for tomorrow we die. (See 22:13.) If all these nations are going to collapse, what is the right reaction? If all things are uncertain and going to vanish, what should we do? In a world where there are so many problems and troubles there are many whose approach to life, now as then, is, 'Let's eat and drink for tomorrow we die.' Isaiah could give Hezekiah the message: your people in Jerusalem have the wrong reaction to all this, they are celebrating when they should be repenting. They should be turning to God and trusting in him and quietly waiting for him to get them out of trouble instead of saying let's have a good time. The 'foreign secretary', a man called Shebna who was negotiating all those treaties, was getting a wonderful tomb built for himself so that when he did die he would be remembered for evermore. Isaiah came marching into the court one day and said to Shebna that God would throw him out of that place as if he were throwing a ball. Shebna would never be in that tomb he was building. The people celebrated; the foreign secretary built a tomb — what a picture! God made it clear that all of this was wrong. God was going to appoint a new foreign secretary called Eliakim. *"I will place on his shoulder the key to the house of David; what he opens no one can shut, and what he shuts no one can open"* (22:22). Here was a foreign secretary who would follow God, who would not give way. He would shut the door to these alliances and none would open. Those words are applied to the Lord Jesus in the last book in the Bible.

Finally, Isaiah looks at Tyre and Sidon. The Phoenician nation had sent sailors all over the world, sailors who were the first to learn to navigate by the stars, sailors who came to Cornwall for tin, sailors who went to India for spices, a commercial empire. Tyre was the richest nation in that fertile crescent, and they believed that in money lies your security. Judah was tempted to make a treaty with Tyre because of their wealth. God said about Tyre that sailors coming back to their home town will stop off at Cyprus and there they will be told that Tyre is no more, and for seventy years Tyre will be absolutely desolate. That happened too, and the centre of the greatest navy and the greatest commerce of the fertile crescent was absolutely deserted for seventy years.

What does all this mean? The key is to be found in 23:9—

The LORD Almighty planned it
to bring low the pride of all glory
and to humble all who are renowned on the earth.
(NIV)

The lesson from this very difficult passage is this: What was wrong with all these nations that God purposed to bring them down? The answer is that they were all too proud, and when God meets the pride of men he humbles that pride, and when he meets the humble, he exalts. So Isaiah's message was to Judah — be humble and trust in God and God will exalt you. Those nations were proud, and God's purpose was to bring them down. The simple fact is that of every nation in that fertile crescent there is only one that is still on the map over 2,000 years later and it is the people of God. Some of the names have reappeared but it is not the same people. The Assyrians have gone, the Egyptians have gone, all the others have gone, and Israel alone is there because they are God's people, and God exalts the humble and he humbles the proud.

8

KEPT IN PERFECT PEACE

Read Isaiah 24–27

A. JUDGEMENT EXECUTED (24)
1. EARTH - PURGE
2. HEAVEN - PUNISHMENT

B. JEHOVAH EXALTED (25)
1. PAST - ACCLAIM
2. FUTURE - ANTICIPATION

C. JOY EXPECTED (26)
1. DEATH - DUST
2. RESURRECTION - DEW

D. JACOB EXTENDED (27)
1. GENTILES - REMOVAL
2. JEWS - RETURN

To try to understand any prophecy in the Old Testament, the first thing to do is locate it in time and space. If you can find the answers to the questions *when* and *where*, you will begin to understand God's predictions in the prophecies. In all the chapters so far in Isaiah I have tried to do this for you. I have tried to gear it into the map; I have tried to gear it into history. Really, the Bible is a book of history and a book of geography, and you need both time charts and maps to get the full message of God. So I am going to begin by locating this message. I want to try and gear it into time and space. When is all this going to happen? Where is all this going to happen?

Chapters 1–12 of Isaiah were concerned with a very small area of land we call the Holy Land, which is no bigger in size than Wales. On a map you can see that the boundaries of Israel were almost exactly star-shaped. Right in the middle lay the city of God, Jerusalem. In the first twelve chapters Isaiah was only concerned with what was happening in the land of the people of God, but in 13 — 33 Isaiah zoomed his lens out and looked at a much broader field. We have already noticed what we called the fertile crescent, the world of the Old Testament, stretching from the Persian Gulf and the rivers Tigris and Euphrates, right round to the Mediterranean Sea, the Red Sea and the Nile. In 13–24 Isaiah's vision has broadened out and he is now looking at the nations around the people of God. But in chapters 24–27 he is looking at the whole world – not that he knew as much about it as we know now but he knew there was a whole earth and that the fertile crescent was not the only bit of the earth. So in 24 – 27 one of the key words, which occurs twenty-five times, is the word *earth*. So we must have a worldwide vision before us. If you go to the Church of the Holy Sepulchre in the city of Jerusalem today they will show you a mosaic star let into the floor of that church. The guide will tell you that is the centre of the whole world, and from God's point of view it is — everything revolves around his city Jerusalem, everything significant is related to that centre. So if Isaiah talks about the land of the people of God in chapters 1–12, Jerusalem is the centre of his thinking. If he talks about the fertile crescent, the whole world of the Middle East, Jerusalem is *still* the centre of his thinking. And if he talks about the whole world in chapters 24 to 27, Jerusalem is *still* the centre of his thinking.

Now we locate these chapters in time. Another key phrase is: *in that day*. It comes in every one of the four chapters and we have to ask: in what day? The answer is quite simple. Whenever the prophets used the phrase *in that day*, nine times out of ten they are referring to the end of the world, to the last day of history, to the day when God ties up all the loose ends, when he brings this world to an end, the day when he puts it all right, the day when he fulfils his plan for the ages — in *that* day. So if we are going to understand these chapters we must keep in mind that they tell us what is going to happen to the whole world at the end of time.

There are two other books in the Bible which do this. In the Old Testament, Daniel; and, in the New Testament, the book of Revelation. Both are concerned with the whole of the world and the end of history. Therefore you would expect that Isaiah would say some things that Daniel and the book of Revelation also say, and we are not surprised to find that at least fifteen to twenty things are said in these chapters about the future which are also said in Daniel and Revelation. The only difference is this: in Daniel and Revelation they are said in an orderly chronological way, but in Isaiah 24 – 27 there seems to be no order at all. If I could put it this way: if you buy a jigsaw puzzle and tip out all the pieces onto the table, you look at those pieces and think: now where do we begin to unravel it and find out what the picture is all about? Then you see a piece and you think, 'I know what that piece is, it's part of a man's head,' and you put it by. You pick out another piece and say, 'I recognise that, it's a corner of a house,' and you put that by. You begin to see the pieces. Gradually they begin to link up and you get a little bit of the jigsaw down here and a little bit there until the whole picture is complete. As far as the end of the world is concerned Isaiah just tips up the box and tips out all the pieces in chapters 24 to 27. They are not in any order, but as you look at this chapter you will suddenly pick up a piece and you will say: I recognise that, I understand that — and then you will pick up another piece, and another. That is what we are going to do here — pick up the pieces to put them together.

Look at some of the pieces. Here are some of the things that Isaiah says in these chapters that Revelation or Daniel also say. First, the whole world is to be judged. Second, the Lord is to return. Third, the sun and the moon are to be changed. Fourth, all tears are to be wiped away. Fifth, the resurrection of bodies will take place. Sixth, a trumpet will be blown. Seventh, a great feast will be enjoyed. Eighth, death will be swallowed up. Ninth, Satan will be vanquished. Tenth, Israel will be gathered together. Eleventh, a new Jerusalem will be built. Twelfth,

God's glory will be seen by the whole world. Did you pick up all those pieces as you read? They are all there and I am going to go through these chapters for you to see where I found them. You will find them all put beautifully together in Revelation.

I agree that all this is rather difficult and strange because when you are discussing the future it is so much more difficult than discussing the past. If I speak about a past prophecy regarding Babylon I can take you to the British Museum and show you the fulfilment of Isaiah's prediction and you will get the point. But how much more difficult it is to understand the future. If you had told my grandfather that you could sit in your living room and watch the Olympic Games in Beijing at the moment they happened he would not have believed you. He would have found it difficult to understand the future. But if you had told him that motor cars would take people he would have believed it because he had seen that, it was past.

These chapters say that we can expect four major things to happen in *that day*. First, we can expect the judgement of God to be executed. Second, we can expect Jehovah, God himself, to be exalted or extolled, to be praised. Third, we can expect tremendous joy which will burst into song. Fourth, we can expect Jacob, Israel, to be extended until her fruit fills the world.

Let us take those four things in chapter 24 about the judgement of God one by one. What an awful picture of desolation in chapter 24 — a dreadful picture of the world, destroyed, burned up. This kind of language in the Bible becomes only too real since that mushroom-shaped shadow spread over Hiroshima. We begin to realise that there can be dreadful devastations in the earth, more dreadful than our forefathers dreamed possible. The first is that nobody will escape it, regardless of their social or financial position. Everybody will be judged. That is a sobering and serious thought which we constantly need to remember. People may escape judgement easily here but there will be a day when no-one will escape. Money will not buy them out of it, religion will not buy them out of it, social status will not buy them out of it; everyone will stand before God, including the kings and rulers, who will stand with their people to be judged.

Why is God going to judge the earth? The answer is given so clearly: because of the guilt of the human race. God's statutes have been violated, God's laws have been transgressed, God's everlasting covenant has been broken — that is all in verse five. This is not God deciding to destroy the earth for arbitrary reasons, this is a righteous God saying: I must destroy the earth because they have broken my covenant, they have violated my statutes, they have transgressed my laws. And you just need to pick up one newspaper to find the truth of that. You do not need to look further than one day's news to discover that men are transgressing God's laws, violating his statutes, breaking his everlasting covenant. I know that not all men have heard the ten commandments but the Bible tells us that God has written on every man's conscience some of his laws, that every person in the world knows that there is a difference between right and wrong, and every single person in the world has gone against what they know to be right. There is not a man or a woman who could look God in the face and say, 'I have always lived up to what I knew to be right and good, and clean and true,' not one, and judgement is coming because of this. There is a very vivid Hebrew expression here. It says that God will take the earth like a dirty bowl, turn it upside down, scrape out the dirt and then scour it clean. That is what God is going to do, he is going to wash up the universe. He is going to scour it of men's disobedience. He is going to take away all this transgression. He has got to do so. How do you think a holy God feels about a dirty, sinful universe? He wants to wash it up and get it clean, and that is why he will make it desolate. The Hebrew (24:1) says he will turn the world upside down and scour it out. In that day, pleasure and happiness will go. I think the saddest part of chapter 24 is the second half of verse 11—all joy has reached its eventide, the gladness of the earth is banished. This is a very sad thing, but it is a picture to tell us that the delights of sin will go. People enjoy the pleasures of sin for a time, says the Bible, but the time is coming when they will not. It says they will even try drinking to get happy again and will not be able to. They will drink strong drink and it will taste sour and they will not feel happy over it. There will come a day when human happiness and joy will go because the earth will be desolate, there will be nothing left to enjoy, to be happy about. The only happiness in that day will be the joy of the Lord. But there is a sad picture of those who no longer enjoy their pleasures.

We learn how the earth is broken (in 24:18) but v.21 now says a most extraordinary thing: that God will do the same to heaven as he is going to do to earth. I wonder if you have ever realised that there is sin in heaven as well as on earth. If you have not realised you will not understand the New Testament where it says we wrestle against spiritual hosts of wickedness in the heavenly places. There has not only been disobedience among men there has been disobedience among the angels, and chief of them was Satan himself who began his existence as one of the angels of God and decided to set up a rival kingdom. And the Bible tells us quite specifically that he persuaded one out of every three angels in heaven to join his rebellion. These have become the evil spirits, the demons, the principalities and powers of evil, the spiritual hosts of evil and wickedness in heaven. God not only has to scour and wash up the earth, he will have to wash up heaven too, and in that day he will do both. God has a day coming when he is going to clean up heaven and earth, and that of course will mean scrapping heaven and earth; the old heaven and the old earth will pass away, and God will have to make a new heaven and a new earth, to create a universe that is as good as he intended this one to be originally. My imagination begins to stick here! I cannot imagine a new heaven and a new earth, can you? But God will have to scour and make desolate and destroy the old one if he is ever going to have a clean universe free from sin. So on earth a purging, a cleaning up, in heaven the punishment of those hosts in heaven who have been disobedient to God. Notice that in this chapter there are only two classes of people: those who lose all their pleasure and those who sing for joy. We will come back to the second group later.

In chapter 25 I can just pick out the notes that are sounded in this symphony. It begins in praise:

> *O Lord, you are my God;*
> *I will exalt you and praise your name . . . .*

People will praise God in that day for two things: the past and the future. You can praise God when you think of what he has done and what he is going to do. If you ever want to praise God all you need do is ask yourself what he has done. What will he do? And your mind will be filled with praise, you will exalt Jehovah.

The key word in the first five verses occurs three times: *ruthless* — v.3, '*cities of ruthless nations*'; v. 4: '. . . *the breath of the ruthless is like a storm driving against a wall*'; and in v. 5: '*the song of the ruthless is stilled*'. I praise God, who brings low ruthless people. You only need to read history to discover that. Study the history of every nation that became ruthless and cruel and you will discover that its days were numbered when it did. Why has he done it? To the ruthless he has done it because he has compassion for the poor and the needy. And in the exile in Babylon all the Jewish nation became the poor and needy. Before they were taken away into Babylon there were only a few who were poor and needy among the people of God, but when they went away into Babylon they all became poor and needy, and they now praise him because he brought Babylon down to the dust and Assyria down to the dust and Egypt down to the dust. Every nation that was ruthless with the people of God, making them into the poor and needy, numbered its days.

To lift your finger against the people of God in ruthless cruelty is to sign your own death warrant before God, and you only need to study the history of the nations to prove that.

What about the future? In verses 6–12 there are some wonderful promises. Look, for example, at verses 6 to 8 — how many things are promised there! Here is a wonderful picture of a feast that God's people will one day enjoy. Look at that statement: he will remove the veil that prevents them seeing God, the covering that blinds their eyes.

Look at the next promise: death will be swallowed up. What a wonderful reversal of the true facts of today. One by one, death opens its mouth and swallows up everybody on earth. Death has been doing the swallowing through history, but in *that day* death will be swallowed up and finished with.

Then we have a lovely picture. Have you ever seen a parent take out a handkerchief and wipe a child's eyes dry because they are crying? Next time you see that, say to yourself: that is the picture of God presented in my Bible, a God who will not just say stop crying, he will himself wipe away all tears from our eyes. When death is swallowed up there is no reason to cry any more; the ultimate enemy is defeated.

The reproach of his people will be removed. Whether his people be the Jews or the Christians they suffer reproach. How many jokes are made about Christians? If you are the only Christian in the office you will have jokes made. God's people suffer reproach. Look at what is happening to Christians in so many other countries in the world where they may be tortured and imprisoned. One day such ruthlessness will meet the Creator and Judge of all. One day the reproach of God's people will be removed. No longer will Jew and Christian be regarded with mockery and joking and rebuke and malice and ruthlessness. One day it will all be put right, and this is the day. We are content to wait for God's time. The Jews had to wait 2,000 years to get back to their own land and it has happened. We have got to wait a long time until evil is banished from the earth, but it will happen and we trust (v. 8) as we wait for the God of our salvation.

Notice the last word in chapter 25 is the word *dust* and that introduces me to chapter 26. One of the richest promises in scripture is: you will keep him in perfect peace. But this is a conditional promise: *only* if your mind is fixed on God. You cannot claim that perfect peace unless your mind is fixed on him. I have lived long enough to see that people whose minds are stayed on God enjoy perfect peace. Peter, walking on the water to Jesus, had his face fixed on him, then, suddenly, his mind came off Jesus and he looked at the waves—and his mind was not stayed on the Lord and he began to sink. You can prove that. If tomorrow morning you lose your peace and serenity I will guarantee it is because your mind has come off the Lord. Put your mind back on the Lord and the serenity comes back. The original context of this promise is this: when the judgements of God come on the earth, when you see the beginning of this desolation, when you see the ultimate judgement of God making desolate this world in which we live, then you will be kept in perfect peace if your mind is stayed on God. Others around you will panic, their hearts will fail them for fear; others will be deeply troubled at what is happening, but you will be at peace if you are alive when these dreadful things happen, *if* your mind is fixed on God.

The contrast in this chapter is between death and resurrection. In a vivid metaphor Isaiah draws the contrast between dust and dew. In the hot, dry climate of the Middle East the body does not go to mould but to dust. We still use in funeral services the word 'dust': earth to earth, ashes to ashes, dust to dust. All those who ruled are dead, they have gone down to the dust.

26:19 is a glorious verse. There is going to be a wonderful new world. But if everything is going to be put right, who is going to enjoy it? Only those, presumably, who are alive when it happens, and they are going to die anyway so they lose it. I could never understand the communists in this regard. They worked for and expected utopia on earth, and who for? The generation who happen to be alive when it comes, a generation that is going to die so quickly and lose it all again. What a hope! What a thing to live for and hope for — a fleeting, temporary utopia. I would think it more sad and more cruel to die if you have got a perfect world, and that is why there is something wrong with death in a perfect world. It states here concerning the bodies of the people of God: 'Your dead will live; their *bodies* shall rise.' Christians say, 'I believe in the resurrection of the body' — only Christians believe that, because they know that Jesus came out of the grave with a body, and the future in that perfect world is a future in a body. Do you realise that I will be able to shake your hand in heaven as I could shake it if we met here on earth? It is as real as that. We shall have bodies in heaven, but bodies that will not grow old and decay, bodies that will not be subject to disease or death.

Finally, in chapter 27, we learn that Jacob will be extended. The key verse is 27:6 (NIV),

In days to come Jacob will take root,
Israel will bud and blossom
and fill all the world with fruit.

But verses 1-3 describe the destruction before then of Assyria, Babylon and Egypt in picture language: the fleeing serpent is Assyria, the twisting serpent is Babylon, and the dragon that is in the sea, Egypt. Why these pictures of serpent and dragon? Because the devil himself, Satan, is referred to in the Bible as a serpent and dragon, and because behind the ruthlessness of Assyria, Babylon and Egypt lies the malice of Satan. Therefore, here we have the destruction of Satan prefigured in the destruction of these three agents of Satan. Leviathan the monster — another word which hints at Satan. After Satan is dealt with, and after the enemies of Israel are dealt with, God is going to sing a new song about Israel as his vineyard.

Notice the contrast with chapter five where God sang about Israel seven hundred years before Christ and he said that it was bringing forth no fruit so he would let the thorns and the briars come in and overgrow it. But now he says, '*Sing about a fruitful vineyard .... If only there were briers or thorns confronting me! I would march against them in battle; I would set them all on fire ...!*' Then we have a marvellous picture of the Jewish nation bearing fruit for the whole world. When God called Abraham, he said: I will bless you, and in you and in your family all the earth will be blessed. That will come true. The seed of Abraham will bless the nations.

The rest of the chapter describes how the exile has purged the nation, how going off into slavery has taken away their altars, their idols, their pagan worship. It has purified them and God has brought them back. Isaiah asks this question: has God smitten Israel as he smote those who smote them? Has he slain Israel as he slew those who slew them? The answer is no. Babylon slew Israel so God slew Babylon, and Babylon is no more, but Israel is still there. Assyria slew Israel so God slew Assyria, and Israel is still there. Egypt slew Israel but God slew Egypt, and Israel is still there. Oh, he smote his own nation, but not as he smote the empires of the world that have vanished.

So in verses 12 and 13 in *that day* a trumpet will be blown. We find that whenever we talk about the day of judgement, the day of the Lord's return, there is a trumpet being blown. Next time you hear a trumpet think of that. When God's trumpet blows, the piercing sound of it will be heard by all, and we find that he promises then to gather Israel one by one from all the places they are, until they are all back. Wherever the Jews are, it seems that God stirs up that nation against them so they might be brought back. If people ask what two world wars achieved I would say that they brought Israel back onto the map through the Balfour Declaration of 1917 and the events of the post-war world.

There is another key word in all these four chapters — the

word *sing*. Again and again in these chapters they sing. In chapter twenty-four Isaiah could hear people singing for joy at the judgements of God. What an extraordinary thing! Yet I want to tell you that in *that day* the world will stop singing. The only people left to sing will be the people of God and they will start singing for joy. We might think of Handel's magnificent Hallelujah Chorus which comes from the last book in the Bible, and it is the people of God singing hallelujah when God destroys human civilisation, marking the end of the world. That singing was born in that vision of the end of human history.

In 24:9 it says: *no more do they drink wine with singing*. In 25:5 *the song of the ruthless is stilled*. I ask you this: does all that I have written here make you want to sing or not? The answer will depend on whose side you are on. If you are on God's side you will sing at the thought his coming to judge the earth. If you are on man's side you will not sing. But those who desperately want God's glory to be seen, those who want God's world to be good, those who want God to have what he meant to have when he created the world, those people want to sing. And when you hear that God is going to judge sin and scour the earth clean and create a new heaven and a new earth, and swallow up death and make it all good, you will really want to sing, and sing with joy. It is interesting that Isaiah predicts that the singing will come from the west to the east in the world, and that the people who will sing for joy at our Lord's judgement coming will be in the west and will call upon the east to recognise the glory of God. I will leave that to you to work out in your own thinking.

9

PRECIOUS CORNERSTONE

Read Isaiah 28–29

A. BLUNDERING JUDAH (28)
1. DRUNKEN STUMBLING (1-8)
a. North (1-6) b. South (7-8)
2. DUMB INTRIGUE (9-22)
a. Lies (9-13) b. Truth (14-22)
3. DIVINE RESTRAINT (23-29)
a. Sowing (23-26) b. Reaping (27-29)
B. BLIND JERUSALEM (29)
1. DRUNKEN STUPOR (1-12)
a. Revelation (1-8) b. Retardation (9-12)
2. DUMB INTELLIGENCE (13-16)
a. Ritual (13-14) b. Reality (15-16)
3. DIVINE RESTORATION (17-24)
a. Reversal (17-21) b. Respect (22-24)

With chapter 28 we enter a new section of the book of Isaiah. Let me just remind you what happened in the first twenty-seven chapters. In chapters 1–12, Isaiah looked at the people of God in that little land which we call the Holy Land. Then he began to stretch out in time and space, and the next eleven chapters, 13–23, were concerned with the whole of what we call the fertile crescent. Not only was he stretching his vision in space he was stretching it in time, from the present to the immediate future. Then in chapters 24–27 he stretched his vision to the whole wide world, right out to the limits of the earth itself, and even included heaven in a side look. He looked at the whole earth, the whole universe, and he looked to the distant ultimate future, the end of the world. So if you are a photographer you will understand when I say Isaiah was using a zoom lens. He started with a close examination of his own country in his own day, then a wider area in the immediate future, then the whole world in the ultimate future, and he zoomed right out to the limits of prophetic vision. But with chapter 28 he zooms right in again back to his own nation, back to his own day, and in chapters 28 – 33 we have a series of sermons that Isaiah preached, probably in the open marketplace, or in the courts of Jerusalem, about the difficulties of his own day and his own people. But that does not mean we will not learn something from what he said, because the faults of the people of God in those days appear again in the people of God today.

Each of these sermons begins with one little three letter word — *woe*. It is there at the beginning of chapter 28, in chapter 30 it is there in verse 1, in chapter 31 it is there in verse 1, in chapter 32 it is there in verse 1, in chapter 33 . . . woe, woe, woe — what does it mean? To us it means a little trouble: come on pour out your woes to me, pour out your troubles. But in the Bible it means something far more and far worse than that. It is a curse; it is the opposite of the word *blessed*. If you say 'blessed is' someone you are pronouncing a benediction of God on them. But if you say woe to someone you are pronouncing a malediction upon someone in the name of God. In Isaiah chapter 6 Isaiah had pronounced a curse on himself. When he saw God in the temple one day, his words meant: O God, my lips are filthy, my speech is dirty, I use bad language. He said: '*Woe to me!*' Now he is going to pronounce the curse of God on a number of faults of his nation at this time. As we pick them out and look at them I think we are going to be looking in a mirror. As we do, I want you to ask: 'Lord, is it I?' Apply it to yourself. Are there any of the things upon which Isaiah pronounced the curse of God that apply to God's people today?

I hope the first one does not. It can do but I think it is usually rare among the people of God: alcoholism. Isaiah pronounced a woe on those who staggered around and stumbled through life because of an addiction to strong drink. The Bible does not lay down a rule of total abstinence for all the people of God; it does lay down that rule for some of the people of God, but it always condemns drunkenness which reduces a man to the level of an animal. Isaiah looked out at his own nation which was by this time divided into the two parts — ten tribes in the north, two in the south. The ten in the north were named after the main tribe, Ephraim; the two in the south were named after the main tribe, Judah. He looks at Ephraim in the north and sees a drink-besotted society. And we know from secular records that one of the failings of Ephraim at this time was that they were drinking far too heavily. It may have been the pressure of world events, it may have been the fear of Assyria in the north, but, whatever it was, the people were saying quite simply: let us eat and drink for tomorrow we die. This had increased alcoholism to a remarkable degree. Isaiah says: look at them in the proud capital city of Samaria, full of drunkenness. And he prophesies that it will all collapse. A nation that is given to alcoholism will collapse morally; spiritually, it will go. So Isaiah pronounces a woe on Ephraim. The message was: you have got this crown of beauty, the city of Samaria, the Lord should be your crown of beauty .... The people should not be proud of their own achievements, they should be proud of him and belonging to him. Having pronounced a woe on Ephraim he lets those in Judah (v. 7) know that they are just as bad. Then he describes an awful situation. Isaiah says here that the priest and the prophet were reeling with strong drink. They stumbled and staggered as they walked about the house of God. When people came to them and asked them for a judgement on some moral issue their speech was slurred, they could not even speak properly. The prophet who had a vision of God could not even get it out in words, he stumbled so much over it and he got all confused. It is a sad picture, but it was happening. And in the book of Leviticus those who were engaged in leading religious worship were absolutely forbidden to touch strong drink before they did so. They must be in absolute full possession of their faculties. It is even more important for a priest to have all his faculties than for a man to keep off drinking while he is driving, for he was tampering with the souls of men, and that is a more dangerous occupation than endangering the physical lives of people by drinking before you drive. The priest and the prophet were reeling with strong drink in Jerusalem, the capital city of God, in the temple.

Isaiah went into the temple one day and he saw a most horrible sight. It is there in crude and direct language – the Bible is direct and it sometimes offends our nice respectability. Isaiah said that he went into the house of God and the sacred tables were covered with vomit. Can you imagine anything worse in the house of God? No wonder he pronounces a curse on it all, no wonder he criticises his own nation for this. I remember going into a public house once when we were on a mission in the north of England, and a man who was three parts gone put down his tankard and turned to me and said, 'There's one thing that gets me closer to God and that's another' (pint of beer). That is blasphemous. It is confusing spirits. On the day of Pentecost everybody thought they were drunk — they were not, they were very close to God — but there is a substitute, a superficial moving of strong drink, that many people confuse with the real moving of the Spirit of God, and this was happening.

Furthermore, this drunken people, when they heard Isaiah's preaching, mocked and scoffed and criticised it. Look what they said. Here I am afraid I have a very personal interest in what they said. Did you notice the alliteration in the first few verses of this prophecy in chapter 28? In the Hebrew the priests were criticising Isaiah for his alliteration. They thought it was childish. Who does he think he is teaching, that he has to rhyme it all up for us line upon line, here a little, there a little? It is amazing how many people who think that they are big, and think that they are grown up, criticise Christian teaching because they say it is for kids. We are older than Sunday school, we are too big for this kind of teaching, it is too childish, it is too simple. Isaiah said to them when they criticised him for this: if you won't take it from me you'll have to take it from foreigners. If you won't take it little by little and rhyme upon rhyme from me, if you won't take simple teaching that makes it clear as to a child .... By the way, if you are ever going to get anything into a drunkard's head you will have to talk to him like a child anyway, and I think Isaiah's words were most apt here. But the truth of God is essentially simple, it is essentially for those who become as little children who are prepared to be taught as children. We are all in Bible school because we are all children and we all need to be taught the word of God, here a little, there a little, line upon line, precept upon precept, building up our knowledge as you would build up a child's knowledge in school. Because the foreigner will speak in a foreign language you will have to take it as a child would, line upon line upon line, here a little, there a little, because you can only take in a foreign language like that. That was fulfilled. They laughed at Isaiah's prophecy of doom, but one day the Assyrians surrounded Jerusalem and they shouted taunts at the people of God in there. They used the Assyrian language and the Jews had to ask each other: what does that mean? And they had to learn it line upon line upon line, here a little, there a little. So much for the intellectualism of those priests and prophets. They were superior. They wanted philosophy, they wanted elaborate oratory. People used to come to the church of which I was pastor who have gone away saying exactly the same thing. A businessman came. He was big, he was a man. And he went away saying, 'It's childish stuff being taught in that church,' and he never came back. But except you become as little children (and learn it line upon line) then the same word of God applies: you do not see the kingdom, you do not understand spiritual truth.

We go a little further here. In a key verse, 28:12, we are told that God said to his people: *"This is the resting-place, let the weary rest", and, "This is the place of repose" —but they would not listen*. The word *rest* is significant. God had said through Isaiah to the people 'I will give you rest', but they would not hear, it was too childish. And to this day Jesus says: 'Come unto me all you that labour and are heavy laden and I will give you rest'. People say it is too childish and they go on with the strain and stress of modern living, and they never find rest for their souls because they never take the yoke of Christ upon them. If they did then they would find rest. 'Rest' is a wonderful word. Consider v. 14. They were scoffing, they were deriding the prophet, they were mocking what he tried to say to them about rest. So Isaiah said to them that they were mistaken in thinking that they could find rest and security in making a covenant with their enemies. For at this time Judah was on its way with ambassadors to the nation of Assyria to try to make peace. The ambassadors came back and said: we have made a pact with the killers and therefore when they come they are not going to kill us. I cannot help thinking of Neville Chamberlain waving the piece of paper at Northolt Airport — 'peace in our time'. You do not get security and rest by making a treaty with a killer, by making a bargain with death, a covenant with the underworld. This is what Judah was doing, and Isaiah said: *You boast, "We have made a covenant with death . . . ."* If you do that with any man, sooner or later, after he has killed the others, he comes after you. That is precisely what happened to Neville Chamberlain's hopes, and it was going to happen to Judah. Where do you rest in complete security?

Verse 16 is a crucial verse in which God says through the prophet, *"See, I lay a stone in Zion, a tested stone, a precious cornerstone for a sure foundation . . . ."* You need to know something about Middle Eastern building to understand this phrase. If you have noticed the flint cottages in Buckinghamshire you have seen the same style. The idea is you build a straight corner and then you fill up the walls with rubble, and the corner holds the wall. If you have seen this in the Middle East, unlike the flint cottage you will see, instead of bricks, stones at the corner, and you will see at the bottom the largest of all, which holds up the corner, the chief cornerstone. Everything rests on that, the security of the building is on it; if you pulled that out, the whole thing would collapse. But if there is a good cornerstone well-laid, the whole building is secure. The chief cornerstone of Solomon's temple weighed 113 tonnes; it holds up the entire corner above the Hebron Valley and you can still see it today. The meaning is: don't go rushing off to Assyria to make a pact, don't go rushing off here, there and everywhere, stay right where you are in Zion; in Zion I am going to lay a chief cornerstone and if you build on that you won't panic, you won't make haste, you won't be ashamed of yourself later.

What was he referring to? We know now because we have the New Testament. Three times in the New Testament this verse is quoted, and it is quoted of Jesus Christ. What Isaiah is saying is this: right here in Jerusalem is the foundation of your rest and your security. You wait here and I am going to lay a foundation stone. That idea gripped the imagination of the New Testament preachers. If you build on Jesus Christ, you have security, you have 'rest' that holds everything else up. Remove Christ from your life and the whole thing collapses. Isaiah warned his people against rushing off, trying to find this foundation for their security in men, it is such a temporary thing. Their covenant with death was useless. A covenant with a killer means that when he has killed everybody else he will come after you.

Now comes this lovely verse, 28:20. The bed is too short and the blanket too narrow to wrap around you. If you are a preacher I urge you to preach a sermon on this verse. When you announce the text you will have interest straight away! The bed is too short and the blanket too narrow: is there a better picture of misery than that? Have you ever tried going camping and had these two things true for you? You try to rest and you just get off to sleep, and you are woken up again and your feet are cold. Then you scratch, and your feet are hitting the end. You just cannot rest or settle down. What Isaiah is teaching in this very vivid phrase is this: if you put your trust in anyone but God the bed is too short and the blanket is too narrow; there is no final rest. As Augustine put it: our hearts are restless until they find their rest in thee. This is a picture of people without God. This is a picture of a life that is not built on the foundation of Christ; a life in which the bed is too short and the blanket too narrow. They cannot get settled or rest or feel secure — something breaks in to disturb them. But I have been a minister long enough to see that in the lives of people who are built upon Jesus Christ the bed is long enough and the blanket is wide enough, and they can rest, and they know what serenity of soul really means.

In the third section of this chapter, having told them that God is going to come with destruction for the land, Isaiah must temper that warning with a word of comfort, and he uses two very simple parables from country life. Does a ploughman go on ploughing the soil all the year round? Does he go on churning and breaking it up for ever? No. He only does it until he has got a good seed bed, and then he sows. The lesson from this picture is: God is not going to plough up his people for ever and ever. He is only going to plough until he has got it ready for sowing something good in it. So the judgement is going to be limited. The other picture is of threshing. He said that you have to be very careful when you thresh that you use the right instrument. If you use a threshing sledge on small seed like dill you will destroy it — you should use a stick, a flail. And so you would use a cartwheel on bread corn to thresh, and this is typical Middle East policy, but you would only go over it once with the cartwheel to separate the corn from the chaff. If you went over it again you would begin to damage the grain. In other words, you must be limited in your threshing or you will destroy what is good. The word of comfort here is this: for your drunkenness, for your stupidity, for your mockery of

God's teaching, God is going to plough you up, but only so he can sow something good. He is going to bring a thresher over you, but only just enough to separate the good from the evil. He is not going to go on ploughing and he is not going to go on threshing after he has achieved his purpose. With the people of God that is exactly what he does. He has a plan even in his punishment. He has a purpose even when he chastises his people. And he does not do it so much that he destroys what is good and is left with nothing.

Now we turn to chapter 29, a chapter of spiritual blindness centred on the city of Jerusalem. The amazing thing to me is that people who can read a scientific book that leaves me absolutely bewildered, who can understand complex philosophy and are brilliant in their work, find the Bible a closed book and cannot understand it. Some of the most intellectual people in the world cannot make any sense of this book because they are spiritually blind. This chapter is concerned with those to whom the Bible is a sealed book.

In the temple at Jerusalem there was a large, square altar. It had horns at the four corners and inside was a grate, and the fire was kept burning there — the smoke went up. They would lay the carcasses of the animals on the fire for the burnt offering and the ashes would drop down in the bottom of the altar. And this was called God's hearth, God's fireplace, or in the Hebrew language, *ariel*. When somebody said 'ariel' they thought of God's fireplace, the place where the burnt offerings were burnt, where the blood ran down the altar, where the fire was always burning. Isaiah now predicts that Jerusalem, the whole city, will become God's fireplace. What is true of that piece of furniture in the temple will be true of the whole city: blood will run everywhere and fire will burn everywhere. That was literally fulfilled. The place was razed to the ground; the blood of those people who lived there flowed through the streets and Jerusalem became God's fireplace. But Isaiah said don't worry, because the enemies who surround the city will be dealt with. God will not allow this to continue forever. Again, it was literally fulfilled. They were dealt with, they were brought down to the dust. In one night 185,000 Assyrian soldiers perished without the Jews firing an arrow. All that is in the first eight verses, and we have looked at that scene already.

Consider vv. 9–12. Isaiah felt that he was just speaking to a crowd of drunks. They were in a stupor, they didn't listen when he told them these things, they seemed to be befuddled. It is rather as though you were trying to wake a drunken man saying, 'The house is on fire, you have got to get out before you burn.' And the drunken man says, 'Wash that?' and takes no notice. We can imagine how Isaiah must have felt as he warned the people. He could see that it was not just when they were drunk that they were like this; when they were plain sober he could not get the message in. Preachers have sometimes felt like this. I hasten to add that I did not feel like this with my former congregation — I was spoiled there. But it is said of some churches one visits that you have to take all your fire with you, or that it is like preaching at a brick wall — they are perfectly sober yet they are in a stupor. What goes wrong? You will find this the whole world over. It seems as if some eyes are closed and minds shut. You tell people of the judgement to come and they cannot take it in. Tell a man that he is going to face his Maker one day and be responsible for all that he has done and said, and he just looks at you as if he is drunk. What has done it? The answer is in the rest of this chapter. If you ask him to read the Bible and he is an intellectual he will say: this book is sealed, I just don't get the message. If he is illiterate he will say: I can't read anyway so there is no point. He does not get someone to read it to him. The problem is religious formalism, honouring God with your lips when your heart is far from him. It is due to 'parrot style' praise. It is due to learning things by heart and repeating them like a parrot in church while your heart is far away. It is due to spending all of the time in worship wondering whether you left the gas on, or thinking about yesterday's football match.

'This people honours me with their lips but their heart is far away.' Do you want to know what sort of worship God loves? Not people who learn a creed and merely recite it; not people who just sing because everybody else is singing and a hymn book has been pushed into their hands; but people whose heart desire is to tell God how much they love him, people whose hearts are full of love and adoration and praise, people who want to worship and who if they could not come to church and if they had to stay at home would still worship because they wanted to. The people of Israel were religious — they had all the feasts, all the services in the temple, the lot — but their heart was not in it. The only worship that God is interested in is heart worship. It will have to come out through the lips but it must start in the heart. This was the reason for this drunken stupor. If people are just coming to church for the outward show of it, if they are just saying things that they do not mean, if it is all formalism that they have learned by heart, then you can preach the word to them and the Bible is a closed book to them. If it is just religion then revelation cannot get through. That was what was wrong with these people.

They said: Who sees us? Who knows what we're doing? And they thought that God did not know a thing about all their intrigues with Assyria. Just because you do not meet God in worship does not mean that God does not see you during the week. Just because your worship and religion are so formal that you never get near the Lord does not mean that the Lord is not near you. Just because I cannot see God it does not mean he cannot see me. So their derision of the prophet was due to an intrigue that they thought God could not see. And Isaiah's message is that your thinking is upside-down. You are the clay, God is the potter. Can the clay say to the potter he doesn't see me? Can the clay say to the potter that he has no sense? Can the clay say to the potter: I will decide what I am going to do; I will intrigue; I will make my own life secure? That is what was going on. We can see that when Isaiah preached to them they just did not understand. They had reversed their thinking and they thought that man was at the top and God was at the bottom: the clay was up there and the potter was down here, and the pot could say to the potter anything it liked. There are many people who think exactly the same way; they think God cannot see them, and they think they can tell him what to do and keep him in his place. Their thinking is upside-down.

In vv. 17–24, again it finishes with a note of hope. Notice that both these chapters have the same pattern. First of all, something about drunkenness, either physical or mental, then, secondly, something about their intellectual attitude of scoffing, but thirdly, always a note of hope. If Isaiah began a sermon with woe he always finished it with blessing. That is a grand combination and the right way around. You cannot tell people of the blessedness of God until you have told them of the curse of God. You cannot tell them of the love of God until you have told them of the law of God. You cannot give them a sense of his mercy until they understand his justice. They will never appreciate his pardon until they have understood his punishment. So this was the way round that Isaiah began the sermon, with 'woe', and finished it with 'blessed'.

Chapter 28 finishes on a note of optimism. One day, he says, these deaf people will hear words out of a book. One day, he says, these blind people will come out of their darkness and gloom, and see the truth and the light. One day the poor and the needy will be lifted up and the scoffer and the tyrant brought down. The fruitful field at the moment of the scoffer will become the jungle, and the jungle of the poor and needy will become the fruitful field. God will turn things right way up one day. It is wonderful to worship a God who is going to do that. At the moment everything is upside-down. At the moment people's thinking is upside-down: man is the master of his fate — glory to man in the highest and God somewhere low down. That is upside-down. They said of the early apostles that they have turned the world upside-down; in fact the apostles were turning the world right way up, but if you are standing on your head it looks the other way. Since the majority of people in the world are walking around upside-down in their thinking, Christianity seems upside-down to them, but really it is right way up to God. God is going to put everything right way up and the poor and the needy will prosper, and the scoffer and the wicked will suffer. God will put everything right one day. He will not let it all go on as it is going at the moment. Psalm 73 is a wonderful psalm when you are depressed about the fact that the innocent suffer and the wicked prosper. The psalmist nearly lost his faith because so many bad people got away with it and so many good people had a rough time, until he went into the sanctuary and then he understood their end, he saw that God would put it all right way up one day, and he was prepared to wait. So one day true religion will flourish, though now there are spiritually blind people, stupid people who cannot take the word of God in because their religion is formalism. And in a church where it is all outward show, where it is all lip service and words are repeated without meaning, you will find that they cannot take much Bible study. In that church they will say: it is a closed book, I just don't get it all. In that church you will not find Bible study because it will not be liked or understood. But one day, and this is the last verse of chapter 29, those who err in spirit will come to understanding, and those who murmur, or the stubborn, will accept instruction. It has been my joy over the years that I have been privileged to preach the word to see this happen, to see men and women come and listen to Bible study and obviously they do not get it and they go away and they say it is childish. Then one day the Holy Spirit touches them, the blind eyes are opened and the deaf ears are unstopped and suddenly they find that this book is the most interesting book in all the world. Suddenly they find that they can understand it, they find it makes sense, it hangs together and they are off on a voyage of discovery that will last a lifetime. Even if they spent five hours every day studying this Bible they would still find forty years later that there was new truth to discover.

10
THIS IS THE WAY

Read Isaiah 30–31

A. FALSE ALLIANCE (30)
1. EGYPT RIDICULED (1-7)
2. ISRAEL REBUKED (8-26)
3. ASSYRIA RAVAGED (27-33)

B. FUTILE RELIANCE (31)
1. EGYPT RUINED (1-3)
2. ISRAEL RESCUED (4-7)
3. ASSYRIA ROUTED (8-9)

Let us turn back to the year 704 BC. The scene is the southern gate of Jerusalem and there are the envoys of Judah setting off for the south. They must go through the dangerous and difficult country of the Negev, the desert which lies between them and Egypt. They take a slow-moving caravan of asses and camels all those miles through the desert. They are charged by the king to go to the north and the south of Egypt, to the town of Zoan in the north and Hanes in the south, and to give this gold and these treasures to the Egyptians, and to get them to come up. But Isaiah had a big placard ('tablet' or 'scroll') and it read: 'Rahab the Do-Nothing'.

Let us look further into this prophecy. You will remember that in the first chapters of Isaiah the political situation was rather different. When he began preaching, the people of God had been through a civil war and they had split into Israel and Judah, and they were now sworn enemies. On the northern borders of Israel were the pagan nations of Syria and Assyria. Now, by the time we get to chapter thirty, Assyria has come right down, round the fertile crescent through Syria and demolished it, then through Israel and demolished it, and is now poised on the borders of Judah. What is Judah to do? Again the political pundits put their heads together. They held a cabinet meeting with Hezekiah and began to plan for envoys to go right down to Egypt. The Egyptians had developed cavalry and chariots and so were seen as invincible.

The interesting thing is that God allowed his people to fight but had forbidden them to have the superior horses and chariots. They were intended to discover that they would win with him, even without horses and chariots. If you read the Psalms you will find this theme again and again: put not your trust in princes; put not your trust in horses; put your trust in the Lord. Putting your trust in superior weapons means that you do not trust God. I always cringe when I hear on national occasions the hymn 'O God, our help in ages past', for the sheer hypocrisy for our nation, or any other nation that is in the armaments race, to sing 'sufficient is thine arm alone and our defence is sure' — the budget does not look like that. I am not preaching pacifism because this nation is not the people of God. But here we are dealing with the people of God, and they were told to fight with God's weapons. That was how they brought down the walls of Jericho, not with superior armaments. Here they were taking the line: Egypt has the horses, Egypt has the chariots, let's send our envoys down, take a lot of money with them and let's persuade them to come to our aid against Assyria. This was like a familiar, modern game of international politics: you fight one another in this war, you are making friends with each other against some new enemy in the next. Treaties fall apart and new ones are made. Of course this is an oversimplification, but when you look at it from God's point of view, is there not a lot of that in it? Always rushing around trying to make a treaty with some stronger nation so that we can avoid threats! Just look at how many political treaties there are today with exactly the same object as this. But the point here is that this was God's people doing it. They should not have been entering into this political intrigue, they had God, and with him they could have sung and meant it: 'sufficient is thine arm alone, and our defence is sure'. They only needed God.

Now we have the prophecy and we can understand the background. Each of these two chapters divides into three parts. The first part is about the Egyptians, the second part is about the Jews and the third part is about the Assyrians. What Isaiah says about each of these groups makes profound sense. You may wonder what ancient or modern politics has to do with your relationship with God. By the end of this study you will see that this has a great deal to say to you. In the first part of each of these two chapters the Egyptians are mocked, derided and laughed at as being utterly useless. Second, the Jews are disciplined and brought back to God, to the trust in him they should have had. Third, of the Assyrians, Isaiah's message is: you have no need to worry about them, they are going to be destroyed (the word 'devoured' is used in both chapters), so why worry? Panicking, chasing around like this trying to find help! — you should be quietly resting in God. In quietness and confidence shall be your strength; in returning and rest you shall be saved. That is the message. When you are in a corner right up against it, when the forces against you are pressing hard on you all around, when it seems as if disaster is imminent, in quietness and confidence in God shall be your strength. I have been long enough in the ministry to see in people's lives that this works, and a poise and a serenity is given to them in the middle of a crisis, when they are confident that God plus one is a majority, and that nothing can prevail against us if God is for us.

The alliance or treaty they were trying to make with Egypt was an act of treason, rebellion against God. They did not consult him about it but they are his people. It was not of his Spirit. Can you imagine those envoys setting out with their big caravan of treasures, and that little preacher standing there with his placard as it were, saying God didn't tell you to go? You didn't consult him before you planned all this. You are making a plan but it is not his. Preachers like that are not very popular. It disturbs things; it is seen as being in bad taste to stick up placards with a direct message. But Isaiah was a prophet of God and he knew that he had to get the message through: you may go to Zoan and Hanes — you may go to the north and the south of Egypt — it is a sheer waste of time. Such obstinacy would bring shame and disgrace. He points out what difficult country they will be going through. The lion and the lioness are in the Negev, there are 'adders and darting snakes' (NIV) — and they were going to take animals and people right through the desert to try and get help. They were likely to lose a good many on the way before they arrived, and they were deliberately putting themselves in danger.

Then comes his message. On Isaiah's sign the first word was *Rahab*. That is a well known name in the Old Testament. I am sure you know about the prostitute who sheltered the spies in Jericho before the walls came down. The name means 'blusterer' or 'braggart' — someone whose mouth is bigger than their life, who is always boasting of what they will and can do, someone who is all talk and no action. The interesting thing is that Egypt already had this nickname in the ancient world. So many times she had boasted of what she would do to other nations, and never did it. She was always boasting of conquering the world and yet she never really liked to leave her own country. So Isaiah gave her another nickname to the known one of 'all talk' and called her 'Rahab sit still', or 'Braggart Sitstill'! Oh, she'll promise you anything, but when it comes to the crunch she won't come. She'll sit still and you'll be overrun, though she boasts of her strength and superiority. The nickname stuck and it was a jolly good name for Egypt in those days. In fact, it turned out to be only too true. Egypt had her own problems with Ethiopia when the crunch came, and she never helped.

From v. 8 onwards, Isaiah stops talking about the Egyptians and he talks about the Jews. What did Isaiah do with this name, Rahab Sitstill? He wrote it on a tablet — that means on a notice board where it could be seen by everybody — and he wrote it to be kept for future generations. He knew perfectly well that the crowd would not listen to his preaching by word of mouth. I suppose if he had not written it we would not have it now.

Why would they not listen to the preaching? The answer lies in vv. 10f. The pew in those days told the pulpit what to say. Perhaps there are times when you would like the same privilege! But in those days when the preachers preached the word of God the congregation objected. Their attitude was: speak to us smooth things, nice things, comforting things. We don't want to be disturbed; we don't want to be upset or offended. They were not the first congregation to demand that from God's preachers, and there are different ways of doing so.

Now let us look at this a little more deeply. One of the most famous preachers in the United States, who drew the largest congregation in New York for many years, was once visited by a newspaper reporter who was doing a series on the secrets of great preachers. He went to this man's church for a few Sundays and he wrote an article in the New York papers about it. He wrote: 'What is the secret of this man's popularity as a preacher? I think it is this: he preaches a comfortable religion that offends no-one.' Could any preacher have a worse epitaph than that? Yet it is what people want. But Isaiah was one of the few preachers who gave what God wanted the people to hear. He told them the truth about themselves and about God, about judgement and chastisement; he told them what God really thinks. This meant that Isaiah never had much of a congregation. He was never a popular preacher, and nor were many of the Old Testament prophets. The people were saying, '*Tell us pleasant things*'; '*stop confronting us with the Holy One of Israel*.' This was not a title the people liked for God, but Isaiah reminded people that God is the Holy One of Israel, and his holiness means he has got to deal with your sin.

We remember that Jesus said, when he preached: '*you who kill the prophets and stone those sent to you*' (see Matthew 23:37, NIV). And they killed him, the greatest preacher there ever was. He warned his disciples that the same would be done to them.

The people were like a high, cracked, bulging wall that will one day collapse suddenly. You have probably seen old brick walls with soil piled up behind them, and they begin to bulge. One day there is a rainstorm, and down comes the wall in an instant. You have seen a fence that is leaning and you mean to put it straight and put a new post in sometime, but you do not do it and one night there is a wind and the drunken fence crashes, and it is all down in the morning. Isaiah told them that was what they were like. They were not straight and upright. A favourite picture of the prophets was that God has a line of holiness and he measures you by a line to see if you are upright, to see if you are straight people.

Then changing the metaphor — and the prophets did not mind mixed metaphors — he changed it to that of a potter's vessel. In the poor homes of those days, if a potter's vessel was broken they would use some of the pieces as shovels, to shovel the ash of the fire away, or to dip the water from the cistern when the housewife was baking. But he said they would be smashed so much that there wouldn't even be a piece big enough to get the ashes out of the fire, or to dip water from the cistern. They would be broken in tiny pieces, and they were, they were broken so much that there was nothing left worth saving within the land of Judah.

If you find that a bit uncomfortable, then look at v. 15. What a wonderful verse this is. We can always get the sense of a verse in scripture if we try and write the opposite. Here is the opposite now. In rushing around and feverish activity you are lost; in panic and fear you are weak. But the opposite of that is returning, repentance, rest, quietness and confidence or trust in God. If you want to be strong, come back and rest in God. I will come back to that in the next chapter. But the sad words that Isaiah said to them in the name of God are: '. . . *but you would have none of it*.' Again I am reminded of Jesus' words: *"O*

Jerusalem, Jerusalem, you who kill the prophets and stone those sent to you, how often I have longed to gather your children together, as a hen gathers her chicks under her wings, but you were not willing" (Matthew 23:37, NIV).

I think all of us who are Christians of some years of experience could testify that when we have panicked, when we have rushed around, when we have gone around feverishly seeking help, we have been disturbed, we could not rest, we did not find strength; but when we quietly got down on our knees and said, 'Lord, I trust you to help me through this; you can make all things work together for good; you can give me the courage to see this through', we found that in quietness and confidence was our strength.

At 30:18, we read: *Yet the LORD longs to be gracious to you*. How could a just God bless people while they were rebellious? How could a just God be gracious to them at that moment? They had to come back first. The Lord waits to be gracious to you because he is a God of justice, and blessed are those who wait for him. If he does not bless us immediately it may be *because* he is a God of justice and he waits until we are right back with him. Then, in verses 19–26, window after window is opened to the gracious mercy of God that they could enjoy: *you will weep no more*. There is guidance: *"This is the way; walk in it."* Notice that the guidance comes as you walk, and if you stray to the right or to the left the guidance comes. God will guide those who trust in him; he will say: this is the way. Maybe you cannot see a way out of the problem or where to go, but God will say 'this is the way, walk in it' — and you go ahead. There is a picture of plenty, a picture of sunshine, a picture of enough food and water, a picture of spacious blessing, and a picture of idols and images thrown away.

The final verses of chapter 30 tell us that the Assyrians will be terror-stricken; God will come against them with his rod, his fire. Notice the word *fire*, and here is the first mention in Isaiah of hell, a valley of fire prepared. And the word is used of the valley outside Jerusalem, the valley of Gehenna, the valley of Topheth, where the rubbish was burned and which our Lord used as a picture of hell. Isaiah's message is that hell is waiting for the king of Assyria. You do not need to worry about Assyria, they will be devoured.

So we come to chapter 31. Again the Egyptians are laughed at. Israel is trusting them because they have superior weapons — they need not do that. Horses are flesh and not spirit; the Egyptians are men and not God. The meaning of this prophecy is this: put your trust in the flesh and you will be let down; put your trust in men and you will be let down — but put your trust in God and put your trust in his Spirit, and you will be saved. So he mocks the Egyptians and says God is wise (and that means practical). They would not trust God because they did not think he was practical, and that horses and chariots were what you needed on earth. Yet God is practical and he can deal with people. You put your trust in him. If you cannot trust him in practical things then you cannot trust him in anything.

I cannot help remembering the words of Napoleon in the famous retreat from Moscow as he crept back with his men in the snow, knowing that this was the end of his power: 'The Almighty is too strong for me.' He did not learn that until he had crossed Europe with his forces. Here were the people of God and they did not realise this. It does not matter what empire arises, what dictator arises, the Almighty is too strong for them. If your trust is in the Almighty you have nothing to fear. Why? Because God is like a *lion*. Now Isaiah speaks of God in two pictures. A lion can deal with a bird, a cat, a dog, a horse, anything. In a vivid pastoral picture, it is as if a lot of shepherds have seen a lion carry off a lamb, and there the lion is growling, with the lamb held between its paws. The shepherds stand at a respectful distance. They shout, they throw stones, and the lion just growls and keeps hold of its prey. You try and approach a lion when it has prey between its paws! Here, God is like a lion and Jerusalem is the prey within his paws.

They may shout but they dare not come near. But God is not cruel, and Isaiah provides another picture — of birds hovering overhead; God will 'shield' Jerusalem, deliver it, 'pass over' it and rescue it.

Isaiah had warned against going to Egypt for security, and he pointed the people to God: *Return to him you have so greatly revolted against, O Israelites. For in that day every one of you will reject the idols of silver and gold your sinful hands have made* (31:6, NIV). What an appeal! Get rid of superstition! It is remarkable how people even in this day of science are superstitious. I have met brilliant, gifted men whose job it was to fly warplanes, those remarkable creations of science, and in the cockpit they had little rabbits and teddy bears and horseshoes. Is it not amazing? It seems that when you put your trust in superior weapons you put your trust in superstition at the same time, and many pilots of these modern fighters would not take off without their charms in their pockets. Superstition, security — what is the answer? The answer is to turn back to God, against whom you have rebelled.

The final verses again tell them that Assyria was finished. There is no need to worry, God will deal with Assyria; no man with his own sword would deal with them And the day came when 185,000 soldiers of the Assyrian army perished by an act of God, with not a single Jewish sword raised against them.

There is one profound difference between Judah putting her trust in Assyria and putting her trust in Egypt. Judah had once been slaves of Egypt, and from Egypt God had rescued her, and he had already proved that he was greater than Egypt. They had history behind them, so they had no excuse for trusting Egypt. After all, with a mighty hand he had brought them out. The lesson I want to draw is this: what is the point of going back to trust the things from which God rescued you when he saved you? In what did you put your trust in the past? Your health? Your money? Your friends? Your intelligence? Your connections? Science? The welfare state? What did you trust to see you through your troubles before you knew the Lord? When you came to know the Lord he redeemed you from putting your trust in these things, and he told you to put your trust in him. To go back to putting your trust in any of these things is an act of treason against God, it is an act of rebellion to him. Most people I talk to seem to put their trust in luck; they hope that their scratch card will have the winning line, that their number will come up. They are putting their trust in luck, in chance, which is why Christians will have nothing to do with luck after they become converted, they would not even buy a raffle ticket; they do not put their trust in this kind of thing. They have been rescued from that, they have come out of Egypt, they are not going to go back to trusting their luck, nor in their health – they are going to put their trust in God; they are going to quietly rest in him. When they do, they will find that they will be saved and that they are strong, that they are quiet, that they are poised, that they are serene, and that they are quite safe. They can say with Paul: *For I am convinced that neither death nor life, neither angels nor demons, neither the present nor the future, nor any powers, neither height nor depth, nor anything else in all creation, will be able to separate us from the love of God that is in Christ Jesus our Lord* (Romans 8:37, NIV). What security!

So we go back to that key verse (30:15a, NIV),

This is what the Sovereign Lord, the Holy One of Israel, says:

"In repentance and rest is your salvation,
in quietness and trust is your strength . . . ."

What a message! The people of God of those days did not take any notice of it; the people of God today need to take notice of it just as much, for we are surrounded by enemies that could easily take us away from God. We are surrounded by pressures; we are in a world in which the hearts of men are failing them for fear because of the political events around us. Happy is the man whose God is the Lord and who rests on the rock.

11

THE KING IN HIS BEAUTY

Read Isaiah 32 – 33

A. SINS LISTED (32)
1. MEN (1-8)
a. True - future (1-4) b. False - present (5-8)
2. WOMEN (9-20)
a. False - present (9-14) b. True - future (15-20)
B. SIEGE LIFTED (33)
1. ATTACKERS (1-12)
a. Heard (1-4) b. Seen (5-12)
2. DEFENDERS (13-24)
a. Heard b. Seen

In the second half of the book we come to some glorious and better known passages, but these two chapters are not very well known; there are not many quotable quotes in them, not many texts that we hear used in worship. Nevertheless, they have a message, even if at first it seems rather obscure.

They are full of contrast. There is a basic contrast between chapter 32 and chapter 33. Chapter 32 is largely concerned with the sin of men, and chapter 33 is largely concerned with the salvation of God. In chapter 32 the prophet comes with a message of gloom and despondency, a message of condemnation, but in chapter 33 he comes with a message of hope. The simple reason for this is that the message of the preacher was always the opposite of the mood of the people. When they were confident and buoyant and optimistic the prophet came with a message of doom, a message of disaster; but when the people panicked and were pessimistic or depressed, the prophet brought a word of hope and optimism. In a sense, a preacher's duty is to bring to people the opposite of their present mood, to balance human sin with divine salvation, to shake the complacent but to comfort the despairing.

We have many more contrasts, and Isaiah was very fond of drawing contrasts to enable people to see the truth: contrasts between men and women, contrasts between the false and the true, contrasts between the present and the future, contrasts between those who attacked and those who defended; between those inside and those outside; between the human and the divine; between what is heard and what is seen.

We begin with a striking statement, which does not excite us and we cannot see the point of it, living in our own times. But, *See, a king will reign in righteousness* (32:1a, NIV) is the most exciting thing you could say in the Middle East, and would thrill people's hearts. I want to emphasise this phrase. The reason why we do not get excited about these words is that (in Britain) we live in a constitutional monarchy in which the poor royal family has little or nothing to do, and if ever they do anything they are criticised. What a changed conception of royalty we have today! We do not live in a kingdom where royalty governs. The real centre of power is of course in the Prime Minister, who within our country has more personal power than the President of the United States (and nowadays, of course, much law-making and some executive power is exercised by the European Union in relation to its member States). So although we sing of the Queen 'long may she reign', in fact she does not rule. Therefore the announcement that a king will reign in righteousness does not thrill our hearts because we cannot see what a king could do, however good he was, and we no longer see the centre of power in the throne.

But if you want to know what a monarch really was, you would have to look at the history of traditional kingship in the Middle East. The king was a 'managing monarch'; power rested with the throne, his word was law. Therefore the crucial factor is this: will the king reign in sin or in righteousness; in selfishness or in consideration for the people? The position could be used by the ruling monarch for personal ends, or it could be used for the benefit of the people. Traditionally, for some hours every day, the king sat and any person in the land could approach him directly with a complaint, an injustice, a right that was not being met, a need that was not being satisfied. There is no need for an Ombudsman — the king is the Ombudsman. This is the concept of royalty lying behind the Old and New Testaments. But I have the feeling that many of us in Britain, because we have an earthly constitutional monarch, tend to treat God as a constitutional monarch, thinking he is there on the throne of heaven but the real decisions are made here. But I remind you that our Lord himself is a *managing* monarch and it is the privilege of every citizen in the kingdom to approach the throne of grace and to bring a need to the King of kings and Lord of lords. That should thrill you. 'See, a king will *reign*' — that is something that we do not know. 'See, a king will reign in *righteousness*' — this was the hope of Israel at this time and Isaiah could hardly have expressed their national hopes in a better way. One day there will be a king who will reign in righteousness, who will be a protection for every citizen. He will be like the shadow of a rock within a weary land, somewhere you can run to be sheltered and covered. He will be a protection, he will be a shelter from the wind, a refuge from the storm. If you had the privilege, just imagine that any trouble you had, any burden that you carried, any distress you were caused, you had the right to go straight to Buckingham Palace and share it with the Queen, who would put it right with all her power. Think of the security citizens would enjoy in a managing monarchy like that. This then is the picture painted at the beginning of chapter 32.

Sadly, this is not a picture of the situation as it was in Isaiah's day. It is a picture of the future, of true government, of righteousness and justice, of a place in which there is right judgement of character, in which the king will have discernment and will call things by their right names and will be absolutely fair — this is true nobility. It is a wonderful thing if you have a righteous, just and benevolent king who will listen to any of his subjects and who will call right what is right and wrong what is wrong. It is a lovely picture, and it is the sort of government that God really intended us to have and for which he made us. A righteous king reigning is God's government.

In vv. 5–8 the present false government is pictured — marked by bribery and corruption. When corruption is revealed at the top you will not be able to arrest the decline in integrity among the people, but where there are rulers of integrity, the example of their influence tends to spread through the rest of society. In Isaiah's day a bad person was called noble, a fool was called honourable — they did not call things by their right names.

Now let me bring that up to date. Who is a successful person? Who is a clever person? According to the Bible the fool is dishonest and the wise man is honest, but in many industrial and commercial realms today you are thought to be a fool if you are honest, and these terms have been turned upside-down. Who is considered successful today? Someone who has got on regardless of the principles on which he based his career, who has made money however he has made it, and so we twist our language. That was what was going on. Language became twisted because ideas were twisted. Conventional, worldly morality was replacing the standards of God. So men were in control whose judgements were wrong, whose moral principles were perverted, whose integrity was in question, and this was spreading down through society. I have lived for a short time in such a society where it was widely known that a certain bribe in a certain quarter would see you through the law courts. Once you have got that corruption at the top in the representatives of justice you cannot stop the rot spreading. When the men in control have wrong judgement then the whole of society will slip. In such a situation Isaiah stands and says that a king will reign in righteousness. What a wonderful hope for a people living in a society like that.

Now let us turn from the men to the women. The men are

in control. By the way, the people of God never had a queen in the Bible, they always had kings. Nations around them had queens — the Queen of Sheba is the best known, Cleopatra is another. In God's wisdom he ordained that men should be the leaders of society, and they were in control and on the throne. The women contributed their own particular nature and sentiment and attitude to the well-being of society, but it was not to be in control, it was to be in contentment by nature. Here I tread warily for I am speaking as a man. But nevertheless, here is what Isaiah is saying: by nature women contribute the contentment, the security, the stability of society. But just as man's virtue perverted becomes a vice, so woman's virtue perverted becomes a vice. And if man's virtue is to judge, it becomes a vice when he judges badly. And if a woman's virtue is to be content with the leadership, it becomes a vice when it becomes complacency.

Here is an interesting fact: in 32:9f the words *ease* and *complacency*, which are clearly a criticism and a sin, are the same words as are used in vv. 17f., but they are translated *peace* and *quietness* —the same word, but there a commendation; a contentment either becomes the virtue of peace or the vice of ease; it either becomes the virtue of quietness and trust or the vice of complacency. The besetting sin of the feminine nature is thoughtlessness and shallow optimism, and the attitude that says, 'Well, I don't see any need for change and I'm quite happy with things as they are — why can't we go along as we have always gone along?' — this is the perversion of a virtue. The true basis for such virtue is not to be content with things as they are but to be quiet and content with God. By nature women contribute contentment and stability and quietness and rest to the menfolk as they rush ahead with their wrong judgements. Not that there is to be a suffragette movement, not that women are to transfer their complacency to an agitated demand for things to be put right, but rather that their trust should be in God to put things right.

The false vice of this contentment appears in verses 9 – 14. Isaiah's prediction of disaster made no impression on the women. They did not believe what he said, they were content with things as they were. Why are you so worried, preacher? Things are alright, we're getting on fine; why is there any need for us to make any changes? What's wrong? Everything is managing perfectly well. When a woman talks like that she is turning the virtue into a vice. She should be content, but not complacent. She should be trustful, but not at ease in a situation like this. So Isaiah tells them that in twelve months' time they will be in mourning. There will be no harvest. Their complacency and ease will be shattered. Just as men are given to the besetting temptation (or sin) of making wrong judgements, women are given to the besetting sin of making no judgements. Mary, the mother of our Lord, is held up before us as an example of feminine thoughtfulness. She was quiet, she was trustful, but not because she was complacent, because she pondered on these things in her heart and she trusted in the Lord. She is held up before us in scripture as an example, as one who was thoughtfully optimistic, whose trust was in the Lord, and therefore she was peaceful and quiet, and that is the impression we get. It was not a false, superficial optimism or a frivolous self-security; it was not ease and complacency, it was peace and quiet.

When I went down to a nursing home in Brighton I noticed as I went in that a text was carved in the stone over the door. It was Isaiah 32:18 – 'My people will abide in a peaceful habitation, in secure dwellings and in quiet resting places'. Indeed it was a quiet home inside and there was no panic, there was quiet and restfulness, but it did not come from complacency, it came from a trust in God. That is to be the virtue of the women in society – a quiet trust in God that stability may be given to the family and the home, and through the home to the society itself.

Where does that true stability come from? Where does that true peace and contentment come from? It comes from the Holy

Spirit. When the Spirit is poured from on high upon people — that is when women are given the virtue of true contentment. So, in v. 15, we learn that the Spirit is 'poured'.

Then (v. 16) justice will dwell in the wilderness and righteousness will abide in the fruitful field. The effect of righteousness will be peace. One of the main faults and difficulties of our world today in trying to find peace is that we want peace first and righteousness afterwards. Here it is stated that righteousness produces peace, not the other way on; when men seek justice and do what is right, the fruit is peace. There is no short cut to peace and security — the only path lies through righteousness and justice, what is right and true and fair. When we seek justice we shall find peace, but if we just seek peace we do not even find it. That is why Christ said, *"But seek first his kingdom and his righteousness, and all these things will be given to you as well"* (Matthew 6:33, NIV). The first thing is first and the second thing follows. The first need of our world is not for peace and security but for justice and righteousness. This applies to our internal peace within the nation. If we want peace between people in the nation, if we want security of property and life within the nation, it is righteousness we shall need to seek first.

Now we turn to chapter 33. Many years elapse between these two chapters, and by the time we enter chapter 33 the people are in quite a different attitude. In chapter 32 they were complacent, they were content. Their attitude to Isaiah was: we can't see anything wrong, we don't have any need to listen to you, everything is perfectly alright. But by the time you enter chapter 33 everything is all wrong and they know it.

Let me paint the picture for you. It is really a most dramatic chapter, though because we do not live in the situation it is not dramatic to us. Those Assyrian hordes by the thousand came down through Israel and Judah. They burned every village and city, they foraged every field and left it utterly wasted. In their track they left a devastated countryside until finally one day they reached and besieged the city of God, Jerusalem. Right round the city they were — 185,000 soldiers around that little city just a few acres in area. During the siege the bread and water diet mentioned in chapter 33 began, and sickness came. We are told in the Bible, in very crude but very realistic terms, that that siege reduced the people of Israel to eating their own dung and drinking their own urine. This is the background of chapter 33. Now the people are not complacent, they are in mortal fear. They know that every other city has fallen, and they can see beyond the troops around them the devastated countryside. Everywhere they look there is sadness and desolation.

One of their biggest problems is water. The city of Jerusalem had no water within its walls. Later, King Hezekiah himself ordered a tunnel 1,700 feet long to be dug through the rocks to a spring in the valley outside the walls, a tunnel that I have walked through, which is still there today, and which was discovered by accident in the 1920s when a boy fell through a hole and they found that he had fallen into Hezekiah's tunnel; but in these days they had no water, and they were short of food.

A very dirty trick was played on Hezekiah by Sennacherib, the king of the Assyrians. Sennacherib offered them peace if they would pay him heavily. In desperation, Hezekiah plundered the treasury and even stripped the gold and silver off the temple itself and took every bit of wealth they could muster out to the troops under a white flag. They took the money and then mocked and laughed and broke the covenant and said they were still going to take Jerusalem. It is mentioned in chapter 33. Covenants are broken. The envoys of peace weep bitterly. Those envoys they had sent out with the money to try and buy off this great conqueror —they wept. Every other city had fallen and there was no human reason why Jerusalem should not fall. That is the picture.

Now Isaiah does not come preaching sin and judgement, he does not come saying you will mourn in a year's time, he comes with a different message. The people know now that they have sinned and they have been too complacent. They know they were wrong to say it could never touch them — they know it and now they need a word of salvation.

Vv. 1–12 describe the scene *outside* the city and vv. 13–24 describe the scene *inside* the city. The first half of the chapter describes the scene outside before the siege was lifted, but the second half describes the scene inside after the siege was lifted, and if you realise that then you will understand everything that is said.

The first verse is a message shouted from the walls by Isaiah to the Assyrians. Standing up on the tower he shouts: a curse on you (remember that the word 'woe' is a curse), you destroyer, you will be destroyed; a curse on you who dealt treacherously, taking our money and still coming to attack us; a curse of God upon you, woe to you. I can imagine that dramatic moment as one solitary figure in the city cries out and curses the Assyrian troops. Then that figure standing on the tower lifted his face and cried, not to the men around the city but the God above the city:

O Lord, be gracious to us;
we long for you.
Be our strength every morning,
our salvation in time of distress.

33:2 (NIV)

The wonderful prayer of Isaiah must have filled the people with tremendous confidence; it is wrung from the heart of one man but it is the echo of the whole city.

Then, having listened to the two things he says, Isaiah invites them to look, first into the future:

The Lord is exalted, for he dwells on high;
He will fill Zion with justice and righteousness.

33:5 (NIV)

Look to the future — look now at what God will do: he will be the stability of our times, abundance of salvation, wisdom and knowledge — look at God. They were so busy looking at the enemy troops, they were panicking and afraid. Look at God! They looked. Now look out at that land beyond the troops, the holy land. The valiant ones cry without, the envoys of peace weep bitterly, the highways are deserted. Covenants are broken, witnesses are despised, there is no regard for man, the land mourns and languishes. Look at the most beautiful national parks in our land, he says, look at Lebanon, look at Sharon, look at Bashan, look at Carmel — these were all beauty spots. They looked, and their attention was drawn to what God was going to do. The word *now* is heard three times: now I will arise says the Lord, now I will lift myself up, now I will be exalted. God acted suddenly. The next morning when they got up there were fewer than twelve soldiers left! How would you feel if you had been in that city? How you would feel would depend entirely on the state of your soul. If you were not right with God you would be afraid. What happened? In 33:14, we learn that the sinners in Zion are afraid. Supposing you said one night: 'Lord, destroy all the wicked people in the earth' — then, when you woke up in the morning, everybody else in your street had gone. How would you feel? If there was any trace of wickedness in you, you would be scared stiff. The God who dealt with them, what is there to stop him coming on and dealing with you? You see it is all very well for people to say: why doesn't God stop a war? Supposing he did, he would have to deal with all that caused the war, and according to the Bible what causes war is selfishness within the human heart. Therefore God would have to deal with all those who are selfish. Do we really want God to act like that? Remember the disciples in the boat on the Sea of Galilee. They said, *"Master, Master, we're going to drown!"* Jesus stood up and did something, and they were afraid. They were more afraid of the Lord then than they were of the storm, because they realised they were in the presence of someone with unique power. Here we have sinners afraid. If God started judging people today and we heard that Mr so and so had been stricken down because he was selfish, and that Mrs so and so had been stricken down because she was a gossip, how would you feel? Would you be glad that God was beginning to remove wickedness from the earth, or would you be on your knees examining your own heart as the judgement of the Lord came near you? A real sense of the nearness of God would make you afraid unless you were right with him.

Why were the people afraid? God has conquered their enemies. Because they are very near to God and they are just beginning to wonder about those things which they had forgotten in their fear, the things that they had done that were wrong and that he was going to deal with. God had come straight through the enemy troops and was heading for them and they were afraid. There is only one sort of person who could dwell without fear in that moment, and it was the person depicted in v. 15 (NIV) —

He who walks righteously
and speaks what is right,
who rejects gain from extortion
and keeps his hand from accepting bribes . . . .

If a commission of inquiry is appointed into a certain industry or social sphere in which there has been corruption, the only people who need to be afraid are those who have had a hand in it. If a man has been upright and straight he does not need to fear the examination of the commission, and that is what happened when God came near Jerusalem that day — sinners in Zion were afraid. Do you want the Lord to return? Fine. Do you want the Lord to come and destroy the wicked? Fine. Do you want the Lord to come and take away all sin out of the earth? Fine. Do you want God to come with flaming fire in vengeance upon those who disobey him? Fine. But are you sure that this would not cause a fear in your own heart? Are you ready to meet the Lord when he comes in power? That is the message here.

In v. 17, Isaiah invites them to look. I remember VE Day —the day when the war was over, the day the fighting had stopped, the day when the boys could come home. On that day if anybody was within a few miles of London they made their way along the Mall to Buckingham Palace. Why? To see the Royal Family on the balcony. It seemed the appropriate thing to do that day, to go and look at the king, to go and celebrate with the leader of the nation. Now here is the picture of Hezekiah coming out onto the balcony of his palace. You will see the king in his beauty and the crowds rejoice —it is a victory day. Your mind would muse on the terror: where was that Assyrian who counted out our money? Now we can go out and get it all back. Where is that man who counted our towers to see how many machines he would need to take the city? You will see no more of this insolent people of an obscure speech whose language you couldn't understand; look upon Zion, your eyes will see Jerusalem, and God will be to her streams of living water — that was the thing that Jerusalem lacked. Egypt had the Nile, Assyria had the Euphrates, but Jerusalem had no water. There is a stream whereof the rivers make glad the city of our God. God himself would refresh them. The Lord is our judge, ruler and King, and he will save us (see v. 22). For those who will be living in Zion, sickness will have been dealt with and sins forgiven (see v. 24).

Their thoughts and hopes centred on a king. Who was this king? Some have thought it was Hezekiah, and certainly in later years Hezekiah was a good king, a righteous ruler, a man who was fair and just. But Christians reading these two chapters have come to that word *king* and have paused and said that there is someone more than Hezekiah, there is another double fulfilment here. When they have read that word *king* three times and seen that the third time it says *The Lord is our king*, they have begun to think of a human king who was yet a divine king, and Christian hopes are centred in a king, not a constitutional monarch, a managing monarch who is to come and bring a kingdom. Christians understand that this means Jesus Christ. *"Where is the one who has been born king of the Jews?"* said the wise men. After Jesus had fed the five thousand, people wanted to make him king. He rode on an ass on Palm Sunday into Jerusalem, fulfilling the prophecy of Zechariah: "*. . . See, your king comes to you, gentle and riding on a donkey . . . .*" And when they put him to death, above his head the sign said: *THIS IS JESUS, THE KING OF THE JEWS*. It was right, even though the people said it in mockery. Your eyes will see the King in his beauty.

We are pressed on every side by enemies, we are in tension, we have sins of corruption and wrong judgements and no judgement within our own hearts, but our hopes are centred in a King and our eyes will see the king in his beauty, and when they do his people will dwell in quiet resting places. The promises of this chapter to the Israelites, the promises to the Jews under Hezekiah, to us find the perfect fulfilment in the King of kings who is to be seen and who will reign in righteousness. To his throne of grace we have access today, that we may come to him and bring our prayer and our praise — and our problems and burdens. The managing monarch of heaven, God himself, and at his right hand, Jesus Christ his Son, will meet his citizens.

12

ENTER ZION WITH SINGING

Read Isaiah 34–35

A. SINNERS DOOMED (34)
1. JEHOVAH'S FURY (1-4)
a. Host of earth (1-3) b. Host of heaven (4)
2. JUDAH'S FOE (5-17)
a. Blood and fat (5-7) b. Pitch and brimstone (8-10)
c. Beasts and weeds (11-17)
B. SAINTS DELIGHTED (35)
1. HAPPY WILDERNESS (1-2)
2. HOPEFUL WORLD (3-4)
3. HEALING WATER (5-7)
4. HOLY WAY (8-10)

Many people treat the Bible as if it were a box of chocolates. They have it around, now and again they dip into it, but when they do they pick out all the chapters with the soft centres. Now this is really not the way to treat the word of God, and when we do so we come up with our own ideas, we do not come up with God's ideas. We have an outstanding example here that we do this. Which of these two chapters do you know best? There is no doubt that one of these chapters has a soft centre and a lovely taste and it is a very nice chapter to read—chapter 35 is a wonderful and beautiful chapter. How we love reading those words: then the eyes of the blind shall be opened and the desert blosoming like a rose. But how many words could you quote from chapter 34 from memory? It has a hard centre, it is a tough chapter, but we need to realise that if you are going to get the truth you have got to have the whole truth and nothing but the truth, and that if you just pick and choose in the Bible and only read and study those chapters that are nice and comfortable you do not finish up with God's truth at all, you finish up with your own choice of truth, your own opinion.

We are going to take these two chapters because they belong together; they are about exactly the same subject and you cannot understand one chapter without the other. They present a perfect balance and contrast between two parts of God's truth. And Isaiah of course never wrote chapter headings. He is on one subject and he deals with the same subject from two different angles in these two chapters and the subject is clearly stated in each.

Look at 34:8a. This is the subject: *For the LORD has a day of vengeance, a year of retribution . . . .* Notice the two words, 'vengeance', 'retribution' (which could be translated 'recompense'). Now turn to that lovely chapter 35 and look at v. 4, towards the end: . . . *he will come with vengeance; with divine retribution he will come to save you*. Both these chapters are about the vengeance and the recompense of God, but viewed from two different angles that subject becomes either a most terrible one or a most wonderful one. In simple terms, when sinners consider that subject it is a horrible subject, but when saints consider it, it is a wonderful subject. Chapter 34 looks at this subject from the sinners' point of view, chapter 35 looks at it from the saints' point of view, and that is the difference.

I frequently get this said to me: that the God of vengeance belongs to the Old Testament not the New, and that this is an old idea that we have grown out of now, and that the Lord Jesus has brought us through to a picture of God as a loving Father, not a God of vengeance any more. Yet quite recently I was expounding to some Christians a chapter from the word of God in the New Testament. Read it: *Do not take revenge, my friends, but leave room for God's wrath, for it is written: "It is mine to avenge; vengeance is mine, I will repay," says the Lord*. That is Romans 12:19 (NIV). And if you go through to the book of Revelation in which the Lord Jesus himself told his church about his Father in the fullness of revelation, there is again the word and the idea that God is a God of vengeance.

If you pick out the soft centres you would never come to that conclusion, but if you eat the whole box and make a meal of it and not just a snack — and take it all — you are bound to come to the conclusion that God is a God of vengeance, a God of recompense, a God who says, 'I will repay'.

Is that good news or bad news? That depends on whether you are a sinner or a saint. God is the same, but people's reaction to the truth that he is a God of recompense will depend not upon God but upon them and upon the state of their mind and heart. Interestingly enough, these two chapters virtually bring to a close the first great section of Isaiah. It is a summary of all the first thirty-five chapters, and then we have a complete break into something quite different. All who have read this and notice that this is the climax and conclusion of the first great part of Isaiah's ministry have remarked on the amazing parallel with the book of Revelation. If you read the book of Revelation through, you will find again that people pick out the soft-centred chapters 20 and 21, about God wiping away every tear from eyes, and the new Jerusalem, and the river of water, and the gladness and joy and light of all that. But if you read chapters 4 – 19 you have chapters which are exactly parallel and which quote from chapter 34 of Isaiah. Once again, you will find that in the book of Revelation many people know the first few chapters and the last few chapters best, and the bit in the middle they do not really know. Again, it has to be said that this of course is no way to study the Bible — it has to be all of God's word or nothing. After all, if God said a thing we must take notice of it, and the great advantage of reading the Bible right through in your private devotions is that you will not pick and choose. There are some books on the market which are helpful devotionally but which have just picked out the soft-centred passages and texts and promises. I think you have to watch that you do not allow books like that to stop you reading the whole truth.

The truth of both chapters is that God will repay, and the New

Testament underlines it. Do not deceive yourself and do not be deceived, God is not mocked. Whatever a man sows, that shall he also reap. I will repay. I will recompense. Vengeance belongs to me, says the Lord. God's vengeance may be delayed a long time, but because it is delayed we should not ignore or forget it. He has appointed a day of vengeance which has not yet come. One day God will repay men for their attitude to him and to his people. There is a day when things will be settled. What will happen on that day? Chapter 34 looks at it from the sinner's point of view, and in both chapters we have a remarkable relationship between nature and human nature. The prophet Isaiah constantly saw God's plan and purpose as affecting both man and the world in which he lives —nature and human nature. That is why he could look forward to the lion lying down with the lamb, and the little child playing safely with snakes —he saw nature redeemed. That is why he could talk about beautiful trees growing up in the place of thorns and briars, and about the desert blossoming like the rose. But that is also why he could talk of fertile areas becoming deserts and becoming inhabited by wild beasts. Nature and human nature go together — sin has affected both, and salvation affects both. It is an interesting thought that God never created desert. There are traces in the deserts of the world of trees and shrubs. In the heart of Arabia I remember an Arab showing me a huge tree trunk that he had dug up in the middle of the sands, and it must have been lying there for centuries in the middle of the desert.

Having set the scene, let us look then at this alarming chapter (34). It describes first of all the doom of the whole world when God repays. In the first four verses we have a horrifying picture of the end of the world as we know it. It describes God's fury or wrath — that is a strong word but it is used in the New Testament also, it is used by Jesus. Why is God so angry? The simple reason is that men whom he put in the garden of this world have made it a desert of sin: they have broken his laws, they have rebelled against him, they live as if he does not exist, they flout his commandments, and this has made God angry for it has spoiled the world he made. This world is nothing like the world that he made. We have no idea of the beauty and the loveliness of the world as it left his fingertips, even the nature around us has been spoiled. There is only one thing that would adequately repay mankind's crimes and it is universal death. Such is the description of the universal death that will come at the end of history — that the corpses will not even be buried, just cast out. This is going to happen as certainly as I write this. Because God has delayed it, because the day has not come yet, it is utterly foolish for us to think that it will never happen — it most certainly will. God has also (34:4a) doomed the host of heaven.

All the stars of heaven will be dissolved
and the sky rolled up like a scroll . . . .

That is picture language; I know that the sky is not a thick sheet of blue parchment and Isaiah knew that too, but God will roll it up as we would roll up a piece of paper and throw it in the waste-paper basket. And: *all the starry host will fall like withered leaves from the vine*. Those stars which he flung into space he will fling out of space and they will fall like leaves in the autumn. It is a dramatic and terrible picture of the last moment in history and the New Testament takes it up, quotes it, enlarges it, and reminds us that this is still true.

Now in vv. 5–17 we turn to the main enemy of the people of God. Down to the south from Israel and Judah there lived the nation of Edom. They lived on the top of a sugar loaf mountain. It is now called Petra, the rose-red city hollowed out of the very rock itself, about 120 miles to the south of the Dead Sea in the dry rift valley called the Arabah. In Isaiah's day, that area was populated and cultivated, and was the main caravan route from the south going further north, one of the most fruitful areas in the whole of the Middle East. Now there is not a soul living there — you come out to see the magnificent ruins of Petra, and you see the animals and the birds of prey.

What happened? Let us go way back in history to a day when a woman was pregnant and had twins within her. Those twins struggled with each other and they were born, Jacob and Esau. How different these twins were from each other. One was a man who was interested in the future and in spiritual things; the other was only interested in the present, and material things. One had his eyes on a heritage and the future, the other would rather have a plate of soup in the present. No people can fall out like brothers and sisters. The closer you are physically related the more you can fall out mentally and spiritually. And just as these brothers had their differences and clashes, the two races that descended from them — the people of Israel from Jacob, and the race of the Edomites, or 'Edom', from Esau — they went on along that line. The Edomites were only interested in things of the flesh, and they hated their relatives, the Israelites, who were interested in the things of the spirit. That hatred lasted for a thousand years and more. When the Jews came out of Egypt and through the wilderness they travelled the famous road, the King's Highway, that passed right through Edomite territory. When they reached the borders of Edom, her own relatives the Edomites would not let her pass up the road, and they made Israel take a huge detour through the dry desert to get back onto the road north of Edom. They would not even help them through. Later, the Edomites so hated the Jews that every time they got the chance to go and raid the country and bring back slaves, or to stop them getting some benefit, they would take their opportunity. Edom stands as a symbol for those who hate the people of God — those who are antagonistic to spiritually-minded people, whether the Jew or the Christian — and the doom of Edom seems more fierce than the doom of the world because of this 'anti' attitude to the people of God. So as we read what is going to happen to Edom we are reading of the particular anger that God has for those who deliberately set their face against his people for no reason other than their jealousy and malice. We will come to the later history of the Edomites, but let me point out three things that are to happen.

The Edomites lived by trading and sheep rearing. In Edom was one town called Bozrah where thousands of sheep were slaughtered. And God says, through Isaiah, there will be the greatest slaughter in Bozrah that has ever been seen there: blood and fat will cover the ground — not that of sheep but of Edom. It is a terrible picture and it came true. Around the sixth century BC the Arabs began to get interested in Edom and pressed down into that area, finally slaughtering the Edomites at Bozrah in just the way described here. The Edomites were almost wiped out then, but some survived. A few survived until the time of our Lord, although they were not able to live in their own country. When Jesus was born, the ruler of the Jews was a man called Herod, an Edomite who had been made king of the Jews by the Roman authorities. And if you want to understand the relationship between Jesus and Herod you must go back to Jacob and Esau, because Jesus came from Jacob and Herod came from Esau. The Jews were ruled by Edomite kings, the Herod family — that awful family still only interested in physical and sensual things. Herod was glad when he saw Jesus, he wanted to see some miracle done by him. Jesus had nothing to say to Herod, calling him 'that fox'. The Jews and the Edomites are symbolised in the relationship between Jesus and the Edomite kings of the Herod family. (The Herod family finally came to a dreadful end when the last of them was eaten by worms, as recorded in Acts chapter 12).

This is the first thing that was to happen to them: their own blood and fat was to stain their own soil. They had killed thousands of the people of God. When Jerusalem finally fell, some years after the time of Isaiah, the Edomites rushed in and took all the plunder for themselves — any Jews who had managed to escape were taken by them and handed over to the enemy, so malicious were the Edomites towards their relatives.

You can learn something of the malice of Edom from the denunciation of their dreadful behaviour described in the book of Obadiah, written some years later.

The second thing that was to happen was that pitch and brimstone would burn their land. It is interesting that this is what happened to Sodom and Gomorrah, which were in the same valley, a volcanic area where there is fire and brimstone just under the surface. So this is not picture language, it is a real threat. The Edomites knew perfectly well that four cities had been utterly destroyed by fire and brimstone, and God says that the same thing would happen to their land.

The third thing mentioned is that their land would be inhabited by wild beasts and wild weeds. If you want to study wildlife, take your Bible with you when you go to Petra. Isaiah is bold enough to invite the reader to check this —none of the animals and birds named would be missing. We see that God is in control of the animals; God's will affects nature as well as human nature. The book of Jonah tells us that God can control a whale or a worm. All creatures are within his sovereign will, and here God makes a list of the animals and birds he will put in the Edomite territory. And thorns, nettles and thistles — go and look at them today — not one of them is missing. The mouth of the Lord has spoken, the Book of the Lord has it, and the Spirit of the Lord will do it. That is my confidence in the Bible, that is why I preach it and preach no other book, for in no other book have I this confidence.

As we have seen, Edom did not repent of her sins; she went on attacking the people of God, and the Herods were the last of the Edomite line, and with them Edom vanishes from history. There are no Edomites in the world today; the Israelites are there, but no Edomites. The name of Israel is in your atlas but the name Edom is gone, never to reappear. Nor are there people living where they lived — the place is deserted, it is only a place for tourists to visit. The mouth of the Lord has spoken. So then we have a picture in chapter 34, first of the whole earth doomed for rebelling against God, and second of Edom as representing those people who have particularly sinned against God's people and who have developed an attitude of malice toward them. I watched a television account of the horrors of the Auschwitz camp, and one felt like shouting at the end: 'Vengeance is mine, I will repay, says the Lord.' To touch his people is to touch the apple of his eye, and we need to remember that. That is why Jesus said, '*Inasmuch as you did it not to the least of these my brethren* . . . .' To touch his brethren is to touch the apple of his eye. There is particular treatment, particular doom, for those who have taken this stand against God's people.

Now let us turn to chapter 35. It is as if the black thunder-clouds roll away and the sun comes out. It is as if you have been walking through a dark wood and suddenly meadows, gardens and streams appear. It is a most wonderful change, and yet it is about the same day, the same year of recompense, the same future — only it is looking at it now through the eyes of God's people. If chapter 34 would make you want to weep, chapter 35 is full of joy and singing. In v.1 the words 'joy' and 'singing' occur; in v. 6, the tongue of the dumb sings for joy; in v. 10, they come to Zion with singing and everlasting joy upon their heads. This is a chapter of singing and joy, and no wonder.

There are four wonderful things about the future for the people of God to ponder upon and to rejoice in. First of all, there is a picture of a happy wilderness. South of Judah was Edom in the Arabah valley. But west of the valley is the Negev desert, and that is the most desolate desert in the world which lies between Judah and Egypt, and there is a whole area there that is in the rain shadow. The winds over the region are either easterly or westerly. If they come from the east they bring no moisture because they cross the Arabian desert; if they come from the west they bring rain. Read the life of Elijah in the light of this — how he sent his servant up to Carmel to look west for a cloud to come, to see the wind change after three and a half years from the east, to bring the rain back. God could bring either fertility or its opposite to his people by just changing the wind direction. If you remember that the Mediterranean curves for Egypt, neither east nor west touching the Negev brings moisture; there is no rain there, it is absolutely barren, and yet it is part of the land that God has promised to his people. God gave it to them, but what is the point of giving them a barren part like that? What can they do with it? That is why they constantly had this problem as they looked south. Why should God give us a patch of land like that? A land flowing with milk and honey, yes, now that's a decent gift – but that desert . . . ? And here is Isaiah saying that God had not finished with the desert. All these chapters look south; they are looking south at Edom; now Isaiah looks south at the Negev. The Jews own land which the Edomites never inhabited because it was no use to Edom either, only inhabited by a few Bedouin folk until recently. So they looked south and Isaiah saw something happening in the desert—crocuses blooming. Crocuses are the first sign of life in spring and they suddenly blaze forth with that lovely orange, mauve and purple. There is a garden that is going to be there. When God made the Middle East he made a garden of Eden, but it is not a garden today. We can plot the garden of Eden on the map — we are told where it was — but go there today and it is a desert, not a garden. Looking south to the Negev, Isaiah could see the wilderness, the desert, singing for joy, with crocuses springing up everywhere. Then he names the beauty spots of Israel — Carmel, Sharon, and Lebanon. It is a wonderful picture and I do not think we are meant to take it figuratively but to take it as it stands. If man can make a garden into a desert, God can make a desert into a garden. All he would need to do would be to shift the winds around a bit and bring a north-west wind over the Mediterranean. It is a wind that has not occurred in the Negev so far, but if you believe that God controls the beasts and the weeds, can he not control the wind? Of course he can, and in the book of Jonah he did, and when our Lord stood up in a boat he did. The Jews today have tried to anticipate this: they have diverted the Jordan through an eighty mile canal into the Negev, and it is beginning to blossom as they bring their water, but all that canal would be wasted if God would just send them the north-west wind and bring water to the Negev, which would become a garden.

In vv.3–4, we see those people whose hearts are failing them for fear. It is a picture of someone who is gripped with dread, a paralysing fear of the future. Their hands are weak, their knees are feeble, their hearts are fearful. The message to them is comforting: God will come and repay. There is no need to fear the future if you belong to God and know that one day he will come with recompense. Why should you dread the future? Why should your hands be feeble? Why should your knees give way if God is going to come and put it all right? He will come and save you.

Vv. 5–7 describe the health that will be brought. The eyes of the blind will see, the ears of the deaf will be unstopped, the lame will leap like deer, and the tongue of the dumb shall sing for joy. Why? Waters shall break forth in the wilderness. There seems to be a connection in Isaiah's thought between the waters and healing and health. For waters will spring. Have you noticed how often water and healing go together? Have you noticed that Jesus said to someone 'Go and wash' —and the blind man went and washed and he came seeing? To a leper called Naaman the prophet of God said, 'Go and wash in the Jordan river.' Here is God's 'spa' in the desert. The water will not only produce the crocus it will somehow bring health.

There is a lovely word here in the Hebrew that does not quite come out in the English. In v. 7, *The burning sand will become a pool*—but the word for burning sand is *mirage*. I do not know if you have ever seen a mirage in the desert, but I have once and it is a fascinating sight. There it is, a lovely pool of water, and you make for it — or you think you do! You can drive as fast as you like but you will not get there. Mind you, if you saw a mirage of palm trees and water in the middle, all you would need to do would be to go twice as far as you see it and you would find it, because in fact it is simply a distant oasis being reflected in the hot air down to you. So that is just a practical hint for travellers in the desert! But so often a traveller has seen it and did not go far enough, so it remained a mirage and, when he got to the place where he thought it was, it was not there. The 'mirage' will become a pool. To press this point further, I think some people do not find the refreshment of God because they do not go far enough towards it. They see it and they go so far, but because things do not happen immediately they give up.

Then Isaiah sees something else. He is still looking south. He sees through the middle of the desert a straight road, an easy road, a safe road, and he can see in his vision the people of God coming up that road towards the city of God, the city of Zion. It is a wonderful picture, and a highway shall be there through the desert. When I visited Petra I crossed the Jordan and up towards Amman, the capital of Jordan. Then from Amman there is a straight road for a hundred miles and more through the desert. We travelled the whole way along this road (which leads through to the Red Sea) in an American taxi. Then you have to leave it and cut down to Petra. So there is a highway through the desert, an amazing road. You can see fifty miles ahead. There is no danger of bandits lurking behind bushes because there are no bushes to lurk behind. When you travel that way you think of Isaiah's vison. He saw a highway coming up through the Negev towards Zion, and the contrast in his mind is with the days when the children of Israel wandered for forty years in the desert, trying to pick a road through the stones and the barrenness. If they had only had a straight road from Egypt they could have been home in weeks instead of forty years. And he sees this vision of a highway, a straight way. There will be no dirt on the highway, no unclean person will walk on that road. There will be no difficulty with the highway – even a fool could keep on it (see v. 8). There will be no danger on that highway, no ravenous beasts. But when we look at the people we see that it is the redeemed, the ransomed and the rejoicing who walk on it, and here we see them singing as they come.

I remember a mining village in south Wales where we once had a procession of witness. As we went past the grey slate cottages, past the pit heaps, between the mountains, as they call the hills there, we sang: 'We are marching to Zion, beautiful, beautiful Zion, we are marching to Zion', and that is what the picture is in this last verse. The ransomed of the Lord shall return – can't you see them? No longer refugees picking their way through the desert, but the redeemed of the Lord singing as they are marching to Zion. What a vision, and all that is to happen when God comes to repay – his people are to come home.

When was all this fulfilled? Some have said it was fulfilled when the Jews came back from exile in Babylon just about a hundred years after Isaiah said all this. I do not think that is it. Some have said it began to be fulfilled in Jesus' ministry. Well, the blind saw and the lame man leapt, but I do not think that is when it was fulfilled. Some people feel that it is being fulfilled today, and when we see what the Jews are doing in the Negev with their irrigation we just cannot help speaking about the desert blossoming. Yet surely there is still something in the future. This day has not yet arrived, and though we have caught little glimpses, little foretastes of it, all that I have written of is yet to be in its fullness. For example, the pitch and the brimstone has not yet overflowed the land of Edom, so even that has not yet been completely fulfilled. One day it will be, and in that day somehow all this earthly fulfilment will be swallowed up in a spiritual fulfilment, and we will look for a Zion not on earth, beautiful though that city is, but the Zion that will be built in heaven and sent down as the new Jerusalem, built there and sent down by God as his gift. And the holy way that leads to the heavenly Zion is to be found in Jesus Christ who said, *'I am the way . . . .'*

13

ROOT BELOW AND FRUIT ABOVE

Read Isaiah 36–37

PROLOGUE (36:1)
The invasion/The occupation (of Sennacherib)
A. REVILING MESSENGER (36:2-37:7)
1. SENNACHERIB'S PRIDE (2-22)
a. To the king (4-10) i. Things ii. People iii. God
b. To the people (13-20) i. Future ii. Past
2. HEZEKIAH'S PRAYER (1-4)
a. Reputation of Jehovah b. Remnant of Judah
3. ISAIAH'S PROPHECY (5-7)
a. Retreat b. Assassination
B. RAGING MESSAGE (37:8-35)
1. SENNACHERIB'S PRIDE (8-13)
2. HEZEKIAH'S PRAYER (14-20)
3. ISAIAH'S PROPHECY (22-29)
a. Words (22-29)
i. Jerusalem mocks Sennacherib (22)
ii. Sennacherib mocks Jehovah (23-25)
iii. Jehovah mocks Sennacherib (26-29)
b. Signs (30-35)
i. Judah (30-32) ii. Sennacherib (33-35)
EPILOGUE (37:36-38)
The retreat/The assassination of Sennacherib

George Bernard Shaw used to say that his education began when he left school, and I can understand what he meant by that because mine did as well. And my two worst subjects, in what was then called the School Certificate, were Scripture and History – now they are both the great loves of my life, and the great interest. I am so glad that the Bible is a book of history, not a book of philosophy or opinions. If you do not like history you will not like the Bible but, once you really get into the Bible, history becomes a completely new subject because God is the God of history. Our faith is based on fact not fancy. It is based on things that happened, the truthfulness of which you can check. So we are not following some 'will o' the wisp' in believing the Christian faith. We have not received a faith that can be shaken. And here in the middle of the book of Isaiah, between the first and the second half, is this little chunk of four chapters of history, a slice of fact on which you can base so much of your faith, and that is what is really thrilling about it. It is centred on a king whose name is mentioned thirty-two times in the four chapters, King Hezekiah, the third king in whose reign Isaiah was the preacher of God.

We are given a kind of prologue in v. 1, a historical setting. The mighty king Sennacherib of Assyria, away up in the Mesopotamian basin with his capital at Nineveh, is marching south-west, destroying everything in his path, and there seems to be no stopping this dictator with ideas of world conquest. Down through Syria he comes, and Syria vanishes; down through Israel he comes, and Israel vanishes; down through Judah he comes and forty-six cities are razed to the ground until there is only one city of Judah left standing — Jerusalem. Sennacherib's object is to get through to Egypt and Ethiopia. If he can conquer them he has the whole world as far as he is concerned. When he reached Jerusalem he made a most surprising decision — not to take Jerusalem but to receive a heavy tribute of money from there, and to march on south to Egypt. Hezekiah scraping together all the exchequer, all the treasury, even scraping silver and gold off the temple, gave all the wealth of Jerusalem to Sennacherib who agreed to march on south and not touch this city. He went about thirty miles further south-west to a town called Lachish, a heavily fortified town, and there began the siege of that place.

For some reason Sennacherib changed his mind again. He thought: Jerusalem is behind me; it is a fortified city, that's a weak point in my rear. I will go back and take it. Calling to him his main political officer, Sennacherib sent him to go back there, destroy morale, get their surrender and then come back. He did not like the thought of a city behind his lines that he had not destroyed. So the deputation went back to Jerusalem, to a particular point just outside the city walls, where the people were crowding. Hezekiah sent his secretary and two others to go out to find out what the Assyrian envoy wanted, and to negotiate.

The place where he stood is very important. He stood by the conduit of the Upper Pool on the road to the Fuller's Field (or Washerman's Field). Now what on earth is important about that? You find out that the Bible never wastes a word. You might think: why say that? What does it matter where he stood? It does matter. Twenty years earlier, God had told Isaiah to go and stand by the conduit of the Upper Pool leading to the Fuller's Field and to say to Ahaz that the king of Assyria was coming to this city. It was the identical spot where Isaiah had said that! There is further significance to this place. The one difficulty of Jerusalem in a state of siege was getting water. An invader who was going to threaten the city would go and stand by the conduit taking water from the pool to the city, virtually saying: I could chop this off just like that. So the Assyrian envoy (the 'field commander') stood by the conduit, the water supply of Jerusalem, and his message was: give it up, you might as well surrender now. He tried to break their morale. Of course he was not to know that, a hundred feet underground, Hezekiah had dug a tunnel a quarter of a mile long, from a spring to a pool in the city. You can still paddle through that tunnel, which was accidentally discovered in the 1890s.

Now consider the speech calling for surrender. It was a brilliant, plausible series of arguments. Do you notice that he did not once call Hezekiah 'king'? The contempt of the man! *"Do not let Hezekiah deceive you. Hear the words of the great king . . . ."* The contempt is clear. He starts his argument like this: *"On whom are you depending . . . ?"* Was it on Egypt, or on God? Were they depending on chariots and horsemen?

The commander even offered to supply two thousand horses if they could put riders on them. Oh the subtle cleverness of it all, because the Jews were no good on horses, they had no experience with them! The subtlety of the Assyrian commander was brilliant. You can imagine the devastating, morale-breaking note in this challenge. The commander made it clear that it was no use their relying on things or people. What about Egypt? Egypt was like a broken reed, and if you lean on that it is like leaning on a sharp pointed, broken stick — it will go through your hand. It was true, and Isaiah had said exactly the same thing just a year or two earlier. Can you imagine what the people in Jerusalem thought of Isaiah now? They would turn to their preacher and say: Isaiah, our enemies are saying the same thing as you, you must be a traitor. Your last sermon is the same as he is telling us now: don't rely on Egypt. It must have been very difficult for Isaiah in the city in those days.

The Assyrian envoy, a brilliant diplomat, had taken trouble to find out the internal affairs of the city of Jerusalem. He pointed out to the people that their king had been destroying the altars all over the country and saying that they must worship at one altar in Jerusalem. The implication was clear: that doesn't look very confident, does it? It looks as if he's a bit scared of all this worship going on. Oh, it was subtle, because Hezekiah had done it for a good reason—because of all the idolatry that was coming up in the provincial centres. True to God's law, he was re-centring the worship of the temple in the metropolis, where it could be kept pure. But the Assyrian envoy subtly appeals to the Jews who did not like their altars being destroyed and their high places going. Besides, said the envoy, God told him to march against the country and destroy it—and that was true, because Israel had sinned, and Isaiah himself had preached that God would bring the Assyrian as his punishment upon his people. So now it looked as if Isaiah was in league with the Assyrian forces. What an embarrassing position for a preacher to be in! Can you see the tension of forces in the city? The Assyrian spoke in a very loud voice—much too loud, and he had even taken the trouble to learn the Judean language, so the people on the wall were all listening to every word. The three people whom Hezekiah had sent out wanted the Assyrian to keep his voice down and negotiate quietly with them in Aramaic. But the envoy had come to speak to the people as well as the king, and he shouted loudly — in Hebrew.

Now speaking to the people, he said two things to them which were aimed at driving a wedge between them and their king. First: he was offering them a wonderful future: you stay in there and you'll be reduced to the foul diet of siege, and you know it. You give in to us and we'll give you enough to eat, enough to drink, we'll give you your own fig tree, your own cistern of water, you'll have everything. Notice the very subtle and ominous '*. . . come and take you to a land like your own . . . .*' They had taken away 200,000 Jews already, and they had not taken them to a better land, they had taken them in chains. It is a subtle offer. If you stay there you are going to starve, as are your children. It is awfully difficult to face a threat to children. Not only is your future better with us but look at the past. There is not a single nation or god that has been able to resist us, why do you think you'll be the first? And the Assyrian commander lists cities that have fallen. Humanly speaking, his argument was watertight, and the people answered not a word. It was a plausible, contemptuous speech, and when the three reported to the king, the king clearly felt that they were finished. He used a vivid metaphor which was often used in the scripture: a woman in childbirth who cannot bring the baby forth — and that is a most dangerous position for both mother and baby, it has the threat of death in it. He had a faith in God inside him but just could not bring it out and trust God. It is a dreadful day, a day of disgrace, a day of rebuke. Why was it a day of disgrace? Because Hezekiah had, alas, done his bit toward bringing this about. Isaiah had told him of this, warning that running off to Egypt would be no protection. Hezekiah now knows that he should never have doubted God.

Hezekiah wants to pray, but he cannot. He feels that he is too guilty himself of the things that have brought this situation about, so he asks Isaiah to pray for him. He can't even say, 'My God' or 'our God', he sends a message to Isaiah and speaks of *your* God. Pray for the little remnant of Judah. Here is a man in desperate straits who is turning to God. At least he went to the right place — the house of the Lord — and that is a good place to go. When you are absolutely at the end of your tether, when you are, humanly speaking, in an impossible situation, that is the place to make for. And if you do not feel you can pray yourself, then get somebody to pray for you. Go to someone and say: look, I'm desperate, will you pray for me? I'm in a state of rebuke and disgrace and distress, will you pray for me? That is a very sensible thing to do, and Isaiah prayed. But he did more than that, he prophesied. He not only gave Hezekiah's message to the Lord, he gave the Lord's message to Hezekiah. His message was not to be afraid of the Assyrian's words. What faith! God says that Sennacherib will go right back to his own country and he will die there by the sword. What an astonishing thing to predict. Only a man in touch with God could predict the retreat and the assassination of such a world conqueror as Sennacherib.

Before we move on to the second chapter of this study, may I apply this to today. Very often today the true people of God, the real believers, seem to the world to be in very much the same position as Jerusalem seemed to Sennacherib. We are only a remnant. We seem to be under pressure, and the world criticises, laughs and mocks, and with plausible arguments seeks to destroy our faith in God. On whom are you going to rely? Do you still rely on the Bible? Look how feeble and ineffective you are! What do you think you can do? How do you think you can survive? People have been saying this for a long time. The world thinks we are finished, that we do not stand a chance of survival. Science seems to many to offer everything we want, and selfish people follow this call. Oh, we get all these offers: You rely on God do you? He didn't get so and so out of trouble did he? When someone is mocking God's people with plausible arguments, the best answer is not our words — there is no need to answer those arguments — the word of God is the answer, and the predictions of scripture for his church are the answer. The church will survive and grow and there is no need to fear that either the word of God or the people of God can be destroyed and finished. The word of God predicts that every other human achievement will be finished, that every civilization on earth will come to the dust, that everything else will fade away —but not those things and people which God has established. Frankly it is enough for me that Isaiah and other prophets say, 'Hear the word of the Lord'. Don't be afraid of all these plausible arguments. This is God's prediction for the future, and therein lies our faith.

So we move on to the second crisis in this political situation. Let us go back to Sennacherib. Where is he and what is he doing while his envoy, the commander, is at Jerusalem? Sennacherib has swept down through Syria and Israel, he has destroyed all the cities in his path, he has taken the tribute from Jerusalem and he has marched on to one of the strongest cities, Lachish (about thirty-five miles away) on his way down to Egypt and Ethiopia to conquer the world. He had sent his envoy back on the fruitless visit to Jerusalem to negotiate with Hezekiah and bring about their surrender. Meanwhile Lachish is under a severe siege. We know about that siege from many different historical accounts, including an expedition in 1935. The whole of Lachish has been uncovered and many interesting things found, including tanks. Did you know the Assyrians had tanks? There are pictures of them. They are on wheels, armoured, with a battering ram on the front. Mounds of earth were built up to the walls, and boiling oil, flaming torches and scaling ladders were used. Modern armaments! Having besieged Lachish, after a fierce battle they took it. The expedition, in its report, said this: conditions on the site leave no doubt that the destruction of level three (level three being the top layer and the one of that period) was the outcome of a fierce struggle. So you can go back to Lachish and see it all there — this is fact, it is history, it is real and it is what God did. I will return to that in a moment.

Sennacherib had left Lachish, and funnily enough he had turned back on his tracks yet again. There was a city called Libnah — not a Jewish city but another which had not yet been conquered. So Sennacherib took his forces ten miles north to Libnah. His commander, returning from Jerusalem, found him and had to report the failure of his mission. The significance of this was that he was now much nearer and within striking distance of Jerusalem again, so things were more tense. One other thing had changed the situation. A rumour had reached Sennacherib (by the way, it is interesting that Isaiah had said he would hear a rumour) that the king of Ethiopia was marching north to deal with him, so he was torn between two things. He had to go and attack Jerusalem and deal with it but he heard that the Ethiopians were coming up after him this way and he did not want to go straight from one battle to another. What was he to do? Should he go and deal with Ethiopia or go and finish off Jerusalem? He decided to try one more thing with Jerusalem: he sent a letter. This time it is not a plausible argument, it is a threat. It is not a confident letter; there is a note of anxiety now. Sennacherib was a little unsure of himself, and he is threatening in anger —not just reviling, *raging* is the word used. Hezekiah gets the letter and he reads it and knows that the army has turned north again and is just about fifteen miles away, poised to come up through the hills and take Jerusalem. But this time the prophecy of Isaiah that he has already had has given him strength. Instead of taking the letter to Isaiah he goes to the house of the Lord again, and this time he prays for himself. The difference in his prayer, the confidence that Isaiah's confidence has given him! The preacher was sure that God was going to look after them, and now Hezekiah is more confident in God. It is the most wonderful prayer that you have read from a king. Here is a king on his knees before the King of kings, and what a prayer. I would like to spend a lot longer on this prayer than is possible here. 37:16–20 is the prayer. Look at the note that each verse strikes. It must have gladdened the heart of God. In v. 16 Hezekiah acknowledges that God is over everything, maker of heaven and earth; that he rules above the cherubim; he reigns, supreme. That is a wonderful beginning to a prayer. After all, if your prayer is going to the throne room of the universe you can expect something to happen. We are not praying to some little god. Hezekiah was praying to Almighty God, who is '*over all the kingdoms of the earth*'. He had a big view of God. If you are going to pray effectively you have to get a magnified view of God: 'O magnify the Lord with me', cries the psalmist again and again. If your prayers are little prayers it is because you only believe in a little god who can only help you in little things and do little things for you. But if you believe in God who is great and mighty, you bring a big prayer. So Hezekiah begins to pray, *"O Lord Almighty, God of Israel, enthroned between the cherubim . . . ."* See how he magnifies God? That is step number one.

Then he points out that it is God they are mocking. He has realised the fundamental principle that if you mock God's people you mock God. Do you notice that is what Sennacherib had done? When his commander came to Jerusalem, he had warned the people against relying on Hezekiah. But when the letter was written (37:10) it said do not let your God on whom you rely deceive you. Hezekiah's prayer meant, in effect: Lord, it is you they are talking about. That is a tremendous thing to realise. So often we are concerned about *our* reputation, what people say to *us*, what they do to *us*, but our prayers should really be concerned with what they are doing to God and what they are saying about *him* — that puts your prayer on a different level.

Prayer must be real, and in v. 18 Hezekiah faces the realities of the situation. He mentions that the kings of Assyria have laid waste all the nations and their lands. He is not shutting his eyes to reality.

In v. 19 we see supreme faith. Hezekiah knew that those lands fell — because their gods were not real gods. What a tremendous insight and diagnosis. They were only wood and stone. They could not help anyone, they could not lift a finger, they could not speak, they could not move. No wonder! If you worship an idol it cannot help you when you are in a jam, it can do nothing, it is just man-made. Even the fortified cities of Judah that fell had these high places and idolatrous altars that Hezekiah had destroyed. He knew why every city but this one had gone: they were all going after idols, and idols cannot save you.

So he comes to his appeal in v. 20, an appeal to God's glory and reputation — a prayer for God's sake, not his. He prays and asks the Lord to deliver, so that people may know that Almighty God alone is the Lord. That is the sort of prayer God answers. If you are praying for conversions to happen in your neighbourhood do not pray, 'Lord, bless our church and bring conversions and change people's lives' — pray, 'Lord, will you do this so that people here may know that you are the Lord and may see your glory and may know that you are among your people and that they belong to you and that it is your power.' Pray like that and God will act because God is concerned about his glory. Hezekiah's prayer was answered mightily.

Isaiah answers first with words. He knew about Hezekiah's prayer — the Lord told him and the Lord gave him the answer to give to Hezekiah. The answer was firstly in words and secondly in signs. Jerusalem would be able to mock Sennacherib. Why? Because Sennacherib has been mocking the Lord. We notice that in Sennacherib's words it is all 'I' —I have done this. God had allowed Sennacherib to come this far, planning his advance. Do you realise that history is in God's hands? God allows conquerors to go so far and no further. God allows all that happens; and God, on his throne over the whole universe, moves nations according to his will. What faith this should give you! A hook would be put through Sennacherib's nose because of his rage and insolence towards God, and he would be led. This refers to a young bull. It was my job on the farm to ring young bulls. It is quite a job to put a ring in their nose because it is the most tender part of their body and it is the only thing you can do to get hold of them and lead them in a particular direction after they are a year old. And the bull was the symbol of Assyria — you can see it on their monuments. I'll put a ring through your nose, says God, and I'll lead you back to your own land. The mockery of it, the satire! And there would be signs for God's people: this year they would eat what grows up naturally from the ground; the second year, what is sown naturally by the falling grain; but the third year they would be able to plough, sow and reap, and they would take root downwards and bear fruit upwards, they would be planted again, and the ravaged land would once again be a fertile agricultural land, Sennacherib going back to Assyria.

So we come to the epilogue, 37:36–38. Consider again the two chapters we are thinking about. Isaiah had predicted that Sennacherib would retreat and go right back to his own capital of Nineveh, and that there he would be assassinated — two very bold predictions, and they both came true to the letter. Funnily enough, the disaster that befell Sennacherib's Assyrian troops is described in three books in the Bible, in the Egyptian history books, and even in the Greek history books three hundred years later. So appalling, so sudden, so inexplicable was this disaster to this great army, the greatest the world had seen to date, that three centuries later they still wrote about it and talked about it. Herodotus, the Greek historian, in 400 BC writes about this disaster. The accounts apparently do not seem to agree, at first. For example, the Jewish account says an angel did it, the Egyptian account says mice did it. Yet these are not contradictory. Here is what happened, and you can read it, whether in the Bible or the Egyptian or the Greek accounts. The Assyrian army had a plague of small rats or mice which ate up all their bow strings, shield straps and quiver straps of the army. Is that not astonishing? Isaiah had said that not an arrow would be shot. This is stretching facts too far statistically to be coincidence. Furthermore, those rats brought with them the bubonic plague, which swept through the camp. Moreover, that expedition of archaeologists I mentioned uncovered a huge grave containing thousands of skulls, a hastily dug grave — a great trench made, and the bodies just thrown in. The army were desperately trying to bury those who had died of this plague. It all happened! Only about twelve men survived, and Sennacherib made off for Nineveh as fast as he could go. He escaped the plague it is true, but when he got home he lost his public image and feeling against him grew, until twenty years later his three sons, arguing as to who should be king in the place of their helpless father, decided to assassinate him, and as he was at his prayers in his pagan temple two of his sons came in and drove a sword through him, and the Assyrian empire was finished. Sennacherib went down into history and that mighty army was no more.

The contrast in these chapters is between, on the one hand, Sennacherib, who seems to me to symbolise and represent worldly self-confidence in power and force, contemptuous of the people of God, with plausible arguments to use against those who dared to put their trust in Jehovah —and, on the other hand, the simple man called Isaiah whose faith was such that he believed that what God says is true and will most certainly happen. Sennacherib has long since been assassinated and buried; Isaiah, being dead, yet speaks, and his words are still very much alive, for God is the God of history and God is the living God, and in that God I put my trust. Nineveh has gone, Lachish has gone — these are just mounds of rubble and ruin in the desert — but the city of God still stands, and to that city millions still look.

14

POULTICE OF FIGS

Read Isaiah 38–39

A. HIS ANXIETY - PRAYER (1-8)
1. DISTRESSED (1-3)
a. His faithfulness
b. His wholeheartedness
c. His righteousness
2. DELIVERED (4-8)
a. The promise
b. The proof
B. HIS APPRECIATION - PRAISE (9-20)
1. GRUMBLING (9-16)
2. GRATEFUL (17-20)
B. HIS ARROGANCE - PREDICTION (1-8)
1. HAUGHTY (1-4)
2. HUMBLED (5-8)

These two chapters have a lot to say to our hearts. They are a picture of a man facing death before Christ rose from the dead. The contrast I want you to keep in your mind here is between how you face death *without* Christ, and how you face death *with* Christ having brought us a living hope by his resurrection from the dead. Later I am going to write about the fact of the resurrection and its meaning.

I wrote earlier that the book of Isaiah is like a sandwich. We are right in the middle of the sandwich at the moment. Chapters 1–35 consist of prophecy. They are the 'bread', if you like. Chapters 40–66 are prophecy again, another slice of bread on which to feed. But in the middle we have this slice of history. Thirty-two times in four chapters the name *Hezekiah* occurs, and it is part of the story of this king's life. It tells us one vital thing: when we get to the end of our resources, when human beings can do nothing more, that is just the point where we begin with God. Man's extremity is God's opportunity —and in chapters 36 and 37 we saw how a nation came to within an inch of extinction, how all the cities of Judah fell bar one, Jerusalem, and how it looked as if she was facing utter disaster and destruction, and how God brought that city back from the brink and not an arrow was fired into it; and that city lasted another 115 years before it fell. It was a reprieve for a city. But what Almighty God can do for a city and a nation he can do for an individual, and chapters 38–39 describe how the king of that city came to within an inch of his own death. He was pulled back by God at the last moment and given fifteen more years. So we can see the same God in these four chapters doing exactly the same thing first for a nation and a city and second for an individual. We are shown a man who had one foot in the grave but was able to pull it out again, by the grace of God. You cannot get as close to death as that and remain the same. We have the great privilege of reading the very words which this man later recorded of his innermost thoughts and feelings.

I want you to imagine that the doctor said to you this morning, 'I'm sorry but you only have a few more days to live. There is nothing we can do.' Imagine that then you were given a reprieve of fifteen more years. How would you feel? What would you think about? How would you behave afterwards? What would you be most likely to do when you had recovered? We see the very sad and sorry spectacle of a man who, when he was faced with death, made vows and promises to God which, when he was made well again, he did not keep. This is human nature and we see it in King Hezekiah. We can be brought face to face with the last enemy and still go back to our folly, self-centredness and pride. There are people who think that death itself will bring a person to God. Do not believe it. Even death does not bring a sinner to the Saviour automatically.

The first thing that strikes us is that chapters 38 and 39 obviously describe a point in time before chapters 36 and 37.

We shall see later why in this slice of history it has been cut in half and the two halves have been put this way round. For 38:6 says, '*I will deliver you and this city out of the hand of the king of Assyria and defend this city*', whereas in chapter 37 we saw the way that God did deliver them. So we are going back over the previous story which we studied above to something which happened earlier in Hezekiah's life, some years before the Assyrians were finally defeated. At the end of this study I will tell you why the Holy Spirit guided this scripture to be reversed in time. But bear in mind we are now retracing our steps to the earlier years of Hezekiah, before he had seen the deliverance of the city. The deliverance of the individual came before the deliverance of the city. Hezekiah was hauled back from destruction before Jerusalem was saved.

Now we consider three things about Hezekiah: first, his anxiety on hearing the news that he would not recover — which led to prayer; second, his appreciation of the experience through which he had passed — which led to praise; and, third, his arrogance some months later, which led to a prophecy from Isaiah. Here are the three stages through which this man's soul passed when faced with the enemy of death.

First, his anxiety. Hezekiah became sick. I do not know what the sickness was. It is described in scripture as a 'boil', but that is a general description used in the Bible for any swelling of the body. It may have been an abscess, a carbuncle or cancer, we do not know. We do know that it was so serious that it brought that man to the verge of death at the age of around forty. He was face to face with death at the peak of his career, having instituted reforms in the nation which were not yet complete, having yet no son to follow him on the throne, which was a very serious thing indeed in that country, no heir to reign after he was gone. Hezekiah was told he was going to die. I do not know what the atmosphere of such an occasion was in those days. I know that today one of the most disturbing features of our society is the conspiracy of silence that surrounds a person when they are sick unto death. I sense from what I read and from what I hear that up to 150 years ago it was more common to let a person know that they had come to the end of their pilgrimage, that they might have an opportunity to set their house in order, to speak to and write to those people they would want to contact, to make such provision for their loved ones as they would want to make, and this was the normal thing. But today — and this is growing evidence of the deep phobia of death which comes out in our drama, in our art, in our philosophy — we dare not face it. We dress up our funerals like harvest festivals, we build our crematoria to look like palaces, and everything is designed to shield us from the greatest fact of life, which is death. I do not know if they were hesitant to tell each other in those days, but I know this: God sent a man of God to tell the king to set his house in order. A believer in the Lord is in a position to do that, and it is wonderful to see how a believer is able to fight and to conquer the news: set your house in order, for you will not recover from your illness.

Such was the news given to Hezekiah, but bear in mind that it was given to someone who lived on the other side of the resurrection. It was given to someone who loved God and who had such a prophet as Isaiah to guide him in his thinking, but never once did Isaiah say a single word about what happened to the individual when he died. We have here the reaction of a man to the news of death who does not yet know of the resurrection of Jesus Christ from the dead, and his reaction is utter despair. His reaction is a pleading prayer: Lord, restore my health, let me live just a little longer, I cannot face death yet, I cannot fight this enemy. And so he was told, knowing perhaps that he would not be able to take the news, and he prayed. He turned his face away from people; he could not look anyone in the face now and he turned his face to the wall and wept like a child. He was going to die and he could not face it and he cried. He asked God to remember his life. He said three things about his reign and his character which were all true and wonderful: he had been faithful, wholehearted and good. Hezekiah was one of the best kings. He was faithful, he could see a thing through. He could stick at it, he was persevering. He was wholehearted in his devotion to God, and it is wonderful when a person is wholehearted and not just half-hearted. Most people when they come to face death think of what they have done that is good in their own sight, or what is good in their neighbour's sight, but what really matters is whether you have done what was good in God's sight. So someone will say, 'Well I tried to be kind and decent. I tried to help people in trouble' — but that is being good in their own sight, because the very first thing that God requires of a good life is that we love *him* and worship *him*. And you will notice that so many people who are good in their own sight have never loved God and do not worship him — they never do a thing for him; they may help Mrs so and so next door, but what do they do for God to show their love for him? To do what is good in God's sight is to put worship first in your goodness. And Hezekiah had done that. He had destroyed the altars of the high places where idolatry took place, he had brought worship back into the house of God in Jerusalem, he had made worship the first thing in his life. Let me never hear a Christian say: so and so outside the church is as good as anyone inside the church. Does that person put worship first in their life? You ask that. Ask them when they last worshipped God and loved him for his own sake with all their heart and soul and mind and strength. That is the first thing in the good life in God's sight, and Hezekiah had done it. Hezekiah prayed, and Isaiah was sent by God with another message: God had heard the king's prayer and was going to give him another fifteen years. Notice that God can give a second prophecy which cancels out the first. For he can change his action, he can change his mind, God can 'repent', and the Bible teaches this. He can change his mind as we change ours. When we repent God repents of the evil that he would do, and that word is used again and again. How would you feel if somebody said to you that you have fifteen more years to live? I think you would see greener grass and bluer sky as you came to church if you had been told that when you had been thinking that it was your last Sunday. You would think: why do people grumble and complain about life? I have just been given fifteen more years to live! Hezekiah must have felt very happy, thrilled that he was given this reprieve. There was a change in his heart and a change in his health, and God granted him more years of life. That has happened and can still happen.

At this point I would like to refer to vv. 20 and 21. (By the way, all this account except for the innermost thoughts of Hezekiah which we are going to study, is to be found in 2 Kings 20 and 2 Chronicles 32, and there vv. 20 and 21 come in after v. 6.) Isaiah said at this point: '*Let them apply a cake of figs to the swelling*'. Notice that God may use means or medicine or some outward sign to someone about their healing. It is interesting that that is what Isaiah felt led to do. We recall that our Lord mixed clay with his own spittle and anointed a blind man's eyes and said: now go and wash that off. Isaiah used a physical sign of healing, and a cake of figs was simply the normal poultice of the day. God would use that to cure Hezekiah of the sickness unto death. Then Hezekiah, still doubting whether a cake of figs could cure such an illness, asked what sign, what proof, there would be. The word of God is so often confirmed with signs following; the miracles confirm the message.

Now we come to a most unusual thing in this story which is sometimes referred to as the 'dial of Ahaz', which could have been one of two things. It might have been a square block with lines engraved around a kind of hollow hemisphere in the stone. The sun would cast a shadow over the lines as it moved round. That is a sundial of those days and they have been discovered by archaeologists. On the other hand, the term sometimes translated *degrees* can also mean *step*, and a much simpler form of sundial in those days was a column, a sort of obelisk, placed on a pyramid of steps. You could tell the time by where the shadow of the obelisk was on the steps, which were carefully built so that they graded the time of the day into half hours or quarter hours. So the sun when it was due overhead at midday would cast no shadow. But while it was climbing up from the east the sun would cast a shadow on the steps on the west and then the shadow would gradually climb up the steps, then, when it went past the shadow, it would go down the steps on the other side. That is how they told the time. Isaiah noticed this dial outside the palace window, and in v.7 we are told that the shadow on the steps would go back ten steps. That would be the sign. Those who deny all miracles and all supernatural events will certainly try and wriggle around this one. I personally find no difficulty whatsoever in understanding this or accepting it. As to describing how it was done there are three possible ways, one of which seems to me the right one. God could of course have moved the earth backwards, or he could have moved the sun forward, or thirdly, what is almost certainly indicated by the scripture: it was a miracle of what is known as refraction, which of course occurs when the clouds are full of moisture and on a very cloudy day the sun is shining down, its rays of course reach the earth nearly parallel, but when it hits the cloud the rays are refracted. It simply needs a particular kind of cloud formation to bend the sun's rays. In London in the 1920s two suns were visible! One morning it caused quite a panic. The real sun was refracted so that two suns were seen, casting a double shadow over the city — it was simply refraction. At the 'stairway of Ahaz' God simply ordered the clouds at that very moment and a cloud came over which refracted the sun's rays and pushed the shadow backwards. I say that I think this is the obvious way it was done because the Bible indicates that it was a local phenomenon, it only happened in the land of Judah and it says that it only happened there — neither the earth nor the sun would move if it only happened locally. The miracle is that God did it at that point. This could not have been a more appropriate symbol to Hezekiah. It was as if God was saying I am pushing your life back; I am turning the clock back fifteen years for you; I can turn your time back as I can turn this shadow back. It was the sign, the encouragement, the comfort, the assurance that Hezekiah needed, and he believed because of the sign confirming the word.

Vv. 9 – 20 (in the style of a psalm) form the key part of this study. We now turn from the outside of these events to the inside and we are given the privilege of probing Hezekiah's heart. He wonderfully laid bare his innermost thoughts and feelings as he faced death. His reactions are the reactions of men to the news that they will not recover. It was all written after he recovered, but he recollects those feelings, and in vv. 9–16 he describes the anguish of his soul when he heard the news. He would be separated from the people and, worse still, he believed death would separate him from the face of God. Notice that. He was frustrated because he was praying; he was weary with looking up to heaven (and of course they did pray with their eyes open.) He was frustrated, knowing that the only person who could help him was the one who was doing this to him.

Why was it that Hezekiah so dreaded death? The answer is that before Jesus came, before the New Testament teaching was given, before Jesus rose from the dead, this was what the Jew looked forward to after death. He knew that some day in the distant future there was to be a general resurrection, but it was the bit in between that worried him. It was that waiting period which he described by the name *Sheol*, which means 'hollow' or 'empty'. It was that great hollow emptiness between his death and that very distant resurrection, which was no real comfort to him when he died, which worried him. Do you remember Jesus meeting Martha and Mary? *"Lord," Martha said to Jesus, "if you had been here, my brother would not have died."* And Jesus said, *". . . Your brother will rise again."* Martha knew he would, but that was no comfort, it was a long way off. We see the typical Jewish reaction to death. It was not that they became extinct at death. I do not think you would dread death if that was just curtains — as if you just went out like a candle blown out, and knew nothing more. If you felt that you went on, but in some kind of half shadowy existence in which you could do nothing, in which you were no better than if you were asleep, in which you could not praise God and could not talk with anyone else, in which you lost everything that is precious to you, you would dread it and say, 'Lord, let me live a little longer, it might bring me a little nearer to that day of general resurrection.' We have here the Jewish picture of life after death. I heard it best described by a scholar in Cambridge. He said that Sheol was like a station waiting room at four o'clock in the morning. If ever you have been in that situation you will understand something of what it meant to the Jew: nothing doing, just a weary existence with no joy, no comfort. So the king dreaded death. Is it not interesting that with the coming of Jesus Christ people say, 'I long to depart and be with Christ'? To be with him, even before the resurrection, is far better. And Paul said that he would rather be without his body, absent from it and at home with the Lord, away from here and with him. Even now that is the difference that the resurrection of Christ from the dead has made. That is the difference that Christ's words to the dying thief have made: *"Today you shall be with me in paradise."* Christians know there will be a general resurrection of the body. But it does not comfort us in the hour of our death if that is a long way ahead. It is the bit in between that we need comfort for. Since Jesus Christ is alive, and since he has assured us that because he lives we shall live also, and since we know that the moment we die we go to be with him, then all the dread of the in-between has gone, Hezekiah's prayer is not the earnest prayer of the Christian now. The earnest prayer of the Christian is the prayer of Paul. His attitude is: I am willing to stay here if you have more work for me to do, but I would rather be off. I would rather depart and be with Christ, which is so much better, even than being in a body here. You see, there are three steps in our existence, as it were: here where we are in the body and where we know the Lord but are not yet at home with him; the second stage where we are absent from the body and at home with the Lord; and the third, glorious stage after the resurrection when each of us will be in a body again. It is good here, it is better there, it is best then. For the unbeliever it is bad here and worse there and worst then. But that is what we look forward to, and when we listen to Hezekiah's innermost thoughts we thank God that we live on the right side of the resurrection of Jesus — it comforts us.

So in vv. 17–20 we find Hezekiah's thankfulness for the fifteen years more. A Christian would be thankful to be taken, Hezekiah was thankful to be left behind.

Now we turn to the rather sad sequel to all this. I would have thought that a man who had been within an inch of death and had been given fifteen more years of life would have lived a sober, righteous and humble life, and certainly he intended to, certainly he promised to walk carefully and in a godly way before his Creator after coming back from the grave. Did he? Let us study what happened afterwards.

A few months later, a group of strange people in strange dress appeared at Jerusalem's gates and asked for the king. They said they had come from the king of Babylon, Merodach-Baladan. They had come for a number of reasons. They said they had brought a present for the king, who was desperately ill and had recovered. Now you cannot just imagine people coming eight hundred miles with a present simply because a man has been sick and got better. You would imagine there must be something more behind it, and of course there was. If you study 2 Kings 20 and 2 Chronicles 32 you will find out what was in their minds. It says they not only came to give Hezekiah a present, they came because they had heard of the miracle that took place in his land of the sun going back ten steps. They also came for a third reason: because they were interested in forming an alliance with Judah to rebel against the might of Assyria. I would have thought they should have come when the king was sick if they were simply interested in bringing a present. You do not take flowers to a person who has recovered, you take them to them when they are ill! The Hebrew word about Hezekiah means 'he became flushed with pleasure and pride'. One translation of the Old Testament says: you're the man who recovered from sickness, you're the person who had this miracle performed. Believe me, one of the awful dangers that comes to those in whose lives God mightily performs a miracle is that they become a spectacle, an object of curiosity, and that this goes to their heads. That is why I think we should be very careful before we give publicity to the healings that God still performs today. It went to Hezekiah's head and he became proud that God had so signally blessed him, and instead of giving glory to God he missed the glorious opportunity of witness. He did not take them into the temple and say, I'll tell you about the God who did it to me, he said, I'll show you my treasures, and he took them into his storehouse and showed them all his precious oil and all his gold and all his jewels, and he strutted about his palace showing them all that he had. After all, they came ready to be impressed and he was going to see that they were not disappointed. It went to his head that God had blessed him. The humility of that king who cried like a baby on his bed with his face to the wall was gone.

After the visitors had left, Isaiah came into the palace, but he was the last person that Hezekiah wanted to meet at that point. Prophets just have a way of coming at the wrong time! Isaiah asked who the group of men were who had just been to see him. Hezekiah said that they had come from Babylon. What had he been showing them? Hezekiah began to feel a bit embarrassed. 'I have been showing them *my* treasures in *my* house.' My, my, my — notice it coming up again. And Isaiah told Hezekiah that after he had died everything he had shown them they would take away. Even his sons would be robbed of their power to have sons and made eunuchs in the palace of the king of Babylon. Those predictions were fulfilled to the letter. Just over one hundred years later the Babylonians came and took away every single thing, and the people living in that city. It is a solemn and awful warning to us. Under pressure and fear of death we might make solemn vows: Lord, if you'll just give me my health in this I'll live for you, I'll do all this that and the other for you. Don't make such proud vows! It is so easy for the sanctity of sorrow to slip away when life is easy and healthy again. It has happened to many of us, and if we are honest there have been crises and difficulties, maybe physical, maybe mental, maybe spiritual, when we have said: Lord if you'll just bring me through this I'll never disobey you again. I'll give my money, I'll give my time, I'll do anything for you. And then the day slips away.

A lady who was not a member of the church came to a funeral. Later she said, 'If I felt that when I died such things would be said about me I'd do everything that minister told me.' What a reaction! But that is not the way that human nature is redeemed. She was not a churchgoer then and she did not become one afterwards. Because you can make your promises when you are in the presence of death, you can make your vows when you realise that you are not here forever, you can make your good intentions when death is knocking at your door and you realise that life is short and fleeting and that in the midst of life we are in death. But it takes more than that to bring us to a place of holiness, because holiness is not based upon fear, it is based upon perfect love which casts out fear. Holiness is based not on one crisis through which you pass but on a daily walk with the Lord. Holiness is based on that relationship which goes on and on.

Hezekiah's last recorded thoughts displayed selfishness. Outwardly he said to Isaiah: that is right and just, that is a good word of the Lord, I deserved that. But inwardly his heart said: but it's not going to happen in my time. That is the last comment on Hezekiah. This good king who had been faithful and wholehearted and had done what was good in God's sight finished up saying, well it's not going to happen in my time. Pride and selfishness crept right back into this poor man's life.

I mentioned earlier that I would explain why these chapters were reversed in time. The answer is this. Chapters 36 and 37 are concerned with Assyria because chapters 1–35 were prophecies about the Assyrian threat. But chapters 38 and 39 bring Babylon onto the scene, because Assyria was to go and Babylon was to become the mighty world empire and was to do worse things to Jerusalem than Assyria was ever able to do. The second half of the prophecy of Isaiah which we begin in the next chapter, with the wonderful majestic words of chapter 40 — *'Comfort, comfort my people'* — are written against the background of the threat of Babylon.

May I close by reminding you again that the real lesson is this: would it not be utterly awful to die without Christ, to go out into nothingness into a shadowy existence of which we know so little, to feel that you are going to be cut off from your people, from God? But, thanks be to God, none of us need face death like that. I do not know how near to death you have been, how ill you have been, how near you have been to an accident or to another's death, but Christian character grows when it is in the presence of death, our understanding of life deepens when we are in the presence of death, and our gratitude to Jesus Christ grows when we face death, because we know that we can face it properly now.

The Right Honourable George Tomlinson, late minister of education in this country, was visited during a very serious illness by a friend of mine in the ministry. My friend said to him, 'Mr Tomlinson, what are your prospects?' And he said, 'They're good: If I get better I'm going to Blackpool to rest with my wife, and if I don't I'm going to heaven to rest with my Saviour.' That is how the believer faces death this side of the resurrection. Let us praise God that the tomb is empty and that our tomb will one day be empty, and that until our tomb is empty our spirits are with the Lord in glory. And I would rather be absent from the body and at home with the Lord. Praise his name!

15

PREPARE THE WAY

Read Isaiah 40:1 – 11

INTRODUCTION TO Chs. 40-66
1. The difference
a. Content b. Context
2. The authorship
a. Division b. Unity
A. WARFARE OF JERUSALEM STOPPED (1-2)
1. PEACE FOR HER SONS
2. PARDON FOR HER SINS
B. WAY OF JEHOVAH STRAIGHTENED (3-5)
1. VALLEYS LIFTED
2. MOUNTAINS LOWERED
C. WORD OF JEHOVAH STANDING (6-8)
1. FLOWERS FADE
2. PEOPLE PERISH
D. WELFARE OF JUDAH STABLE (9-11)
1. SOVEREIGN HELP
2. SHEPHERD HEART

The book of Isaiah is a kind of Bible in miniature, as I said right at the beginning. There are thirty-nine chapters and then twenty-seven chapters. In the Bible there are thirty-nine books in the Old Testament and twenty-seven in the New. Furthermore, there is obviously a great change of atmosphere between the Old and New Testaments. When you read Isaiah right through you discover that there is the same contrast. It is rather like beginning to read the New Testament when you read chapter 40. Indeed, it begins with words which are applied to John the Baptist right at the beginning of the New Testament: *'A voice of one calling: "In the desert prepare the way of the Lord . . ."'* (Isaiah 40:3, NIV). This is a difference that we have got to notice straight away. I want to deal here with what is called a critical question, a question of authorship. Such is the change between the first part of Isaiah (1–39) and the second part (40–66) that many people have come to believe that the second part of this book was not written by Isaiah the prophet at all. Many have been taught this as definite fact.

There are two ways we could approach this. One is to ask what the change is in the two halves. Another is: who was the author of the two halves? Let me look at the change first before we discuss the question of who wrote it. It is like passing from the storm clouds to the sunshine. In fact, someone has said that it is just as if a pneumatic drill has stopped and the peace and quiet that follows is in such contrast. You get used to the noise and then suddenly it stops, and the peace and quiet is quite enjoyable after all the battering away. It seems that Isaiah uses a pneumatic drill during chapters 1–39. He keeps hammering at them the judgement of God; he keeps battering away at their souls with the charge of idolatry and injustice. Then, at the end of chapter 39, suddenly the prophecies are quite different, the whole atmosphere is quite different, and we must ask why.

I suppose the first verse and the first word of chapter 40 give us the theme for the rest of this book: *Comfort*. Let me say straight away that the word *comfort* does not mean coddle — though that is how many people interpret it. It literally means to be 'with strength' — *fort*. You know what a fort is and it comes from the Latin *fortis*, from which we get 'fortitude'. And to *comfort* a person is to put strength into their soul, to put steel into their heart, not to put cotton wool round their body. So often people say to the preacher, 'Why don't you comfort us? Why don't you preach sermons of comfort?' Well if you mean coddling sort of sermons to tell you everything is alright and you're jolly good people that is not the sort of comfort any pulpit should give you! To comfort is to put strength into you. Strengthen my people, fill them with fortitude, fill them with courage — that is comfort. And the Holy Ghost is the Comforter.

Look how he transformed those disciples hiding behind locked doors, frightened of the Jews, into blazing apostles who were ready to die for Christ. They had been comforted, they had been filled with strength and courage. And to comfort a sick person is not to say, 'There, there, there are always some worse off than you, you know' —that is coddling them. To comfort a sick person is to fill them with strength and courage to face what they have to face. 'Comfort my people.' We should not say that softly, and yet it does say speak tenderly to Jerusalem. But comfort is a strong word. The rest of Isaiah is not designed to humble the people of God and to break them down, as the first thirty-nine chapters were, they are to build up the people of God, to strengthen them, to comfort them, to make them hopeful, rejoicing, confident and unquenchable.

We notice that there is a quite different use of the word *righteousness* in the first and the second halves of this book. In the first half *righteousness* means God must punish his people. In the second half of Isaiah *righteousness* means God will save his people. And righteousness can mean both. If God is righteous and just and fair he must punish his people when they go wrong and he must save his people when they are being wronged. It is this change in the meaning of the word *righteousness* which has led people to think that somebody else wrote it. This change of subject from condemnation to comfort, from punishment to pardon, from justice to mercy, from war to peace, is reflected in the vocabulary, the style, the grammar and indeed in the whole layout of the next part of the book. If you had not seen these two parts under the same name Isaiah it is doubtful if you would have thought they belonged to the same prophet or the same book.

The next thing is that not only is there a difference in the *content* of the book there is a difference in what we call the *context*. One of the immediate and obvious things is that in the first half it is Assyria that we constantly hear about, and then suddenly Assyria is cut off in chapter 39. From then on it is

Babylon that we are hearing about — quite a different enemy. Furthermore, and here comes the real problem, the historical background of the second half is 150 years later than the first half. The events described in detail in the second half of Isaiah took place 150 years after Assyria left Jerusalem alone. This may not have been a problem to your mind. You can read through, and as I said if you treat the Bible as a chocolate box you would never find this problem, picking out all the chapters with the soft centres. If you have just picked out these chapters with the soft centres you would have picked out Isaiah 40, Isaiah 42, Isaiah 53, Isaiah 55 and Isaiah 61 and you would know them quite well, but you would not know the other chapters at all. I find that some church members only know the bits in this second half that Handel put to music in his famous *Messiah*. Others know the chapters I have mentioned. But the other chapters of this second half are among the least known passages in the Old Testament, and I will prove that to you as we study it. They really are little known, and if they were better known people would say, 'Well I can't fit this in.' The things described in these chapters did not happen until 150 years after Isaiah. Of course that would be no problem if it was a simple matter of predicting the future, but it is not predicting the future, it is actually preaching to that day. This is unique among the prophets. Many of the other prophets predicted something that was yet to happen. That is quite normal in scripture and quite common. But here is a prophet not just predicting but actually preaching to people who lived 150 years after he did — and that is the problem. He is not just saying certain things will happen, he is saying now that these things have happened you ought to be like this. He is preaching to a congregation that has not been born yet, he is preaching long after his death. I think it would be helpful if I tried to give you a little thumbnail sketch of what happened in the 150 years between the last chapter and this one.

We begin the gap in the year 701 BC. Sennacherib and the

Assyrian army were defeated by God and went back home to Assyria, and Jerusalem was saved. That is where we left Isaiah in the last chapter. What happened for the next 150 years? Hezekiah died about five years later. You will remember that he had been near death and had been given fifteen more years to live. It would have been better if he had died fifteen years previously, because during that time he had one son, and that boy grew up to be the most wicked man they had ever had on the throne. At first as a boy king, and then as a man, he was wicked. His name was Manasseh, and he did not follow his father's love for the Lord, and his father's love for the temple. He began to play about with idolatry again, erecting altars, images and idols. When Isaiah told him that his father would not have done that, Manasseh ordered a hollow tree trunk to be brought, and Isaiah's body to be tied and pushed into the tree trunk, and then he ordered the tree trunk to be sawn into logs for his fire. If you read Hebrews 11 about those who were sawn asunder, that is referring primarily to Isaiah. The whole situation went to pieces. For that evil, God's punishment came again.

Manasseh was carried off as a prisoner to Assyria some years after he had done that dreadful thing, and he was followed on the throne of Israel by another boy king. But he was a good boy. Isn't it strange how you can get changes from one generation to another? His name was Josiah, and he began to put things right again. They were always going up and down, right and wrong, good and evil. Josiah, the boy king, ordered the temple to be cleaned. It was very dirty. Going through an old cupboard they discovered a copy of the book of Deuteronomy, which had not been read for a long time. When they read it, Josiah saw that, according to this book, God had a right to wipe the people out, because of the things that were being allowed in the land. In the year 621 BC he began to put things right according to the law. Josiah was helped in this by another prophet who was himself a boy, a teenager when he was called — Jeremiah. Jeremiah said that he was only a youth, but God told him not to be afraid of their faces; he would be with him. Jeremiah took up the threads of Isaiah's work. Jeremiah watched all the reforms that the boy king Josiah was making, and saw that the people were not really with it. It is one thing for a king to order idols to be destroyed, but if the people still want them in their hearts you have not reformed the nation. So in spite of the good things that the good king Josiah was doing, Jeremiah was a gloomy prophet. And he said that it was no use. The city was going to be destroyed. There is no comfort in Jeremiah. You read it through. It is all: don't you believe that this is going to put things right. Now I am afraid Jeremiah was alone in this. There were dozens of false prophets and preachers who said: no, no, we'll preach what Isaiah used to say, that this city will be safe. But Jeremiah said: no, it won't. In spite of what the king is doing, your hearts still love the idols and you'll go back to them as soon as you can, and God will destroy this city. Of course, Jeremiah was right.

But in the year 607 — a century after the last events that we studied in the previous section — something happened. What little bit that was left of Assyria, with its capital, Nineveh, was destroyed and finished by a new nation that was getting bigger and bigger in the Mesopotamian basin — the nation of Babylon. Now Assyria was off the map and Babylon was on the map, and gloomy Jeremiah said that it was Babylon that would come and destroy the city. When Josiah died, an evil king came to the throne who reigned for three months then was thrown out, and another evil king came, Jehoiachin. When the evil king came he said we must put this Jeremiah to death. And Jeremiah was in danger of his life.

However he was right and 598 BC — just about six hundred years before Christ and a hundred years after Isaiah — the army of Babylon came. They besieged Jerusalem and they took away as prisoners the royal family, the government, the military leaders, the lawyers, doctors, and every influential person. They took 20,000 people. They allowed the others to go on living in

Jerusalem, but of course it was chaos without their leaders. That was the first time, and still Jeremiah went about saying I told you so, and they still did not like gloomy Jeremiah. People do not like Jeremiahs. He was a very lonely figure. They did all sorts of things to him. He said it was still not finished. Believe me, those Babylonians are coming back because you still haven't put right what is wrong in God's sight.

Among the people carried away to Babylon was a man called Ezekiel. It was his job under God to hold together the people carried away. And he did so by giving them the word of the Lord in Babylon. Just a few years later (in 587 BC), the Babylonians came marching back, this time to wipe out Jerusalem altogether. Jeremiah and a few Jews fled to Egypt and Jerusalem was besieged for eighteen months and reduced to famine and pestilence, and finally the whole place was razed to the ground. Jerusalem, the city of God, was left without a single Jew in it. The only two preachers of God were Jeremiah, down in Egypt keeping some Jews together, and Ezekiel up in Babylon, keeping the rest together.

Thirty-eight years passed, and the suffering of the Jews in exile got worse and worse, until it reached rock bottom. Now they were suffering for their sins all that time. But a king came to the throne who decided that the Jews were not even going to be allowed to worship their own God in Babylon, which they had been allowed to do until then. For the first time their sufferings were due not to their sins but to their righteousness. They were no longer suffering for the bad things they did, they now began to suffer for the good things they did in God's sight, and it is that change which means that a righteous God would not now punish them for their sins but rescue them for their righteousness. Do you see the difference? A righteous God would have to punish his people for doing wrong, but a righteous God would also have to save his people for doing what was right. That is the point at which Isaiah chapters 40–66 become relevant. At that point the prophecy comes to the people of God: it is soon going to be over, you are soon going to go back. God is coming now to save you because now you are not suffering for the wrong things you did in his sight but for the right things you do in his sight. From now on you are going to be saved from your suffering. *'Comfort, comfort my people . . . .'* And almost everything said from Isaiah 40 onwards refers to that point in time, and Isaiah is going to teach this: Babylon is soon going to be conquered by a man called Cyrus, king of Persia. And the king of Persia will allow you to go back to Jerusalem and rebuild it. Therefore you are going to see that the preaching in this section is 150 years after the preaching we have been studying previously. That is the problem. These chapters, then, are addressed to a different place and a different time from the first half of the book.

If we were discussing simply a human book there could be no question and no answer but that somebody else must have written this part of the book of the prophet Isaiah. I cannot preach as a human being to people 150 years ahead. I cannot preach a sermon now that will be perfectly relevant and just the word of God to a congregation in the year 2160. How could I do that? Humanly speaking, it is impossible. So, many scholars today talk of a man they call Deutero Isaiah, or second Isaiah. They talk about someone else. They do not know his name so they simply call him second Isaiah. They say he must have lived in Babylon in the exile 150 years later. They point to the fact that the time and place are far removed from Isaiah the prophet. They point to the fact that Isaiah's name is not mentioned from chapter 40 onwards. They point to the fact that the events which took place are not mentioned as predictions but as actually having happened. They point to the fact that Jeremiah's prediction of the captivity showed no knowledge whatever of Isaiah's. They point to the silence of 150 years and ask why nothing was said during that silence. They then say this must be the work of another preacher. Well, I just want to stop and say that I do not think the question is settled that easily, for we are not just dealing with a human book, we are dealing with a divine book. We are not just dealing with a book that comes from a human author but from a divine author. And God is a God who knows the end from the beginning. God is a God who is perfectly capable of preaching to a congregation 150 years ahead and perfectly capable of enabling an inspired man to do so.

Furthermore, there are a number of arguments that would confirm for me that it was perfectly possible for Isaiah the prophet to have done this preaching. The first argument is this. Until around 160 years ago, every Jew and every Christian believed this was from Isaiah. You have got to explain why no-one had any inkling that it was someone else right from the very beginning to then.

Secondly, the New Testament quotes from both halves of the book, and when it does so it says 'as Isaiah the prophet has said', so even the New Testament writers were wrong, according to the scholars who believe that there were two authors to this book.

Thirdly, the phrase that Isaiah the prophet used for God was always the 'Holy One of Israel', a phrase hardly ever used by anyone else. It only occurs five times in the whole of the Old Testament outside this book. Inside this book it occurs twenty-six times — thirteen times in the first half and thirteen in the second. That is an extraordinary fact.

Fourthly, the local colouring of chapters 40–66 is Judean and not Babylonian. The trees, the mountains, the scenery is described as by one who knew Judea and not one who knew Babylon. There were no mountains in Babylon, there were in Judea. The trees mentioned — the myrtle, the cypress and the others — were not found in Babylonia, not by someone living in Babylon, they were found in Judea. These chapters are written by someone living in Judea, not someone living in Babylon.

Fifthly, if these chapters were written by someone else it seems to me utterly incredible that such a wonderful prophet should have been forgotten. I just cannot understand how a man who could preach things like this could ever be forgotten and his name vanish from history when we have the name of every other prophet.

Finally, when the Dead Sea scrolls were discovered in 1948 there was tremendous excitement. Would all these chapters be in one book in Isaiah? Because the Dead Sea scrolls were 1,000 years older than any copy of Isaiah we had up to that date, and our knowledge of the book of Isaiah was carried back 1,000 years nearer to the time. The copies of the Dead Sea scrolls do not go back to the time of Isaiah but to 100 BC. Before their discovery the earliest copy of Isaiah we had was 900 AD. Scholars asked: will it be from two authors? Will it be in two books? To their surprise they discovered that the book of Isaiah as early as 100 BC was in one book and attributed to one author. That has begun to shake the theories of those who feel that there must be more than one author behind this book. I can only say, therefore, that my own understanding is this: because I believe this to be a divine as well as a human book, the balance of the evidence for me is that here we have a miracle of preaching. Here we have a man, Isaiah, who by the grace of God was not only able to predict the captivity in Babylon 150 years before it happened, but was able also by the same Holy Spirit to give a message which was preserved and which was given to them 150 years later.

A man once gave me a sealed envelope and he had written a letter inside it for someone I knew. He said, 'I want you to keep that envelope and I want you to take it to a certain person in ten years' time.' I kept that. By a miracle of grace I managed to find it ten years later in my study among all my papers, and I took it and I delivered it ten years after it was written. It was a message the man saw would be needed by a young boy ten years later. It was quite an unusual privilege to take a message to a boy ten years after it had been written. Why should not God say to Isaiah the prophet (who was the first to predict that

Babylon would come and take them away into slavery): Isaiah, I want to give you a comforting message to give to them that they may read when they are at the bottom of their suffering, that will lift them out of their depression, lift them out of their fear, and lift them back into my presence. I personally believe that is what was done and that chapters 40–66 were not preached but written, that they were kept for 150 years, that they were taken or sent to the people of God in exile, and that 150 years later they began to read what a dead man had written. And here we are reading these words. I see nothing impossible or even improbable in God doing just that. However, if you feel, looking at the evidence that somebody else, some unknown prophet of whom we have never heard, wrote these chapters, then quite frankly it does not alter anything in them. It does not really matter which *man* the word of God came through, it is the word of God to the people 150 years later. If we put the words in that setting we shall find their original meaning, and finding their original meaning we can apply them to ourselves.

Now I will apply this letter to us. *Comfort, comfort my people* — not coddle them but strengthen them. And in vv. 1–11 we have four voices crying in the night, in the darkness and suffering of God's people. These are words to read when you are going through it. When you are suffering for your faith, read Isaiah 40–66. The voices begin with a whisper and end with a shout. They begin: *'Speak tenderly'* and they end *'lift up your voice with a shout'*. The voices are very difficult to discern. Whose voices are they? I do not really know, but these voices in the night, coming without face and without form, lift up the people of God.

The first voice is clearly the voice of God or the voice of an angel bringing a message of God, (40:1–2, NIV)—

Comfort, comfort my people,
says your God.
Speak tenderly to Jerusalem,

and proclaim to her
that her hard service has been completed,
that her sin has been paid for,
that she has received from the LORD's hand
double for all her sins.

'Speak tenderly' is the traditional phrase for a couple wooing one another. God is wooing his people, drawing them into his love. Speak tenderly to her, it's all over, she has suffered more than enough for the wrong she has done. What good news that would be.

The expression rendered in NIV *hard service* literally means 'conscription'. When we had conscription and national service it was always good news to a young man in Her Majesty's Forces when he was told: your conscription is over, your demobilisation is at hand. That conscription was settled to the exact year by the prophet Jeremiah. Now Isaiah's word said that it was over, his letter could be opened. The people had gone through all these years of suffering, punishment for their sins. Now it was over. The pardon for their sins is announced. That is the first voice.

Is the second voice that of an angel or a prophet? I do not know, but it speaks of a way being made straight. When a monarch was going to visit a place, a road might be built for him. The Middle East is full of such roads. I remember seeing the main road in Addis Ababa, Ethiopia. It was a broad, straight road which led absolutely nowhere. It suddenly stopped and you had to turn off it to get to the rest of the city – a magnificent road built for the emperor. It was not built to go anywhere, it was built for him to come to his palace or parade his army. It was built for him to show his majesty. We see the same thing sometimes in Western countries. (I have seen in Rome a great, straight road which Mussolini built purely as a highway for himself to parade his troops, built right on top of some ruins of the Roman forum). You would not build a narrow, twisting, rough road for a king, you would level it out like a motorway, you would reduce the hills, lift the valleys, smooth the rough places. You would build a straight, broad, level, smooth highway for the king.

Those poor people suffering as slaves in Babylon were being told that their king was going to come through the desert to them: so get ready! Everybody will see his glory. There was no literal highway built through the desert to Babylon, that was picture language, but I am sure every Jew in Babylon was thrilled to hear that news: the king is on his way, get a straight road ready. Prepare as you would for a monarch coming.

It is no wonder that when we come to the New Testament these words were applied to John the Baptist. What was his job? It was to prepare the way of the Lord. It was to announce the coming of the King, the Messiah, the Christ. Through all the bumps and the roughness of human hearts, by calling people to repentance John was making a straight highway into the lives of people for the King when he came — that was his task. So at the beginning of the gospel is a voice crying in the wilderness, '*Prepare the way for the Lord* . . . .' The significance is clear: the King is coming, get ready for him; make the pathway into your hearts straight and broad and smooth for the King to come. When he comes he should come straight in. But the original prophecy was to the people in Babylon, letting them know that God was going to come through the desert to them. They were to get ready for his coming, and get ready to see his glory. It is a wonderful message.

The third voice affirms that, '. . . *the word of our God stands for ever'* (v.8b, NIV). Those people had been thirty-eight years in slavery and that is a whole generation. You reckon three generations come and go every century. The leaders who could have fought for them and led them back to their own land had all gone. A new generation had been born in exile. Babies had grown up who never knew the promised land. Something of the tragedy of this comes across. The people are likened to grass.

No wonder the prophet used the imagery of flowers. Babylon was a great place for flowers. The Hanging Gardens were one of the wonders of the world which people came from miles around to see — 'hanging' because Babylon was as flat a billiard table. It was the alluvial plain of the Tigris and Euphrates, flatter than Norfolk. So they built their gardens up artificially on walls and they hung their flowers. But all flowers fade and grass withers when the wind blows on it from the desert. The breath of the Lord comes, and the flower fades and the grass withers. Our human lives are just like the flowers. They flourish and then they reach their prime of beauty, then they begin to flag and they wither and pass away.

The message here means: don't worry that your leaders have died; don't be afraid that the people who led you have gone; don't feel that everything has slipped away from you, there is one thing that is still the same: the word of God abides forever, it stands. I could apply this personally. If your church meets in an old building, a hundred years ago different people stood there, different people sat in those pews. There is no-one in the church worshipping now who was there when it was built. They have all come and gone. The leaders will have come and gone. All flesh is as grass. The flower fades. But there is one thing that is exactly the same in a church as it was when it was opened, and that is the Bible. We may use a new version to bring the language up to date, but the word of God stands forever. I tell you this: if the church that you attend is still there one hundred years hence, you will not be in it, but the Bible will be the same. And if the people's confidence is in the word and not in any flesh, then that church will still be there and the same preaching will still be there. I read some of the sermons preached from many years previously at the church of which I was once pastor and it was the same gospel, the same word, that I preach now. It is my job to gear people's faith to the word that stands forever. So that is why I think it was most appropriate that God had given this word to his prophet 150 years before.

It gave them confidence. The word of God stands forever. This word is still relevant. I preach these words over two thousand years after they were written, and you will find comfort and help and strength in these same words. Is that not amazing? Even when heaven and earth pass away, this word shall not pass away. That is the glory of it. And as we learn from Peter in the New Testament: you were born again not of perishable seed but of imperishable. You were born of the word of God which lives and abides forever. Peter quotes Isaiah chapter 40 to prove it.

The message of the last voice means that the welfare of Judah is strengthened. The last voice calls upon Jerusalem when it is re-established, to speak to the whole district of Judah. We are back again in the city, and when Jerusalem was established all the district of Judah was re-established. Without the capital they collapsed but with it they would be back again. So now the prophet says: get back to Jerusalem and become a preacher of the good news; say to Judah, behold your God.

Now we have a wonderful picture of this. God is not only a mighty conqueror, he is a tender shepherd. Some people are so tender that they cannot be much help to you because they are not strong enough. Some people are strong but they cannot help you because they are not gentle enough. The people who can really help you are those who are both strong and gentle. You need that combination. And our God is a God who is all mighty and all gentle, all tender. It is a picture of a conquering hero who will come and slay his enemies and a shepherd who will gently lead his people home. That is the combination that we need and find in our true heavenly Father. We worship a God who has all power, who could destroy this world with a word as he made it with a word; but he is a God who is tender too. So when God comes with his might to rule, when he comes to deal with the Babylonians, then he is going to lead you back gently like a shepherd. He comes as a soldier, he goes back as a shepherd. There is a lovely touch here of a shepherd leading his flock. There is a little lamb that cannot keep up with the flock. The shepherd bends down, picks the lamb up. He gathers the lambs in his arms, he will carry them in his bosom. The shepherd slows the flock up and gently leads those that are with lambs. What a picture!

So the prophet has told those Jews in exile God is coming, that he is coming in might to deal with the Babylonians, he is coming in power to slay them, and then his power will change to gentleness. He will take his people — the women expecting babies he will lead gently; the little children — he will watch over them and he will bring them five hundred miles back again. What a difference to the journey out, which we know took three months. They had been forced to march so fast that pregnant women fell and died in the desert and little children were too tired and fell and were left to die there — that is how the Babylonians had taken the people into exile. But God will gently lead them back, like a shepherd with his flock.

16

WINGS LIKE EAGLES

Read Isaiah 40:12–41:29

A. JEHOVAH'S GREATNESS (12-26)
1. HIS MIND (12-20)
a. Creator of things (12-17) b. Like what? (18-20)
2. HIS MIGHT (21-26)
a. Controller of people (21-24) b. Like whom? (25-26)
B. JACOB'S GRUMBLES (40:27-41:29)
1. FAINT NOT (27-4)
a. God's power - Israel (27-31) b. God's performance - heathen (1-4)
2. FEAR NOT (5-29)
a. God's presence - Israel (5-20) b. God's prediction - heathen (21-29)

Pearls in oysters are caused by a tiny piece of grit getting in through the crack in the oyster shell and setting up an irritation. To protect its soft body from the irritation the oyster clothes the grit with that lovely smooth coating which we know as the pearl. Therefore at the heart of every pearl there is a piece of grit which originally caused irritation, pain and suffering. As we go through the Bible, when we come across a promise of God that is a 'pearl' of his wisdom you will find at the heart of it a piece of grit, a pain, an irritation, a suffering. Most of our deepest insights into God's character and love come when we are in the middle of suffering. And the fact that Isaiah chapters 40 – 66 contain many of the most precious promises and passages in the Old Testament is not accidental. They were written to a people who were suffering, and suffering very badly.

Let me paint the scene for you again. They were away from home. They had been away for nearly seventy years; they were slaves in a foreign land. Their city lay in ruins, five hundred miles away, burnt to the ground. Many of their children and old people had died. The rest of them had been taken away in chains and force marched across the desert. They now lived in a most depressing place – Babylon. We have noted that the terrain was flat. The only things that stood up from the plain were the things which man had built. No wonder in Babel or in Babylon men were always trying to build things up. Whether it was a tower to reach to heaven, or the famous Hanging Gardens of Babylon, there in that flat place in which you could see nothing of God's creation except the stars and the sun and the moon, there the children of Israel, the people of God, languished for seventy years. And they suffered increasingly through those years, until in the time of which we speak a new ruler was persecuting them for their religious outlook. They were suffering now not because they were doing wrong but because they were doing right. They were suffering because they believed in God, not because they did not. So there is a change in their suffering. To those poor people who had honestly come to the conclusion that God was no longer interested in them, that he had forgotten all about them, that he was not going to do a thing to help them in their suffering, came those words: *'Comfort, comfort my people'*. But we have seen the pearl of comfort in Isaiah chapter 40 – God is gently going to lead them back to their own place.

In 40:12ff, the first point is this: have you got a big enough view of God? The more you know God, the bigger your view of him. Of course we start off in life with a very little view of him. As children we may have thought of God as a kind of Santa Claus up in the clouds, an old man with a beard, very much like ourselves but much nicer. We have such a little view of God. Even many adults have a little view of God, as a God who just helps you out when you are in a jam, a kind of heavenly supermarket you go to just to get things. Isaiah chapter 40 shows us that our view of God should be big. If you are in trouble, if you are suffering, if you are going through it, the first thing you need is a big view of God. Isaiah tries to magnify their vision of God. The bigger your view of God, the smaller your troubles — it is as simple as that. The smaller your idea of God the bigger your troubles. Isaiah says, '*Who has measured the waters in the hollow of his hand . . . ?*' All through this chapter and the next he has his hearers looking up. That was all they could do, and it is one thing I would find very difficult to do. I was brought up among the hills and I love the hills. The only part of God's creation they could look at was the sky. In these verses Isaiah communicates something of the greatness of God. Think of the greatness of the mind of God. We are told today that we know more and more about less and less, and that is true. We are discovering that there is so much knowledge packed into the universe, so much to know, that we have to specialise even to catch up with one little area of knowledge. So each specialist knows more and more about less and less, and one human mind can only begin to master one tiny area of human knowledge. You cannot possibly catch up with all the knowledge that we now have, yet we are just at the beginning. It has been said that the human race has learnt more about the universe in the last few decades than was learnt in the previous two thousand years. What must the mind of God be like, that had all that knowledge in it to begin with? —the God who packed the atom, the God who made all this, the God who thought it all up. Every piece of knowledge we have gained we have had to acquire from someone else. If you could put all the knowledge of every brain in the world together into one brain, you would still not have come anywhere near the mind of God. What a mighty God we have!

In contrast to all that, don't you feel small? Of course you do. The nations are just like a drop in a bucket. Do you not see now how utterly foolish it is to try to portray God with an image? To take a piece of metal or wood and to start shaping it and say: that's like God. However big you made that, it would still be petty and could not convey his greatness. I am afraid that as soon as you make an idol you try to cut God down, and that is wrong. It is utterly ridiculous. Isaiah laughs at the idols, he mocks them, he laughs them out of court with sheer sarcasm. How can a man think that he can make anything like God? No idol, no image, could ever convey the greatness of God, and in our worship we are never to use images of God. If we did, we would not be worshipping him. Lift up your eyes on high and consider who created the natural order.

Vv. 21–26 move on from God's *mind* to his *might*, from his thought to his acts. He is as great in his might as he is in his mind. Isaiah rebukes and chastises the people of God for forgetting what they have been taught. He asks his hearers whether they have not known. Had they not heard? Had they not known this from the beginning? If you were brought up from a young age to know that God is the Creator, then when your troubles get so big that they get bigger in your sight than God, I say to you ask yourself this question: Did you not hear? Did you not know? Have you not heard this from the beginning that God is far greater than your problems, far bigger than your sufferings? You were taught this from the beginning. We have no excuse for grumbling.

He who sits above the circle of the earth is able to destroy your enemies. He brings princes to nothing. Not only does God create things, he destroys people. Scarcely are they sown, scarcely planted, when God blows upon them and they wither and die. I have seen this. Out in the desert in Arabia we tried to grow a garden outside the wooden hut which we used as our place of worship. We watered it three times a day with a hose, and of course if you can get water it is like growing a thing in a greenhouse out there. And up sprang the things we had planted, almost in hours! I have got colour pictures of my little garden planted to try to bring a little greenery into the barrenness of the desert. Three weeks after it grew, we had the hot desert wind and a sandstorm. Next morning there was not a trace of a green leaf, it had all gone! This is the Middle East geography, and it is being used by the prophet. Those mighty princes, dictators like Sennacherib, Nebuchadnezzar, scarcely are they sown, scarcely are they planted, and God blows on them —and they go. Have you forgotten that? Clouds arise and tempests blow by order from God's throne. Have you forgotten that God can cut a man down to size? Have you forgotten that God is in charge of history? Have you forgotten that he deals with the enemies of his people? Scarcely are they planted, scarcely sown, when he blows upon them and they wither. Look at all the world's dictators and see how they fell. Since God is the Holy One, the only ruler of princes, to whom will you compare him? Get a good view of God and you are not afraid of man any more. If you fear God you will fear no-one else.

Isaiah says, *Lift your eyes* .... The Babylonians worshipped the moon. The people in that flat place looked up, but Isaiah is not, of course, encouraging his hearers to look up to worship the heavens. His message means: look up; who made all those? Who called them out? Who set them in their place so that they are there to be relied upon? Already by this time sailors were navigating by the stars. It was the Phoenicians who discovered that the stars were always there and worked out how they moved. They discovered that you can rely on the stars in heaven and that each night they would be there. They were the sailors of the world; they went everywhere guided by those stars which God had put in the heavens. I know that we are not to think of heaven as a big black sheet with God pinning stars on. I do not think they were thinking like this. They were simply describing how it looks to us, just as if I talk about the four corners of the earth I do not want you to think I believe the earth is square! This is phenomenological language — it is how it appears to man. They say God put the stars in their place and not one of them is missing; they stay there, you can rely upon them. Who did this? God, by the greatness of his might. So what are you going to say God is like? And whom are you going to say God is like? Of course with our knowledge of the universe we can now have a bigger view of God than Isaiah. We know something of how many stars there are. They used to think in Bible days there were about 6,000 as that was all you could see. Now we know that there are thousands upon thousands. They did not know the vastness of space. Now we know that it is millions and millions of light years. We know how big it all is, so we have no excuse for having a little view of God, its Creator.

May I suggest that next time you have a big trouble, next time you are really weighed down and going through it and having a rough time, you go out on a clear night and stand for half an hour and look at the stars and ask yourself who created them. I have found that this is a big help. I remember one night away up in the Shetland Islands I was going through a crisis, a really difficult time. That night, I went out into the hills above the ocean and walked for hours over the moors, under the starlit sky. When I returned, my problem was right-sized. It is because we get things out of proportion that we forget that God is much greater than our problems. But if we only look at our problem and our suffering, our suffering gets bigger.

We come to v. 27. Now the people were grumbling, and we are told what they were saying. The people of God had been in exile for so many years, suffering, without their homes, their temple, all that they loved and cherished, and they thought God was no longer interested in them and did not care. May I point this out: when suffering comes, some people say that there is no God. But the people of God never did that. They never ceased to believe in him. What they did feel was that he was not helping them. They never said: Why should there be this suffering if there is a good God? They came to the conclusion that God was not bothering with them, that he had forgotten about them, that he was no longer interested. If you are a Christian and you belong to the people of God I do not think you will ever come to the point where you say because of suffering there is no God. The most you could say is God has forgotten about me, for he seems uninterested in me. You would still believe in a God, but you might feel that he did not care. That would be your problem and it is completely different from denying his existence. It is, rather, a doubt concerning his character. So Jacob was grumbling, Israel was grumbling: they thought God had forgotten about them, could not see them and did not care. Isaiah's answer follows in vv. 28ff. You can look up and see every one of those stars so far away; God can see every one of you.

The message in this passage is both 'faint not' (40:27 – 41:4) and 'fear not' (41:5–29), and there are two points under each heading. The first is addressed to the Jews, and the second to the Babylonians. To the Jews: remember my power. To the Babylonians: remember what I have performed. Under 'fear not', the message is: remember my presence. And to the Babylonians: remember my predictions.

Faint not nor fear — how do we do that? First of all, we do it by remembering that God never gets tired. We get tired, we get weary. The Bible has to keep telling us not to be weary in well doing. Don't get tired of serving the Lord; don't flag in your zeal. I have the feeling that our problems get too big for us when we are tired. Do you not find that? It is when you are tired that you get things out of proportion. It is when you are tired that a little problem gets you down. It is when you are tired that you get irritated. We run out of energy. How often do we say of little children tearing around breaking up the happy home: where do they get their energy? But even children get tired! We look at a young man in all the vigour of his manhood, in the prime of his life. He is able to study for hours then go out and play football for hours, then go out and be romantic for hours — where does he get all his vigour? But even youths shall faint and be weary, even young men get tired. Even the power of the sun is running down and burning up, so I am told. All power of a natural kind wears down — the rocks give up their radioactivity. But God's power never reduces. And those who wait for the Lord will find that he keeps giving them strength. They shall fly, they shall run, they shall walk. I would have put it the other way on, wouldn't you? I would have built up to a nice climax. I would say they walk, they run, they fly. But no, Isaiah quite deliberately says they fly, they run, they walk — walk being the climax. Some have thought he was referring to the physical ages of man. When we are a youth we fly. We rush up those clouds of idealism. We want to mount up with wings as eagles. Then when we are middle-aged we begin to run instead of fly. Then by the time we get past fifty we are walking and we watch the young ones fly. I do not think it means physical ages, I think it means spiritual ages. When you are first a Christian you want to fly, and indeed you do, and God gives strength to you to be filled with that exuberant buoyancy which lifts you above everything. Then you run, but you know the climax of Christian strength is to keep on walking — not the flights of one's early love but that daily trudge year after year, when God gives you the strength to walk worthily of your high calling. It is easier for God to make us soar up suddenly like the eagle, and it is harder for us to learn to walk and not faint. I have been greatly impressed with the saints of God who, thirty years after their conversion, are still walking steadily with the Lord and not fainting. They have had their flights, they have had the times when they ran, but like Paul they had learned to walk and to keep on walking. They who wait for the Lord will renew their strength. They shall mount up with wings as eagles, they shall run and not be weary, they shall walk and not faint. That is Christian life, continuity.

In 41:1-4 there is an appeal to the Babylonians: Let's talk. The kingdom of Babylon lay in the muddy flat plain at the head of the Persian Gulf. Five hundred miles away was Jerusalem, and the Jews had been brought through the desert into exile in Babylon. Babylon thought they were top dog. They had already defeated Assyria and others. They were the great nation Babylon, great Babylon, the name that has gone down into history as a mighty empire. God said, you Babylonians, not only can I give my people strength if they wait for me, I can use my strength against you — and I stir up someone from the east. In the east was a tiny kingdom, ruled at that time by a man called Cyrus — just a little king of a little kingdom. But God said: I am stirring him up. And stir him up he did. If you read the story of Cyrus you will be amazed at the phenomenal conquest he made of all the nations around him. It is the most fantastic story of military conquest in history. So fast did he march that there was a proverb that his feet never touched the ground, and that proverb is in Isaiah 41:3.

> *He pursues them and moves on unscathed,*
> *by a path his feet have not travelled before.*
>
> (NIV)

The literal Hebrew is 'without touching the ground'. So swift were his conquests that his feet did not touch the ground. Who had made that possible? See v. 4. God was raising him up for a particular purpose. Do you know what that was? Let me jump across the years. Cyrus was going to defeat Babylon and then he was going to discover that in fact it was the God of the Jews who had enabled him to do it, and he was going to let the Jews go back to Jerusalem and he would let them rebuild the temple because of this. That was why God raised him up. Cyrus was a pagan, not a Jew. He did not belong to the people of God. But God is over everything, in charge of history.

So in 41:5–29 the refrain is (in vv. 10, 13, 14) 'fear not', because all the nations around Cyrus were afraid of this young conqueror. They were trembling. From secular records, a Greek historian of this period said they were rushing to their priests, to their idols, and saying, 'What's going to happen? What's the future? What's this man Cyrus going to do?' And the oracles were silent and the priests were silent. So they started making new images and saying to the images, 'Tell us the future.' All this is mocked in vv. 5–7, where we are told that the craftsman encourages the goldsmith —people are busy building idols to try and save them from Cyrus! It is sheer mockery. We know that Babylon and two other kingdoms to the north (Lydia and Media) were rushing around asking the gods what was going to happen now that Cyrus was coming. But God's lovely message for his own people is: fear not. Next time you are down in the dumps, next time you are going through it, next time you think that God has forgotten all about you, read Isaiah 41:10. The rest of the verses (to 41:20) describe how God will help his people and restore them, refresh them and get them back into their own land; how he will make them a people who leave their mark on the world. You may feel like a worm (see v. 14) but God would make his people a threshing-sledge (see v. 15) that would leave its mark —and his people have certainly left their mark on the world.

Finally, from 41:21 onwards, God turns to the Babylonians again, and the heathen priests are challenged to produce any predictions they have made that have come true, or to predict anything about the future and see if it happens. Of course, only God knows the future.

Then, in v. 25 we read that God stirred up one from the north, from the rising of the sun. According to my geography the sun does not rise from the north. What does this mean? It is just one of those apparent contradictions in scripture that is absolutely true. Now remember we learnt in v. 2 that God stirred up one from the east, Cyrus. How do we reconcile it? Very simply. Cyrus was east of Babylon. He called his little kingdom Persia. It looked as if Cyrus would come from the east, but he did not. The first thing he did was to go north and conquer Media and make one kingdom of the Medes and the Persians. I am sure you have heard the phrase 'the laws of the Medes and the Persians' — Cyrus did that. Then he came on to Babylon. So it is perfectly true that God stirred him up from the rising of the sun in the east and brought him from the north. He came from the east and from the north and attacked Babylon. Poor old Nebuchadnezzar built a wall seventy miles long, a hundred feet high, and twenty wide, between the Tigris and the Euphrates. He dug four canals between the rivers and thought he had defended himself. But Cyrus marched straight through, and he let the people of God go back to their own land —and God did that.

In conclusion, remember that nature and history are God's workshops. The God we are to worship made the universe, he is Maker of heaven and earth; and he rules over all human history and governs all princes. To me the most amazing thing is this: that God is my Father, and he loves me. If you just have a big view of God and that alone, you would not love him. You would revere him, you might worship him, but you would not love him. But I love him because God who made those stars — and has ruled the history of the world — invites people to call him 'Father'. As you wait for him you will renew your strength. You will rise up with wings like eagles. You will run and not be weary. You will walk and not faint.

17

SING A NEW SONG

Read Isaiah 42

A. A PEOPLE - ALL JEWS?
1. ACTUAL - JACOB?
2. IDEAL - ISRAEL?
B. A PERSONIFICATION - SOME JEWS?
1. GENERAL GROUP?
a. Remnant? b. Righteous?
2. PARTICULAR GROUP?
a. Prophets? b. Priests?
C. A PERSON - ONE JEW?
1. PRESENT - MAN?
2. FUTURE - MESSIAH!
a. Jews - Christ b. Christians - Jesus
A. RELIABLE SERVANT (1-4)
B. RIGHTEOUS SOVEREIGN (5-17)
1. PAST - PREDESTINATION (5-9)
2. PRESENT - PRAISE (10-13)
3. FUTURE - PROMISE (14-17)
C. REBELLIOUS SERVANT (18-25)

In all Bible study one of the best things to do right from the beginning is look for key words. If necessary underline in your Bible those that seem to stand out. (Do not be afraid of writing in your Bible.) At this point we have hit the most important key word in the whole of Isaiah, and I am going to have to spend most of this chapter looking at just one word, and helping you to try to understand what it means. It is the word 'servant'.

Consider how this theme runs through the rest of Isaiah: *"But you, Israel my servant, Jacob whom I have chosen . . . ."* (41:8). *'You are my servant'* (41:9), *"Here is my servant whom I uphold"* (42:1); and 42:19; 43:10; 44:1f.; 44:21; 45:4; 48:20; 49:3, 5, 6, 7; 52:13; 53:11. I think I have proved to you that this is a key word!

What does 'servant' mean? Even more important: *who* is it? You would not believe how many books have been written on this question. I have one book in my library that sums up the views that have been expounded since Isaiah used this word 'servant' and you could fill a library with the books that have been written on this one issue.

It is comparatively easy to answer the question: what is a servant? Mind you, in a few years' time that word will have gone right out of our language. It is rapidly disappearing. Nobody likes the word 'servant' nowadays. It implies that a person is subservient to another, and in our modern democratic age we no longer talk about a servant — employee, perhaps. The days in which private homes were filled with servants have disappeared. Like the word 'kingdom' the word 'servant' is therefore losing its meaning. But I think we can still basically answer the question by simply saying that a servant is a person who is at the disposal of someone else, to obey their will, to do their work, to represent their interests. Therefore when God says, *"Here is my servant"*, he is referring to someone who is at his disposal to do his will, to do his work, to represent his interests, and we must therefore ask about whom Isaiah is speaking when he describes this person, this servant who is at God's disposal. That is where we get into the question.

A famous professor of Old Testament theology, S R Driver, decided to write a commentary on the book of Isaiah, and when he reached this word 'servant' he became so confused and perplexed, so overwhelmed with the meaning of this one word, that he finally abandoned the entire commentary and it was never published. If a professor is overwhelmed it is quite understandable if some of us are too, but I am going to try to clear the way through the jungle of the many opinions that have been given, and I am going to give you some of other people's opinions, then I am going to give you my own, and ask you to search the scriptures and see whether these things be so.

When Philip (in Acts 8) jumped up into the chariot of the

Chancellor of the Exchequer of the kingdom of Ethiopia, he found him reading Isaiah — one of the very chapters in which the word *servant* occurs. He asked Philip who the prophet was talking about — himself or someone else. That is the question we have to answer now. We know the answer Philip gave, but we have got to begin much further back than that and realise something of the problem.

Broadly speaking, there are three different answers that have been given. First, that when God says *"Behold, my servant"*, he is referring to all the Jews, treating them collectively as a nation, and saying that this nation is his servant, this nation is for him, to do his will and his work in the world. The second answer is that 'my servant' does not refer to the whole nation or all the Jews, but does refer to some of the Jews. It is a personification, a bit like John Bull or Uncle Sam or some such figure as that, summing up a particular group. Particular groups within the Jewish nation are God's servant or minister (the same word, incidentally). Then there is the third view that the servant of God is only one Jew. There have been at least twenty-five guesses as to who that one is, within that view. All the Jews, some Jews, one Jew; three different answers — a people, a personification, a person — which is the right answer? Or are all three the right answer? Or are two of them the right answer? That is the question we have to face.

Let us begin with the first answer. It is quite obvious that in at least half the texts that I have referred to, the first answer is the right one. In at least half those references *my servant* is defined as Jacob or Israel, and both names are given. That undoubtedly refers to the nation of God, the Jews. I cannot quarrel with that. There is one God in heaven and his purpose was to choose one people on earth to represent him. God's method of reaching people is not to speak to all of them at once but to speak to one of them and ask that person to tell the others. That is how he has chosen to work. He has not chosen to speak to the Russians, the British, the Americans, the Africans, the Chinese all at once, he has chosen one nation and spoken to them, then told them to speak to the others. That is God's method. You might criticise it — I am sure some people always seem to think that they could find of a better way of doing it than God has done it. But God chose one nation to speak to all the others — just as he does not directly speak to everybody in your town. He will speak to you, and then you go and tell them. That is why if we do not tell them they may never hear. God has chosen this way and it is a very good way of doing it. He told the Jews that they were to be his witnesses. Jesus said to his disciples, "*. . . you will be my witnesses . . . .*" God has not chosen to tell everybody the truth but to tell some people the truth and to tell them to go and witness to it. That is why Jesus said, quite fundamentally, "*. . . for salvation is from the Jews.*" No-one will ever be saved except through what God said and did to the Jews. This is a Jewish book that we are reading and I am now expounding. Christ was a Jew. All the twelve apostles were Jews. God gave them salvation to give to us, and that is how it comes to us. In that sense the Jews as a whole nation are his people, his witnesses, his missionaries, his servants, and every Jew was intended by God to be a missionary. From the very first call of Abraham, God had made it quite clear that in him and in his seed all the families of the earth would be blessed. That was Abraham's job, his service. The greatest tragedy of history is that the Jewish nation never became a missionary nation. They never fulfilled their service. Happily, some of them did. The apostles did and others did, but as for the nation they never actually did — they were not good servants. How would you get on training a domestic servant who was totally blind and stone deaf? I do not think you would get on very well training them in housework. Yet here we have:

"Who is blind but my servant,
and deaf like the messenger I send?"

42:19a (NIV)

The tragedy of the Jewish nation is that they could not see the truth themselves and they could not hear what God was saying to them, therefore he could not use them as he longed to do and as he planned to do when he called them. They were given something to give to the whole world, and by the time Jesus came they had so lost interest in that work that the court of the Gentiles in the temple had become a place of business and money-changing, and if you were not a Jew you could not even pray in the temple of God — there was no place for you. That is the situation, and incidentally that is why Jesus cleansed the temple. God's intention and plan was that the whole national history was to be a testimony about God to others, and his people were to speak about him, but they never did. Therefore there has been a division among scholars and students of the Bible as to whether the words 'my servant' refer to Israel as she actually was or as God had intended her to be, as the double name — the human name 'Jacob' and the divine name 'Israel' — would seem to suggest on this interpretation. There is such a tension within the whole Old Testament. Either way, that is the first interpretation, and at least half the references to 'my servant' in Isaiah obviously come in this category: my people, my servant, my servant Jacob, my servant Israel; the whole nation meant to be missionaries, intended to serve God by being witnesses. But, and this is the problem, there are four passages in these chapters in which the words 'my servant' cannot possibly mean this. Here are six reasons why these four passages cannot be fitted into the first answer.

In these four passages:

(1) The servant is anonymous.

(2) The servant is talked of as *he* and not addressed as *you*, which is true of all the passages labelled 'Jacob' and 'Israel'. It seems to begin to emerge that there is someone else in God's mind.

(3) The prophet is clearly describing one person.

(4) The character of God's servant is absolutely perfect and righteous — my righteous servant. The nation was never like that.
(5) The things which 'my servant' is going to do were never done (and never could be done) by the nation as a whole.
(6) This clinches it: the mission, the task, of 'my servant' is *to* the people of Israel, and therefore it must be someone else.

The 'servant' described in Isaiah 53 cannot possibly refer to the nation. What the servant does there they never did and could not have done. So we are left with this conclusion: of the passages which mention the words 'my servant', half of them obviously refer to a people (all the Jews), but the other half of them cannot possibly refer to the whole nation.

So we move on to the second answer that has been given. Does the second group of passages, which refers to 'my servant', actually refer not to *all* the Jews but to *some* of them, a group of Jews within the nation, either in general terms, those who survived physically, the remnant — or those who survived spiritually, the righteous or good ones? Do the good ones have a ministry to the bad ones? Is the 'servant' really a group of ministers to the whole people of God? That leads to the particular definition of them as either the prophets or the priests. I have encountered all those four answers. Some scholars have said that 'my servant' in these four passages refers to a remnant, those who physically survived, to the righteous, those who were better than the others, to the prophets who spoke the word of God, or to the priests who ministered in holy things. But I want to say that I do not think that this explanation can possibly be fitted into the picture. Still we are up against the fact that none of these four passages gives any hint that it refers to more than one man. None of these passages refers directly to prophet or priest, to remnant or righteous, and therefore it is a pure guess, a speculative hypothesis, and we move on quite quickly from this to the third one.

Do these four passages refer to one Jew? If so, who? The majority of students of the Bible have come to this conclusion: that God was speaking not only of the nation as his servant but of one person within the nation as his servant in a special way. That has been held by Jew, by Christian — by Catholic and Protestant students of the Bible. If this is so, then who is he? Here, opinion is further divided: there are those who think it was somebody alive in the days of Isaiah, and those who think it was someone yet in the future (as from Isaiah's day). From those who have thought it was somebody in Isaiah's time there has been a great list of candidates suggested, but it is interesting that both Jew and Christian ultimately came to the conclusion that these four passages (the first of which we looked at in chapter 42, and the last of which is Isaiah 53) are describing God's Messiah.

Moreover, Jews and Christians came to this conclusion at the same time. The Jews came to it without connecting it with Jesus. But as far as I can discover, Jewish students of the scriptures only began to think that this 'servant' referred to their expected Christ about the time of Jesus, they did not think it before then. Isn't that amazing? — and for another thousand years Jewish scholars said that the 'servant' is the Messiah. In the Middle Ages, however, the Christians began to use these passages so forcefully in their preaching that the Jews departed from this interpretation and jumped back to the first interpretation instead, and said that it meant that in every case. Jewish students today usually refuse to take that earlier view that this 'servant' refers to the Messiah, largely because they have become so embarrassed with these passages. Christians read 'he was wounded for our transgressions', and they say to the Jewish nation: can't you see this is your Messiah dying for your sins? But there is a veil in their minds and so most cannot see it, so they no longer believe that the 'servant' means the Messiah. But for a thousand years they did and for two thousand years Christians have done.

Let me therefore take the Christian understanding of this

'servant' in Isaiah. Until around two centuries ago Christian students of the Bible were unanimous that 'my servant' referred to Jesus, and they based it on a number of things. They based it on the fact that Jesus himself made this interpretation. He said, "I am among you as one who serves". He wrapped a towel round his waist and washed the disciples' feet. He quoted from Isaiah 53, interpreting his death in terms of this servant who was to be wounded for the transgressions of others and bruised for their iniquities. The early preaching in the Acts of the Apostles called Jesus again and again the '. . . servant Jesus'. (See, for example, Acts 3:13 where Peter, after the healing of the lame man at the temple, said: *"The God of Abraham, Isaac and Jacob, the God of our fathers, has glorified his servant Jesus."* (NIV). Later, to the crowd, he said, *"God raised up his servant . . . ."* Even in prayer they gave Jesus this title. In Acts 4 we have a prayer of the early church in which they say, *". . . your holy servant Jesus"*. It became a title of Jesus. They took the word from Isaiah and they linked it up with our Lord, the servant Jesus. In the epistles you get the same thing, Christ Jesus who had been in the form of God thought it not robbery to be equal with God, but made himself of no reputation. He took upon him the form of a servant — and you will find running right through the New Testament this link between the servant of Isaiah and Jesus of Nazareth. It is no wonder that right through church history until two centuries ago every Christian believed that the servant in these four passages was Jesus, and that when you read them you must think of your Lord. But then the critical scholars of Germany began to cut the Bible up. They began to say that Isaiah didn't write all of Isaiah. They began to say that it came from this that and the other person. They began to question everything in the Bible. And my sad news for you is that many professing Christian scholars no longer see this. Indeed, having been taken through these chapters in Cambridge University I was taught that the servant is no longer thought of as Jesus. It is a tragic thing that after holding this faith for two thousand years, Christian scholars should depart from it.

What, then, is the answer to this situation? Let me summarise like this: is the 'servant' of Isaiah a people, a personification, or a person? All the Jews, some of the Jews or one Jew? There is one group of scholars today who say that it must be one or other of these options —but quite frankly you cannot do it, all these 'servants' will not fit into one or other of those categories. So we dismiss the idea that we must choose between them.

At the other end of the scale are those who say that you can actually treat the 'servant' as *all three* —that the servant may be thought of as a kind of pyramid, first it was all the Jews, then it was some, and then it became one, and that in fact you can trace this evolutionary development. The difficulty with that, which looks neat on paper and sounds plausible, is that there is nothing at all in scripture about that middle bit, and it is impossible to establish that the word 'servant' ever meant *some* of the Jews. So we can actually cross out that middle stage!

We are therefore left with two meanings of the word 'servant' in Isaiah. It refers either to the whole nation or to one person within it. Every one of the passages in Isaiah can very simply and easily be fitted into one or other of those two meanings and the whole thing becomes clear. To recap briefly, here was the problem: God chose Israel to be his servant, a light to the nations, a witness, a missionary movement —but the trouble was they never did become that. What was wrong? The answer is they were sinful, they did not do what God told them; they would not obey his laws, they would not obey his mandate. How could he possibly put that right? Of course some might say: well, he could have chosen the British to do it, or he could have chosen the Russians, or any other nation, but the same thing would have happened because everybody is in the same sinful condition! The only answer that could meet the need was provided by God. One Jew who was perfectly righteous would bear the sins of all the other Jews in order to save the others from that which prevented them from being his witnesses — and we see the whole pattern. In order for the nation to be God's servant somebody else had to come and do something — to bear their sins — so that, having got rid of their sin and disobedience, again they might become the missionaries. That is exactly what happened with the apostles. They were Jews. They were part of the disobedient nation yet Jesus died for them and took their sins away, and they became witnesses of Christ and of God, to the ends of the earth, and the church still is witnessing. That is the new plan. Jacob, the old nation, was a sinful nation. Who is blind like my servant? Who is deaf like my messenger? So can you see now why, as you read of God's plan in Isaiah, the word 'servant' is used with two meanings? There is the 'servant' who was no good and the 'servant' who was completely good; the 'servant' who was sinful and spiritually blind and deaf, and the 'servant' who saw it all and heard it all and was not spiritually 'blind' and was not deaf, but came to lead the blind out of their darkness and to open the ears of the deaf. This was the plan of God. So in a real sense Jesus fulfilled the calling of the nation. He was part of it, he embodied it in himself, he was a Jew, and he did for the first time what God had intended every other Jew to do, and be, a light to the Gentiles.

Now you should find that you read Isaiah 42 and understand it completely. The first passage about Jesus is vv. 1–4. Indeed, chapters 42–53 present the life of Jesus, and they start with his baptism. May I give you a literal rendering of the Hebrew of 42:1 — *"Behold my servant whom I uphold, my chosen in whom I am well pleased. I have put my Spirit upon him . . . ."* What do those words remind you of? When Jesus was baptised, the Father said, " . . . *with you I am well pleased"* —Jesus knew the scriptures, and knew perfectly well that was a quote from Isaiah 42 — and that he was God's servant.

The thing that happened immediately after the Father said 'I am well pleased' was that he anointed Jesus with the Holy Spirit — and again it is a fulfilment of v. 1. It is no wonder, therefore, that as we read these words we find a perfect description of

Jesus — Jesus was God's servant, whom he upheld; Jesus was God's chosen in whom the Father was well pleased; Jesus had the Holy Spirit put within him; Jesus will bring forth justice to the nations. It is Jesus we are talking about now.

Look at v. 2, which tells us about the meekness of Jesus. He will not shriek or yell in an excited, hysterical manner. What a contrast to many 'celebrities' in the public eye in the world today! Jesus will not move people like that, and he never did. Have you ever gained the impression that Jesus spoke quietly and in a restrained manner? (Incidentally, the phrase 'raise his voice in the street' is not against open air preaching — it is about advertising oneself, pushing yourself to try to be impressive, to try to get in the public eye.) Note the meekness of the servant of Isaiah 42:2, the gentleness in v. 3. It is a lovely message, that he will not break a bruised reed, and a dimly burning wick he will not quench. We see the gentleness of Jesus with people whose life is ebbing, with people who are downtrodden, with people who are fading, with people who are battered by life — there is the gentleness of Jesus. Yet he will still be absolutely just and fair.

We are reminded in v.4 that Jesus will never fail or be discouraged—and he will establish the will of God on a universal scale. All Jesus' enemies will be under his feet. We fail, and we get discouraged sometimes. If you look at the RSV at the bottom of the page you will find that the verbs of v. 4 are the same as the words of v. 3. Jesus will never burn dimly, nor be bruised. Matthew chapter 12 quotes the whole four verses as a fulfilment.

Verses 5–17 are concerned with God (who is the Creator) speaking to his servant Israel. First, in vv. 5–9, he is calling his people to look back; he had called them to be his servant, to open the blind eyes and bring prisoners out of the dungeon. God's people should be praising him (see vv. 10–13; they ought to be singing a new song, praising him all over the earth). But vv. 14–17 show us that God would come and do it himself.

He would lead the blind. Why should that be? Have you ever asked somebody to do something and they are either so dull or so stupid or so slow that you say: here, I will do it?

In vv. 18–25 he describes this rebellious servant Jacob. *"Who is blind but my servant . . . ?"* Most of the very people on earth who should have seen God most clearly and should have helped others to see him most clearly are in fact the most blind to him. That is the tragedy. You try going as a missionary to modern Israel, and tell them Jesus is the Christ – and see what happens. Paul writes of a veil in their minds even when they read the scriptures. They can read Isaiah 40–53 yet not see Jesus. They read that he was wounded for our transgressions but they cannot see the cross.

Who is blind like the one committed to me,
blind like the servant of the LORD?

42:19b (NIV)

– the very people who should have been leading the blind. He would come and do it himself, and that is why Jesus quoted Isaiah, proclaimed recovery of sight for the blind (see Luke 18f). Do you see how it all fits in? We are called to be servants of the Lord. Jesus exemplified this and fulfilled what Israel failed to do.

18

JEHOVAH'S WITNESSES

Read Isaiah 43:1–44:23

A. FORMATION OF ISRAEL

1. (43:1-7)

a. Procured by God (1) b. Protected by God (2)
c. Precious to God (3-4) d. Preserved for God (5-7)

2. (44:1-5)

a. Predestined by God (1-2) b. Privileged in God (3)
c. Productive for God (4) d. Proud of God (5)

B. FUNCTION OF ISRAEL

1. (43:8-21)

a. Them - declare (8-9) b. You - witnesses (10-12) c. I - am (13-21)

2. (44:6-8)

a. I - am b. Then - declare c. You -witnesses

C. FOOLISHNESS OF ISRAEL

1. IDLENESS (43:22-24)

a. You have not wearied yourselves (22)
b. I have not wearied you (23) c. You have wearied me (24)

2. IDOLATRY (44:9-20)

a. Worthless workmanship (9-11)
b. Mundane materials (12-17) c. Ignorant illusions (18-20)

D. FORGIVENESS OF ISRAEL

1. (43:25-28)

a. Forgive and forget (25-26) b. Sinning in time (27-28)

2. (44:21-23)

a. Forgive and forget (21-22) b. Singing in space (23)

Chapters 43 and 44 are constructed on the same pattern. Each of them says four things. We often find in scripture that in one chapter something is said and in the next chapter much the same thing is said in a different way. This kind of repetition (which sometimes also occurs in one verse) helps to bring the truth home by way of emphasis. So note the parallel and notice also the similar key words which appear in both chapters at the same point.

Let us begin by asking why we study the Old Testament. Somebody came up to me and said, 'You know, I got much more out of your Bible studies when you were in the New Testament than in the Old' — and some people have the feeling that now we have the New Testament we can scrap the Old; now we have got the full revelation in Christ and need not go back. But there are two things we need to remember. Firstly, the God we worship is the God of Abraham, Isaac and Jacob. In the New Testament, God need not repeat what he has already said in the Old. Jesus in his teaching assumed that his hearers knew all that God had already said about himself. He did not need to give a complete picture of God. If Jesus emphasised the love and the mercy and the fatherhood of God, it was not because he was preaching a different God but because he was assuming that every one of his hearers knew the Old Testament and knew about God's greatness and justice, and his judgement —truths which had already been revealed. Our Lord was not changing people's view of God, he was filling it out. You will remember that the Old Testament was the Bible not only of Christ but of the Christian church, for a long time. Before the New Testament was written the church just had the Old, and it was the Old that they studied. If you do not study the Old Testament but only the New, you will get a distorted view of God. The solid foundation of our view of God is to be found in the Old Testament, and the Lord Jesus loved the book of Isaiah, quoted from it frequently, based much of his life and ministry upon it, and obviously assumed that his hearers knew it.

Secondly, we recall that in the New Testament Paul draws a picture in our minds of a tree that has been cut back for the time being, the tree of Israel, and grafted into the trunk is the stock (or the shoot) of the church. We, as Christians, as the people of God today, draw our sap, our life, from the roots of the old people of God, Israel. Indeed, the point of studying Isaiah is that you are studying your own roots and you can draw life and sap from that root, to grow and be fruitful.

That is why we are studying Isaiah 43 and 44. They both begin with the phrase 'but now', which means that there is going to be a significant change in Israel's situation very soon. God is going to do something new: he is going to change their circumstances. When Augustine was converted (a professor of logic in Milan university but an immoral young man), the bishop of Milan, Ambrose, advised the young Augustine to study first in his Christian life Isaiah, and particularly chapters 40–66. Would you tell a new Christian convert to study those first? I am not sure that I would, but that was the advice given and it was a wonderful foundation.

Because chapters 43–44 are so parallel I am going to build up the picture and put it all together under the headings: Formation of Israel; Function of Israel; Foolishness of Israel; and Forgiveness of Israel.

FORMATION OF ISRAEL

First we have a section in which the key word is 'formed'. The Lord is 'he who formed you'. It is a wonderful word. To 'form' means to shape or make something. I love making things, I find it very healthy. I can always see where I have been when I have made something with my hands, and there is a sense of achievement. It is most satisfying to get a vision of it in your mind, perhaps to draw it and then to shape it, to create something. God loves doing that and the reason why we love doing it and find joy in it, whether it is a garden or a garage or a dress, is that we are made in his image; he loves forming things and so do we.

One of the things God formed was a nation, a most unusual nation, a people called 'Israel'. They were called 'Jacob' originally but he changed their name to 'Israel', and he kept calling them by both names to remind them of what they were and what they became after he formed them and fashioned them. So we have certain key phrases in both sections — 'Jacob', 'Israel' are key words, 'formed' is a key word, 'fear not' are key words, 'waters', 'rivers', 'streams' are key words, and the word 'name' is a key word.

In each of these chapters four things are said about this nation. The first is that this nation was *procured* by God — he bought it. One of my favourite bedtime stories as a boy was entitled *Twice Mine*. It is about the little boy who made a boat, took it to the seaside and the sea swept it away and he lost it. But somebody found it again and sold it to a secondhand shop in the town, and the boy saw it in the window and had to save up his pennies and go and buy back the thing that he had made. He ran up the street clutching his boat and shouting. 'Twice mine, it's twice mine.' When somebody said, 'Why are you shouting that?' he said, 'Well I made it, I loved it, I lost it, but now I've bought it back again so it is twice mine.' It is a good story for preachers to tell children — and in a real sense Israel was twice God's. 43:1 refers to God's creation and redemption of his people. Most people belong to God only by creation, but the people of God belong to God twice over.

As the sign of his ownership *he* gives them their name. The only creatures that you can name are your own. The only children that I have ever named are my own children. The only things I have a right to name are the things that belong to me. God can say: I created you, I redeemed you, I have called you by name, you are mine. That is the first point. God created the whole human race, but the unique thing about Israel is that among all the nations of the earth they are God's nation twice over. He redeemed them from Egypt.

Secondly, he *protects* them. They have a peculiar protection because they are twice his. When they pass through the waters he is with them. That happened in history. It is not a metaphor, it is historical fact. One of the most remarkable photographs I have seen was taken from 150 miles above the earth, looking down on the Red Sea, Egypt, the Nile delta and the Sinai peninsula. It is the most marvellous colour photograph of the Red Sea. Looking at that picture you can almost sense God looking down and there trapped in the desert are his children, with Egypt to the north of them, desert to the west of them, the Red Sea to the east, and the mountains of Ethiopia to the south; but he leads them through the waters of the Red Sea. They knew what it was to go through the waters and have God with them. We of course can take this spiritually and metaphorically, and it is true that when you go through the floods he will be with you. A flood of responsibilities, a flood of troubles pile up and we feel overwhelmed, flooded, but God is with us, he protects us.

The other threatening thing mentioned is fire. Walking through a fire, his people would not be burned (see 43:2b). That is a historical fact. Just about the time to which this refers, three men (Shadrach, Meshach and Abednego) were thrown into a boiler, the furnace that heated Nebuchadnezzar's palace. They were thrown into that fire to be burned alive because they would not bow down to a huge image set up by the king. They said to him that God was able to save them from the fire; they were not going to bow down before the image. What courage and faith! God did save them, and those three came out of the furnace. These things happened literally, and they still happen metaphorically too. They happen spiritually. Sometimes the fires of affliction go through you, sometimes the fires of persecution break out, and God brings his people through, who may say, with tremendous courage: we will not worship any other God; if he does not save us physically, we still trust him.

The third thing to notice in vv. 3–4 is that Israel is very *precious* to God. He would rather have them than any other people. Historically, God did exchange other nations for the life of Israel. Where is Assyria now? Where is Babylon now? But where is Israel now? —still there! God loves his people, so fourthly, they are *preserved*. They may be scattered over the whole world but God can bring them back. He has done that time and again in history, and we are living to see him do it again as they are brought together after being without their own land, their own nation, their own money, even their own language. God gathers them again. It is one of the most remarkable things in history, the re-gathering of God's people. He created them, he formed them, and that is truth number one in chapter 43.

Chapter 44 takes up the same theme. Here are the same words 'Jacob', 'Israel', 'formed', 'fear not', 'rivers', 'streams' — but now four new things are said. The first is that Israel was *chosen* by God — they did not choose him, he chose them. Predestination is one of those doctrines over which, tragically, there is heated argument. The way some people talk about this issue, the only One who has no right to have a free will — choice — is God! They think *they* should choose, that it should be men who choose him. Why should it? God is God, why should he not be free? Do you believe in the free will of God? I do. Why did God love the Jews? I will tell you the Bible's answer: because he loved them, that is all. Not because they were loveable. There was nothing in them that made him love them more than anyone else. There was nothing more attractive or more desirable about them. It was sheer love that chose them. Why should God choose us to be his people? Why should he ever step into our lives and confront us with himself? I cannot understand that. There is nothing in us that God would find more loveable or attractive than anyone else. Why should he have chosen you to have the privilege of studying his word and being part of his people? I just do not understand, I leave it to him. The word 'elect' is used in scripture, and election means choice — and God chose the Jews. I do not know why, just that he did. That the Jews are what they are not because they chose God but because God chose them is a very important truth.

The second thing mentioned here is that they are *privileged*. He is going to pour out water for them to drink. He is going to pour out the fire of his Spirit upon them. Here is fire, now not as a threat to their life but as a blessing; the rivers of water they need, and the fire of his Spirit that burns, as it did on the Day of Pentecost. Here is a promise to their descendants — that God would pour out his Spirit. Do you know that when God finally did that it came on 120 Jews? That promise was fulfilled as described in Acts 2.

Thirdly, they will be *productive* for God, they will be fertile, they will be fruitful, they shall spring up like grass amid waters.

Fourthly, they will be *proud*. Here is the amazing thing: many of God's ancient people are ashamed of the fact that they are God's people — they are embarrassed. But they will be proud to say they are the Lord's, they will write it on their hands. Now tattooing was forbidden to the Jew. God's word forbids you to tattoo your body, as you probably know from Leviticus. But they were going to write on their hands so that many people would know they are the Lord's.

FUNCTION OF ISRAEL

Why did God make Israel? That is a very important question. When somebody has made something, the first question is: what is it for? When you look at the Jews and the nation of Israel, when you see how God has lavished attention upon them for these thousands of years, you ask: why? What is it all for? What is their purpose? And the answer comes out in the second section of each chapter. Again there are certain words that we notice in both chapters — words like 'declare', 'witnesses', 'I am', 'redeemer', 'king of Israel'; and phrases like 'apart from me there is no God'. What do they mean?

First of all, in 43:8–9 God challenges witnesses of other gods to tell what the future holds. Only God can do that, man cannot. He knows what is going to happen and Israel are his witnesses.

Now 43:10 is the verse from which a certain cult gets its name. This verse is the most important verse in the Bible to the Jehovah's Witnesses. "*You are my witnesses,*" *says Jehovah.*

They have ripped that text out of its context and applied it to themselves, which we shall question in a moment. This verse is speaking to Israel. By the way, whenever you see the word 'LORD' rendered in capital letters in the Bible it means that the original word there is the one sometimes rendered *Jehovah*. In Hebrew they wrote the Old Testament without vowels, using only consonants. That sometimes creates difficulties in translating. This is the sacred name of God, so sacred that the Jews stopped saying it for centuries and therefore it is difficult for us to get back and find out what it was. We know what it means: 'I am'. But we do not know how to pronounce it. Certainly 'J' is pronounced as a Y and 'V' is pronounced as a W. So it certainly was not pronounced 'Jehovah'. But sometimes people put two vowels in and make it *Yahweh* — you may well hear that, but about 750 years ago they put other letters in and made it 'Jehovah', as an anglicised rendering. *You are my witnesses*, says 'I am'. Have you ever noticed how often those words were on Jesus' lips? *'I am the bread of life'*; *'I am the light of the world'*; *'I am the good shepherd'*; *'before Abraham was, I am'*. When Jesus was put before the chief priests and asked, '*Are you then the Son of God?'* he replied *'You are right in saying I am'* (see Luke 22:70, NIV) —and signed his death warrant. The soldiers in Gethsemane wanted Jesus of Nazareth, and he said *'I am he'* (see John 18:6). Jesus used this name for himself for he was Jehovah, he was Yahweh. *'You are my witnesses'*, says Yahweh – says I am. Have you noticed how often the phrase 'I am' occurs through this book? *'I am he'*, in v. 10. *'I am the Lord'*, v. 11; v. 13 — *'I am God and henceforth I am he'*; v. 15, *'I am the Lord'*. In 44:6, *'I am the first and I am the last'*. God is the great 'I am' —not an 'it'.

We notice that three verbs are used of Israel and three of God in 43:10–11. In v. 10, Israel was to know God, to believe him, to understand him. The three stages of knowledge of God are: to know about him, to believe in him and to understand him. I wonder what stage you are at. Do you know *about* God? Do you *believe in him*? Do you *understand* what he has revealed about himself? Then you can be a witness to God, telling others about him. You cannot be a witness unless you know, you cannot be a witness unless you believe what you know, and you cannot be a witness unless you understand what you believe. But if you do all those three things you can be a witness for him.

Three verbs apply to God in 43:12. He *declared*, he *saved*, he *proclaimed*. What does that mean? Well, he declared what he was going to do before he did it, then he did it, then he announced what he had done. That is how God's words and deeds fit together, and we are witnesses to those three things. The Old Testament tells us what he was going to do in Christ before he did it, the Gospels tell us what he did, and the epistles tell us what he had done, after he did it. So, because I know God and believe in him and understand what I believe, I can witness to what he predicted, what he did and what he announced had been done. These are the verbs connected with witnessing, and Jesus told the twelve disciples: you shall be my witnesses. They knew him, they believed in him, they understood him, and then he wanted them to go around the world proclaiming what he had done. That is witnessing, and the Jews were called to be God's witnesses. There is never a biblical mention of a missionary society, God's plan was for a missionary nation.

The Bible never argues about the existence of God — it assumes that 'I am' exists before everything else and that you have to explain the existence of everything else. That is the right way round in our thinking. You should not say 'I exist, this building exists, but you have got to prove that God does.' Start by saying: God exists, now how on earth did this building get here, and how did I get here? That is the right way to argue. The same three thoughts occur in 44:6. *"I am the first and I am the last"* —means I was there before everything else, I'll be there after everything else. God is always there. A silly, childish question which we think is a puzzling question, is not puzzling at all — the question 'who made God?' It is an illogical question, like asking who made what was never made, or about a square circle. God always was, so the question who made him is a ridiculous question. By definition *God* is everlasting and it would be absurd to ask who made the one who is everlasting.

In 44:7 there is a challenge to other people to foretell what is going to happen; and then, in v. 8, "*You are my witnesses*" — God's people are to tell others. Then we read: "*Is there any God besides me?*" There is only one God in heaven and there is only one people of God on earth to tell the rest. This is amazing. In those days they believed that each nation had its god. Babylon had its god, Syria had its god, Egypt had its god or gods, and Israel had her God — so it was generally understood. The claim that the prophets made was this: only one of these actually exists. The God of this tiny little tribe in the Holy Land, that God is the only real one. That was a remarkable claim which many people refused to believe, quite naturally. After all, what would you think if somebody came to you and said my faith is the only true one? But that is what the people of God do say. That is the exclusive claim of Christianity — that Jesus Christ is the only way, among all the religions of the world. "*I am the way and the truth and the life. No-one comes to the Father except through me*" (John14:6, NIV) — this is an exclusive claim, and the Bible is exclusive of all other religion and all other gods.

FOOLISHNESS OF ISRAEL

The third section of each chapter is concerned with the foolishness of Israel: on the one hand idleness, on the other idolatry. In spite of all that God had done for them the two things that they did were these: first they got tired of God and of worship. God's people can do this sometimes. You can get tired of God, tired of bringing your sacrifices. Idleness — they became weary and did not bother to go to the temple. God's people do this sometimes, too. The other sin, idolatry, was much more serious, and this was the besetting sin of the people of God. In spite of the fact that there was only one God and they knew it, they were forever taking bits of stone and bits of wood and carving them. The prophet laughs at such folly: You take a block of wood; with half of it you cook your dinner and the other half you say that's god. Isn't it ridiculous? Here is this poor chap slaving away. He is so weary. He has a drink of water and then he chips away at the stone working all day and then he says, now save me —and the thing doesn't budge an inch. It is sheer sarcastic ridicule, and sometimes the best way to deal with foolish religion is to laugh it out of court. How absurd to cook your dinner with half your god and then set the other half up and pray to it! That is idolatry and it leads to a deluded mind that cannot understand what the truth is and that has deceived itself.

FORGIVENESS OF ISRAEL

But there is a fourth section to each of these two sermons. It is on the forgiveness of Israel and the key words are *remember* and *transgression*, which occur in both chapters. In chapter 43:25ff and 44:21f, we see that God is a God who forgives and forgets, as long as his people remember. God says *"Remember these things"*. Memory plays a great part in true relationship to God. You need to remember what you have heard in church, to remember what you have read in the Bible, remember what God has told you and done for you — remember!

"Remember these things, O Jacob,
for you are my servant, O Israel.
I have made you, you are my servant;
O Israel, I will not forget you.
I have swept away your offences like a cloud,
your sins like the morning mist . . . ."

44:21-22a (NIV)

Staying on a farm in the Lake District, at six o'clock one

morning, we looked out of the bedroom window and all the valleys were filled with mist. The peaks shone out above it. I dashed out to take a photograph. I had to take it at that time because by half past six it had all gone and you would not have believed the scene of half an hour earlier. It looked like another world when the mist had gone. That is your sin — God can deal with it like the morning mist if you remember him and what he has done for you. Forget him and he won't forget your sins.

So finally we have a chapter in which the choir starts and the trees come in and the mountains come in and the sky comes in, and the depths of the earth come in —and the whole earth is singing. There is a poem about a man who was converted and then went out and felt the whole countryside was singing. Have you ever felt like that? Have you gone out of church and felt the trees were clapping their hands? That is how you feel when you have been forgiven, that is how you feel when you realise that God has forgotten your sins, and when you realise that God has not forgotten you. That is how you feel when *you* belong to the people of God twice over, when you have been created and redeemed. Then the word that was said to Israel will be true of you: you are my witnesses. The message means: you have been chosen to go and tell the world. God formed and created you that you might fulfil the function of communicating to the world. Even when you sin and are foolish, he wants you to remember that his forgiveness is waiting and he will send you out singing again. Now we have drawn sap from the roots of Israel for ourselves.

19

NO OTHER GOD

Read Isaiah 44:24–46:13

A. SOVEREIGN (44:24 - 45:13)
1. REDEEMS JEWS (24-28)
2. RAISES GENTILES (1-13)
B. SAVIOUR (45:14-25)
1. INSTRUCTS JEWS (14-17)
2. INVITES GENTILES (18-25)
C. SUPPORT (46:1-13)
1. CARRIES JEWS (1-7)
2. COUNSELS GENTILES (8-13)

Isaiah has a bigger view of God than almost than any other prophet. Furthermore, Isaiah has as much to say to the Gentiles as well as to the Jews as any other prophet in the Old Testament, with the possible exception of Jonah—so we have in this prophecy of Isaiah many things that are said to the Jews and then to the Gentiles.

This passage we are looking at now conveys to us three truths about God: he is *above* us as our Sovereign, *alongside* us as our Saviour, and *underneath* as our support — the everlasting arms. Here are three wonderful truths. If you do not get much else from this study then just say those three things. God is my Sovereign above me; he has every right to reign over me and tell me where I go and what I do; he is alongside me to be my Saviour, to help me in time of trouble, to rescue me when I am in danger, to be with me when I am tempted; and when I feel I am sinking under life's alarms, when I feel that I am being overwhelmed, I remember that God is underneath me to carry me and support me all the day long.

Isaiah presents these three truths to the Jew and to the Gentile and elaborates this theme by making the message slightly different to each. As Sovereign, God redeems the Jews and raises the Gentiles. As Saviour, God instructs the Jews and invites the Gentiles. As support, God carries the Jews and counsels the Gentiles. So here we have six points, all of which come out of our study. Why does Isaiah speak so much to the Gentiles? The answer is very simple: because he can see absolutely clearly that there is only one God, and if there is only one God then he has to be the God of the whole world. If there is no other God you have to tell the Gentiles, otherwise they will never be able to have faith.

Returning for a moment to chapter 43, at the end of v. 10 we read,

"Before me no god was formed,
nor will there be one after me.
I, even I, am the LORD,
and apart from me there is no saviour."

(NIV)

44:6 ended,

"I am the first and I am the last;
apart from me there is no God."

(NIV)

The theme of there being no other God – the God who is righteous and Saviour, the rock – then continues. See 44:8 of the same chapter, 45:5, 14, 18, 21, 22b and 46:9. I think I have made my point, and Isaiah has made it. The key point is this: 'there is no other God'. That comes home. Isaiah believes in hammering a point home, and he hammers it again and again until you have really got the point. The first of the ten commandments said, *'You shall have no other gods before me.'* In Isaiah the teaching here is that there are no other gods besides God. You can pretend to have another god, you can delude yourself into another religion, but you have not got another God because there is not one. If the God of the Jews is the only God who exists, then quite obviously we have got to get the Gentiles in too. If there is only one God then we have to bring people to that one God. This cuts right across modern thinking which believes that all religions are much the same and that everybody is heading for God and for heaven. I get that frequently in this country: after all, it is claimed, we all worship the same God; after all we are all going to the same place — but that is rubbish! There is only one God and there is only one way to that one God, and if we do not tell the Gentiles about the God of the Jews, and tell them of the only way to get through to him which is through Jesus, they will not get through to God. This is why Isaiah says so much to the Gentiles.

We have already thought about the name of God and we note that when the Jews are addressed the four letters rendered Yahweh, 'I am I am' are used — for that is what those letters mean. The Jews knew God's name and nobody else did. They alone of the nations of the earth knew God's name. But in Isaiah, when the Gentiles are addressed, that name is only used when it is explained. The Gentiles, not knowing God's name, had to use not a name but a title. By the way, you can usually tell fairly quickly a believer from an unbeliever. An unbeliever may talk about God but a believer will talk about the Lord. Have you noticed that? It is because the believer knows who God is. All Gentiles use the title 'God'. Even an atheist has in his very category a-*theist* – the name God, 'theos' right in the middle, so that even the atheist uses the name 'God'. But it is the believer who says, 'The Lord supports me; the Lord saves me.' The unbeliever says, 'Well, I believe in God', or 'I don't believe in God', but he has to use the title 'God' and not the name 'Lord'. That is how we can tell when Isaiah is speaking to one or the other.

In 44:22–28 the Jews are being addressed. God is sovereign.

He created, stretched out the heavens and spread out the earth. That is language used of pitching a tent. When you do that you stretch out what is above you and spread out what is below you. These are precisely the words used here. God erected the universe rather as we erect a tent on the beach! That is not to suggest that the sky is just a big sheet of canvas with stars painted on it — this is picture language — but it is as easy for God to stretch out the heavens as you stretch out a tent on the beach. It is as easy for him to spread out the earth as you make the sand smooth inside. That is how God made things — he is sovereign and does it as easily as that. Anybody who tries to frustrate God will be broken on God's laws. I can defy the law of gravity by jumping off a cliff, but I don't break the law of gravity, I illustrate it. Those who try to defy God's laws break themselves on those laws.

God frustrates the omens of liars and makes fools of diviners and makes men's wisdom look silly — and how he does that! The Bible makes it clear that men in their wisdom did not find God. You can have a string of degrees after your name, but that does not mean you have found God, nor does it mean you will find it any easier to find God. It could make it much more difficult for you to find God because you trust in your own ideas. God makes men's wisdom look silly, and to some of the simplest people he gives wisdom and knowledge of himself. Out of the mouths of babes and sucklings there can come forth wisdom. God in his sovereignty can do things with men and things without men — he is independent of us. God redeems the Jews, and here he lets the Jews in exile in Babylon know that he is going to bring them back, rebuild their cities and see that the temple in Jerusalem is raised again. That must have been balm to their souls. For many years they had thought of the ruined cities back home. How would you like to be carried off from wherever you live and know that your house had been burned to the ground, that everything there was just a devastated area of rubble and ruin, and you had been taken off as had your family and your elderly people? Imagine you had gone off into slavery somewhere, and your thoughts were of home all the time, wondering if you would ever see it again. Some of the older ones were dying off and children had been born who had never known home. You would long to get back. And then the prophet came and said God is sovereign, he is going to rebuild. It must have been very exciting.

But the most surprising thing is that God now gives his people a name to watch — Cyrus. It is there in the last verse of chapter 44 and the first verse of chapter 45. Watch that name, for it is an amazing one. The most astonishing thing about it is this: as we noted earlier, God was giving them a name of a man who would help them 150 years before he did. Of course that is not unusual for God, but it would be to us. If I said to you I can give you the name of a man who will pull Britain out of her economic problems 150 years from now you would be astounded —and so would I! But God would not be amazed. He knows the end from the beginning, he can declare it before it happens. God named the good king Josiah three hundred years before he was born. You will find it in 1 Kings. God said that there would be a good king (Josiah) who would put to death the evil priests who had led the nation astray. God knew your name long before you were born — did you know that? —and Isaiah the prophet writing these things down to help his people in the future, long after his death, observed that Cyrus was the name to watch —Cyrus would bring God's people out of Babylon; Cyrus would rebuild for them. And it all came true to the letter.

I must digress for a moment and tell you about this fascinating man Cyrus. The Jews had been taken 400 miles through the desert on a forced march, during which many of them had died. They had been taken away to Babylon and were slaves in exile there. Babylon was strong and powerful. Babylon is the same place as Babel where they tried to build a tower reaching to heaven. It has become a byword in the

Bible for godless civilisation. God's people thought they would never get away from that place, but then there had been a time when they thought they would never get away from Egypt, had there not? The same God who got them out of Egypt was going to get them out of Babylon. To Egypt God sent a man called Moses to do it, but now, here is the astonishing thing, he was going to send a man called Cyrus to do it, and Cyrus was not a Jew, though Moses was. Cyrus was not even a believer in God, Moses was. This is one of the most surprising things in the whole Bible: God was going to use a man who did not even believe in him, who was not even part of the people of God, to get his people out of Babylon. The sovereignty of God in choosing whom he would to accomplish his purpose stands out in this passage.

How did it happen? There was a kingdom called Persia, and a kingdom further north called Media. There were other kingdoms — Asia Minor, Lydia — and these kingdoms were strung out around. On the edge of Persia was a tiny area ruled over by a sheik, as we would call him today — and Cyrus was just a little leader of a clan or a little tribe, yet he was destined to become one of the greatest figures in history. The first thing he did was to conquer Persia, ruled over by one of his cousins, incidentally. Persia accepted him gladly because he was a much better king than his cousin. He then swept on up to Media and conquered that. Now he had a pretty big empire called the empire of the Medes and the Persians. I am sure you have heard the phrase 'the laws of the Medes and Persians'. His laws were very wise and therefore they never needed altering —in fact they could not be altered. Then Cyrus swept on to Lydia and to Asia Minor. There was no holding him. But he was not a cruel tyrant, he was a good man, and every country he took over was thrilled that he was now reigning over them. He was the man who fought for the underdog. That is the reputation that Cyrus has in Greek literature.

Here is the interesting thing. We know a lot about Cyrus

from Greek literature because he even pressed forward right into Greece. But we also know quite a bit about him from Hebrew sources and we are given two different pictures — not contradictory but a tremendous contrast. In Greek literature, everything said is about what he was, a noble man, a pure man, a man of integrity, a man of health, a man of wisdom, a man of generosity, a man of simplicity. They hold him up and say: that's the ideal man, a great man, follow him as your hero. Greek literature, like the books of Herodotus and Xenophon, are full of Cyrus. But, when you turn to the Hebrew account of Cyrus there is not a single word about what he was, not a single good thing is said about him; not a single thing is said about his purity, integrity or generosity. Everything in the Hebrew scriptures about Cyrus is about what he did. Frankly, that is just the difference between the outlook of the unbeliever and the believer. I have noticed this at funerals. When we have buried the mortal remains of a saint of God, unbelievers can only talk about the goodness of the person who has been buried; believers talk about God and all that God did through the person. It is a difference of outlook. The unbeliever worships man's nobility and says what a good person they were; the believer says that everything good in man comes from God. Because the more we know God the more we know this: every scrap of goodness there is in a person is due to God. God is the source of all goodness and therefore we attribute it where it belongs. So whilst the Greek literature praises Cyrus as a good man, the scriptures teach us that he was God's man, and we praise God for what he accomplished through him. It is a very striking contrast, a different way of looking at a person.

Nevertheless, Cyrus is called (in 44:28) 'my shepherd'. And in 45:1 there is an even more extraordinary word used: 'anointed'. To term a Gentile 'anointed' and 'shepherd' would have been astonishing to a Jew. Christians, too, can find it hard when God uses someone who is not a Christian to be his instrument of salvation.

In chapter 45 God begins to speak to Cyrus, calling him by name. Cyrus did not even know Yahweh/Jehovah. As far as I can tell Cyrus accepted the Persian religion basically, though he seems to have picked up every religion he conquered. He adopted the religions of those countries and added their gods to his, and he finished up with quite a bundle of them. When he took Babylon he thanked the gods of Babylon for letting him in. When he took Media he thanked the gods of Media for letting him in. We know from Jewish history (a Jew called Josephus recorded this) that when Cyrus came into Babylon somebody showed him the chapter we are now considering. Somebody showed him Isaiah 45, and he read it through. The Lord told Cyrus what he was doing for him, with the words, *". . . so you may know that I am the Lord, the God of Israel, who summons you by name."* Do you know what Cyrus's response was? Cyrus believed that, and was ready to help rebuild Jerusalem. It is wonderful to dig through history and see how God had his hand on this pagan conqueror, and to learn how that man believed.

What was the Persian religion? They believed in two gods, one of which was believed to do all the good things and one all the bad things, and they were really fighting all the time. That is basically the religion of Zoroastrianism, and it could be said to be a very convenient sort of religion because it explains very quickly who does all the bad things in the world and who does all the good things. Since neither is stronger than the other we are just left with good things and bad things *ad infinitum*. You can see how the religion worked itself out. But God's message to Cyrus says this:

> *"I am the LORD, and there is no other;*
> *apart from me there is no God."*
>
> 45:5a (NIV)

We see from that and the surrounding verses that one of the

things Cyrus had to learn was that there is only one God and therefore God is responsible for bringing both prosperity and 'disaster' (NIV) which is translated 'evil' in KJV. Some people have jumped at that translation of the word and said: now we know where evil came from, God did it. However, we must not jump to that conclusion but look more carefully. Whilst the Bible teaches that God allows Satan to test human beings (see the book of Job), Satan is only capable of doing evil things in the world because God allows him to and gives him enough rope, this does not of course mean that God actually causes moral evil. And the meaning here signifies something *physical,* not moral evil. It means suffering, calamity — so one translation correctly brings out the meaning: I make 'weal' (not a very common word) and create 'woe'.

Now we come to a greater difficulty. From v. 9 it is obvious that God was trying to tell the Jews why he had chosen Cyrus. God has a perfect right to use anybody for his purposes. To grumble because Cyrus is a Gentile and an unbeliever is like a piece of clay on the potter's wheel questioning the potter. Or it is like saying to a mother who is just producing a child: that's not the sort of child you ought to be producing. It is a silly, ridiculous thing to turn round to God and say: what sort of children are you having? Not only does God have a right to use Cyrus, he is right to do so: *'I will raise up Cyrus in my righteousness . . .'* (45:13a, NIV). Sometimes God uses the most unlikely means.

Professor Johannes Warns was one of the greatest theologians in Germany. His book on baptism is one of the finest books you will ever read on that subject. He was a professor three times over, with a string of degrees to his name. But God used a Salvation Army washerwoman, somebody scrubbing his front doorstep, to lead him to the Lord. He could have said: 'I'm a professor, why does God choose that person to lead me to him? Surely he should send me an intellectual.' God will choose anyone. I know a man who was converted because a little girl climbed onto his knee and said, 'Daddy, why won't you come to church?' God can use the most unlikely person to help his people, and here he uses Cyrus.

God is not only sovereign, choosing whom he will, using whom he will, God is *saviour*. And the word 'saviour' is used twice over in the next section which I am going to deal with briefly. First, he is saviour of the Jews and second he is saviour of the Gentiles. He is saviour of the Jews because it was to them that he gave his word. It was to them that he spoke what is his truth, and he did not do it in secret, he spoke to them as it were on the stage of the nations; he spoke to them in the exodus; he instructed the Jews. The exclusive claim of the Bible is that you will only find God as the God of the Jews — Jesus said to the Samaritan woman at the well, *". . . salvation is from the Jews"* (see John 4:22b, NIV). That is exclusive, but it is exclusive in order to be inclusive, for the invitation should go out from the Jews. Turn to me and be saved all the ends of the earth. The invitation is to all if the instruction was only to the few. This Bible was given to the Jews, to the few, but the invitation is to all: to turn away from your idols which can't help you, and turn to God, who is just and who is saviour. How can God possibly ever be both? How can he be just and punish me, and be saviour and forgive me? The answer is found in Paul's letter to the Romans where he teaches that God is both just and the justifier of whoever has faith in Jesus.

There are echoes in the New Testament of much in this chapter. *'Before me every knee will bow'* (see v. 23). Who is this about? It is about Jehovah, and about Jesus. Do you notice again and again that things the Jews were told are true of Jehovah are quoted of Jesus in the New Testament? It is really through Jesus that God became the saviour who comes *alongside* us, and echo after echo of Jesus occurs. Read through the rest of chapter 45.

Finally, we come to chapter 46. God is not only our *sovereign* above us, choosing whom he will, using whom he will; he is not only the *saviour* alongside us, he is instructing the Jews in his truth and inviting the Gentiles to be grafted in and draw sap from what he has given to the Jews; he is the *support* underneath. The first thing is he *carries* the Jews. At this point Isaiah gets sarcastic again, in the name of the Lord. In 46:1ff he begins to talk about the idols of the Babylon religions. There is the idol of Baal and the idol of Nebu. Do you know that the kings always used to call themselves after the gods: the idol of Baal, Belshazzar; the idol of Nebu, Nebuchadnezzar. These were the 'gods', little wooden things, stone things and gold things. People would bow down to them and say save us. One day they would just be loaded onto animals and taken away. So they have been — taken away to the museums of the world, loaded on the backs of beasts and taken away by conquerors. This happened, and there is not an idol left in Babylon today. You will find them in the British Museum and other museums of the world.

Here is the question that arises: does your religion carry you, or do you carry your religion? It is a big question. If you bow down to idols you have to carry them around and into the temple. You place them, and they don't move when you do. If you want them in a better place you have got to carry them there. So here is a picture of these poor people who have spent hours making an idol, then they hump it down to their temple. They have to carry their god. There are many people who have to 'carry' their religion. They go to church as a burden, a duty — something you have to 'support'. But I go to church not because it is a duty but because it is a delight. I need it desperately because I want support during this week, and I get that support when I worship God and give him the place that is rightfully due to him. So in v. 4, God says to Israel, "*. . . I will carry you.*" Imagine a mother carrying the baby. Even before birth we talk about a woman 'carrying', and God says, *"you whom I have upheld since you were conveived."*

If you are an unbeliever, if you really do not know Christ,

then you still think of religion as something you have to carry. You say: I'm never going to join that church, they'll have me doing this, that and the other before I know where I am. They'll get me tied up, load me with this and that, I'll be giving money and time. I'll just have far more to carry if I ever go near that church. The real truth is that you don't need a religion you have to carry but a Saviour who carries you. The reason members do so much for the Lord is because he carries them, and because he gives them the strength to go on, the blessing to do it and the fruitfulness in it. Do you have to carry your religion as the Babylonians had to carry their idols, or does your God carry you?

Again there is the affirmation in 46:9 (NIV)

"I am God, and there is no other"

—and then, in v. 10b,

"I say: My purpose will stand,
and I will do all that I please.
From the east I summon a bird of prey . . . ."
(NIV)

Cyrus's banner consisted of an eagle with outstretched wings. God had told him what to do.

Finally there is an appeal in vv. 12f to the stubborn, stiff-necked people who will not let God carry and deliver them, because they do not like his means of deliverance. It is an appeal to the Jews who do not like the idea of Cyrus saving them. We are reminded that there is a call to those who do not like the idea that they need Jesus, do not like the idea of the cross for their sins and do not want to walk in his way. *"I am bringing my righteousness near . . . ."* I say to anybody who is not being saved by the Lord: when God draws near to you in power to save, seize your opportunity, because his salvation will not be delayed.

20

THE FIRST AND THE LAST

Read Isaiah 47–48

A. DESTRUCTION OF BABYLON (47)
1. SUPERIORITY - DISGRACE (1-4)
2. SADISM - DARKNESS (5-7)
3. SENSUALITY - DEATH (8-9)
4. SECURITY - DISASTER (10-11)
5. SUPERSTITION - DISMAY (12-13)
6. SELFISHNESS - DERELICTION (14-15)
B. DEPARTURE FROM BABYLON (48)
1. SINS OF JUDAH (1-8)
a. Their reputation (1-2) b. Their resistance (3-5)
c. Their rebellion (6-8)
2. SAKE OF JEHOVAH (9-22)
a. His reputation (9-11) b. His revelation (12-16)
c. His redemption (17-22)

The text of this sermon which Isaiah preached is at the end of the passage and is the best known verse in all of these two chapters: *"There is no rest for the wicked."* That has become a proverb in the English language, and it is the lesson we are to learn now. There is no peace for someone who is out of God's will for their life. One of the main reasons why so many people are lacking peace, and why so many people are looking for peace, is precisely this: that the root cause of their *dis*-ease (and that is a very interesting word) is wickedness.

In chapter 47 we are given a picture of the wickedness of people who do not know God and do not belong to him — pagans, like the Babylonians. But then, in chapter 48, we are shown the wickedness that can occur in the people of God, in believers, those who know God — among those being saved by God. These are different kinds of wickedness, but they still take away peace.

Chapter 47 predicts the destruction and judgement of one of the greatest cities there has ever been. The name itself stands for all that is worst in human civilisation — a large selfish, sinful, pleasure-loving, profit-making, cruel, godless empire. The very name *Babylon* is used throughout the Bible to signify godless human society.

It begins of course in Genesis 11 with some men who set out to build a city with a skyscraper whose top would reach into God's province itself, into heaven. For the name *Babel* is the same as *Baby*lon, and it shows the same dreadful character of men who in their pride forget all about God and say: we will live in heaven, we will build, we will make ourselves a name, we are man-centred, we worship ourselves. In the building of the tower of Babel you can see all the materialism, the militarism, the totalitarianism, and the other *—isms* which you read about in your daily newspaper. Their pride and godlessness was such that God came down and smashed that civilisation. The first attempt to build Babylon ended in utter confusion and they had to separate. God confused their speech. They could not correspond or converse with one another. But man does not give up that easily. When God judges man and destroys something he has made, very soon afterwards you will find man trying to build it up again and rushing into the very things which caused that judgement to come. I am reminded again of Winston Churchill's final volume of The Second World War whose subtitle is this: 'How the great democracies triumphed and thus were able to resume the follies which had so nearly cost them their lives.' That is human nature—we never learn. Just as they built up Babylon and God destroyed it the first time, they still did not learn, and up it went again.

I have mentioned that Babylon was situated in a land that is flat. It is the alluvial plain of the Mesopotamian basin with two rivers, the Tigris and Euphrates, running through the mudflats. Therefore anything that man builds can be seen a long way off. They built Babylon with its towers reaching to heaven so that the whole area might look across the plain and say: there is great Babylon. They had to build their gardens on the buildings, so people could see them, it was so flat. So they built up terraced buildings, and the gardens were up on the terraces, and the foliage hung down over the buildings. The famous Hanging Gardens of Babylon were one of the seven wonders of the world. For culture, for trade, for religion, for pleasure, Babylon was the place to live. It gradually sucked into itself people who came for a variety of reasons: businessmen came to make money; lustful people came because of the backstreet clubs; captives were brought to be the slaves to build the buildings. It became a cosmopolitan metropolis. God was defied in that metropolis. Such is the story of the second city of Babylon. The first was destroyed; the second Babylon reared its head.

The interesting thing is that in the Old Testament, which mentions the second city of Babylon again and again, there is not a single word of appreciation of Babylon's Hanging Gardens, culture, strength, commerce, the crowds who came to live there, not a word of commendation. Instead there are just curses flung from the lips of angry prophets who saw in Babylon the very heart of the human race's attitude to God — a pride that said: we can do without you, we are secure, we are safe, we are strong, we can rule the world.

We have seen that from 43:11 to 46:9 there has been the recurring theme: I am, and there is none besides me. [I am the LORD, or I am God.] But do you see what Babylon was doing? Babylon was saying: 'I am god'. Humans worship themselves, and this is the heart of human pride: glory to man in the highest. I am the captain of my fate, the master of my soul — such things have been said by humanist philosophers, those who have put man in the centre of their thinking rather than God, those who have looked to themselves and their own knowledge, wisdom, resources, might, power and pleasure; those who have lived with self right in the centre, and who even if they have not said it with their lips have said it with their lives. Babylon's pride was seen not only in building the tower of Babel, reaching into heaven and virtually saying we are going to live in heaven, but in building up a civilisation that did not care that much for God. It had its religion, but in spite of its religion it still said: I am and besides me there is no-one else. Only God has the right to say that. God had said it in chapters 43 – 46, and we see now in chapter 47 that mankind is saying exactly this of itself. Here is the summit of human godlessness: I can do anything; we can achieve all that we need to achieve; we can save ourselves. But if you worship yourself, you turn your back on God.

Isaiah 47 points out a number of wicked things in this godless society for which God was going to send an appropriate punishment. Here we see the kind of wickedness of the unbeliever that robs him of his peace. First of all, there is the *superiority* of this Babylonian empire and capital. She is always pictured as a woman—here and throughout scripture. At the end of the Bible she is called the great prostitute of the world, the great harlot. But here she is described as a queen, as a mistress of the kingdoms, and that is what she was. Babylon, as a royal lady, tender and delicate, reigned over the whole area. Many nations looked up to Babylon as to their mistress, and she controlled the affairs of men from her throne. In crude but simple language the prophet pictures her stripped naked and pulling grindstones around and around, which was the task and the appearance of a female slave. For the utter pride, regarding herself as the queen of the nations, she would be dragged down to the level of a simple slave girl, naked and labouring away to grind flour. You can imagine some of the feelings of an individual lady to whom that happened, and it did happen to individual ladies of those days. They were stripped and made to pull grindstones, those who had been tender and delicate and never done a day's work in their lives. This picture was applied to the whole of Babylon. Their luxury was to give place to this dreadful disgrace.

The second thing in which they were wicked was their *cruelty and malice*. God gave into Babylon's hands his own people, to punish his own people. But, and here is the point, there is a line of moral decency beyond which you do not go in treating your captives. One of the meanings of the symbol of the Red Cross during times of war is that it stands as a reminder, to both sides, to treat their prisoners within the bounds of humanity. God himself has told us that he will hold men responsible for their inhumanity and sadistic cruelty to one another. Read through the first chapter of the book of Amos where he condemns six nations, who had never even heard of the ten commandments, for their cruelty to those whom they captured in war. God notices what is done to prisoners of war. In particular, Babylon showed no mercy to the elderly, who of course are most hard hit by being taken away captive. It is not so easy to take the sufferings of captivity when you are older. Far from pitying the aged they laid heavier burdens upon them to kill them off so that they would not have to feed and look after them. They worked them to death. For that they would go into 'darkness'.

The third thing was their *sensuality* — they were lovers of pleasure. If you wanted to 'paint the town red' you made for Babylon. The backstreets were full of every perverted pleasure you could imagine. It catered for and exploited this lust of men, and we know from secular records something of the immorality that accompanied this wild search for pleasure in Babylon. It took refined and crude forms, but one of the things that a pursuit of pleasure does to a man's soul is to divert him from the realities of life, and one of the realities of life is death, and sooner or later death is going to rob you of those pleasures. But while you are pursuing them you forget all about the fact that one day death is going to come. So the prophet says one day you will become a widow and lose your children. In fact in one day they did just that. King Belshazzar was killed, and according to secular records some three thousand of the people of Babylon were crucified by Darius. In one day Babylon became a widow and a mother without children.

The next thing mentioned is she had a *false sense of security* in her wickedness. Her sense of security was due to her wisdom and her knowledge. Babylon was the seat of science and culture. She not only drew the tradespeople to herself she also drew scholars, lecturers and students. A person who has gained a great deal of knowledge may feel sure they can cope mentally with all their problems. But against that security, with the idea that the *status quo* will continue forever, there comes the prophet's warning of the sort of disaster of which you have no knowledge. You can feel secure until you have personal knowledge of insecurity. It may be that you have never had any really serious illness in your life. You therefore tend to feel secure because you have never known how low you can be laid and how frail life is. They had no knowledge of disaster in this secure, wicked, knowledgeable place, but that does not mean that it cannot come. Because I do not know much about a thing it does not mean that I am secure from it. Such 'security' is nothing! Human wisdom and knowledge do not show people the knowledge of the judgement to come.

Isaiah mentions the sheer *superstition* of this city, a religious city. Man is religious, and with all his wisdom, pleasures and security, he often likes to have religion, of a superstitious variety. It seems to me extraordinary that sometimes the greatest brains can accept superstitions with credulity. I read of Sir Oliver Lodge and Sir William Crookes, two of the greatest scientists and thinkers we had in this country, yet they both fell for spiritualism, completely swallowed the whole thing and wrote for it. How could two great brains like that fall for such a thing? Why, when they had such wisdom and knowledge in Babylon, should they have had so much astrology? The prophet is not talking about astronomy but astrology, of trying to read one's fate in the stars. You know: if you meet a black cat tomorrow you are going to have lots of money and go on a nice holiday, all generally phrased so that sooner or later something clicks and you fall for it. But the Babylonians were up to their eyebrows in sorcery, incantation and astrology. They are going to be utterly confused by that, wearied with many counsels. Sometimes life is like that. If you ask advice from too many people, you may be dismayed by all that they say.

Finally, there is their *selfishness* as the people pursue their commerce, traffic and trade. People came to Babylon from all over. They came to live there, and the suburbs grew with the houses of wealthy traders. Its situation at the head of the Persian Gulf was just right for trade between east and west. But the point the prophet now makes is this: when the crisis hits you, the people who only came to you for trade desert you. It is as if you have a group of sales representatives who meet once a week for lunch, and what draws them together is that they are all in commercial jobs. Their moneymaking holds them together. They meet and they make friends. But if you took away their jobs as salesmen, that group would split up. Those who have laboured and traded together cannot save each other. They will go as quickly as they came when the profit motive is removed. If that is what the city is built on, the city will collapse — and that is precisely what happened. There is no society so lonely or so loose as that which is built on commercial motives alone.

Now Babylon has gone. In a day, said the prophet, it will go, and in a day it was conquered. On November 3rd, 538 BC, Babylon fell —in spite of the fact that it had a wall of defence forty-five miles long and twenty-one feet high. Cyrus the Mede came, and he diverted the river that ran under the wall of the city and through the city and out the other side into one of the canals that Babylon had dug. Then he marched his army through the dry riverbed and took that supposedly impregnable city easily. She became a widow and a mother without children overnight. Human pride had a third go at setting up this city. In spite of God's judgement on the tower of Babel they built it in the days of the prophets. In spite of God's judgement after the prophets, they tried to build it again, and the man who thought of doing it was Alexander the Great, the Greek conqueror. As he pressed eastward with his mighty empire, he said: I will rebuild Babylon as my capital in the east. That was his intention. And, at the age of thirty-one, suddenly one night Alexander the Great died and he was never able to put one brick on another on this city. God said it will not be rebuilt, and when God speaks his word stands.

But is Babylon gone? The answer of the New Testament is physically it has gone but spiritually it is still very much with us. 'Babylon' is the name used in the New Testament for every godless city that is in the same attitude of pride and godlessness, the same living for pleasure and profit, rearing its imposing buildings to man's glory. Therefore Rome is called 'Babylon' in the New Testament, in the first letter of Peter, because Rome had this same spirit of self-sufficiency, superstition, cruelty, and ultimately of pride in its own military might, mistress of the kingdoms.

Even more important, the Bible predicts that at the end of history godless human civilisation will head up into one world government with a mighty metropolis which will be exactly what Babylon was on a more limited scale in those days, erected to man's glory. It will be fostered by science, by human wisdom and knowledge, trade and commerce, and the pursuit of pleasure. This gigantic metropolis of godless pride is described, both in its peak and in its downfall, in Revelation 16–19.

The message of Isaiah chapter 48, addressed to the people of God, is: get out of Babylon (see v. 20.) Lest the Jews become proud themselves because their enemy Babylon is to be destroyed, God reminds them, firstly, of how they got in to Babylon (vv. 1–8) and secondly of why they get out of it (vv. 9–22). How did they get in? Quite simply, because of their own sins. They would never have been there if they had not sinned against God. Three sins of the people of God are mentioned that brought them into Babylon and robbed them of their peace.

The first sin is *formal religion*. I have called it their 'recitation' because they had all the right words on their lips but their lives did not match up. They professed to belong to God, they claimed to belong to the holy city of God, yet it was not in truth or in right, meaning not in sincerity or reality. They said that they belonged to God and the holy city, then they lived as if they belonged to Babylon. That takes away your peace. If you recite all the words, sing and say all the right things in church, the right words are on your lips, but if your life during the week does not say that you belong to God, nor that you look for a city whose builder and maker is God, then this is one of the first things that robs God's people of their peace. It is wickedness in God's sight because he hates hypocrisy in religion. 'This people honours me with their lips' (said Isaiah and Jesus) —but their heart is far away from me.

The second thing is their *resistance*. They had iron necks and brass foreheads. What a vivid description! Have you ever known somebody like this? Have you ever been like this? An iron neck? Some people are stiff and proud — and with a brass forehead you cannot get anything in there. We would say it's like talking to a brick wall, because 'bricks' are the usual hard things in our life. But it is the same figure of speech. The interesting thing is that the idols and images of Babylon were made of brass, iron, wood and stone. What he is saying is: you are just like those idols. Might as well talk to an idol as to you. Just imagine a church full of little stone figures of people all around. I would have great fun preaching to a congregation like that! It would be utterly frustrating, useless. But, says the prophet, that is the second thing in the people of God that is wicked and robs them of their peace. Imagine them sitting with brass foreheads and cast iron necks, thinking: I am not going to admit I am wrong, I am not going to humble myself, I am not going to sit and listen to that, I am not going to take that in, I am just going to switch off and think about the football match yesterday. This is so easy for us to do and it robs us of our peace.

A third thing that God mentions through the prophet to the

people of God is the fact that from the very beginning they were in a *rebellious attitude*. (See v.8.) From the very beginning Jacob's name was 'usurper', or someone who rebels. God's people were rebels all the way through. The story of the history of Israel is one rebellion after another toward God.

Now God tells the people why they are going to get out of Babylon. It is not for their sake but for his. It is his reputation that is at stake. He had given his name to them. Do you realise that Jesus gave his name to every Christian? A *Christ*ian bears the name of Christ. His glory he will not give to another; having given his name to his people he cannot cut them off as he can cut Babylon off, because people could forever afterwards say: Well, God failed with his own people, how could he succeed with anyone else? He cannot cut Israel off — and there is the name of Israel still in the atlas! God cannot cut that name off because it is a name he gave and it would reflect on his name if he did. What he can do, and what he must do as we will see in a moment, is to put them through the furnace of affliction so that they are refined. The Lord chastises those whom he loves so that they do not disgrace his name. I chastised my children as you chastise yours. They are letting the family down apart from anything else if they misbehave. It is for the sake of that family discipline and honour that chastisement must take place within the family.

God then talks about his revelation, both in nature and history. In nature he spread out the heavens and stretched out the earth. How often has he said that in the book of Isaiah! We must never forget that God is the Almighty maker of heaven and earth. Then there is his power in history, this revelation in history. God refers to loving Cyrus, that pagan conqueror, to calling him, bringing him and prospering him. God is in charge of nature and history. It is for the sake of spreading that revelation in the world that God is calling his people out of Babylon again. It is that his redemption might be known by the world. How do I know that God is a redeemer? Because he redeemed the Jews. How do I know that God is a saviour? Because God saved his people. God says in 48:20 that he is bringing his people out of Babylon, and then he wants them to tell the whole earth: God redeemed us from Babylon. And we know that God is a redeemer, by reading the history of the Jews.

Sadly, not all the Jews would get out of Babylon. Some of them had become so much involved in the trade and commerce there that they stayed. God gave them a chance to get back to their own country. They need not have worried about the desert. God got them through the desert the first time and caused water to gush from the rock. Above all, they were to come out remembering that there is no peace for the wicked. I would have thought that text (v. 22) would have been better at the end of chapter 47. Surely, after all the wickedness of that pagan city Babylon, then is the time to say there is no rest for the wicked. And alas, Christians have often thought that this text applied primarily to the unbeliever, to the person who does not belong to the people of God. But this text is deliberately said to those who have been chastised and disciplined by God in the furnace of affliction. It is a reminder of this: wickedness in the believer, in the people of God, robs of peace. The wickedness in the people of God may not take the crude forms of sadistic cruelty or living for pleasure. It can do, but it need not take these cruder forms of superstition and the other things of Babylon, but there are refined wickednesses, of hypocrisy in religion, rebellion against God's word, and a resistance to where he wants to lead us. This is wickedness no more and no less than the superstition and the selfishness of Babylon. In both cases it will rob you of your peace. When the people of God have been through a time of chastisement and discipline, and come out of it again and get out of Babylon, they must remember all the time that they will go back into Babylon as captives of those things unless they remember why God disciplined them and remember what makes for their peace. So the phrase 'no peace for the wicked' applies to all people, whether they belong to God or not. And when the world cries, 'Peace, peace, where can we find peace?' the preacher of God must reply very clearly: When you find righteousness you will find peace. And the most poignant verse in this second chapter is the verse where God cries out,

"If only you had paid attention to my commands,
your peace would have been like a river,
your righteousness like the waves of the sea"
48:18 (NIV)

We shall never have peace or righteousness until we learn to deal with our wickedness, and until we see it as that, and until God deals with it in forgiveness and in sanctification.

21

CAN A MOTHER FORGET?

Read Isaiah 49–50

A. JESUS (49:1-7)
1. SALVATION FROM GOD (1-6)
2. ACKNOWLEDGED AS A PRINCE (7)
B. JACOB (49:8-50:3)
1. DELIGHTS OF SALVATION (8-13)
a. Physical - from suffering? b. Spiritual - from sin!
2. DOUBTS OF SUFFERING (14-3)
a. Wouldn't remember (14-21) b. Couldn't redeem (22-26)
c. Shouldn't reclaim (1-3)
C. JESUS (50:4-11)
1. SUFFERING FROM MEN (4-9)
2. ATTACKED AS A PROPHET (10-11)

I do not mind telling you right at the beginning that we have a difficult passage here. In chapter 49 there is a change in the prophecy. Certain things drop out that had been in the forefront. Certain other things that were in the background come right to the front, and certain new things appear. For example, the name 'Babylon' and the name 'Cyrus' drop out altogether. We leave history behind with chapter 49, and that does not make it any easier to understand. But, on the other hand, the 'servant of God' — this strange, mysterious figure striding through these pages — comes right to the front, and we have to look at him more than anyone else for a while.

The big change that occurs is this: in chapters 40–48, God is going to deliver his people from their *suffering*. But from chapter 49 onwards he is far more concerned to deliver them from their *sin*. It is this change which explains all the other changes. If I may put it like this: in our Lord's own ministry he began by helping people in their suffering. He caused the blind to see, the deaf to hear, the lame to walk; he healed the sick, cleansed the leper, raised the dead. He was helping people out of suffering. But through his ministry there is a change. He becomes more and more concerned with people's sin rather than their suffering, until finally at the cross he is dying for their sin. That is the kind of switch of emphasis that we find in Isaiah 40 onwards. We are already studying the life of our Lord. He is the servant. And when we get to Isaiah 53 we shall be right at the foot of the cross and studying someone who is dying for people's sin.

Now let me explain by saying this: I remember going to see a man in hospital who was desperately ill and the doctors did not think he would pull through; he was full of promises to me as to what would happen if he got better, saying that if God would just get him better then he would come to church and he would do this and do that —he was going to put his life right if God would only relieve his suffering. As it happened he did get better, but he did not come to church and he did not put right all the things he said he would. Exactly one year later I was visiting that man in his final illness. Here was a man who thought that if only he could get out of his suffering he would be right; that he could put his own life right if God would only save him from his suffering. The Israelites in exile in Babylon no doubt thought the same way. If God will only get me out of this trouble, if God will only get us back to our own land, we will never do anything wrong again. That is easier said than done.

I remember speaking to a women's meeting on the subject of gossip (not because that is necessarily the main sin of women – far from it!) A lady came to me afterwards and said, 'I am never going to gossip again.' Now that is easier said than done! The same goes for a man as for a woman. The Israelites may have said: Lord if you will only get us back home we will be alright, we will live as you want us to live. The one thing that God had to teach them through Isaiah was this: I will need to save you not only from your suffering but from your sin if you are ever to be right with me and serve me. So the rest of the book of Isaiah is not really about their suffering but about their sin. Most of us pray when we are in suffering: Lord, get me out of this pain, get me out of this sorrow, help me through this trouble. But God longs for someone to come and say: 'Lord, save me from my sin' —because that is really what causes most of our suffering, and our suffering would be quite different if our sin had been dealt with. It was so with the Israelites in exile. They were in exile because of their sin. Therefore they should have been crying to God, 'Lord, save us from the sin that brought us into suffering.' That would cure the whole situation.

Having given that introduction to these two chapters, let me say that there is a kind of sandwich here. The first part, 49:1–7, is about this servant of God, whom we now know to be Jesus himself. Then comes a whole section when he talks to this wayward nation of Jacob or Israel. Then comes the final part of this sandwich: back to the servant again, or back to Jesus again, and we shall read the final part thinking of Jesus. We have already studied the meaning of the word 'servant' and we came to the conclusion that in some passages it is God's servant Israel or Jacob, and in other passages it is God's servant Jesus, and there is no doubt who it is in chapter 49.

In 49:1–6 the servant is speaking about God; in v. 7 God is speaking about the servant. What do they say? Let us go through verse by verse. The servant is saying that God called him before he was born. If ever there was predestination, there it is. Before ever he made any choice himself, God called him while he was still in his mother's womb. That applies to other people in the Bible. Jeremiah said he was called from his mother's womb. Paul said that he was called from his mother's womb. God can decide before a person is born what they are going to do.

The servant's mouth was 'like a sharpened sword' (v. 2) and Jesus' certainly was. In Revelation 1 he is described as he is today, and from his mouth there comes a broad, two-edged sword. There were two types of Roman sword — a long one and a very short-bladed one exactly the shape of a human tongue. This picture appears again and again. The word of God is sharper than any two-edged sword, living and active. The tongue of God can cut, and cut very deep. When God speaks, it cuts right through to the marrow, right through to the heart. That is how you can tell the difference between human words and God's words. Human words can cut, but only God's words can cut to the very depth of your being. Sometimes when you are listening to the word of God something seems to stab your heart right though. The servant of God would have a mouth that was sharp, that would cut, lay bare, be a surgeon's knife, and could slay. I think of the times when our Lord's tongue was like a sword. He said, 'You are like whitewashed tombs'; He spoke of Herod, as 'that fox'. He could say a word that ripped away the veneer with which people covered themselves from others, exposing their very depths. He knew what was in men, and his speech would be like the prophet's tongue that cuts.

In the servant, God would be glorified. We can see his glory reflected in something or someone else. God always meant that the Jews should glorify him. The word *glorified* here is a translation of a Hebrew word meaning, literally, to burst forth. Something that has been hidden can be seen.

Now we come to this problem of v. 3 —If this is about Jesus, why is he called 'Israel'? The answer is very simple and we have it a few chapters earlier: God called the nation of the Jews to be his messenger, his witnesses, that he might be made visible to the whole world, and they failed him utterly. They rebelled against him, they refused his word. Jesus would be the servant. That is precisely what has happened.

Verse 4, in which we see the real humanity of Jesus, describes the discouragement he would encounter. He said to his own disciples, *"How long shall I stay with you?"* The greatest discouragement was expressed on the cross: *"My God, my God, why have you forsaken me?"* But notice at the end of v. 4 the servant's trust is in God to put it all right.

Verse 5 describes the task of the servant of God, Jesus: to bring Jacob and Israel back to God. That proves that this servant is not Israel, it is someone else. Jesus is charged with the task of bringing God's people the Jews back to God. But in v. 6 it is made clear that the servant will not only be used to bring God's people back but will be a light to the Gentiles, the nations, the peoples, that his salvation may reach to the ends of the earth. We suddenly see the broadening out of this servant's task.

Verse 6 is quoted many times in the New Testament. When Jesus was a baby and his parents brought him into the temple to dedicate him to God, an old man called Simeon saw him and said, *"For my eyes have seen your salvation"*. He went on to say that this baby would be "*. . . a light for revelation to the Gentiles and for glory to your people Israel.*" Simeon knew the book of Isaiah. Paul quoted this verse many times. Whenever the Jews refused to listen to Paul he simply went next door into the next house or the next lecture hall and spoke to the Gentiles, and said to the Jews that Jesus is to be a light to the nations. He quoted this verse again and again to the Jews to justify his preaching to the people who were not Jews. It is a most important verse. Indeed, what I want to emphasise is that if you do not know Isaiah well, there is a whole lot of the New Testament you will never understand.

Verse 7 switches the picture — the first use of the word *despised* about this servant. God speaks about the servant as the servant has been speaking about God. This servant will be deeply despised and abhorred by the nations. That is the first mention in Isaiah that this servant will not get on very well with men. It is going to get worse and worse through Isaiah until we come to chapter 53 where no-one desires him and where he is put to death as a criminal. But here is the first mention of trouble coming to the servant of God, Jesus. God will reverse this one day, and kings and princes will one day bow down before the one they have despised. I think of that Royal Academy picture by Charles Butler entitled 'King of kings'. It has five hundred personal portraits of rulers, princes, sovereigns, dictators, all standing around a central figure of the King of kings, Jesus Christ. Each of them is taking up the attitude that they adopted in life. Napoleon stands with a supercilious look on his face. Edward the Confessor bows and offers his crown to the Lord. Behind the King of kings cowers the prince of this world, Satan. It is a wonderful picture. One day the role will be reversed. Those who despised and abhorred will acknowledge. I find this a frightening verse. One day Jesus will be on the judgement seat, and standing before him will be a man called Pontius Pilate, to be judged. One day Jesus will be on his throne, and standing before him will be an evil man called Herod. One day Jesus will judge, and standing before him will be Annas and Caiaphas. One day standing before Jesus will be Adolf Hitler and all the dictators of this world. It will be a complete reversal of history. Before the servant of God all the rulers of man will bow. What a picture! And that is the ultimate picture of God's servant. He may be despised, he may be rejected of men, he may be abhorred, he may be the subject of contempt; people may dismiss Christ, and they can do that by dismissing his people, for inasmuch as they dismiss his brethren they dismiss him, but one day the roles will be reversed and God's servant will be seen to be on the throne. All this is helping us to fill out the picture of Jesus that they had in the Old Testament — the servant of God. We are beginning to see an outline emerging of someone who is called from his mother's womb and named from before his birth; someone who will have a tongue sharper than any two-edged sword.

Now read 49:7-13. This turns to Jacob, the people of God. Here we have a natural sequel to what we have just read. We have been describing the Saviour, now we consider salvation and the delights of it. It is one of the loveliest passages in this section. The main question is what sort of salvation is it describing — physical or spiritual? When you read it through for the first time it appears to be physical salvation from suffering: the prisoners coming out of prison, the people in exile in Babylon wending their weary way home and then feeding on the pastures of the hills. Yet v. 8 is used again and again in the New Testament to describe a spiritual salvation from sin. 2 Corinthians 6:2, having quoted this very verse says, *now is the time of God's favour, now is the day of salvation*. There is no doubt that these words may be used in a spiritual sense for our sufferings due to sin and the salvation that we have in Christ Jesus. No wonder then that in v. 13 we shout for joy.

This prophecy is about God's salvation. *They shall not hunger nor thirst. Neither scorching wind nor sun shall smite them*. That is quoted in Revelation 7, of those who have come out of the Great Tribulation and washed their robes white in the blood of the Lamb.

We move on to 49:14–50:3. I hope this will help you in your daily life. When you suffer, when you go through it, your mind gets twisted, unless you are very careful. If life has treated you badly, if you are bruised and broken by the experiences through which you have passed, your thinking about God can get distorted. You might begin to doubt or question him. People who are suffering sometimes say things about God that they would never say if they were not suffering. There are three things that the Israelites, this nation of Jacob, were saying about God that they should never have said. They did not believe that God would save them and that they would sing for joy at their salvation. They had been through so much suffering that they said, firstly, that God would not remember them; secondly, that he could not redeem them; thirdly, that he shouldn't reclaim them. So they stopped believing what God was saying through the prophet. Let us look at their doubts. One of them may be yours.

First of all (from vv. 14–21), they were saying that God would not remember his people. This verse is about a woman forgetting her own child. The Israelites were saying: seventy years and God has forgotten us. Seventy years is an awfully long time for human memory. You can forget things after seventy years very easily. But seventy years is nothing to God; a thousand years is as a day. They had overlooked this and were thinking that God had forgotten all about them. It is sometimes very easy to think this way. When life is going so badly and things are on top of you, your little heart says: God has forgotten me. But simply because you find it easy to forget him does not mean he finds it easy to forget you. There is a wonderful argument from God: 'Can a mother forget the baby at her breast?' In some rare and dreadful cases that may be possible, but can God forget Israel? Never!

The Bible forbade tattooing. There is a definite command in the book of Leviticus not to tattoo the body. It was a habit that they picked up in exile, from the Babylonians. They would puncture the skin and push dye in, in very much the same way as tattooing is done today. But, in a most daring metaphor here, God says: I have tattooed you on the palms of my hands. I noticed when I worked for my living that some of the men I worked with had, for instance, 'Sally' written on the arm, and perhaps even a drawing of Sally, tattooed, graven there so that they would not forget. You have to be very careful before you do that, as you are going to live the rest of your life with Sally! The Babylonians would tattoo someone's name upon some part of their body. Upon the palms of their hands they would have it punctured and the dye put in and a name would be written there. Every time they used their hands they would be reminded of the person they loved. God says: I have tattooed your name on my hands. He could never erase the name 'Israel' from his hands. Whenever he did anything with his hands he remembered that they are the work of his hands. What a picture that is, and it is as true of the people of God today as it was then. It is as true of the Christian as the Jew. Your name is engraved on God's hands. Charles Wesley mentions that at least a dozen times in his hymns. What a thought for the Christian, that you are tattooed on the palms of God's hands. Picture language, yes, but what a truth.

God says *'your walls are ever before me'*. There is a picture, the picture of the walls of Zion, and you cannot erase that from God's hands. When we talk of the palms of God's hands I cannot help thinking of nail prints there. In that way the hands of the Son of God are tattooed with his people, and for the rest of all eternity his hands are marked with the marks that speak of those he came to save. We can just let our minds float on through this wonderful verse.

That section finishes with a picture of the re-population of the land of Israel, and the people of Israel asking: where did all these people come from? So many people had been born in exile that when they got back to the little land of Israel they crowded it out and said the land was too narrow. In fact the population did come back to God's land.

The second temptation to doubt in their suffering was not that God would not remember them but that even if he did he could not do anything about it; that Babylon was too powerful; that it had been a fatal move to let his people go to Babylon; that the situation was hopeless. This doubt is expressed in 49:24. Can the prey be taken from the mighty? Or the captives of a tyrant be rescued? People languishing in prisoner of war camps and concentration camps felt that. Can anyone free us from the hands of a tyrant? Even if God did remember us, what could he do about it? Have you ever been in a situation where you have been tempted to think like that? But those who hope in God will not be disappointed. He is more powerful than the most powerful tyrant on earth and captives will be rescued from the fierce. God will contend with those who contend with you. Remember that God is all mighty and all powerful. There is no situation too strong for him to deal with.

I am afraid that even in small things we deny our faith at this point almost every week. We get into a situation and we get worried about it. What is worry but denying that God is all powerful in that situation? If we worry, we are saying that God cannot control these circumstances, that we are in the grip of forces that he cannot move. If we worry, we are breaking faith. But those who wait for the Lord shall not be put to shame. When we get agitated, when we wonder what is going to happen next, when we are disturbed, when we say that God could not possibly put something right (and we might say that in our thoughts as well as in our deeds and words) we are denying the faith.

The third doubt they had was even more serious. They doubted whether God *should* have anything more to do with them. Some people in Israel were saying: we deserve to come here, we can see that, and in fact God should never have us back. They were actually teaching that he had got rid of them forever. Sometimes I come across a Christian who is tempted to say this: 'Oh, I've just sunk too low this time, God would never have me back, he shouldn't — I'm just too great a sinner; after all he's done for me . . . I feel I've committed the unforgivable sin.' Some of the Jews were thinking that God had finally cut them off, as if he had divorced them. Divorce was allowed in the Old Testament under certain very limited circumstances and it was absolutely final. You could not have that woman back again, it was settled. Some Israelites were saying God shouldn't have them back, or they got the picture of debt rather than divorce, and were thinking that it was as if God was in debt and had sold them into slavery. A father who was in debt could sell his children on the slave market to pay his bills. But if he did he could never have his children back again. What does God say? In 50:1 he asks where the certificate of divorce is — or which creditor had he sold them to? This is meeting them at the point of their doubt.

God admits that it was for their iniquities that they were sold and for their transgressions that their mother was put away. But then he asks them a series of questions. He is letting them know that the real reason why they would not come back was not on his side but theirs. Why was it that when he called no-one answered? Why is it when I came there was no-one to meet me? May I just give you a little advice here. If somebody comes to you, a Christian who has sinned and who has suffered for that sin, and says, 'I am no good, I am beyond redemption now, God couldn't have me back now, God has cast me away forever,' then the reply to that is: 'Prove it. Why is it when God is calling that you won't answer? It is you who are putting yourself beyond God, not God who has put you away. It is you who are cutting yourself off.' I have found the most difficult thing with such people in that kind of doubt is to persuade them that the fault is on their side, not God's. He would have them back. He offers forgiveness. Our gospel is the gospel of the second chance, it is the gospel of forgiveness for those who repent. It is the gospel of 'Come home again' to the prodigal son. It is the prodigal's fault if he does not answer when he is called. If he says, 'I am beyond redemption', that is his answer, not God's. If he says, 'God should not have me back, I have just sunk too low,' that is his judgement it is not God's. You must say to such a person: you prove to me that God has done this and I will prove to you that when he calls it is you that is not answering. Is God's hand shortened that he cannot redeem? This assumes that God has a short arm and that he cannot reach far enough down to get people back from the bottom. A person who has sunk very low into sin, who has got very down in degradation, a person who has messed up their life, ruined their self-respect and their reputation, a person who has sinned crudely and who has paid the bill, a person like that says: I am too low down for God to reach me. And you will meet people who doubt whether God can save them because of this. And your answer is God has a long arm and can reach down as low as you are. His arm is not short that he cannot redeem. That is a verse that I love to roll my tongue round, to savour in my heart.

So God has dealt with all three unwarranted doubts. He had not forgotten his people. They were tattooed on his hands;

he could redeem them and deal with a tyrant. He had not cast them off or sold them. They were still his. Even though for their sins he let them go into affliction, he had not cut his people off. There are wonderful promises in this passage.

Now there is another part of the sandwich. Quite abruptly, as if God is impatient with this discussion of their doubts, he turns them back to the real subject: the servant. The servant speaks again, as he did at the beginning of chapter 49. Somebody has called this 'Gethsemane'. Here we have even more clearly the fact that God's servant is going to suffer. First he is going to speak. He will have a word to sustain him that is weary. And he will have this word for others because God's servant will listen to God first. Morning by morning God wakens the servant's ear to hear. The servant was not rebellious. God's servant, Jesus, listens to the Father and he does not rebel as Israel did. He listens, and therefore he can help others who are weary. If you are ever going to speak to those who are weary, and help other people, you will only do so because you listen to God. Those who listen to God and do not rebel against his word will be able to help others with their words. That is the description in vv. 4–5, Jesus as God's servant did not rebel against God's word but listened to him morning by morning. We know from the Gospels Jesus had an early morning time with his Father and listened before he spoke that day. He prayed before he preached, listened before he spoke, and had a word to sustain him when he was weary.

But now look at 50:6. *"I gave my back to the smiters and my cheeks to those who pulled out the beard. I hid not my face from shame and spitting."* This is God's true holy servant speaking, and he is describing indignity, brutal physical violence, insult and shame, through which he has to pass. We are being prepared all the time for Isaiah 53. Notice that in the last servant passage we had those words *despised* and *abhorred*. Now we have even more detail, we have plucking out the beard. Do you know that apart from being a most painful thing it was considered the greatest insult you could give to a Jew, and to spit on him, to abuse him. Here we learn that the servant of God would be personally abused. Of course we know how this came true. This is our Lord's trial being pictured. They slapped him on the face and said, "Prophesy." They spat upon him, the Son of God. That is how they treated God's servant.

But the rest of this passage describes how the servant of God will allow God to put this right. He will not try to avenge himself. At his trial he will leave it to God to contend for him. (See 50:7.) *"Therefore have I set my face like flint"* —the only other place in the Bible where that phrase occurs is when Jesus set his face to go to Jerusalem. Jesus set his face to go through with all the indignity and pain because he believed the Father would vindicate him and put it right (as he did). In v. 8 we have the trial. *Who then will bring charges against me?* Where is Pilate today? Where are Annas, Caiaphas and Herod today? Where are the mob who shouted 'Crucify him'? They have all worn out like a garment. The moth has eaten them up. They have died. Where is Jesus today? God has raised him from the dead. Read all this and meditate upon the servant of God who comes to save not only Israel but the Gentiles from their sin.

Finally, in vv. 10–11 we have both an encouragement and a warning: an encouragement to those who trust in the name of the Lord and obey the word of God's servant, and a warning to those with *flaming torches* which they 'set ablaze' (NIV). Notice that the words *obeys* and *trust* occur in v. 10. Who is there who trusts and obeys the servant Jesus? Thankfully, there are some. But there are also others who are constantly firing fiery darts at him, and those who do this are warned that they will lie down in torment.

We leave this rather difficult passage with some very precious thoughts: first, that you are tattooed on God's hands. How can he ever forget? Second, God's arm is long enough to lift you up again.

22

BEAUTIFUL ARE THE FEET

Read Isaiah 51 – 52:12

A. PROPHECY - MAN (51:1-8)
1. PAST ORIGIN (1-3)
a. Abraham b. Adam
2. FUTURE DESTINY (4-6)
a. Nations b. Nature
3. PRESENT POSITION (7-8)
a. Righteousness b. Reproach
B. PRAYER (51:9-11)
1. EXODUS - out of Egypt (9-10)
2. ENTRY - into Zion (11)
C. PROPHECY - GOD (51:12-52:6)
1. MAKER'S STRENGTH (12-16)
2. JUDGE'S WRATH (17-23)
3. REDEEMER'S GRACE (1-6)
D. PRAISE (52:7-10)
1. HEAR - words of peace (7-8a)
2. SEE - deeds of power (8b-10)
E. PROPHECY - SELF (52:11-12)
1. ACTIVE WILL (11a)
2. CLEAN HEART (11b)
3. QUIET MIND (12)

Something of the spirit of Jewish nationalism comes out in this chapter. The name *Zion* occurs again and again, and the name *Jerusalem* keeps cropping up. The reason for this is that Jewish hopes are centred on a city situated in the Judean hills. Do you know that for 2,000 years God's people have greeted each other at the time of the Passover with these words: 'Next year in Jerusalem'? Their hopes and dreams are centred on Jerusalem. Christians' hopes are centred on a city, not the old Jerusalem but the new Jerusalem, a city whose builder and maker is God —not a city that men build up from the earth but a city that God will send down from heaven. So these two chapters, which talk of the earthly hopes of God's people set on an earthly city, we can lift up to an altogether deeper level and look to the new Jerusalem, adorned like a bride for her husband coming down out of heaven. The feet of those who came with good tidings in this chapter are the feet of those who said the earthly Jerusalem is to come. But now that verse, to Christians, means something quite different, and it is quoted in Romans 10 of those who preach the gospel, who announce a new Jerusalem coming, who have even better news, and whose feet are more beautiful because their good tidings are more wonderful. That gives the setting of the chapter.

You can split these two chapters into five parts: a prophecy, prayer, another prophecy, praise, another prophecy. Prophecy is when God speaks to men; prayer and praise when men speak to God. So there is this kind of double sandwich here: a prophecy—God speaks to men; a prayer—men speak to God; another prophecy—God speaks to men again; praise—men speak to God; then a final prophecy and God speaks to men again. Three times God speaks. The first time he tells them to think about men, the second time he tells them to think about God, and the third time he tells them to think about themselves. It is a very clear outline so we are going to think of other people, God, and ourselves. Out of that grows prayer and praise, and it is bound to do so. That is why in the church in which I was the minister we had our worship after our Bible study. We listened to God speaking to us about others, about himself and about ourselves, then we prayed and we praised, and our worship became a response to him.

Each prophecy begins with a sharp command: Wake up! That is a good command when you are preaching. The prophet wakes up his hearers. It is a stirring prophecy and all through these two chapters God is trying to wake his people up, get them going and let them really see that he is alive, and let them be alive themselves.

The first prophecy is addressed to those who seek the Lord. Indeed, the rest of this prophecy will be quite dead to you unless you are seeking the Lord. It is addressed to those who are seriously looking for God and really asking him to deliver them from their troubles and tribulations. Those who pursue deliverance, and seek the Lord, listen. The message to such people is this: If you are really seeking the Lord then there are three dimensions you should consider: first, consider what God has done in the past for others; second, consider what God is going to do in the future for others; third, you should consider what God is doing in the present. When you are seeking the Lord your mind is full of questions such as: Could God deliver me? Could he really change my life? If I do find the Lord this morning, will it last? If I find the Lord now, what about tomorrow morning at work when people reproach me and ridicule me for having a faith? Will my knowledge of the Lord survive that? Will I be able to see it through in the face of others?

The answer to these questions is: the past, the future and the present. In vv. 1–3 you go back in your imagination to the past, and in a vivid picture it is said:

> *"Look to the rock from which you were cut*
> *and to the quarry from which you were hewn . . . ."*
> 51:1b (NIV)

You did not make yourself, God made you. The Jews did not make themselves, God quarried them. Out of the rock of the human race, God quarried a special stone which he called his own people. He dug them out. You notice they did not dig themselves, he quarried them, he dug them out of the nations to be his own people. They are to look to their origin, back to the beginning, and consider this. Of course this was very appropriate. They were slaves in Babylon. They were a long way from home and thought that God would never get them back. They had doubts as to whether he could ever put them in the promised land.

Where did Abraham live? The answer is he lived in a place called Ur of the Chaldees. 'Chaldees' is the same as Babylon. God took just one man, and brought him all the way round to Canaan and settled him there – and made the one into many. If God could get Abraham out of there and settle him there, can he not do something for you?

Then another memory comes back. Go back even further. In the beginning this area was called the garden of Eden. Look in Genesis 2, note that the Euphrates ran through the garden of Eden. We are going to go back even further than Abraham, right back to Adam. God is not only going to take you like Abraham and plant you, he is going to put you in a garden again. God is able to do this. The wilderness of Judea will be like the garden of the Lord, with all the communion with God that was enjoyed in the garden of Eden. That is the meaning of vv. 1–3. You go back to the quarry from which you were hewn. I think of the country in which I live. This nation has been a Christian nation for many centuries. Missionaries came. The first Christian martyr was a man called Alban, a Roman soldier martyred at St. Alban's, and ever since then the gospel has been known in this country. King Alfred was a Christian and wrote the ten commandments out for the people, as well as burning his cakes! All through our history we have a quarry from which we were dug, and people have known God, and here we are. Need we doubt that God could help our nation again? Go back not only to the nation from which you were quarried and the church from which you were quarried, go back to the family from which you were quarried. You may have Christian parents, Christian grandparents, Christian great-grandparents – and the Lord delivered them from their distress, why should he not deliver you? Consider the past. Go back to the quarry from which you were dug and consider what God did for your forefathers, and then come back to him.

The second consideration should be the future. We now turn to the future in vv. 4–6, and we ask what is going to happen. Two things are described that God is going to do. The first is that he is going to bring justice one day. God is going to put right all that is wrong. He is going to restore what has been destroyed. God is going to make the good blessed and the evil cursed. The nations are waiting for this. The truth is that, deep down, every human heart is waiting for the day when wrong will be put right, evil will be punished and good rewarded; when the world will be seen as a world of justice, law, rule and order, when the wicked do not get away with it and the good are not pushed around. Justice and righteousness will prevail, and God is going to bring that about. That is the first thing to consider.

The second thing to consider is that God is going to destroy everything you can see. Consider the heavens, the stars, the sky, the clouds, the sun, the moon, and consider the earth. God is going to dissolve all that and put it away as you put away your old winter clothes and put on your spring ones. He is going to put away the heavens and the earth. In the light of all this, what sort of person ought you to be? The answer is that when everything you can see goes, when the church which you attend goes, and when the sky above it goes, there is one thing that will still be there: your deliverance, your salvation.

The third thing we are to consider is the present. If you live a good life, if God's righteousness is in your heart — if you live an upright life, a straight life, a clean life — one thing is absolutely certain: you will be ridiculed, you will be reproached, you will be reviled. The world is crooked and does not like a good man. The world is sinful and does not really feel comfortable in the presence of a saint. The world is dirty and a clean life is a constant challenge to it. Therefore, when God's righteousness is in your heart, not just on your lips but in your life, then sooner or later you run into the reproach of men, and this worries those who seek the Lord. I have had people say to me: I have become a Christian but you know, I couldn't keep it up where I work, or where I live, or in my family. They would drag me down again. I know that if I tried to live right that they'd make me crooked again. But God says of men who reproach and insult the believer: "*. . the moth will eat them up like a garment . . . .*"

When my wife and I lived in Aden we used to have to guard against what was called the woolly bug. If you have lived in the tropics you may know what this is. You just do not leave any garment exposed if it has wool in it, or you will pick it up and it will look like a lace curtain, whatever it looked like at the beginning. The woolly bug is mentioned in 51:8: *the worm will devour them like wool* — that it is what we now call the woolly bug. It is a very healthy reminder to you: when those people are getting at you, the woolly bug will get at them. It is a vivid way of putting it. But it stops the fear of reproach when you realise that it is they who are in the dangerous position, not you; that they cannot eat up what you have, but they can be eaten up by what they do. I have noticed this again and again: when a Christian lived in an army or RAF barrack room among others who tried to knock the faith out of them, who tried to drag them down to their own dirty level, I have noticed that they could not eat up what that Christian had, but that what they did ate them up and destroyed something in them, and they lost something. They did not cause the Christian to lose something, they made him all the stronger, but they lost something, the 'woolly bug' ate them up. This is the message: don't be afraid about those who will ridicule you; you are seeking the Lord, don't have any fear about keeping it up, the ridicule that you might experience. God's righteousness will last for ever, and his salvation through all generations.

At this point the conversation is reversed. God has spoken to Israel, now Israel speaks to God. Israel tells God to wake up (see 51:9). That is a very naughty thing to say. The psalms had been written by now and the people knew them, and one of the psalms says that the Lord neither slumbers nor sleeps. But here Isaiah is saying to God: wake up; put on your strength. They are going to have a severe rebuke at 52:1, where God is going to say: *You* wake up. You put on your strength. It is not me who is asleep. It has been said: if God seems far away from you, which one of you moved? Sometimes, when we cry to God and ask where he is, what he is doing and why he does not seem to be delivering us, God is telling us that it is we who need to wake up and do something.

However, their prayer is nevertheless a wonderful prayer. After they imply that God is asleep or tired, which they should not have done, they plead with him to do something again. They remembered that once upon a time the whole nation had been in captivity. They had been slaves. The nickname they had for Egypt was Rahab, the prostitute, and the nickname they had for Pharaoh was the dragon. They were saying: God, you dealt with Rahab, you dealt with the dragon, and your people came out and they came back. They had considered the past and they had realised that God can do it and so they are praying: do it again. That is a prayer God loves to hear. The prayer that God waits to hear is: do it again; you are the same God; we are your people, we are in need, revive your work.

Visiting Wales, I could not help remembering the great revivals that built the chapels, most of which are more than half empty now. It is around a century since a great revival swept through that country, and I found my heart saying: Lord, you did it then, you delivered your people from their lethargy, do it again. This prayer is like that. They recognised, as the Welsh recognised, that when this happens they will start singing. Reference to music in the Old Testament and the New follows God's deliverance. The first mention of God's people singing is in Exodus 15, after they had crossed the Red Sea. All true song of praise is born out of an experience of God's deliverance and salvation.

The prayer mentions the coming out and the coming in, and

says do it again. You brought them out of Egypt and into Zion and they sang, do it again. Now God speaks again and he bids them now think, not about other people but about him. His people were to remember three things about him. If you are seeking the Lord you must seek the Lord as he is. A minister was once asked by a student in Cambridge this question: 'I have been seeking God for ten years and I can't find him. What is wrong?' The minister very wisely answered, 'God has been seeking you for more than ten years, however have you missed each other?' When the minister spoke to the student it turned out that the student was not really looking for God, he was looking for his *own idea of God*, which is quite different. If you are seeking the Lord you have to seek God *as he is*, and if you have made up your own idea as to what he is like, and then you seek that, you may never find him because your idea may be wrong. There is only one God, and there are three things you need to remember when you seek him: he is your maker, your judge and your redeemer. You need to think first of his strength and power, second of his wrath and his anger, and third, of his grace — and then you will find God.

Think first of God as maker. Here are God's people praying to God, and 51:13 tells us that they had forgotten him as their maker. When you pray, it is easy to forget that God is the creator. If we remembered that God created all this, we should have no doubts as to what he could do. We would never have any doubts about his power and his strength. We would never say: Lord, *if* you can do anything, do it. We would say: Is anything too hard for the Lord? You are the maker. You made me, you made the world I live in, you made everyone else, the stars in the sky . . . . When you pray, you pray to the creator who laid the foundations of the earth and stretched the heavens like a tent over the foundation of the earth. Remembering that God is our maker, we will never be afraid of man. If you are afraid of anyone else you have forgotten that the Lord is your maker. If you fear God, you fear no-one else. If you remember that God is the maker, you need not fear anyone or anything. For God the maker is in absolute control of everything he has made, therefore why are you afraid? Are you afraid of thunder and lightning? God made the thunder and the lightning. Doesn't that put a different complexion on it? All fears basically go back to this: we forget that the Lord is our maker and he is in charge.

Secondly, remember that God is your judge and he does punish sins; he is angry with those who disobey him. You need to remember his wrath. Do you know where the gospel begins in the New Testament? It begins with this: by nature we are children of God's wrath. By nature we make him angry. By nature his wrath abides on us because by nature we are disobedient children, and we need to remember this. Here the prophet pictures God's people as a woman lying in a drunken stupor on the pavement, and not one of her sons will even pick her up. This was a very vivid picture. The prophet's message is: you are not lying there in Babylon in that stupor because of wine, you are lying there because you have been made to drink the cup of God's anger. It is a picture of a nation in slavery. Do you notice that God can give that cup to anyone to drink? Does this strike a chord with you? There was a day many centuries later when Jesus Christ knelt in Gethsemane and said: if it be possible, let this cup pass from me. What cup? There is only one cup that the Lord ever talked about, and it was the cup of his anger against sin. And God can give that cup to anyone to drink. For these seventy years of exile in Babylon God has been giving the cup of his wrath to his own people to drink, and that is why they languish and lie in that stupor.

But now he has taken from them the cup that made them stagger, and would put it in the hands of their tormentors to drink. (See 51:22f.) Soon we will come to the most thrilling chapter Isaiah 53 where God took that cup and he gave it to his own Son. We need to remember that God is judge and he must give to someone the cup of his wrath to drink. He must either give it to the ones who have disobeyed him, as he did to Israel in the exile, or he must give it to someone else. The truth of the cross is that Jesus had to drink what otherwise you and I would have to drink — as Israel had to drink — the cup of God's wrath. But God took it from them and gave it to the Babylonians — they drank and they fell into a stupor, and they were unable to stand up, and staggered around. The cup of staggering it is called, the cup that causes people to fall and stagger. I cannot help thinking of Jesus staggering under the cross — the cup of staggering which he had to drink. They offered him wine to drink but his stupor was not due to wine.

Thirdly, we need to remember God's grace as our redeemer. He is our maker from whom we came in the past, our judge to whom we go in the day of wrath, and in the present our redeemer who offers us now his grace in the day of salvation. What does 'grace' mean? It means it is free, and the key word in 52:1–6 is the word 'nothing'. You were sold for nothing, you will be redeemed for nothing. You got into sin without paying, you will get into salvation without paying. This is what grace means. It is so difficult to persuade people that salvation is for nothing. They would much rather pay. I am afraid we all have that bit of pride in us. We do not like charity, we do not like gifts, we prefer to pay.

I stopped at a little garage to buy some petrol on the way to Wales and I saw some rather intriguing chewing gum which I thought would keep my children quiet for the rest of the journey. So I said, 'I'll take a packet of that as well.' He said, 'Well take it free, there you are, it's a gift.' 'No,' I said, my pride coming out. 'I'll pay you,' and I put some coins on the counter. So he took another pack and he threw that out! He was determined to give me a free packet, which I finally took! It is like that between us and God. God's offer is your deliverance: it's free, just get up and take it; you don't buy it, you don't earn it, you don't work for it, you don't have to be good for it, just take it. He redeems you for nothing now, if you'll take it as a free gift. But we are so proud if we won't.

Here is the picture of God: our maker — he made us in the past; our judge, before whom we shall stand in the future; but the God who in the present says: you wake up. I was talking to some children in a service about the meaning of grace. I put a bar of chocolate on the pulpit and I said, 'Now that chocolate is for the first person who will come and get it. It is quite free. I am not charging you anything.' I just waited, and the children's eyes were off me and on that, but nobody moved until one cheeky looking little boy jumped up, ran up and grabbed the chocolate and ate it for the rest of the service! But they had got the message of grace. There it was for nothing, but somebody had to get up and take it, and until they did it was no use to them. Which is why chapter 52 begins with the words, *Awake, awake, O Zion, clothe yourself with strength* (Isaiah 52:1, NIV).

That is what God says to people who say: I have been looking for the Lord and I can't find him; I am seeking the Lord, I want to be saved, I want to be delivered but I can't get through. The answer is: wake up, come and get it, take it for nothing. Say: Lord, I accept your salvation as a free gift for nothing. I know that you are my maker and that I came from you. I realise that you are my judge and that I am a child of your wrath and that you are angry with my sin, but I come to you now, I wake up and I accept your free salvation. That is how you find deliverance, and that is why in Ephesians Paul says: *Awake thou that sleepest*. Wake up if you are seeking the Lord. The fault is not that God is asleep but that you are, not that he is tired but that you are. Awake, put on your strength O Zion. That is the answer to their prayer in v. 9 of the previous chapter. They said, *Awake, awake, put on your strength O arm of the Lord*; he told them to awaken and put on their strength. It meant: come and get it; I am going to deliver you if you wake up and take what I offer you for nothing. You are lying like a drunken woman with nobody to pick you up, but get up and put on your beautiful garments as a bride. Stop being a drunken woman and come as my bride. That is why the new Jerusalem is described as a bride in the New Testament.

We come to a lovely passage of praise in chapter 52. It has inspired many hymns. *How beautiful upon the mountains are the feet* . . . . Why are the feet beautiful and not the mouth? The answer is: because the feet carry the mouth to where it is needed. It is the missionary's feet that are beautiful because the feet take the missionary to where the good news is needed. What is the point of shouting good news if you are not near the people who need to hear it? Here is a picture of Jerusalem lying in ruins, a few people living in shanty shacks, and suddenly they see over the Judean hills a man running. When he comes near he says it is alright, they are coming back, Jerusalem is going to be rebuilt. God has comforted his people. What good news! To publish peace is great news. Paul takes up this verse — the evangelist, the gospel preacher, is this man whose feet are beautiful. (See Romans 10:14ff.) It is my task today, and it is every preacher's task, and it is every Christian's task, to tell people 'peace' — a peace the world cannot give or take away — to tell them that God reigns. What good news it is in a world of chaos, so utterly broken and divided, to tell people God is in charge. The Lord God omnipotent reigns. He is on the throne. That is good news. That is peace, and it brings peace to the heart when it is realised that God is on the throne. 'Your God reigns!'

Not only will they hear this good news, they will see it, eye to eye. It is wonderful what God says, even to see it, but you hear the gospel before you see it. You hear it, you believe it and then you see it working. Seeing follows hearing because believing is based on hearing, not on seeing. They say seeing is believing, but it is not, because once you have seen there is no more room for faith. Hearing is believing, followed by seeing, and they shall see, and when they see they will sing. We have singing again! So we have a wonderful note of praise that even the ends of the earth shall see the salvation of our God. And that is beginning to be true.

Verses 11–12 are the most important verses of the study and now we turn to this prophecy from God to man in which he invites them to consider three more things. The first prophecy told them to consider other people, past, present and future; the second told them to consider God as maker, judge and redeemer; the third tells them to consider themselves, their will, their heart and their mind. If you are going to seek the Lord, the final thing is a response to him of your heart, mind and will, your total personality.

First your will. You must go to God. *Come out from it and be pure .....* God knew that many Jews would not leave Babylon and face the hazards of rebuilding Jerusalem. So God says that the first thing is get out. You have to make the step, to launch out in faith — that is an act of your will. Secondly, your heart must go clean. You must leave behind anything that would defile, and just carry the vessels of the Lord. Go with a heart that is undivided. Don't try and take the treasures of Babylon with you. Cut everything off, and go with a heart that is pure and that has only one desire — to do God's will. That is repentance in a nutshell. God will be in front of you and behind. Let your mind be quite clear as to what is happening. Let it be quiet and trusting before him. Let your will be active, depart.

23

LAMB TO THE SLAUGHTER

Read Isaiah 52:13–53:12

A. HIS ASTONISHING SUCCESS (13-15)
1. EXALTED
2. MARRED
3. REVEALED
B. HIS ABHORRENT SORROW (1-3)
1. MISUNDERSTOOD
2. IGNORED
3. DESPISED
C. HIS ATONING SUFFERING (4-6)
1. SMITTEN
2. WOUNDED
3. SUBSTITUTED
D. HIS AFFLICTED SINLESSNESS (7-9)
1. OPPRESSED
2. STRICKEN
3. BURIED
E. HIS ACCEPTABLE SACRIFICE (10-12)
1. PERPETUATED
2. SATISFIED
3. REWARDED

We have been tracing the way in which Isaiah is the whole Bible in miniature, and in the chapters immediately after 40, through to chapter 53, there are four sections, all of them songs, about someone who is not named but who is described in detail as *my servant*. There has been a great deal of debate about these songs, which are to be found in chapters 42, 49, 50 and 53. They begin with a lovely picture of a rather gentle person who will not lift up his voice or cry out. Then as you move through these songs about 'my servant' we come to the one in chapter 50 which introduces a new note: my servant will suffer. Then in chapter 53 there is death and burial, horror and tragedy. Yet mixed with the tragedy there is a note of tremendous triumph about the servant having his days prolonged even after his death and burial.

There has been much scholarly debate about this. What is his identity? No name is given. There are no words from his lips, just a description of what he is, what he will do and what will be done to him. Most Jewish scholars today insist that the suffering servant described by Isaiah represents, in a kind of corporate personality, the nation of Israel suffering for the Lord. Certainly this little nation has suffered more than any other. But that explanation is not convincing. It is a sad fact that many Christian scholars have also come to the same conclusion. In chapter 53, for example, you find that this suffering servant is suffering for 'my people'. How can 'my people' suffer for 'my people'? Then at the end of chapter 53 it talks about this 'righteous' one. No, that explanation just will not hold water.

I was delighted to read a moving testimony by a Romanian Jewish doctor, Dr Thomas Adler, who found himself in a forced labour camp on the Russian frontier during the Second World War. He escaped to find that almost all his relatives had perished in Auschwitz. He then became a Zionist and finally reached Israel with a group of illegal immigrants from Cyprus, in the period in 1948 when the British were trying to keep them out. He then found himself among Israeli intellectuals studying Hebrew history and archaeology, and he began to read the Hebrew Bible with growing interest, especially the prophets. The verses that struck and embarrassed him were: '. . . he was wounded for our transgressions, bruised for our iniquities, the chastisement of our peace was upon him . . .', to: '. . . for the transgression of my people was he stricken.' He kept wondering what those words meant, and he came across the work of rabbinic commentators who related them to the suffering people of Israel. Then he asked why it says that *he* was pierced for our transgressions, *he* was bruised for our iniquities, by *his* wounds we are healed. He knew something of the Hebrew linguistic debates around that issue. After careful consideration he concluded it must mean a person, not the people of Israel, it must be a chosen servant of God. The key emerged when he read: *'He was assigned a grave with the wicked, and with the rich in his death . . . .'* Suddenly he remembered the account of Joseph of Arimathea, a rich man who offered a new grave for a chosen servant of God. He bought a New Testament and read carefully through the Gospel of Matthew. Then he understood: the chosen servant of God numbered with the transgressors, and who bore the sin of many and made intercession for the transgressors, could only be one person, Jesus of Nazareth.

It is exciting when a Jew reading his own Bible is convinced. So we are going to look at this chapter now and read in it the story of Jesus of Nazareth. The Ethiopian eunuch in the chariot reading this very chapter asked Philip for an explanation. Who is this of which Isaiah speaks? Beginning at this scripture, Philip declared to him Jesus.

I have mentioned a number of passages which are songs. In the English this does not come out, but they are Hebrew songs and they are songs with the broken style of someone who is weeping while they sing – particularly chapter 53. It comes from a broken heart; it is a sobbing song. It has a broken rhythm and a sombre, tragic note. It is composed of five verses, each of which makes up three English verses. So if you have a Bible you do not mind writing on you could just put a line under each of the three verses – the last three of chapter 52 and then you can divide 53 with three little lines into four stanzas, three verses each in English, one verse each in Hebrew. I mention that because it is a Hebrew characteristic of poetry to give us in the first line of each verse the theme of the verse. So when we read each block, each section of three verses in English, it is the first few words that unlock the whole verse in Hebrew. The theme is announced and then expanded.

So we can pick up five themes from this chapter and I am going to give them each a title. The song begins with God singing. God is a singer, as I am sure you know. He will rejoice over us with singing. I think we are the only religion in the world that believes in a God who sings. That is why we sing so much. So the song begins with God singing and it ends with him singing. That is why at the beginning and the end there is a note of triumph. For God sees these events as his greatest victory. But in the middle it is man speaking, and the middle three verses have this sad and sombre note about them. What man sees is tragic. Man sees his own sin, the need for someone to die horribly for it, the sheer injustice of an innocent suffering for the guilty, and that is sad. It is this mixture of sadness and gladness which surrounds us when we come to the cross.

From man's point of view the story of Jesus' death is one of the saddest stories there has ever been. From God's point of view it is a victory — triumph, not tragedy. So there is this sandwich: God's triumph, man's tragedy, God's triumph. We shall see how it moves from God speaking, 'I', 'he', to man speaking, 'we', 'our', and then back to God.

The first heading I suggest could be: *The Great Reversal.*

See, my servant will act wisely;
he will be raised and lifted up and highly exalted.

Isaiah 52:13 (NIV)

Here we have a theme — a servant who will be exalted. The language here is piled up: 'raised', 'lifted up', 'highly exalted'. This is the great reversal. Someone at the bottom of the social ladder appears at the top. Nations and kings are startled, not only by the fact that a servant is now at the top but also by the servant's appearance: scarred, disfigured. The last glimpse the world had of Jesus, this servant on earth, was of a disfigured, agonised human form. His face was scarred, his back was in ribbons, his side was scarred, his hands were pierced, his feet were pierced, his human form was out of joint, the bones were sticking through. He was emaciated. That was the last memory that all but believers had. That was the last thing that the priests saw, the last thing the Romans saw of that tortured frame. Here there seems to be a clear indication that when this servant appears at the very top he will still bear the scars of that experience, and they will still be seen. I think we had all taken it for granted that his hands and feet would still show nail prints, but maybe we have overlooked that his side would still show the gash, that his back would still be scarred and that his forehead would still be ripped with the thorns, when we see him at the top. It means there is glory in scars, they are not incompatible.

There are many who have never heard or seen, and one day they will be astonished. Who is this? And what has been done to him? Why is he so high? That is how the song begins. It is as if God gives the end of the story first so that we do not get too depressed by what follows; it is as if the last chapter is revealed, we have read the last page. That is the first verse in the song. When we come to the communion table and share bread and wine we begin by remembering that our Jesus is exalted high above all the kings and the nations and we worship him, high and lifted up.

We turn to the second Hebrew verse — 53:1–3 in the English and I call this verse *The Great Rejection*. Who believes what I have just written? What newspaper in the world would publish a headline that Jesus will one day be on top, that Jesus, this scarred, crucified servant of God, will one day be King over the whole world? No newspaper would dare to publish such a headline. They would be regarded as having become unbalanced in their judgement. Nobody does believe this until the Holy Spirit removes a veil from their minds and enables them to see Jesus seated at the right hand of God the Father.

The future kings and nations will be amazed, but are they amazed today? Not in the slightest. Are they impressed today? Not the slightest. And because they have not believed our report — and they are not impressed now, having only seen him on earth as the scarred servant — the arm of the Lord is not revealed to them. His saving power is not theirs either. Only those who believe such a report know God's mighty arm to save. So the second verse shows the contrast between God's view of Jesus and man's view of Jesus when he came the first time. Shall I tell you what God's view was? God looked at this world and what he saw was a desert, a dry ground, a barren, infertile land. When some astronauts came back from the moon they said one of the most glorious sights was to see earth with its colours, its blue and its brown and its green, and they were thrilled. They said they saw nothing as beautiful out among the heavens as the earth. But God does not see it like that. When God looks down on the earth he sees barren desert. Why? Because God's plan in making this planet earth and in putting people on it was that he might have a family that loved him, people who would worship him, live for him and obey him, because they wanted to. And what did he get? He got a dry ground, so dry that not one single person had ever given him what he wanted. He had spent much time, much labour, much love on this planet. He had given us a lovely place to live in, he had given us health and strength. He had given us the capacity to look up to him and to pray. He had made us in his own image. Yet all we like sheep went astray and everyone turned to his own way —until the Father sent his Son Jesus, who grew up before him like a little green shoot out of dry ground. The Father watched his Son in Nazareth growing up, and for the first time he had a plant growing in a desert, a root out of dry ground, precious, unique. This spoke at last of life. Now there was the power to transform the desert.

What did men see? Just the opposite. They did not take any notice of Jesus. There was *nothing in his appearance that we should desire him*. I take this to mean, and I hope this will not come as a shock to you, that Jesus did not look anything out of the ordinary. That is important. Many of the Sunday school pictures we were brought up on showed Jesus as such a dashing, handsome, tall, outstanding person that everybody would look at him in a crowd. But I believe that when he walked the streets of Nazareth he looked very ordinary. That is the Incarnation. People who had known him thirty years said: Isn't this just the carpenter's son, the ordinary boy from down the street? I do not believe that God gave him the advantage (or disadvantage) of being extra handsome, and this I believe is why there is no description of his physical appearance in the Gospels — because somehow that was not what struck people. The only physical feature mentioned is his eyes, which struck people in an extraordinary way.

Furthermore, this boy and this man was not I think, as many pictures portray him, a kind of cheerful cheerleader, always laughing and smiling. He was someone who saw the sadness of life, a man of sorrows and acquainted with grief — and a man like that is not very popular. People do not like to be reminded of the unhappy things, they want comedians, entertainers. So it says: as one from whom men turn away. He was not, I think, 'the life and soul of the party', as we may sometimes have assumed. He saw the sheer sadness. Growing up as he did, like a green shoot, he was aware of the desert around him. Loving the Father as he did, he was very much aware of those who did not. Living a sinless life as he did, he was only too aware of the sinful world into which he had come, and this caused him grief. So he was not popular, and people just turned away from him, and that is all you need to do to crucify Christ. As one, literally, we turned our backs on him and looked the other way when he went by. He was despised and we did not care.

What a comment on the human race. Jesus comes and disturbs us, he puts his finger on the sensitive spots. He shows us our sins. We were happy before he came. Why did you have to come and spoil it all? Why do you have to remind us about spiritual things? Why do you have to challenge and disturb us in our complacency? So the world just turns away when Jesus is mentioned; that is not quite the sort of thing to talk about in polite society. The world does not care. That is the great rejection. Notice that it was not so much a positive rejection as simply a turning away, a turning towards the things that were more cheerful, a turning away from a man of sorrows acquainted with grief. Let's see if there's anything good on the television instead. That is all it means — the great rejection — and it is all in Isaiah's song.

Notice at this point that Isaiah is speaking 750 years before the events of which he speaks took place, yet he says *we*. There is a sense in which all the human race before that event and all the human race after the event is included in this *we*. For it is natural to us to turn away from such things. It is our fallen nature not to want to be reminded of the griefs and sorrows of this desert area. We are included. Isaiah is including himself. He is including his contemporaries — centuries before the cross. We turned away. At the very most the world sees him as one of the figures of history. Some might see him as a great teacher. But as a root out of dry ground, as the precious green shoot to give God pleasure — the world does not see him as that. He tends to convict us and we want to be happy and complacent. So still we can read this in terms of ourselves. I want to say that unless you see yourself in the *we* of vv. 1–3 you will not see the wonder of the truth in vv. 4–6. Until a person feels involved and responsible for the rejection of Christ they will not understand the glory of saying he was wounded for our transgressions. If you are not in the first *we* you cannot be in the next *our*.

Once we have seen ourselves in the *we* of the great rejection, rejected of men, rejected by *me*, we are ready for vv. 4–6, the next great verse in the Hebrew song. I call this section *The Great Replacement*. Surely he has borne our griefs. It is the pronouns all the way through this next verse that matter: he, our, we, his, he, our. This is a marvellous verse. We are involved in a double way. Not only are we involved in causing his sufferings by rejecting him, we are also involved because we should have been suffering those things instead of him. We should be there. We were on the giving end and we ought to have been on the receiving end of his suffering. It is a shattering realisation. You see, in those days men had a simple equation: sin led to suffering. That is a profound truth and you will never get away from it. It runs right through the Bible, it runs right through life. But there is one mistake they made, and which people still make today. The person who is suffering is not necessarily the person who has sinned. And we esteem him stricken by God and afflicted. In other words, we thought he must be suffering for his own sins, and to this day most of the Jews have believed the same thing, and not a few Gentiles have said that he was an impracticable idealist and he got what he deserved. Isaiah thought that way at first. He had this simple equation, but the book of Job is a challenge to that equation, for Job's comforter said to Job that he must have sinned an awful lot to suffer; suffering is always due to sin so you must have sinned. The whole book of Job is crying out against this, and Job knew it was not true. He did not know why he was suffering, but it was not suffering for his sin. Job cries to God for vindication, but God was showing that through Job he had a purpose in allowing someone to suffer innocently. Job was tasting just a little of what Jesus tasted such a lot. When Jesus suffered, people thought he was being smitten by God, cursed as everyone who is hung on a tree. That was their law and they looked at this emaciated form dying on a cross and thought that he must have sinned a great deal.

Did he deserve it? The answer is no, *we* deserved it. Here we have the supreme example of the innocent suffering for the guilty. *He* was pierced for *our* transgressions; *he* was crushed for *our* iniquities . . . . By *his* wounds *we* are healed. You see the 'he', 'our'? That is a remarkable statement. It was necessary because all we like sheep have gone astray. You really have to look after sheep to understand this. I thank God for the little experience I have had as a shepherd. It opens the Bible up to me in so many ways. But you know, sheep are so so stupid!

They scatter, they go in twos and threes, they panic, they go the opposite way to the direction in which the shepherd is trying to get them to go, to help them. All we like sheep . . . . And the Lord has laid on *him* . . . . Like sheep we wander round, sometimes in twos and threes, sometimes on our own. We were all trying our own way to live and there is something in us that just wants to do this. It is the problem with the world. When you boil it all down in simple terms there would be no problems in this world if all of us went the Shepherd's way. It is precisely because every individual, every community, every nation wants to go its own way that we are in the mess we are in — and the Lord took all that and heaped it on this one person. Here we have reached the heart of the cross. It is a substitutionary theory of the atonement (forgive the theological language) and it is amazing what an offence this is to people, even many theologians. Yet here is the stark truth — and until we are prepared to accept this we have not truly understood the cross. If you try and say the cross was an exhibition of love, or if you try and say the cross was an example of being true to your convictions at the cost of martyrdom, or if you try to say that the cross was anything but substitutionary atonement, you have missed the deepest note of the cross. The simple truth is that there was an astonishing replacement. On the cross, Jesus replaces you. That is where the wandering sheep ought to have been, and the great replacement is that, 'bearing shame and scoffing rude, in my place condemned he stood.' You will never get away from that in the cross, though it offends some people's moral and intellectual integrity, they say. George Bernard Shaw was one such man. He said: I just don't believe that a man can pay for another's sins. He said that forgiveness is a beggar's refuge; we must pay our own debts and play the man. It sounds good British stiff upper lip courage but it is tragic. He was another sheep who wanted to go his own way, to be saved his own way even, to get to heaven in his own way. There is only one way, and that is to say: Jesus bore my sorrows, he carried my griefs. I went my own way and the Lord loaded all the results and penalties of guilt and shame on him, and so he died for me.

That then is *The Great Replacement*, but I have not finished. He has replaced me there, and here is the other side of it: he therefore will replace me here. The great exchange — it is not a fair one but it is a most wonderful one — is this: that by his stripes we are healed. The punishment that brought *us* peace. Listen to it: all our iniquity on *him*, all our sorrows on *him*, all *our* sicknesses, *our* sufferings piled on *him*, a man of sorrows and acquainted with grief. And in its place he has piled on us his peace, his shalom, his wholeness, his health. What an exchange! What a replacement! That is the deeper truth of the cross. It is not just that he took your sins on him, it is that he is offering his life to us. It is an exchange, a replacement. So where we ought to be, he is; and where we are, he is — and that is the great replacement seen by Isaiah.

We move to vv. 7–9, the fourth verse in the Hebrew, which I want to call *The Great Restraint*. The first phrase again gives us the theme of this section. He was oppressed and afflicted yet — and here comes the great restraint — he opened not his mouth. That is one of the most remarkable things about the story of the crucifixion — the silence of our Lord Jesus. It impressed Herod, to whom Jesus had absolutely nothing to say. It impressed Pilate. And Jesus remained silent to his question. When you think of the things Jesus might have said! When a man was crucified the only thing he could hit back with was his mouth. And other accounts of crucifixion say that when a man was strung up there, pinned like a butterfly to a board and could do nothing to his tormentors he used to shout and curse and swear and call down blasphemies and obscenities upon the people who were doing it. That was normal. We know from the story of our Lord's crucifixion that the two thieves, both of them, at first cursed and swore. One of them later realised he was wrong to do so. But they did the natural thing, and the sheer agony and torment released a man's mouth when they crucified him, and so he was usually gibbering and cursing until finally he drifted off into madness and uttered things that made no sense. It was the normal reaction to open the mouth. When you consider that Jesus, had he opened his mouth and said certain things, could have got off that cross and could have blasted them into eternity; when you consider that there were twelve legions of angels waiting for his voice; when you consider that a word from the Lord Jesus could still a storm and curse a fig tree; when you consider what he could have done if he had opened his mouth – is it not amazing, the great restraint? Like a sheep before its shearer, he opened not his mouth. From the epistle of James we learn that if you can control your mouth, if you can learn to keep your mouth shut, you are a perfect man. And here was the perfect man – he could control his mouth, so he could control every other part of his body. That is why it says he had done no violence, neither was there any deceit in his mouth. He himself is the truth and therefore he only spoke the truth. When he opened his mouth on the cross you listen to what came out: not one word of condemnation, not one word of cursing, not one word of calling his heavenly Father to punish them for what they did. As a sheep before its shearers, this was the great restraint. It is an aspect of the cross that we often overlook. It was the testimony of the dying thief: this man has done nothing amiss. It was the testimony of Pilate's wife: this is a good man. It was the testimony of the Roman centurion: truly this was the Son of God. They all could see it, and one of the things that convinced them of the truth was that he opened not his mouth and he did not hit back even with one word, yet he was oppressed, afflicted, spat upon, stripped, exposed, mocked and flogged.

Finally, there is *The Great Reward*. We have reached the last verse, and half way through it we switch back to God as the singer – from tragedy to triumph. What is the key phrase? It was the Lord's good plan to bruise him. Who was responsible for the death of Jesus? You could line up a lot of people, you could put them in the dock one by one. You could say Caiaphas and Annas, you were responsible. You could say to the Pharisees, you were; to the Sadducees, you were; Pilate, you were; Herod, you were; the Roman soldiers who nailed him to the cross, you were; his disciples who ran away, you were. So who was responsible? I tell you that in the last analysis you have to say God was. As Peter said on the day of Pentecost: you, with the help of wicked men, put him to death . . . . But God by his determined foreknowledge, by his plan, he delivered him up. There are two ways of looking at the cross. You can either see it as the rejection by the human race of this man of sorrows, the turning away, the wanting rid of him, or you can see it as God's will, God's plan, and you will have to say he has put him to grief, he has done it.

Why would God do such a thing? Why would he cause such innocent suffering? If ever you can ask the question 'Why should the innocent suffer?' it was here. Even Jesus himself asked the question. He opened his mouth once towards God with the question: "My God, my God, why . . . ?" It was God's plan. In the last analysis the suffering servant prospers because God's will shall prosper in his hand. There is only one plan that prospers finally: God's will in the hand of one who is willing to be obedient to that will.

What was God's plan? What is the reward? What is the result coming out of all this? Wonderful things. First of all, what comes out of it for other people and then what will come out of it for the servant himself. First, what comes out of it for other people.

Consider the joy and satisfaction of bringing a baby into the world, as well as the pain. A woman will go through the agony, will sometimes draw near to the valley of death to bring life. But the look on her face when she sees her offspring! It has all been worth it. The joy of bringing life into the world. This is why Jesus went through it. He shall see his offspring and be satisfied. Offspring? Every single day there are thousands of people being born again as the result of this travail of his soul. The word is *labour*, the travail of his soul, for when Jesus was going through that six hours of agony he was bringing people to birth. He was prepared to go through with it because so many would find life.

How can Jesus see his offspring? He was raised from the dead and so he sees his offspring born — new spiritual babies born, new lives come into the world, and he will be satisfied, and every bit of the agony was worth it. To put it another way, every person who is justified becomes one of his offspring, accounted righteous — through the death of Jesus Christ we are counted righteous in God's sight. We are counted as among the good people, not because we are good but because Jesus died to make us good and that we might be forgiven. Once again there is a wonderful replacement. He was counted a transgressor that many might be counted righteous. Do you see the exchange? Again he takes our place and we take his and we become a shoot out of a dry ground, a plant out of a desert world, and that pleases God. So he sees the travail of his soul and is satisfied.

What is there for him in this? Back to God in the last part of this stanza. *Therefore I will give him a portion among the great, and he will divide the spoils with the strong*. In Hebrew language God is saying he is the greatest. Kings and nations shall be startled when they see him highly exalted. Why should God do this? Because his servant was willing to go to the limit of obedience. He poured out his soul to death. Because he was prepared to go to the limit of humiliation he was counted a transgressor. Because he was prepared to go to the limit of sacrifice he bore the sin of many. Because he was prepared to go to the limit of love he made intercession for the transgressor. He went to the limit in every way you can imagine. From the human point of view the cross was a tragedy, but from God's point of view it was a triumph.

This chapter is in a sense a miracle in words. It has the stamp of God on it. That all this should be written 750 years before it happened, even including that astonishing verse — *He was assigned a grave with the wicked* [and wicked is plural there] *and with the rich* [singular] *in his death* . . . . Normally, the crucified were thrown into a common grave for criminals. That is what they appointed for him. How then did a rich man ever get involved? Joseph of Arimathea is talked about 750 years before he did what he did. So great a miracle of words does this chapter contain that people have said: 'Oh, it must have been written after the event; It has been changed to fit the facts; it has been subtly altered so that now it reads like a prediction.' They said that until 1948. Nobody says it any more. Do you know why? Because you can go to the shrine of the scroll in West Jerusalem and you can look at a total copy of the scroll of Isaiah dated 100 BC, a century before the cross, and you can see there before your eyes a copy of Isaiah 53, and you can read these words there. God predicted.

There is something even more wonderful. Who wrote these words about Jesus? Jesus himself wrote them. For 1 Peter 1:10 says that the Spirit of Christ was in the prophets testifying beforehand of his sufferings and the glory that should follow them. What does that refer to? It refers to many passages, but supremely to Isaiah 53. And after his resurrection, Jesus came back to his disciples and showed them everything in the law and the psalms and the prophets that was written about him. He had written it about himself. For this suffering servant who has no name in Isaiah, and who did not have the name Jesus at that stage, was the eternal Son of God whose Spirit inspired prophets to know and write about his death and resurrection.

The biggest miracle of words in this chapter is that I find I am included. Nearly 3,000 years ago I was predicted. For there am I: 'He was wounded for our transgressions' —and that includes me, and it could include you and it could include everybody if they will believe our report. If they hear and believe this report of this event — the Son of God dying on the cross for our sins — then the arm of the Lord will be revealed in their life. The power of God to save will be revealed, and they can remember the man who died for another — the Son of God who died for all. If you do not yet know Jesus as Saviour then consider that we have just studied a word of God written 3,000 years ago about you. You turn to your own way like a sheep. And all the results and penalty of that God laid on him. If you believe, tell him so. Say to him: I believe that preacher's report, now lay bare your arm. Show me that you can include me. If you have already known this, and all this refers to you, then when you read this chapter you will say 'Hallelujah, that's me, that *our* includes me,' then celebrate. Let your soul praise the Lord!

24

WHILE HE MAY BE FOUND

Read Isaiah 54–55

A. DESERTED WOMAN (54)
1. HER CHILDREN (1-3)
a. Increase (1-2) b. Influence (3)
2. HER HUSBAND (4-10)
a. Love (4-8) b. Loyalty (9-10)
3. HER HOME (11-17)
a. Prosperity (11-13) b. Protection (14-17)
B. DISSATISFIED MAN (55)
1. HIS BUSINESS (1-5)
a. Commerce (1-3a) b. Command (3b-5)
2. HIS RELIGION (6-11)
a. Repentance (6-9) b. Revelation (10-11)
3. HIS GARDEN (12-13)
a. Song (12) b. Sign (13)

Chapters 54 and 55 belong together and they both follow chapter 53. That all sounds a bit obvious but let me tell you what I mean. Chapter 53, which is the climax of this book, is all about the cross, and our Lord dying for our sins. Everything that follows in the whole of the prophecy of Isaiah depends on this. The rest of this book (54–66) is full of promises. But we must not pick them out of their chapters, for very often the verse in front and the verse after tells us what the promise really means. When Christ died he became the 'yea and amen' of all God's promises. All the rich truths that we shall now study are dependent on the cross. It is only because he was wounded for our transgressions that all these wonderful things come true. That is why the first word in chapter 54 is *'Sing'*. You can only really sing after you are the right side of the cross, and a person can only really sing the praises of God when they know that God laid on Christ their iniquities. So the chapter flows from chapter 53.

The linked chapters 54 and 55 are addressed to Israel, and chapter 54 treats Israel as if she were a deserted woman, but chapter 55 is addressed to a man. So ladies tend to understand chapter 54 best and the men will understand chapter 55, but I think we can all get quite a lot from both.

The woman of chapter 54 has no children, no husband, no home, though she once had all three. This is a vivid and compelling picture of the city of Jerusalem as it was when Isaiah was saying all this. It is a compelling picture of the ruined capital of the Jews when the people were away in Babylon as slaves in exile. Jerusalem looked like a woman who had been robbed of her children, her husband and her lovely home in which to live, and these are the three things for which a woman would live. Of course, in our society there are many other openings and callings for women, but in the Middle East and in those days there was only one opening and that was to get married, have a home and look after children. The only things that would make a woman sing would be to have plenty of children, to have a good husband and to be able to create a home for them. Isaiah the prophet — taking up these three desires of a woman, and particularly a woman who has been deserted and lost these things — indicates that these are going to be restored by God.

Take the first. Most women want children, and, for many, the larger the family the better. It was the desire of Israel to have many children, that she might grow and become a large family in the earth. But here is Jerusalem, deserted, empty, burnt to the ground, with no-one living there. As a woman who has been robbed of her children, she is frustrated and unhappy. But the message is: *Sing, O barren woman . . . .* She was going to have a great big family and lots and lots of children, so had better start building on some spare bedrooms! Of course, living in tents you do not build a spare bedroom over the garage, you simply sew another sheet on the end and lengthen your cords and strengthen your stakes. Indeed, living in tents is very much more adaptable to a growing family than living in houses made of bricks and cement. So in those days all they would do would be to add a bit on to the tent at the end, and in picturesque language, which they would clearly understand, he says, now you get a few spare bedrooms on that tent of yours, lengthen your cord, strengthen your stakes, get a bigger tent. Your family is going to increase and you are going to have lots of children running around. And that is precisely how they got ready for more children. William Carey, of course, made that verse famous when he started the Baptist Missionary Society so many years ago. He used this phrase about lengthening cords and strengthening stakes to encourage the church to believe it would have many more children, and to extend its vision to a bigger family that would include people overseas, so he used these words to the church — but the prophet is speaking to Israel.

A mother may also want to see her children grow up and go out into the world and influence it. Many a mother has told me proudly something like this: 'I have got one son teaching physics away up in Leeds University; I have another son who is a doctor down in the West Country . . .' and she proudly tells me how the children she brought up have spread out into the world and are now influencing and serving the human race. A sense of this comes out in v. 3. Not only is Israel going to have more children after the exile than she had before (the desolate one will have more children than the married one), she is going to see them spread to the right and to the left, or literally from the Middle East to the east and to the west, until they influence nations and possess desolate cities. One of the things I have predicted is that we shall see a continued expansion of God's people, for they have been given this task of spreading and influencing and leading the world.

One final thing about the first three verses: notice the word *barren*. Have you ever studied that word in scripture? Some people ask me: what are all the chapters about with all the *begat*s in? What possible use is it to us to know that so and so begat so and so? The interesting thing is that such passages usually come to a full stop with the word *barren*. Study Genesis 11 for example. It is all *begat*s until you get to Sarah and just there the thing stopped, for Sarah was barren and it looked as if it all came to a full stop. But when things come to a stop humanly speaking, divinely speaking they have just started —and Sarah had a child. Then that child Isaac married Rebekah and she was barren. All her sisters had children, but she did not. Just when things seemed to stop, God stepped in and Jacob was born, and Jacob married Rachel, and though Rachel's sisters had children, Rachel was barren. You notice how God steps in at this word *barren* and says that is not the end of the story. Samuel's mother was barren, John the Baptist's mother was barren — God steps in and the *begat*s start again! So we have a miraculous intervention here. The woman is Jerusalem, she has no children and, secondly, she has no husband. There was a time when God was her husband, but he left her; he was angry with her and he deserted and forsook her, and this happened to the bride which was the holy city of Jerusalem. She felt: God my husband has left me and he will never come back. I have not only lost my children I have lost my husband. She felt desolate and forsaken.

So we move to vv. 4–10, which begin with those wonderful words *Fear not*. In a Bible study group out in Aden with the RAF boys, I said to them, 'Go away and study your Bibles this week and find out how many times the Bible tells you not to be afraid. You take the book of Genesis; you take Exodus,' and so on, and I dished them all out a few books to read. They went away and they came back, and they discovered what others have discovered, that there are 366 occasions in the Bible when you are told 'fear not'. One for every day of the year and one for leap year for good measure! And to this woman who thinks that her life stretches before her as a lonely and desolate experience, the message is: Don't be afraid, your husband has not left you permanently, he will come back. God is your husband, the God of the whole earth he is called, and he has only forsaken you for a moment. He is angry with you, and he has every right to be, but he is coming back to you. He has not divorced you. That of course was said earlier in chapter 50: *This is what the* L*ORD says: "Where is your mother's certificate of divorce with which I sent her away? . . ."* (Isaiah 50:1, NIV). In other words, I have not divorced you, but I was angry and I left you for a time, but it is only for a moment.

The two things that every woman wants in a husband, and which she has a right to have, are love and loyalty. In the Hebrew language those two things are expressed in only one word, *chesed*, a lovely word. We have no English word that covers both meanings. Our English word 'love' is often so debased that it does not carry anything of loyalty in it. But the Hebrew word means loyal love, a love that never lets anybody go. Do you know why we use a ring in marriage? It used to be believed that a nerve ran from that finger up the arm to the human heart and that when you put a ring round that finger you were surrounding the heart nerve with something that has no end — in other words with a loyal love that would never let someone down: for better, for worse; for richer, for poorer; in sickness and in health. Of course there is one thing that breaks that human relationship, namely death. But God's love is not like that. He does not say 'till death us do part'. He says here *'You will forget the shame of your youth'* — that was their bondage in Egypt — and *'. . . remember no more the reproach of your widowhood'* — that was their bondage in Babylon. The husband would come back with deep compassion. There is a contrast in v. 8 between the wrath he had for a moment and the everlasting kindness that will come back. God may be angry with his people for a time, but it is always temporary. He is not angry with us forever, says the psalmist. His everlasting love will replace his anger. The history of the Jews is the history of God's everlasting love coming back and claiming them for his own.

Not only will there be love, there will be loyalty. Whenever you see a rainbow your thoughts no doubt as a Christian will go back to Genesis and the days of Noah. The rainbow is God's 'wedding ring' with the human race — the covenant 'ring' with which he encircled the earth when he promised to Noah that he would never again destroy the human race in that way, and it is a promise he has kept. Israel reminds him of his days with Noah. Just as he promised him he would never destroy society again in that way, he promises them that he would never rebuke them; he would never wipe them out. The only explanation we can possibly find for the survival of the Jews is of course that promise of God, the covenant he made. A Russian philosopher called Berdyaev and the German philosopher Hegel both tried to explain history in philosophical terms. They both reckoned they could explain everything bar one. The only event in history which neither of them could fit in to a deterministic philosophy of history was the survival of the Jews. So we have God's steadfast love in v. 10. The mountains may depart and the hills be removed, and that would be a catastrophic disturbance. Even if it happened, God's love would be steadfast ('unfailing', NIV). Steadfast love there translates only this one Hebrew word *chesed* which means a love that never lets someone down, never lets them go, a love that is absolutely loyal. In these days we need to remind people that true love is loyal. Whatever happens, whatever the other person does, such love goes on. It is so easy to make promises in a wedding service. I shrink inside when I hear a starry-eyed couple making such solemn vows: 'till death us do part' — do they know what that means? You hear them say 'for richer for poorer, in sickness and in health', and then you read 1 Corinthians 13: *Love is patient, love is kind. It does not envy, it does not boast, it is not proud. It is not rude, it is not self-seeking, it is not easily angered, it keeps no record of wrongs* (1 Corinthians 13:4–5, NIV). That is not sexual love there, it is not human affection described there, it is steadfast love, and unless a couple find the steadfast love of God they will not be able to keep those vows in spirit as well as in letter, with a loyalty that comes from the love of God.

This deserted woman called 'Jerusalem' has lost her children but she is going to have a big family, and she is told to get ready for them. She has lost her husband but he is coming back again and will be loyal to her. He has not let her go; he was only angry with her for a time. She has lost her home, but she is going to get it back again. One desire of a woman, I think, is to make and furnish a home, creating an attractive, beautiful place where she and her family can live. Here we have this instinct ascribed to the nation of Israel. She wanted somewhere to live that would be attractive and secure, and God is saying to Israel, this desolate woman, that he will see that she gets that. Jerusalem will be rebuilt, and the rebuilt city will be far more beautiful and attractive than anything before. Precious stones would be used in its construction. Of course that has not become literally true yet. Jerusalem was rebuilt, but of ordinary stone, limestone from the hills of Judea, so some people have asked whether God will keep his promise. The answer is that he will. He is not referring to the old Jerusalem, he is referring to a new one. He is not referring to the one *they* are going to build. What people could afford to build a city of sapphire? Only God is wealthy enough to do that. The last book in the Bible describes the city of God, the new Jerusalem, coming down out of heaven, a city whose builder and maker is God, not a city that men build up, but a city which God builds down, as it were. He is creating a new Jerusalem for his people to dwell in and one day we shall live in a most wonderful city. There is no reason why you should not take those stones literally, is there? God creates precious stones; he created them rare down here, but is there any reason why he should not create them by the ton, and build a city incorporating them? The glory of that city is so wonderful to think of when you read of it in Revelation.

Not only will this city be the most beautiful and attractive home for God's people, it will be absolutely secure. They will enjoy his protection as well as his prosperity. This is something that the Jews have already begun to find and which God's people in the church have already begun to find, but which will of course be experienced ultimately, when we get to the new Jerusalem. But it is already true now, and the truth is this: *"If anyone does attack you, it will not be my doing; whoever attacks you will surrender to you"* (Isaiah 54:15, NIV). It is strange that people do not learn this lesson that if you attack the people of God you fall because of them. No dictator, no nation has got away with an attack on the people of God, and they fall because of them. From the second part of the twentieth-century we have seen several concerted attacks upon the Jews, and this verse is still relevant.

Why will their attackers fall? The answer is very simple. God is their protector (and a husband is a protector, which is why, historically, a wife walks on the left arm of the husband so that his right arm might be free to use his sword or fist to protect her); he is a husband of Israel and his right arm is laid bare whenever she is attacked. There is no need for God's people to be afraid of the weapons others deploy, because he made those who made them (the 'blacksmith' or arms manufacturer). Moreover, he made the man who wields the weaponry. Here is very simple down-to-earth language. No weapon forged against God's people will prevail. God has shown this right through the centuries. The ultimate weapon of 3,000 years ago was not the nuclear bomb but the iron chariot, which was invincible. If you did not have chariots you did not stand a chance against them. Israel had no chariots and Sisera had come against her with chariots. Humanly speaking, anybody would have said: I know which one will win, Israel's enemy has far superior weapons and numbers. But God is the God who made Sisera and the chariots, and therefore Sisera lost. I have stood on the top of Mount Tabor looking down over the plain below, and listened while a young Jewish boy told me how Sisera was defeated down in that valley. A most vivid description, and he spoke as if he had watched it yesterday. The protection of God is there and this is the heritage of the servants of the Lord, and their vindication.

Chapter 55 is addressed to the men. Three things that a man is concerned about are mentioned here: his business, his religion and his garden. I begin by painting the background to all this. God's ancient people gained a tremendous reputation for being gifted in business, for trading. This was learnt when they went to Babylon, situated as it was at a strategic point in the then known world —at the meeting point of east and west. So of course there was opportunity to trade, and Babylon was the centre of commerce and prosperity. The Jews were taken in exile across the desert to Babylon, and there they began to learn to make money and many became traders. This chapter was written to tell the Jews that this was not their calling, not why God gave them their gifts, which were to be used for something else. In fact, making money does not make a person content. I have met so many people now who have proved by their lives that this is the case. They are left thirsty and hungry, so they think they will be satisfied by making even more money, extending the business even further. But this does not satisfy and it never will.

So the first part of this chapter is relevant to those whose interest has become their business. It is an invitation: you are still thirsty, you are still unsatisfied, you are still not content. In all the money making and trading, you still do not have that which really satisfies. Why do you spend your money for that which is not bread and your labour for that which does not satisfy? Why are you living for something that can never fill the aching void inside your heart? Come and buy something without money. Here is a wonderful proposition: something free, something being given away. Of course, if you offer something free people always suspect and say there must be a catch. You do not give away something like that free, you charge for it and you make money on it! Here, to these Jews in exile, God is inviting thirsty people: all your trading has not satisfied you; come and drink — not just water but wine and milk. And don't bring your cash, it is free! It is a wonderful invitation to those who are unsatisfied with money. Here is the richest of food for the soul.

The alternative is this: the true 'business' of Israel was not to make money but to lead the nations of the world to God, to be a leader, a commander, a witness to the peoples of the earth. Those gifts which they have demonstrated so wonderfully in making money were given by God to lead the nations to God. Their gifts for exploiting an opportunity, for planning ahead, perseverance, for being at the right place in the right time, are gifts God gave them to be witnesses and it is a prostitution of those gifts to turn them all into business and money making. So God's message means: If you listen to me and come back to me I'll put you in a different kind of business. What David was to you, you will be to the world. What was David to you? He was your leader. He was your witness to God. Peoples you never knew will come running to you and say we want to know you — not because you are a money maker but because you know God, because you have something they haven't. People who did not know you will run to you because of the Lord your God. You will be able to help them and tell them.

It is the tragedy of history that Israel used her gifts in commerce rather than to command the nations. I have the feeling she is beginning to recover her vision, her destiny, and the way some Jews are talking today they are beginning to realise that Israel's role in the world is a spiritual one, a role of leadership, a role of command, a role of witness. What David was to the nation the nation is to be to the world. *"See, I have made him a witness to the peoples . . . ."*

God is talking to Israel now as a man, and the next thing a

man is interested in is of course his religion. Men do not usually like church but they are religious. So often they develop their own religious societies and ceremonies. Deep down, men want a faith by which to live, they want to know the truth; they want what God has to offer them. I really believe this. I proved it in the armed forces. At first I wondered what it would be like to have an entirely male congregation, and there are many men who are very shy of organized religion, but I discovered that deep down they want the truth about how they can believe in God.

What is the secret of true religion? It is two-fold. First, you will never get anywhere until you repent. That is the hardest thing for a man to do. It is much easier for him to 'support' religion, to patronise it with his money and his time, than to come and acknowledge that his ways and thoughts are sinful and that he needs to repent and seek the Lord. You will never come to realise that your ways and your thoughts are wrong until you measure yourself by the right standard. As long as you measure yourself by someone else, you think that you are all right. But that is the wrong standard. The standard is God's ways and thoughts, which are that much higher than ours. God's ways and thoughts are perfectly clean, honest and upright. A man needs to measure his standards by God's standards, not what others think, say and do. We need to know that it is by God's standards, which are so much higher than man's, that we will be judged, not by man's standards. When we stand before God it will not be according to our own ideas or other people's that our lives will be measured but by God's ways and thoughts.

So a man needs to to repent. We ask: when, how and why is he to do so? First, when should a man repent? The answer is: while the Lord is near. Sometimes we are so busy getting and spending, laying waste our powers, that God seems far away. But there come moments — it may be a bereavement, it may be a sudden disaster, it may be the sound of a hymn coming out of a church door — when there is a sense that God is near. Billy Graham was perfectly right at the end of his sermons to say you may never have an opportunity like this. God may be nearer to you now than he has ever been before. Suddenly something confronts a man with God. It may be some danger, some great difficulty, some huge responsibility; God is near, he should seek the Lord then. When death comes, God departs from a man's life forever. A great gulf is fixed at death between a man and God if he has not found him first. Seek the Lord while he may be found.

How should he seek him? The answer is by turning away from what he is and turning to God. Let him forsake his evil ways and his unrighteous thoughts — turn his back on those and turn his face to God and say: God, I am finished with that. That is repentance. Repentance is not being sorry but it includes being sorry enough to stop! It is something you do, not something you feel. True repentance is saying I forsake my evil ways and my unrighteous thoughts, I stop them and I turn to God and I seek him.

Why repent? The answer is that he may have mercy upon you. God's mercy can only come to the penitent, that is why. People who think that God's mercy is for all are mistaken — it is for those who repent. So let him return to the Lord that he may have mercy on him, and that he may abundantly pardon. God's forgiveness just waits for the penitent.

Man also needs to know that true religion is based first on repentance on his side and, second, on revelation on God's side. He needs to know the truth. Where will he get it? From other men? No. From his own head? No. The answer is that there is a parallel between God's word and the rain and the snow. Like the rain and the snow, God's revelation, God's word, God's spoken thoughts, have come down from heaven to earth. Truth starts in heaven, comes down and affects the earth and it changes it. It produces something in the earth. It produces seed for the sower and bread for the eater. That is a business proposition and it is in business language. What is a businessman interested in? His returns, and what will prosper. He will close down an aspect of his business that has no return and no prosperity in it. Here is the proposition to these business Jews of Babylon.

The best business to be in is the word of God. I am in that business and it is a most prosperous business. The word of God does not return empty, you get good returns from the word of God! One afternoon I was with Gideons International. They are a group of businessmen who have been persuaded to part with thousands of pounds of money, and apparently with no return financially. It is a most extraordinary phenomenon. Here they are pouring their money into what some would say was a business flop. Do you know why they do it? They do it because of Isaiah 55:11, which assures them as businessmen that they are putting their money into something good. It assures them that God's word has a return and that it is the best business to be in. So thousands of businessmen all over the world are in Gideons International pouring their money into what does not bring them back a penny in cash, but they are putting it in because they believe the word of God prospers and does not return empty, it comes back with interest and the investment is worthwhile. They have hundreds of stories to tell them that in prisons, hotels, hospitals and all over the place, the word of God has returned with interest, saving lives forever — so they pour their money into it. This is true prosperity. I believe that when I preach it accomplishes what God means it to accomplish and it does not come back empty. No real sermon on the word of God comes back empty. It changes lives, it plants new thoughts, seeds are sown in the heart, and it feeds hungry souls.

Finally, when a man comes home from work, he may be interested in his garden. All of us have a touch of the gardener in us, and in fact we were made to be gardeners. Adam was a gardener — 'and God who made him sees that every proper gardener's work is done upon his knees', and he is going to put us in a 'garden city' one day. Gardening — study that in the Bible. Nature around us is man's garden, and when man responds to the call of God he goes out in such joy and peace that the garden sings. *The mountains and hills will burst into song* .... When you are right with God, you appreciate nature and the workplace does not confine your thoughts.

In vv. 12b–13, we learn that one day nature itself will be completely renewed. We are already beginning to see a bit of that in the Middle East, but this is really referring to the day when the whole creation, which is groaning and travailing, waiting for the revealing of the sons of God nature itself will be restored from a wilderness to a garden. One day, God will restore his garden. At the moment he allows us to, but one day he will. This refers to the day when he will transform nature —and those thorns and thistles which came in with man's curse in Genesis 3 will go out with man's blessing, and when there will be a new heaven and a new earth and a new garden, and we will be interested in God's garden. In *that* garden we shall be 'nearer God's heart than anywhere else on earth.'

25

NO PEACE FOR THE WICKED

Read Isaiah 56 – 57

A. ACTIONS (56)
1. RIGHTEOUS (1-2)
a. Blameless b. Blessed
2. IMPOTENT (3-5)
a. Emasculated b. Eminent
3. ALIEN (6-8)
a. Interested b. Integrated
4. WICKED (9-12)
a. Dumb b. Drunk
B. ATTITUDES (57)
1. RIGHTEOUS (1-2)
a. Perishing b. Peaceful
2. IMMORAL (3-13a)
a. Lustful b. Lying
3. ASHAMED (13b-19)
a. Humbled b. Healed
4. WICKED (20-21)
a. Tossed b. Tormented

With chapter 56 we enter a new section. The first was 1–39, the second 40 – 55 and the third is 56 – 66. There is such a definite contrast and difference between these three portions that some, I believe mistakenly, have thought that three different people must have written the three parts. But others, equally scholarly and understanding, are quite sure that one man wrote them all. The differences are largely explained by the fact that they are about different things, and you write differently about different subjects.

Very briefly, chapters 1–39 are addressed to the nation of Israel *before* they went off into Babylon as prisoners. It was a warning that they would be taken off unless they put right their wrong and evil ways. Chapters 40–55, as we have seen, were in fact addressed to the nation of Israel *during* the time they were prisoners in Babylon. And all the geography and the language presupposes that they are in Babylon, that flat country and that trading city. But when you move from chapter 55 to the last section you realise that the latter is addressed to Israel *after* their imprisonment in Babylon, and is almost entirely concerned with getting back to the land and how they are to behave when they get there.

So we are on the last lap. Sigh of relief! We have been a long time in this wonderful prophecy, and it is heavy going, especially if you have not done much Bible study before. Nevertheless, we are going to see it through to the end and before too long we shall reach the grand climax in chapter 66. We will be looking at the counsel, the wisdom, that God expressed for his people, to get them back into their own land and to enable them to behave properly when there.

Just look back at 55:12 for a moment. We notice the promise that they would go back. Mountains, hills and trees of the field are mentioned, and the scene is not Babylon but that of the first sight of the promised land as they return. So from now on they are within sight of their land: you are going out in joy and peace and there before you are the hills of the promised land and the trees that you left behind. What a relief to leave behind the flat, barren area of Mesopotamia and see again the trees and the hills. But the great question before us now, which 56 — 57 answer, is this: who will go back? Will everybody go back? Is there any qualification needed for those who return to the land of God's promise and blessing? Yes, there is. Go back again to 55:7, *Let the wicked forsake his way and the evil man his thoughts. Let him turn to the LORD, and he will have mercy on him, and to our God, for he will freely pardon* (NIV). In other words, before they return to Israel they must return to God. That is the condition or qualification for getting back. If they want to live where God blesses them and protects them and where they enjoy peace and prosperity, then they must first live in God. Here is the profound lesson that I want to underline. If you are going to live in God's blessing you need first to live in God. If you are going to know a place of God's peace and protection, then first you need to know God. This is the moral qualification for enjoying God's blessing and peace, signified in the Old Testament by the land of promise; and, for us, involving the work of the promised Holy Spirit. If we are going to enjoy blessings from the Holy Spirit then we must return to God. If you have lost the joy and the peace of your salvation, if you have lost the close walk with God you once had, you cannot go straight back to that, you must first return to God then you can return. This is the qualification.

That raises a question: what are wicked ways and what are unrighteous thoughts that you have to leave behind as you return to God? Chapter 56 defines wicked ways; chapter 57 defines unrighteous thoughts. Chapter 56 is largely concerned with our actions, our ways; chapter 57 is concerned with our attitudes and thoughts. So if you want to know what 55:7 means (*Let the wicked forsake his way and the evil man his thoughts*), then you must read 56 – 57. I could have called chapter 56 'Ways', and 57 'Thoughts'. Here we have clearly portrayed for us the kind of thing that prevents us from enjoying God's blessing and getting back to him, and which we have to leave behind.

So we turn to chapter 56. The first verse is full of big words, words that are so big you can hardly begin to define them. Words like justice, righteousness, salvation, deliverance — four great big words that I could not possibly begin to look at now; you need to know your whole Bible to understand what they mean. But, in brief, the first two words are what God demands from us, and the second two words are what he does for us. He demands from us justice and righteousness and he gives to us salvation and deliverance. These are the two sides of biblical teaching. Justice means being fair. Righteousness can be simply understood by crossing out the middle three letters:

it is rightness — being upright, if you like. God demands of his people that they be fair and straight. But he also gives to his people salvation, which is the same as our word 'salvage', which means taking something that is perishing and useless and making something worthwhile of it — to save. And deliverance means setting free. Here we have the two sides and God emphasises them because his morals are related to his miracles. God performs miracles when the morals of the situation are right. You cannot divorce his wonderful miracles from his wonderful morals. That is why he links his deliverance with their justice and uprightness. God is not a God who performs miracles just anyhow, he performs miracles in accordance with moral principles and the two are related. Therefore he says: on your side if you are going to enjoy my blessing and going to get back to the promised land you must keep (and that is a strong word and it occurs three times in the first two verses, meaning not just once in a while when you feel like it but all the time) — justice. You must keep yourselves from any evil, you must keep the Sabbath and you must do continually what is right. That is the blameless life which God demanded of people. The blameless life will be the blessed life. Blessed is the man who does this and who keeps this. These are the two sides of what is meant by a righteous person. A righteous man is a man who is blameless before God and therefore blessed by him. He keeps what is right and therefore he is blessed. If you want to live in joy and peace in the land of blessing and promise, then these two things are needed: blamelessness on your side and blessing on God's, and the two are linked. A righteous man is one who keeps what is right and fair and is therefore blessed by God in the doing of it. That is one of the Old Testament beatitudes. Blessed is the man who does this.

At this point we raise two questions which were being hotly debated among the Jews in exile. Who would get back to the land of promise? God told them: whoever keeps my covenant and Sabbath and keeps away from evil. But there were two special groups about whom the Jews were very divided in discussion as to whether they could go back or not. The first were the group called the eunuchs. Who are these and what was the problem?

Well, in the ancient world when people were taken away as captives, to prevent those people multiplying and therefore dominating the country in which they were prisoners, certain drastic and cruel measures were taken. Sometimes the male children were all destroyed, as Pharaoh tried to do in the days of Moses. But more frequently the cruel and awful mutilation of robbing the men of their powers of sexual reproduction was followed. In other words, they were made eunuchs by a simple operation on their body and they were emasculated. Many of the leading men of Israel were made eunuchs in Babylon. There is indication in scripture that both Daniel and Nehemiah may have been deprived of the power to have children when they were taken captive. You have to read between the lines and you have to read the Hebrew, but the hint is very definitely there. Here is the problem. In the Old Testament there is a law (Deuteronomy 23:1) which stated that a man who had lost his sexual powers was not allowed within the tabernacle of worship—was not allowed to attend the services. Israel in Babylon had a lot of leading men who were now eunuchs and by their own law they were forbidden to approach the house of God. Could they therefore go back from Babylon to Israel? There was a great debate going on as to whether they could. God says, I will tell you what my answer is. I look at a eunuch and I do not look at his physical condition, I look at his moral condition, and if he keeps my covenant and observes my Sabbath and does what pleases me, then he can come back to my house. There is no reason why he should not. So all your discussion about eunuchs is a waste of time, they can come back. The one condition for living in my land of blessing is that they keep my covenant. Furthermore, says God, because this has happened to them as my people I will give them something even better than sons and daughters. They will have a monument in my house so that their name will be remembered, not because they have had children but because they will be remembered for themselves. And of course the names of Daniel and Nehemiah are still 'monuments' before God, eunuchs and yet there they were, people of God. That is God's reward, in a sense, for their suffering.

The second group of people about which there was a lot of discussion was a group of Gentiles. They did not belong to the people of God at all. When the Jews went to Babylon they took their faith with them. They could not take their temple, they could not take the sacrifice, but they did take the word of God, they did take their faith in the Creator, they did take their prayers and their praises and their psalms, and they sang the songs of Zion in a strange land. Their religion made a profound impression on Babylon which was full of all kinds of pagan superstition. The religion of the Jews was such an impressive, pure religion, and it began to have an effect. Other people began to say do you mind if we slip in at the back of your services and just observe the worship? They said: no, you come in. After a bit these people at the back began to join in. This happens wherever people worship God. You get people coming along who are impressed with the faith of God's people and after a bit they find themselves joining in the worship and beginning to tag along. Then from time to time a person will say: Look I accept your faith, I believe in your God and I want to be part of you — and they are welcomed into the fellowship. Therefore, a number of pagan people (Babylonians, Gentiles) had been coming along to their worship because they were interested in the God of the Jews and had become committed to this faith and had accepted the Jewish God and believed in the Creator. So the question arose when the Jews went back to their own land: what was to happen to these Gentiles, Babylonians who joined in their faith?

The Jews were tempted to say you will not be able to come with us because the promised land is for Israel. You can go on worshipping our God but you will have to stay here. Now look at 56:3, *'Let no foreigner who has bound himself to the* LORD *say, "The* LORD *will surely exclude me from his people."'* (NIV). In other words, when God told the Jews that he was going to take them back to their own land, these Gentile worshippers in their synagogues thought they were going to be cut off from God's people, but they were not to be left behind. And from verses 6–8 we have a most wonderful promise of God: that the temple, when it was rebuilt, would have a place in it for Gentiles. From now on the temple was not to be solely the Jewish place of worship but a house of prayer for people of all nations who believed in the same God, and this is when it started. By the time Jesus came, the temple was being rebuilt by Herod on the pattern of Nehemiah's temple and the biggest court of all was deliberately called the court of the Gentiles. It was there so that Gentiles could come and pray in Jerusalem. But the Jewish traders had filled this outer court of the Gentiles with market stalls, selling animals, doves, sparrows, all sorts of things, for sacrifice. The place had become a noisy market place in which you could not possibly pray. You could not get a minute's quiet there. It was that court that Jesus cleansed. He was so angry that they had made it impossible for Gentiles to come and pray to the God of the Jews by turning that outer court, which was meant to be a house of prayer for all nations, into a den of robbers. When he cleansed that place, Jesus quoted Isaiah 56. We see once again that God will treat everybody on the same basis. It does not matter whether you are a eunuch or a Gentile or a Jew if you keep God's covenant. That brings you into blessing and promise. That entitles you to live in his house. God is no respecter of persons. He looks at moral qualities – he looks for righteousness, and it is on that basis that he accepts or rejects.

Finishing the chapter in a kind of reverse argument, the prophet shows that the Jewish leaders themselves might not get back. So here is the other side of the coin: someone who was not a Jew could come with righteousness, and someone who was a Jew might be debarred because they lacked it. He now finishes with a description of the wickedness of the Jewish leaders. Of course there were two kinds of leader. There were first of all the prophets whose job it was to speak to the people on behalf of God; and there were the priests, whose job it was to speak to God on behalf of the people. This kept the two-way communication between Israel and Jehovah. The prophets were therefore the watchmen of Israel. It was their job to tell Israel when there was danger coming, when there was sin, when things were going wrong. And the priests were the shepherds of Israel. It was their job to look after the flock. You could say they were the 'watchdogs'. That is what the prophet suggests. They should bark when there is something coming. But he says of the prophets: the watchmen are blind, they are all without knowledge. They do not speak when they should. They seem blind to the sins of the people. Dreaming, lying down, loving to slumber, they have a big appetite. They were no use at all so they were disqualified from going back. Furthermore, the priests, because they had no temple or sacrifice, had forgotten that they still had a job to do. But they were not shepherds. They were too busy having a good time themselves, getting drunk every day. I am afraid this was historically true. The prophet is saying that eunuchs and Gentiles will get in and prophets and priests will be kept out. That is because God demands righteous actions, and since he does not get that from the latter they cannot come, and since he does get that from the eunuchs they can return. Jesus was teaching the same thing when he said to the religious leaders of his day that tax collectors and prostitutes get into the kingdom before them. So God does not look at your physical condition, he does not look at your heredity; he does not look at your religious office, he looks at your life and says: is this a person who keeps my covenant? And of course in the exile the one part of the covenant which distinguished God's people from everyone else was the keeping of the Sabbath. It made them different from every Babylonian. Therefore God singles this out for the Jews when they are away from their own land. He says that if a righteous man keeps the Sabbath he can come into his promised blessing. If a eunuch keeps the Sabbath he can come. If a Gentile keeps the Sabbath he can come. But the prophet and priest cannot come because it is the difference between the righteous and the wicked that decides whether they come.

Now we turn to chapter 57, which moves from actions to attitudes. Let me say straight away there is a bit of a problem with this chapter, which you will find mentioned in some books. The things described there are not things that Israel did in Babylon, but things they did before they went. So some have thought that chapters were misplaced. It sounds as if the prophet is talking to the people as if they had never been in exile. But there is a very simple explanation for this which I hope will commend itself to you.

They are now going back to their land and God is warning them to remember what they did in the land that caused them to leave, and they are warned against going back to that. There were certain temptations they had there that they did not have in Babylon, and God is reminding them of what happened long before they left, probably in the days of Manasseh, many years before the exile. I mention that in case you get mixed up with all the dating of this.

The first surprising thing is this: God reminds them that at that time all the good people were dying off young. What would you feel if that happened in your town? Just assume for the moment that you read every week in the local paper that somebody else, a good Christian, had died, and that this began to be out of all proportion, and the churches began to empty and all the righteous people were being carried off in death. Would you think about that? Would you wonder why you were being left if all the good people were dying? The Bible does say that a time is coming when this will happen, and the reactions to it will be very interesting. There will be a time, according to Jesus, when there will be two women grinding with a hand mill, and one will be taken and the other left. There will be two men working in the field — one will be taken and the other left. This was happening in Israel before the exile. The good people, the righteous people, were dying off young and they were going off one by one and no-one noticed, no-one understood what was happening. No-one said, why is it do you suppose that all the good people are dying off? Have you noticed? There's Mr so and so. He went off last week quite suddenly. And Mrs so and so. They died and no-one noticed, no-one understood what was happening. What was happening was this: God was taking the righteous people out of the nation to be with himself in peace before he took it off into exile. That is an extraordinary thing, but it was happening, and God says: *The righteous perish, and no-one ponders it in his heart*. No-one said: Dear me, all the other good people are going and I'm not feeling so good myself!

In a time of disaster it would be much better to die and be with the Lord and be in peace, and that is what happened, so the prophet reminds them that the righteous were resting in peace shortly before the exile and that God took away the righteous people one by one before the others were taken off into exile. You would expect a good God to do that. You would expect a just God to do that, and that is precisely what he was doing.

Notice in v. 2 two important words: *peace* and *rest*. The good people were enjoying that now, lying in their beds laid out for burial. You will notice that when we get to the end of the chapter the two words occur again, for there is no rest or peace for the wicked. Whilst the righteous were taken out of that situation by God into rest and peace, the wicked were not taken out.

What was the wickedness of those who were left? Here there follows the most awful description. I really dare not go into detail about this, except to indicate just what it is all about as you may wonder. The immorality of Israel before their incarceration in Babylon was dreadful, truly horrible. They were so busy discussing (in 56:3–5) those who had too little sex that God reminds them that in the days before the exile they had too much sex. That was the qualification or the disqualification. This happened because Israel had departed from her own pure faith and worship of a holy God, and had adopted the religion of Canaan, Baal worship. I do not know if you have ever studied this but you only need to read a little about it to feel revolted by the immorality of it. Let me just indicate a little and that will be enough.

They practised their religious rites deep in the valleys, in the clefts of the rock, underneath the trees in the woodland or on top of high mountains – in other words, any place where they were not overlooked (see 56:5,7). Their rites were those of a fertility cult which worshipped sex. They had what they called symbols mentioned in v. 8 –huge wooden carvings of the male and female genital organs with which the worshippers would excite themselves. They did not so much have priests as priestesses who were ritual prostitutes and were visited by the worshippers. So they had huge beds. I have said enough to indicate the kind of foul religion that they had adopted, in which immorality was rife. So they were disqualified from living in that land and they were turned out of it. You will find the prophets Hosea and Amos and others constantly speaking against this and warning the nation of Israel of it, but they took no notice. They were so busy worshipping sex in this way that they hardly noticed that the good people were dying and that God was removing them one by one. You would imagine that a lot of unwanted children would come into the world because of this, and that is perfectly true. What did they do with the illegitimate children that abounded? The answer is they used them in sacrifice. They killed the children as a sacrifice to the god Baal, and that is mentioned in v. 5: *"...you sacrifice your children in the ravines and under the overhanging crags"* (NIV). They used perfume in this: *"You went to Molech with olive oil and increased your perfumes"* (57:9, NIV). It is all there, and it was a weary business. Trailing up a high mountain made them very tired (v. 10 says, *"You were wearied by all your ways, but you would not say, 'It is hopeless.' You found renewal of your strength, and so you did not faint"* (NIV). Of course such licence would exhaust, physically, morally and spiritually, but they kept on at it. That is what was happening. It was a lustful religion which led to a deterioration of their character and integrity, which made them a lying people. That kind of thing leads to deceitfulness and it did in the nation. In vv. 11ff., we see God's judgement. It is a very sad chapter in their history. There is sarcasm and irony: *When you cry out for help, let your collection of idols save you!* They will be swept away as with the breath of the wind. It is a biting description and criticism of their immorality. God now instructs them as they are going back to that land, to the area of the world where that kind of evil religion was still practised. They must not go back to that or they would lose the land again. That is what lost them their blessing in the first place. A lying attitude was the result of their lustful religion, and a religion that is immoral will soon lead to immoral character and conduct. If you worship an immoral god it will make you immoral, and that is what had happened.

The passage 57:15–19 is one of the most wonderful in Isaiah. This is not a hopeless condition. Even though God demands righteousness, and the people were unrighteous, nevertheless, he will accept a man who is ashamed of what he has done and who comes with a humble and contrite heart. Here is the only ground on which we dare to come to worship God. If the people wanted God's land then they were to come back to him, humble and contrite, ashamed of what they had done. They had to come back to him and he would accept them. Note 'the high and lofty one' of v. 15, and look back to v. 7: 'a high and lofty hill'. It is not the high and lofty mountains we should look at, it is the high and lofty God we should consider! God is holy;

his ways are higher than our ways. His thoughts are higher than our thoughts; they are holier than our thoughts. So we should lift up our eyes to him and come to him humble and contrite. Never forget that God is high and holy. You can have a kind of worship which is 'pally' with God. Don't get me wrong, we have an intimacy with him, which we are allowed to have in Jesus, calling God Father, but we should never forget that he is the high and lofty one who inhabits eternity, whose name is holy. Therefore, if somebody comes proud and deceitful into God's presence, what an offence this must be to him. The high and holy one should have humble and contrite people. We are to be humble because he is high, contrite because he is holy. That is why we ask for his forgiveness when we come before him. When we come as humble, contrite people God says he will forgive us. He knows our backsliding, he knows our ways, but he will not be angry with us forever when we come like this.

The word 'peace' (v. 19) is the most wonderful word in the Bible. So many people have marched about with it written on banners – but I wonder if they understand it. Do you know what the word 'peace' means in the Bible? It does not mean the cessation of hostilities. It does not mean what we mean by peace when we agitate for peace. In the Bible it means four things: to be in perfect harmony with yourself through a forgiven conscience; in perfect harmony with other people through love; in perfect harmony with God through righteousness; and in harmony with nature. That is peace, and everything else would follow if you had those four things. A Jew meeting another in the street will say *shalom* – peace be to you, peace. Jesus died to give us peace. Here the prophet promises peace to those who are humble and contrite. You notice that he promises peace to two groups in v. 19 – those who are far off and those who are near. What does he mean? He means peace to the Jew and peace to the Gentile – the Jew who is near to God and the Gentile, the one who is far off.

It is worth looking now at just one sentence from Paul's

letter to the Ephesians where he takes up this quotation from Isaiah. He is talking about Christ dying on the cross. Paul says that in the cross,

His purpose was to create in himself one new man out of the two, thus making peace, and in this one body to reconcile both of them to God through the cross, by which he put to death their hostility. He came and preached peace to you who were far away and peace to those who were near.

Ephesians 2:15b–17 (NIV)

This broke down a wall of partition between Jew and Gentile. It was because Paul was accused of taking Gentiles through that wall that he was finally arrested. But Christ at the cross broke that wall. Peace was preached to those who were near, the Jews, and to those who were far off, the Gentiles.

Finally, in 57:20–21, Isaiah comes back to a contrast with the wicked. Notice that both chapters begin with the righteous and end with the wicked. What is wickedness? What is righteousness? We are beginning to see. Between the righteous and the wicked, Isaiah has discussed two groups of people (eunuchs and Gentiles), but he has shown that there are only two sorts of people in God's sight — the righteous and the wicked.

What then are the wicked like? The word here means quite literally they will be out of joint. That is a most vivid description. 'No rest' means to be out of joint. It is a word meaning dislocated, in pain and unable to do things. There is no rest for the wicked, and here there is a picture of the tossing sea whose waves are always on the move. You go to the beach and see the waves are always moving, always bringing up the debris from the seabed, always tossing up flotsam on the beach. This is how the wicked are. They are always on the move, always restless, always bringing up dirt from the bottom, and there is no peace for them either. They cannot have peace; their conscience must torment them sooner or later. They cannot have peace with themselves, they cannot have peace with others and they certainly cannot have peace with God. So these chapters finely divide into two groups those who have the promise of going back to the land: those who were righteous — whatever their blood, whatever their physical condition, whatever their station in life — and those who were wicked, whatever their status in life, whatever their race. So the promised land was for those who met God's conditions, and if they could not meet his demand for righteousness then he was prepared to accept a humble and contrite spirit. For one who threw himself upon the mercy of God there was peace. In exactly the same way, when all this is taken through into the New Testament the promised land becomes the kingdom of heaven and the same conditions apply. God's demand is righteousness. The wicked cannot go to heaven. And we see what wickedness is. It is not perhaps what we thought it was, and we realise that all of us have been wicked in God's sight. But God will take to heaven the righteous man who keeps his commandments. But who can do that? The answer is none of us can. So God will accept in place of righteousness the humble and the contrite heart, and will give peace and healing to those who repent and believe, acknowledging him as high and holy. Why is he able to do that? The answer is because of the cross, because of the righteousness of Jesus Christ which he has accepted for the sins of the world. That is why these quotations from Isaiah 56 and 57 are related in the New Testament to the cross. And the peace that comes to the Jew who is near and the Gentile who is far off — the Jew who is in the inner court of God's house, the Gentile who is in the outer court — is the peace that was made by the blood of Christ on the cross. God will welcome to heaven itself, to promised blessing, to rest and to peace, all those who come with a humble and a contrite spirit, and he heals them.

26

NO-ONE TO INTERCEDE

Read Isaiah 58–59

A. THEIR GOODNESS - FOR GOD (58)
1. RITUAL IS NOT RIGHTEOUSNESS (1-2)
2. DENIAL OF SELF (3-5)
a. Greed b. Anger
3. DUTY TO OTHERS (6-12)
a. Physical b. Spiritual
4. DELIGHT IN GOD (13-14)
B. THEIR BADNESS - TO PEOPLE (59)
1. PRAYER IS NOT PRACTICE (1-3)
2. INJUSTICE TO OTHERS (4-8)
3. INDICTMENT OF SELF (9-15a)
4. INDIGNATION IN GOD (15b-21)
a. Repay (15b-19) b. Redeem (20-21)

People often ask me about the problem of unanswered prayer. Somebody will say: I asked God for something and he never gave it to me; I prayed very hard about it, and it didn't seem as if my prayer had any answer. Like all other major problems, the problem of unanswered prayer is dealt with in the Bible. The first thing we should ask when we have the problem of unanswered prayer is the question which is answered in Isaiah 58 – 59. Here is the very first and largest reason why prayers are not answered. There are other reasons and other factors, but this is the first one we should think about when we fail to get through. Many people really do not know whether they are through; they really do not get any response. They express what they wish to happen and that seems as far as it gets. What has gone wrong? Why does God not answer? Surely he loves to answer prayer. Surely a father loves to speak with his children. Surely a heavenly Father wants to give to his earthly children what they need. Why then does he not answer our prayer?

The Jews had this problem in the period we are concerned with. They had been in captivity and in exile away from their home, away from their land, away from God's blessing for two generations (allowing a generation to be about thirty years). During that time they had prayed night and day: Lord, take us back to where we belong; Lord, set us free; Lord, put us again in the land of your promise and blessing. They prayed earnestly every day together for this and the heavens seemed like brass and they could not get through, and their prayers were not answered. They began to ask why. Then somebody thought: perhaps we are not doing enough; perhaps we should do something as well as pray, we should fast. So day after day they went without their food and they prayed. They dressed in sackcloth and ashes and said: Lord, will you take us back? Still no answer. So some people said: We are not observing the Sabbath as much as we ought to. So they observed the Sabbath and they prayed again: Lord, take us back home. But still they did not get back home. What was wrong?

Isaiah gave them a very simple but devastating answer. Next time you have an unanswered prayer, ask whether this is not the reason. The reason was two-fold. First he said there is something wrong with your goodness, and secondly, there is something wrong with your badness. The first is the one I want to write most about because it is the more difficult thing to realise. Do you realise that we need forgiveness for the good things that we do as well as the bad things? This is just one of those truths that people do not seem to get. It is so easy for people to think: Well, I'm a mixture of good and bad; I need forgiveness for the bad part of me but the good part of me is surely acceptable. But Isaiah says you need to look at your goodness as well as your badness to find out about what is wrong and causing the blockage. So in chapter 58 he talks about what was wrong with their goodness and puts it in inverted commas. Then in chapter 59 he just underlines what they realise is their badness. And both of these things come as a blockage. You cannot get through to God when there is something wrong with your goodness or when there is badness.

Look at chapter 58. It begins by telling the prophet to lift up his voice like a trumpet. You cannot ignore a trumpet! I used to play the cornet in my earlier days, until somebody made some rather rude remarks about it and I lost heart! But if I were playing a trumpet in your presence you could not ignore what I was doing! A trumpet was used in the ancient world to warn people. It was the equivalent of an air raid siren in those days. They would blow the trumpet to warn of the approach of the enemy. The prophet is virtually being told: let your voice be an air raid siren; let your voice be a warning to them; let your voice tell them that something is terribly wrong, something dangerous is very near. Cry aloud, don't spare your congregation, don't consider their feelings, don't consider their sensitivity. Let your voice be like a trumpet that blasts them into waking up. That is strong language, and preachers like that are not usually very popular — preachers who spare not and who shout like a trumpet — but that is what the prophet is told to do, because they will not realise what is wrong unless he does so. They honestly think that they are good people. That is why he has got to blast away at them. They honestly think that they are a nation that does righteousness. We read in v. 2 — *as if they were a nation that does what is right*. What made them think that?

The answer is in verses 1 and 2. They went to the service of worship every day —not just once a week as you may do, but every day. They were enjoying studying the word of God when they went to worship, they delighted in it and because of this they thought they were righteous people, and they were not the last to have made that dreadful mistake. People who go to church frequently and who listen to Bible study regularly and who enjoy it are very much tempted to think that because of that they are righteous people and that God will listen to their prayers. No such thing! The prophet with a devastating trumpet voice says that ritual is not righteousness. Religious observance, religious activities, even when you enjoy them, do not make you a righteous person. That is one of the most important lessons we ever need to learn.

The two parts of their ritual in their exile in Babylon were fasting and observing the Sabbath — but they could not offer sacrifices any more (they had no temple in which to do that). So here were the two things that made up their religion in Babylon and they observed them very dutifully but felt that God had not noticed (see 58:3). And there are many people who feel as they did: We have gone to church every Sunday and yet you don't answer our prayers. We have given money. Somehow you don't get through to us. What is wrong? The answer is God does not like ritual, unless it is backed up with righteousness. He does not like religion unless it is backed up with the life. And he does not accept what we do on Sunday unless Monday to Saturday matches up. That is the simple truth, and how we need to learn this. It is so easy to think that because of what we do on Sunday we are accepted people to God, and that he will answer our prayers and bless us. I would say that it is what you do from Monday to Saturday that is the real test of whether God can accept your prayer.

We take fasting first. Fasting is commanded in both the Old and the New Testaments. It is a thing that the Jews did, it is a thing that Christians are to do. Our Lord Jesus said *when* you pray, *when* you give alms, *when* you fast. He did not say *if* you pray or *if* you give or *if* you fast — he assumed that his followers would do all three. Fasting is something that many Christians have never even begun to learn to do, and do not even know what it is for, but it is part of the Christian life, as praying is, and as giving is.

The Jews fasted like this. They went without food for a day — probably from sunrise to sunset, although we are not sure about that. Not only did they do without food but they did not put on their best clothes, they put on sackcloth and ashes as an outward sign that they were humbling themselves. Then they walked about all day with their heads down, bowed. This they thought was fasting. Sadly, some people still think that if you do without food you have fasted. But that is not a fast acceptable to the Lord.

What in the Lord's sight is true fasting? It will include three things: a denial of self; doing our duty to others; and delighting in God. These three things make doing without food a righteous act. But doing without food and not doing these three things is mere ritual and does not get through to God.

Take denial of self. These people were denying themselves food but they were not denying themselves. It is funny that people still think that fasting is denying yourself *something* (sweets during Lent or cigarettes for a month). It is not — it is *denying yourself*. And if you indulge yourself in anything else while you fast, it is not a fast. It is utterly foolish to deny yourself something and indulge yourself in another direction. I remember a man telling me that he had given up cigarettes in Lent. But his wife told me that he became unbearable to live with! This is not fasting — it was ridiculous because he was indulging his own temper and irritability. To do without something is no virtue if you simply indulge your temper instead. The Jews in Babylon may have done without food but they kept their shops open — business as usual — and they exploited and oppressed their employees to make money. In other words, they denied themselves food but indulged themselves in greed. So if you go without food but indulge yourself in some other way do not think that God will take any notice of that — it is just two-faced.

True fasting is not just denying yourself but doing your duty to others at the same time. It is not only to take something away from you, it is to give that something to someone else who needs it. That makes it a truly righteous act and not just a ritual fast. Look at vv. 6ff. Loosing chains of injustice, working for people's freedom, looking after the hungry and giving the needy clothes — that is the other side of it: you do without something that they might have it. That makes a real fast because you recognise not only that you deny self but that you do your duty to other people.

This duty to them is not only physical but mental. It is to stop pointing the finger at people (see v. 9) and stop speaking wickedness. It would be very much more relevant if somebody said, 'I'm going to give up gossip for Lent.' That is real fasting. If they said, 'I'm going to stop pointing the critical finger and speaking wickedness at and about others', that is good fasting, it is doing your duty. We would soon find that this would get an answer to our prayers (see v. 9). If you pour yourself out for the hungry, if you do your duty to others and if you really see that this is all part of living the Christian life, then look at the blessings that come. The Lord will guide you. Did you grumble that the Lord did not guide you? Could it be that you were not doing your duty to others? He will satisfy your needs. Why did you not have those good things when you asked for them? Could it be that you were unwilling to share them with others? He will make your bones strong. I am not quite sure what that means but it sounds good. You will be like a watered garden, like a spring of water that never fails, and your ancient ruins shall be rebuilt. I am sure that was quite literal to the Jews, but things that had died in your life could be rebuilt and made strong again.

We move to verses 13–14. We now turn from fasting to the Sabbath. God had told the Jews that one day in seven you give to him. They were not to do anything else on that day. It was not just a matter of attending synagogue, not a couple of hours on the seventh day, but one day in seven given to him, a holy day, the last day of the week. We discover that they were not giving that day to God. They gave some of it when they went to worship, but not all of it. What did they do with the rest? First of all, they travelled. That is the meaning of the word *feet* at the beginning of v. 13. Having worshipped, they then took the opportunity to make it a day of travelling. They also kept their shops open. They were in the synagogue and no doubt they got a Gentile who did not go to the synagogue to keep it going. But, again, on the Sabbath they still pursued their own business, or if you like the other translation they still did their own pleasure in the course of the day that should have been God's.

Furthermore, they talked idly. They spent an awful lot of the day in useless conversation. There is plenty of time for that elsewhere in the week. But on this, the Lord's day, it was an opportunity for their conversation to be on the Lord's things. After all, we get very little time to talk of deep and spiritual matters and here was the very day on which to have such a conversation, to go home after worship and have lunch and instead of just chatting about other things to talk about what had been learned that day in the synagogue. Do you do this on Sunday? I heard of one family where the children asked the parents, 'What did you learn in Bible school this morning?' That is great! The parents used to go home and ask the children: 'What did you learn in the children's meeting?' It is a very good thing to talk these things over when you go home for lunch. It is the Lord's day, the Sabbath, Isaiah reminds the Jews. It is not the day for you to travel, it is not the day for you to keep your business, it is not the day for you to seek your own pleasure, it is not the day for idle chatter, it is a day kept for God's sake and to honour him.

Let me say that I am no Sabbatarian. I do not believe that Christians are under the Jewish law. I do not believe we are under the law to give a tenth of our income. I do not believe we are under the law to give a seventh of our time. But shall we who are under grace — and who have so much more to thank God for than the Jews ever had — do less than they did? That is my question. God forbid! Therefore Sunday becomes, for the Christian who is able by his duties to do so, a day to give especially to the Lord and to honour him in — though not because we are under the Jewish law. We delight to do so. I did not want my children growing up feeling that Sunday was a day of 'thou shalt not' — it would not have been a delight. I wanted my children to delight in Sunday as a special day to which they looked forward, a day that they would honour, a day that would be God's day which they would delight to have. And I wanted my children when they grew up and earned money to give so much of that to the Lord not because they had been told you must but because they had been told you may. We are not under law but under grace, but grace has its obligations of gratitude, love and generosity.

Furthermore, Jesus taught that in the three things of which we have been speaking secrecy is absolutely essential. If you give donations, then keep them secret and anonymous. Do not parade your giving, do not go around the place talking about what you give to people, what you have given to the refugees or what you have given to the church. And when you pray and delight in God, go somewhere quite quiet and do it for him alone. I used to advise men in the forces not to pray in their barrack room as a witness. That is not what prayer is meant to be. The other lads would soon find out they were Christians in other ways, but they should go somewhere private, shut the door and pray in secret to their Father. And when you fast don't let anybody know you are doing without food. I know this has difficulties in the family. You must just help them to understand, but you must not parade it. Jesus said it must be secret, and then it is true devotion to God and he accepts it. Some Christians have to work on Sunday. That is not a sin and it is not wrong — they are not under law, they are under grace. But we who are free to give a day to God, let us do that. It is not that there is anything wrong morally with golf or gardening. After all, if you cannot ask God to bless these things you should not do them at any time of the week. But if we are free to give God one day in seven for his thoughts and his activities shall we not do so as a delight and not a duty?

Here then is the first grand lesson of chapter 58. What may be blocking your prayer and shutting heaven's ear to you, the first thing that makes your prayer dead, is this: that your religion is not righteousness, that it is Sunday religion, and that it is not matched up with your life Monday to Saturday; there is no denial of self behind your self-denial, there is not the duty to others in their need — both physical and mental — being fulfilled by you. And your relationship to God may have become a duty rather than a delight. Dealing with these things can turn our so-called 'goodness' into real goodness.

Before we leave this chapter, there is something else which is very important. I meet plenty of people who get the point of this chapter and then swing right over to the other extreme. On the one hand are those who say ritual is all right without righteousness but then some swing right to the opposite end and say righteousness is all right without ritual. That is the opposite error and equally wrong. It is just as silly to say I can live a good life without worshipping God, I can live a good life without being connected with church, I can live a good life without reading my Bible. There is a 'religious' side to true Christian living. The two go together: worship and work, religion and righteousness, and God will accept fasting from food when it is backed up with these other things. He does not say don't fast, he teaches us: don't fast by itself. Fast plus . . . , Sabbath plus this . . . . He never told them to ignore the Sabbath. So we have this perfect balance: worship and work, religion and righteousness – either without the other is not God's intention. It is his intention that we should go to church and worship him. It is his desire that we should fast and pray and give. It is his desire that we should observe religious acts, not because they are duties —but because they express our deepest love for him.

Now we turn to chapter 59. Once again the chapter begins with a statement, then backs it up in three ways. The statement is to the effect that prayer is not practice. We prayed, said these Jews, we asked God to take us home, we have pleaded with him, we have fasted, we have observed the Sabbath – what is wrong? And here comes the answer a second time: not only is your goodness not real goodness but your badness is real badness. Have you ever felt that God is not listening? That is what the Jews were thinking at this time. They were beginning to think God must have gone deaf. Here I am shouting and he's not listening and he can't hear me! Or perhaps his ears are alright but his hands have shrunk and he can't reach me now. His hand isn't long enough to stretch down to Babylon and lift us out of this trouble. But in fact there is nothing wrong with God's hands and ears – his hand is not short that he cannot reach you and his ear isn't deaf that he can't hear you! The prophet teaches that real trouble is *your* hands and *your* mouth: "*For your hands are stained with blood*" (v. 3) and "*Your lips have spoken lies, and your tongue mutters wicked things.*" It is not that God cannot listen, it is that he does not. It is not that he cannot hear (v. 1) but he does not hear (v. 2). The psalmist said this:

If I had cherished sin in my heart,
the Lord would not have listened;
but God has surely listened,
and heard my voice in prayer.

Psalm 66:18f. (NIV)

If your prayer does not get higher than the ceiling, the first question to ask is: am I cherishing sin in my heart? Is there some secret affection for a forbidden thing? Is there something in my life that I am hanging on to that God told me to let go? Is there some habit, some attitude to someone else that is wrong and yet that I enjoy? Is that the reason? For there is only one thing that creates a barrier between us and God and it is sin.

Your sins have separated you from your God. Your sins have hidden his face from you. He cannot see you because there is a great black curtain hanging between you, and written across that curtain in big letters is the word 'sin'.

Here the badness of the people of God is simply portrayed. I have divided up personal pronouns. Notice in vv. 1–3, 'you', 'your'; in vv. 4–8 'they', 'their'; in v. 9 to the first part of v. 15 'we', 'our', 'us'; and finally verses 15b to the end of the chapter, 'he', 'him'. So first of all we have *you* — prayer is not practised and that is your trouble. Secondly, we move to *they*, and what is happening is described. Integrity is going. I once spent an afternoon in the Home Office speaking with the then Permanent Secretary. He had been some years in the Department and he had all the crime figures coming in to his desk. I was asking about crime in this country, and about morals and so on. I said, 'What about crime, is it rising?' He said, 'Is it rising? Out of all proportion to the rise in population.' 'And integrity?' 'Oh that's going down.' I said to him, 'Why? Do you ever think why it is going down?' He replied, 'Well no, I just don't understand it.' I continued, 'Do you think it's a coincidence that church attendance has been dropping now for decades? Do you think there's any relation between that and this?' 'There might be,' was his answer. We had a most interesting chat. But he was quite open to admit and talk about the facts as we all know them. Pilfering is on a gigantic scale. Ask any large firm. I knew of a small branch of a high street retail chain which allowed a fantastic sum to its manager each year just to offset shoplifting from the open counters. Everything above that sum he had to find out of his own pocket. This is the world we live in. Integrity and justice are going as people lie and deceive.

We notice that in v. 9 the prophet switches from *they* to *we*. It is a tremendous step forward in your relationship to God when you can switch from *they* to *we*. It is so easy to say, 'Oh, aren't they dreadful? These people ruining the country.' It is always 'them', somewhere else. But at this point Isaiah is letting us know that this is true of us. It is good when a preacher can say that, and indeed when anyone can say that. We are all in this. We have all been unfair, we have all told our lies. We have all been unjust to others, we have all got iniquity in our heart. And when you really see God face to face you realise that every one of us has contributed to the world's evil at some point or another. Every one of us has made this world a more wicked place than it was before we came into it. So the prophet, this great man of God, says that justice is far from us. We are to blame (see v. 12). We learn halfway through v. 15 that if you try to be good you are simply exploited by others. People have said to me: if you try to be honest at work you are simply exploited; if you try to be kind and helpful they simply take advantage of you. They tell me that it doesn't pay to be honest today, nor to be kind and good — everybody else looks after themselves. So even he who departs from evil makes himself a prey (see v. 15). I might be reading the Sunday papers instead of the word of God written over two thousand years ago. But when you can put yourself into it and say forgive us *our* trespasses — not, 'Lord, take all those wicked people out of the world, punish all those dreadful people who work iniquity' — then you are really going to get through in prayer; when you say forgive us *our* trespasses. I'm in it too, Lord. I cannot just say *they*, I must say *our*, *us*.

Now he switches from *us* to *he*. What does God think about it? Here the prophet draws a veil away from heaven and we see that God is displeased. He says no-one will intervene. He would have to come and put it right himself. Putting on his armour, God came. He put on the breastplate of righteousness, he put on the helmet of salvation, he put on the garments of vengeance, he put on the mantle of zeal and down he came to deal with it. When God comes, two things are going to happen. The first is that he is going to repay the wicked for their injustice. Look at v. 18 (NIV), *According to what they have done, so will he repay wrath to his enemies, and retribution to his foes* .... God will repay wickedness. People may get away with pilfering from the firm now, but he will repay, and men will fear his name. Do you know why we do wrong? It is a very simple reason. It is because we do not fear God. Now we might laugh at him, mock at him, debate him in a television studio as if he does not mind being debated about. There is no fear of God. After all, you would not steal if you feared him and believed that he will repay you for that theft. You would not 'borrow' either time or property from the firm if you feared him and realised that one day he will repay.

But there is one other thing. We should finish in utter gloom if this were the end of the chapter, but it is not. Just as if you sting yourself with a nettle, somewhere near it you will find a dock leaf to rub on (and I am told that is not an old wives' tale as chemically the juice of the dock leaf neutralises the acid of the nettle and it does work), in our Lord's word you find justice and mercy growing together. And wherever you find the promise of the judgement and the wrath of God to come, somewhere near it you will find something to rub into the wound. At the end of the chapter it tells you that to those who turn from their transgression God will come not to repay but to redeem. That is the good news with which we finish. It is a condition that we turn from sin. We need to repent of our part in the world's troubles and turn to God. Then when he comes he will put on us the breastplate of righteousness and the helmet of salvation, not the garments of wrath or the mantle of fury. When Paul quotes from 59:17 (in Ephesians 6) he does not quote the latter part of the verse. God can put on you the breastplate of righteousness and the helmet of salvation; he can put his Spirit upon you and his words in your mouth, and those words you will pass on to your children and grandchildren. That is what can straighten up this old world of ours.

To listen to and obey the word is, I believe, the answer to the situation in which we are in. The scripture plus the Spirit at work within us will remove the injustice, the wickedness and the iniquity from our hearts. That is why I believe that in church we are doing more for Britain than anyone else could ever do, and that wherever people and their children and their grandchildren are being taught the word of God and told of his Spirit we are doing more to establish that righteousness in the land than anyone else could. The task is urgent.

In these two chapters there has run a double contrast between righteousness and sin, light and darkness. In the Bible, light is always moral light, righteousness; and darkness is always sin.

27

ARISE, SHINE!

Read Isaiah 60–62

A. GLORIOUS CIVILISATION (60)
1. GLORY OF THE LORD (1-9)
2. WEALTH OF FOREIGNERS (10-16)
3. WALLS OF SALVATION (17-22)

B. GLAD CITIZENS (61)
1. SPIRIT OF THE LORD (1-4)
2. SERVICE OF FOREIGNERS (5-9)
3. GARMENTS OF SALVATION (10-11)

C. GLEAMING CITY (62)
1. HAND OF THE LORD (1-5)
2. RESPECT OF FOREIGNERS (6-9)
3. WORDS OF SALVATION (10-12)

That the book of the prophet Isaiah is the Bible in miniature, as we have suggested, becomes ever clearer as you study it. The contents of the two sections of Isaiah are like the contents of the two Testaments in the Bible. The first thirty-nine chapters tend to concentrate on the judgement and the justice of God and the sins of the people, with promises of salvation to come. But when we get into the chapters from 40 onwards, it is as though we are reading the New Testament. Chapter 40 begins with a voice crying in the wilderness and we think of John the Baptist and the beginning of the gospel in the New Testament. By chapter 42 God's servant, whom we now know to be Jesus Christ, steps into the pages. From then through the next few chapters we have the life of Jesus portrayed in Isaiah, hundreds of years before the Incarnation. In chapter 53, as we saw, we come to the death and resurrection of Jesus, who was pierced for our transgressions. Then in chapter 55 we had the preaching of the good news, equivalent to the first preaching of the gospel in Acts by Peter. And so on, through the New Testament. Chapters 60–66 correspond to the book of Revelation. The next three studies cover the three main subjects of the last part of the New Testament: 60–62 cover the new Jerusalem, 63–64 cover the final judgement, 65–66 the new heaven and the new earth. If you have a Bible with cross references at the foot of the pages you will discover that from chapter 60 onwards there is a reference to the book of Revelation at the foot of every page. That just gives you the setting. Therefore, from chapter 60 onwards, God is unveiling the future. The Greek word for unveiling is transliterated as 'apocalypse', which is why we call it the 'Apocalypse of John'. An 'apocalypse' draws back the curtain from the future. People read horoscopes, study the stars and so on, but in fact only God can draw aside the veil from the future of the world. This he has done, and he has shown us as much as we need to know about the end of the world to keep our faith balanced and sane.

One of the problems in discussing the future is that it is so difficult to imagine it. We can imagine the past much more easily than we can imagine the future. If I were to give you a lecture on social life in Britain one hundred years ago, even though you were not alive then, with a little bit of imagination you could see the reality of it. But if I were able to describe to you social life in Britain one hundred years hence you would find it very difficult to imagine. If I had told my grandfather in the 1930s that one day he would be able to sit by his fireside and watch things happening in Japan he would have laughed, he would have thought me crazy! When we come to those sections of the Bible that are about the future it can be difficult to imagine these things happening. But I want to say to you that everything God has promised to do in the future he will do, and however difficult it is to imagine such things happening, they are going to happen as certainly as the things that he has promised in the past have already happened.

All these three chapters say exactly the same thing, but they approach the same subject from three different angles: chapter 60 approaches the subject from a world angle; chapter 61 approaches it from the angle of the people; chapter 62 from the angle of the city itself —but all are about the new Jerusalem, the Zion of the future which God is to establish.

The first chapter sees the new Jerusalem as the centre of a world civilisation, as the capital city of the universe. Notice how often the words *nation* and *king(s)* occur (see 60:3,11,12,16). Here is a world civilisation with the nations and the kings all coming to Jerusalem to God's city – not to New York, not to London, not to Tokyo, not to Babylon but to Jerusalem as the centre, the focal point. If you go to Jerusalem today and visit the Church of the Holy Sepulchre, there in the stone floor is a large inlaid silver star. The guide will point to it and say that is the centre of the world. I do not know how it got there or why they say this, but in a sense it is true, it is the meeting point of Asia, Africa, Europe, and if you include the Americas, now virtually linked by modern transport so closely to Europe, this is the centre of world civilisation. Look at the world from one angle and you will see hardly anything but sea. Look at it from another angle and you can see all the continents, and if you take your pen and put it in the middle of it, you will land on Jerusalem. It is the centre of the world in which people live. This is the vision for the future. What is making kings and nations come? The answer is in vv. 1–9, it is because that is the only place in the world where they can clearly see the glory of the Lord; or, to put it very simply, because the rest of the world will be in darkness and that will be the only place in light. And people in darkness go to somewhere that has some light. Darkness and light in the Bible indicate moral and spiritual qualities. Here we have a wonderful situation. *"Arise, shine, for your light has come . . . ."* This is God's light, God's glory. God's goodness is shining on you, and the rest of the world is in darkness, and they are all coming to see how you got that light. They want the light, they are seeking the light, and so they come.

The language of vv. 1–3 is the language of an eastern dawn, which we never see in Britain. We see a slow change from darkness to dawn. At night we see the slowly gathering shadows of the twilight and the gloom of sunset. But in the Middle East the sun seems to jump up. One minute it seems to be dark and then, before you know where you are, there is the sun blazing down upon you. It is a wonderful experience to watch the sun rise in Jerusalem. Coming up over the Mount of Olives, suddenly the sun is there in the sky. There is no slow change, the sun springs into action. That is why the psalms speak of the sun as springing into his circuit, coming forth like a bridegroom out of his chamber, jumping into being and shining upon people, and suddenly the city of Jerusalem is bathed in full sunlight.

So God's glory is here, and people know that here they can find God. God is shining in this place, even as darkness covers the earth. So the nations and the kings come. This is what Jerusalem has to give to the world. In one sense Jerusalem as a city ought not to have survived: it is not on a river, it is not on a main trading route, it is not on a prominent site. It has no natural reason to survive, unlike the ancient cities of Babylon, Assyria and Egypt which have not survived. Is that not remarkable? I think it is just as big a miracle that Jerusalem is on the map as that Israel is, when all those other cities which really had an obvious point have gone. But there is only one thing that Jerusalem had to offer the world, and that she still has to offer, and will offer more gloriously in the future: *The glory of the* L*ORD rises upon you* — and the nations will come for that. That is the picture. They will come from the east and therefore they will have to come on the 'ships of the desert', the camels (see 60:6). From the west they will come in ships, from Tarshish (somewhere near Gibraltar, the place to which Jonah fled, the furthest extremity of the Mediterranean Sea). They will come from the north, they will come from the south. Jews will come, Gentiles will come — everybody will be making a pilgrimage to Jerusalem, because God's glory will shine there. The sails of the boats coming up the Mediterranean will be like doves coming to their dovecote, fluttering up in the wind and bringing the sons and daughters of Israel back home. It is a wonderful picture, difficult to imagine. Can you imagine all the world making a pilgrimage to Jerusalem to get the light of God's glory?

Not only will the people come but the wealth of the world will come. They will not only bring themselves they will bring silver and gold. The wealth of the nations will be poured into God's city. That point is mentioned in 60:5 and v. 11, and again in 61:6. The Jews have done so much trading, and here God is going to give wealth to them. Here it will be poured in voluntarily to their city without their having to work for it or do business for it. We will see why in a moment.

So vv. 10–16 move on to this great immigration of foreigners bringing their wealth with them. They will not even be able to shut the gates, day or night, because the pilgrims bringing their wealth will come in, and that wealth will help to build the city and its walls. With v. 11 we come to something we also read about in the book of Revelation. For of the new Jerusalem in Revelation it is said that the gates will never be shut — there will be free movement day and night. In the Middle Eastern cities, gates were shut every night for safety. I have stayed in little towns in the heart of the Arabian desert inside the walls, and each night the gates were shut tight.

Furthermore, nations that do not come will perish. That sounds a bit like blackmail to some, but that is not what is meant. It is a simple fact that when the glory of the Lord is available, and the light of the Lord is shining, the people who refuse to come to it will perish. When God is shining clearly and inviting people to come and bathe in the glow of his glory and they refuse to come, then they will perish. It is a simple statement of fact that nations that come will be blessed but that nations that do not come will perish and be utterly laid waste.

Even the physical glory of the city will be wonderful. The walls will be built, the gates will be opened, the buildings will go up and trees will be planted. I live in an area that is heavily wooded — and how beautiful the trees are. From time to time man has had dreams of garden cities and has built these places in which trees have been planted to beautify the place where people live. According to my Bible, the new Jerusalem is to be a garden city. The leaves of the tree will be for the healing of the nations. And here we are shown a tree-lined city (the cypress, the fir and the pine). Did you know that since 1948 millions of trees have been planted in Israel alone? It changed the whole scenery of the land. *The sons of your oppressors will come bowing before you.* Here is a reversal of Israel's former position in the nations.

The next thing chapter 60 teaches is that, because of all this, this city will be the most desirable place to live in. People will say: you ought to go and live there if you can. If you can get inside, those walls are safe (called 'Salvation'). If you can get through those gates, you will praise God. According to vv. 17–22 there will be prosperity. With all that wealth pouring in they will not use common building materials. Instead of bronze, gold; instead of iron, silver; instead of wood, bronze; instead of stones, iron.

There will be justice. The Jews had known evil taskmasters, but the 'governor' in Jerusalem will be peace, and the ruler 'righteousness'. There will be peace —no violence, no destruction, no devastation, no war. There will be light. There will be no sun and moon, and with this we are reminded of another reference in the book of Revelation, where it says of the new Jerusalem that there will be no need of sun or moon. When God shines, then his glory is enough light and the city is bathed in a glow. Of course, when God is not present even the sun goes out, as it did on that dreadful day when Jesus died. How we love a sunny morning. Isn't it pleasant walking to church when the sun is shining? What will it be like to walk in the glory of the Lord to worship him? The days of mourning will be over; there will be no sorrow. Goodness will be there. *Then will all your people be righteous*. Have you ever wanted to live in a town where everybody was good? Can you imagine that? This is where our imagination boggles. We find it difficult to imagine, but Jerusalem will be like that. All this is primarily for God's glory. The final question we ask about chapter 60 is: when will all this happen? *In its time* (see v. 22). When? I postpone that question to the end.

Let us move to chapter 61, which has a different theme. The key words of chapter 60 were 'glory', 'glorious', 'glorified' – occurring there nine times. But in chapter 61 that tends to drop out and another group of words comes in: 'rejoice', 'exult', 'joy', 'gladness'. Now we are not looking at this world civilisation that is full of the glory of God, but at the citizens of this city, and as we look we see how glad they are. Why are they happy people?

At this point the prophet speaks in his own name, quite personally. He was addressing people who were in captivity, far from the city of Jerusalem – in Babylon they were slaves, they had lost their homes, their land, everything. Many of them had lost their children and their old people as they trekked 500 miles through the desert, force-marched in two months. And they were so sad they could not even sing. They hung up their musical instruments on the trees. To these people Isaiah said:

The Spirit of the Sovereign LORD is on me,
because the LORD has anointed me
to preach good news to the poor.
He has sent me to bind up the broken-hearted,
to proclaim freedom for the captives
and release from darkness for the prisoners.

61:1 (NIV)

I can think of few more lovely things to do than to tell people good news. Just think of those moments when you have been able to take good news to someone — have you not felt thrilled? But you did not need the Spirit of the Lord God to say that, did you? Why then did the prophet Isaiah need the Spirit of the Lord to anoint him just to tell them the good news? The answer is two-fold, as it is for me when preaching the good news.

Firstly, without the Spirit of the Lord you would not have any good news to give, because how would you know that the future was going to be bright? It takes the Spirit of the Lord to reveal to us what the future is, what the good news is — and without the Holy Spirit I would not have any good news to preach.

Secondly, without the Holy Spirit's anointing you would not believe the good news. You would say: I just can't accept this. But the Holy Spirit can anoint a preacher in such a way that you are absolutely convinced that what he says is true. Think of the great good news of the forgiveness of sins, that God can wipe your slate clean. You could find that very difficult to believe. You could say: I can't forgive myself for doing these things, how can God forgive me? I can't forget these things I've done. How can God wipe them out if I can't forget them? The good news of God needs the Holy Spirit's anointing both because the person who announces it must be convinced of its truth, and because the people to whom he announces it must be convinced. In v. 1, the prophet comes to tell these weary, disheartened, disillusioned, sad people, that the Spirit of God had anointed him to give them good news. They were going to be set free. They were going back home. And they believed it because he was so anointed.

But as we read these words we think of how one day Jesus went back to the synagogue in his home town where he had been brought up as a boy. He was invited to preach before his relatives and neighbours. That, I know from experience, is one of the hardest things to do. They knew you as a child. They knew you as you grew up. In Nazareth they said this about Jesus:

Isn't this Joseph's son? He was handed a big roll of parchment and he unrolled it to this very chapter, and began:

> *"The Spirit of the Lord is on me,*
> *because he has anointed me*
> *to preach good news to the poor . . . ."*
>
> Luke 4:18 (NIV)

He read on, then he stopped at a comma, and then he sat down. The preachers in those days sat to preach, which is quite a nice idea! But that is what the phrase *ex cathedra* means – from the seat – and to pronounce *ex cathedra* is to pronounce from the throne, from the seat of your authority. Jesus sat down and spoke, and he said: *"Today this scripture is fulfilled in your hearing"* (Luke 4:21, NIV). Just as Isaiah was anointed to bring good news to the poor, Jesus was claiming the same: I have exactly this anointing on me and if you want to know why I am preaching sermons now and why I am healing the sick and raising the dead and cleansing the leper it is done by the same power that anointed Isaiah. But do you notice where Jesus stopped reading? Isaiah's good news to the Israelites in Babylon was: . . . this is the day of God's favour and the day of the vengeance of our God upon your enemies. Jesus did not read that, but not because he thought God was so loving that he would never have vengeance. God is a God of vengeance – the New Testament says that. '*Vengeance is mine, I will repay,' says the Lord* (see Romans 12:19). It was because Jesus did not come to inaugurate the day of vengeance of our God – that is yet to come. But he did come to bring the day of God's grace, so he stopped reading where he did. Isaiah went on because it was the day of God's vengeance against Babylon when he preached. So the Spirit of the Lord brought the good news.

61:5–9 states what will be the relationship between the foreigners who come and live in the city of God and the Jews who were already there. The answer is the foreigners will do all the manual labour. Lest you immediately begin to jump to wrong conclusions here, I will explain why. They will say to the Jews: you have God, you can teach us about God, you can share God's glory with us. We want you to be set free from daily labour because we want you to be our ministers. The Jews will be called ministers of God, and the foreigners will feed the flocks and be ploughmen and vineyard workers. That is rather like what my congregation did for me. In order for me to minister to them in the things of God and spend time preparing the food for them, they went to their daily work and by their gifts they supported me. Just as within our home my wife has to go out and shop and come back and prepare the food and cook it and is released from daily employment by my earnings so that she can feed the family, in exactly the same way there is no distinction of honour here, there is simply a division of function. This is what will happen in the new Jerusalem. The Jews will all be the priests and the ministers and the others will all do the work so that they can give time to this. If I may add, my work is very much like my wife's. It may take her a couple of hours to go out, shop, come home, prepare and cook and put it on the table —and it is gone in twelve minutes flat! And in the same way it takes about ten times as long to prepare a meal in the form of a sermon for Sunday morning as it does to give it. But that is the whole point of setting someone apart to do this, and the Jews will be set apart here to be ministers so they will be supported: *you shall eat the wealth of the nations and in their riches you shall glory*. You will not need to run businesses to get your money, they will give it and say: will you be our minister? Will you teach us? You have got the glory of the Lord, will you share it with us? So instead of dishonour they will rejoice in their lot. And in their land they shall possess a double portion. God's covenant with them is that they will be seen to be a people whom he has blessed.

61:10–11 indicates that they will rejoice, exult, not in the money they are getting, not in the position they get, not in the honour of being ministers and priests — they will not rejoice in any of these things, they will rejoice in the Lord because he has clothed them with the garments of salvation. Two pictures are drawn now: a wedding, with the bridegroom getting all spruced up and the bride getting adorned and beautified. That is the first picture. They are both as attractive as they can be, and the prophet says that as a bridegroom decks himself, as a bride adorns herself, God's people will be beautified with the garments of salvation. Changing the metaphor, God will cause righteousness and praise to spring up out of his people, like plants in a garden — most attractive.

Chapter 62 looks at the city. And the prophet cannot keep quiet until all this happens, until the city of God is like a crown in God's hands, like a royal diadem. God will hold Jerusalem like a crown of jewels in his hand. And new names will be given. No longer called 'Deserted' or 'Desolate', but 'Beulah' —married, with a family, somebody sought by others. Then in vv.6–9 the prophets, the watchmen on the walls, will not be silent nor are they to rest until this happens. Again foreigners are particularly mentioned, because they will respect the property of Israel and will no longer take from it and ravage the crops and take the wine — they will leave Israel to have her own products in peace.

Finally, in vv. 10–12 comes the magnificent appeal. Go through the gates, get the road ready, get the stones off the roads. so the people can come easily and smoothly and quickly. *'See, your Saviour comes!'* The words of salvation must go out to the ends of the earth to prepare for this great day. That I believe is happening now. The chapter ends with this tremendous statement that the people shall be called the Holy People. The Jews have been called many other things in their time, but in that day they shall be called the Holy People, the Redeemed of the Lord; and the city, which again has been called many things and has been divided and forsaken and destroyed, will be called 'Sought After', and 'the City No Longer Deserted'.

So when will all this happen? It is as if the prophet is looking through a telescope. If you look at a range of mountains through a telescope they all look as if they are together, but if you were to go and explore, then you would find that between the first one and the second was quite a long journey, and so on. It is as if Isaiah is looking at three or four different periods of history through a telescope and sees them all together, and sees the whole development in one glimpse. Undoubtedly a little bit of all this came true when they came back from exile, from Babylon. They brought with them the wealth of Babylon to rebuild the city, so they did indeed rebuild the city with the wealth of other nations. But only a little bit of these three chapters came about then. The nations did not seek Jerusalem for God's glory. So you cannot just say that fulfilled all of it. Then we think of 1948 when the State of Israel was re-established. Some people think that that is when all this was fulfilled, and certainly the wealth of the nations poured into Israel and is still doing so (look at the size of the German reparation figure), yet the nations still do not seek Jerusalem for God's glory, perhaps because God's glory is not yet shining fully on them. So I do not think that is the fulfilment, although I think we are seeing in our day even more of these things coming near. There is a period at the end of history to which we give the name 'The Millennium', which means a thousand years, a period mentioned in the book of Revelation in which Jesus will reign on the earth in righteousness and peace. I can see even more of this being fulfilled in that period, and that will be after our Lord has returned to earth. And in that Jerusalem one can see so much of this coming about. Yet I still do not think all that we have studied in this section will be fulfilled then. Right at the end of the Bible is the new Jerusalem, a city not built by men on earth but built by God in heaven and sent down from heaven. Like a bride adorned for her husband, a city whose gates shall always be open, that the kings of the nations might come in, a city in which there will be no sun and no moon, for the glory of the Lord will shine upon it. When I study that city I find that everything we have studied in this section is fulfilled. So, in a sense, I have the feeling that the prophet is looking through his telescope, if I can put it that way, and he can see four mountain peaks of history. But he is ultimately looking to the city whose builder and maker is God, a city which Abraham himself looked for. So if we would look for the ultimate and final fulfilment of all that is said in these chapters I think we need to look right through all these to the final city of God which we yet look for, sent down from heaven. How do I imagine a city 1,500 miles square coming down out of heaven to earth, God's metropolis? I cannot imagine that, but I honestly believe I see it, and that is part of the great Christian hope for the future.

28
TREADING THE WINEPRESS

Read Isaiah 63 – 64

A. FUTURE ANGER OF THE SON (63:1-6)
1. VINDICATION (1-2)
2. VENGEANCE (3-4)
3. VICTORY (5-6)

B. PAST GRIEF OF THE SPIRIT (63:7-14)
1. LOVE (7-9)
2. LAW (10)
3. LEADERSHIP (11-14)

C. PRESENT SILENCE OF THE FATHER (63:15-64:12)
1. COMPASSION (15-19)
2. CO-OPERATION (1-7)
3. CONSIDERATION (8-12)

In chapters 60 – 62 we studied the promise of the new Jerusalem. Later we shall study the promise of a new heaven and a new earth. But in 63 – 64, we look at a serious revelation of the future, which to some people spoils it all! There are many who hope that the Bible is a kind of 'happily ever after' book where everything goes on swimmingly into a glorious future, as novels used to do. The Bible does in a sense, and when God draws a veil back from the future he shows us wonderful things: a new Jerusalem, a new heaven, a new earth wherein peace and righteousness dwell. But one thing about this revelation of the future spoils it for many. The book of Revelation in the New Testament, which contains some of the most lovely passages about heaven and the new Jerusalem, is found difficult by some because it includes a revelation of something that is going to happen in the future which is most terrible and awesome. This comes out at the beginning of Isaiah 63. Looking through his prophetic 'telescope' into the future, having painted the glories of the new Jerusalem, the prophet suddenly notices something which shocks him, stirring him up to prayer. This 'something' is a solitary figure of a man striding towards Jerusalem from the south-east, who is strong and clothed in splendid garments. Yet in the vision this man is splashed with bright red all over his clothes and he is marching on Jerusalem.

He is coming from a place called Edom. Incidentally, the name *Edom* means red. It is related to the name *Esau* which also means red. For Esau was a hairy man of red hair. Esau was Jacob's brother, and from Esau descended the Edomites who lived just to the south-east of Jacob's descendants, the nation of Israel. So the Edomites and the Israelites were closely related, cousins who were originally descended from twin brothers. Yet within this blood relationship there was a deep hatred. It is often those who are closely related who have most antagonistic feelings towards one another. Edom and Israel, I am afraid, lost no love between them. The hatred was largely on Edom's side. When the Jews were taken away into Babylon in captivity do you know what their relatives the Edomites did? Did they come to their aid? Did they try to help them? No, they did not. Their behaviour was terrible, so in Obadiah we read some of the most severe curses upon a nation that a prophet ever uttered, so—

As you have done, it will be done to you;
your deeds will return upon your own head.

Obadiah v. 15b (NIV)

Recall again the saddest psalm in the Bible, Psalm 137, when they hung their harps up in the trees and said

If I forget you, O Jerusalem,
may my right hand forget its skill.
May my tongue cleave to the roof of my mouth . . .

Psalm 137:5f (NIV)

That psalm finished with these bitter words:

> *O Daughter of Babylon, doomed to destruction,*
> *happy is he who repays you*
> *for what you have done to us—*
> *he who seizes your infants*
> *and dashes them against the rocks.*
>
> Psalm 137:8 (NIV)

What a thing to say! Yet they are just saying out of the bitterness of their hearts that Edom helped to dash their little ones to pieces; that in the day of calamity they took advantage, looted their goods and cut off fugitives. That was Edom, and Edom must go down into history as the descendant of Esau, the man who for a plate full of soup sold his heritage and lived according to the flesh and hated those who lived according to the Spirit.

It is from Edom that this strange figure strides into Isaiah's view. He looks as if he has been treading wine. To make wine, the grapes were put in a heap and jumped on with bare feet, and of course the juice splashed up and their clothes were stained. This man, striding from Edom, the red country, was splashed with red. At first Isaiah thought he had been treading the winepress. The capital of Edom was Bozrah, which means 'winepress'. It was the centre of a wine industry. So Isaiah, looking into the future, sees this majestic strong figure coming from Edom for Jerusalem and says: Who is this? And the figure does not reply by name and simply says, *"It is I, speaking in righteousness, mighty to save"* (Isaiah 63:1, NIV). No name is given, so we are still left in the dark. But Isaiah asks a second question. Why are his clothes splashed with red? Has he been treading out wine? The answer is no, he has been trampling out blood. A most solemn thought now comes. This figure coming to put all things right has also come to destroy things that are wrong. And Edom has just been destroyed. He has trampled them out in his anger against what they did to God's people.

Here is a terrible picture of someone who brings vindication, which means putting everything right — someone who is mighty to save and who yet must judge and destroy, and who has been trampling that wicked nation of Edom underfoot. As they did to others, this figure on his own has done to them. Indeed, he emphasises this. He said, *"I have trodden the winepress alone; from the nations no one was with me"* (Isaiah 63:3, NIV). So with his anger and wrath he brought vengeance to those who wickedly took advantage of the difficulties of his people.

Who is this? Unless we can answer that question we are not going to understand this chapter or apply it to ourselves. The answer is that it is Jesus Christ. And this is a most solemn thought about Jesus Christ that many people refuse to accept, though it is written right through the Bible. It is that one day Jesus is coming back as Judge. He came the first time as Saviour, and the first time he visited this planet of ours he was pierced for our transgressions, bruised for our iniquities, the punishment that brought us peace was upon him. When he came the first time he was punished for the sins of the whole world. When he comes the second time he comes to punish the sins of the whole world. That is the teaching of the Bible. It is strange but people will cling to the 'meek and mild' sentimental view of Jesus that excludes this. That is why many people do not like the book of Revelation, because it says exactly the same thing. The curious fact is that people who will not accept this still have it on their lips. They will go to church and they will recite the Creed and say 'from thence he shall come again to judge both the quick and the dead' — and yet they do not believe it. And if it has a catchy tune to it they will sing about it. They will sing 'Mine eyes have seen the glory of the coming of the Lord; he is trampling out the vintage where the grapes of wrath are stored'. We sing it because it is a nice tune that you can march to, but listen: it *is* true that one day Jesus Christ is going to trample out the vintage where the grapes of wrath are stored. In the book of Revelation we have a picture of Jesus Christ with his garments splashed with blood. We have these exact words of Isaiah 63: 3 quoted of the Lord Jesus Christ in Revelation 19. This is the answer to the question of v. 1, *Who is this . . . ?* The answer is it is the Son of God, coming at the last of human history to deal with all those who have been wrong and wicked, to punish and destroy. That is the full truth about Jesus Christ. He is Saviour and Judge. God has appointed a day in which he will judge the earth by Christ Jesus. This is the terrible revelation of the future in chapter 63. Who is this who is coming? Why are his garments red? It is Jesus, coming to deal with Edom, coming to deal with all those who have dealt wrongly with his people. We know from Matthew 25 that the principle of judgement is this: we are judged by our attitude to Jesus Christ, and this is revealed in our attitude to his brethren: "*. . . whatever you did not do for one of the least of these, you did not do for me.*" The disturbing thought is this: this figure of vengeance, this anger of the Son, is now marching from Edom to Jerusalem. Unless you see that point you will miss the rest of the study.

Let us now turn from the future to the past. The prophet has had a glimpse in the future of Jesus coming in judgement and in anger against wickedness. If you and I could catch a glimpse of that, the first thing we would think about would be our past. They say that a drowning man recalls all his life in a flash. I do not know if that is true, I have never drowned! But I do know this, that people who face death can be made to realise that it is appointed to a man once to die, and after that the judgement. And when they do realise that, it is their past that they think of. So here, when the prophet sees Jesus coming as Judge in the future, the first thing he thinks of is the past of his own people. Are they fit to meet the Judge? The answer is no they are not, they have grieved the Holy Spirit. 63:7–14 shows how they grieved the Holy Spirit by abusing the love that God had showered upon them. Unrequited love is tragic. God's love has been showered upon this world of ours, it has been showered upon every one of us. Above all, it was concentrated upon his people — his steadfast love. That love, goodness and mercy are portrayed in vv. 7 – 9. Surely with all this they would be faithful to him, and not deal falsely?

I remember going to see a mother who had adopted a boy many years before I knew her. She had slaved to the bone to bring him up, showering upon him all that he needed. She had nursed him in his illness. She had got him to a good school. She had done everything she could for him. Then one day he ran away from home, at the age of sixteen, and he took all her life savings with him. That was the reward she got for the love she showered upon him. The grief and the sorrow were so deep, that was when she sent for me, and it was a heavy burden to have to face — the grief of love that has been showered upon someone and then abused. God said: surely they will not deal falsely. Surely they are my people. Surely this love would keep them faithful. And so he became their Saviour. He was so sympathetic toward them in their need that in all their affliction he was afflicted. In all their sufferings, he suffered. Do you not think that a parent who loves a child suffers more than the child when the child suffers? Have you not seen that? In his love and his pity God redeemed them, and he carried them as of old as a father carries his young son. But (see v. 10) they rebelled and grieved his Holy Spirit.

What does true love do when a child rebels? Laugh? Forget? Say, 'Well, boys will be boys, we'll forgive and forget'? May I tell you that true love must discipline that child. Sentimental love would not do it but true love would. If you love your child you cannot bear to think of them going on in rebellion and developing a character that will become increasingly self-centred. So love chastises. Whom the Lord loves he chastises. *What father is there who does not chastise his children whom he loves?* (Hebrews 12). If you are not disciplined of the Lord, says that chapter, you are a bastard and not a child of God. If God loves you, he disciplines you. He had given them his law to obey. Having loved them and redeemed them from Egypt, he told them how they were to live. But they broke his laws and rebelled and they grieved his Spirit. They turned God into their enemy. Verse 11 does not include the word 'he' in the original Hebrew, so cross it out if it is in your version. Then he remembered the days of old of Moses his servant. Who remembered? Not God, but the people who had rebelled. Verse 10: 'then they rebelled'; v. 11: 'then remembered'. When the Lord chastises and disciplines, you remember. When you are going through it, you remember. When the Lord becomes your enemy, you remember the days that he led you. They remembered the days he parted the Red Sea and brought them out. They remembered the leadership he gave them under Moses; they remembered how his Holy Spirit led them like cattle into the valley to perfect rest. Notice three times the Holy Spirit is mentioned in vv. 10–14: the beginning of v. 10, the end of v. 11, the middle of v. 14. The Holy Spirit was the guide and the one who was grieved when they went astray. And we grieve the Holy Spirit when we rebel against God's love. God had given them his love, he had given them his law, he had given them his leadership, and they had abused all three.

Therefore this figure striding with vengeance and anger against the evildoer is marching straight for Jerusalem and the people of God. And Isaiah realises, as another prophet did, that judgement begins with the house of God, and that God is no respecter of persons. You may go to church, you may be religious, you may try to be good, but that does not absolve you from judgement. So God must be fair to all, and if he must punish wickedness in Edom he must punish wickedness in Israel. If he must punish wickedness in the world he must punish wickedness in the church. Why should we think that God has favourites? So this figure strides for Israel and comes straight for the city of God.

It is this appalling tension that Isaiah now puts into a most wonderful and moving prayer which is one of the most honest prayers I have ever read. As we look into this prayer we shall see the tension. The tension is between, on the one hand, an eagerness for the future to come, an eagerness to live in this new Jerusalem, an eagerness to be part of this glorious future; and, on the other hand, a knowledge that one is not ready, that there are things in the life of the people of God that are not ready for the Judge to look at. I have known this in Christians who were reaching the end of the road. I have talked to them when they knew that they were near the end of their earthly pilgrimage. The tension was there. On the one hand they wanted to be in heaven, they wanted to be in glory. On the other hand their own unworthiness was seen with even greater clarity. The memory of the things they had done and the things they should not have done seemed more real. And there is this awful tension: I want to be in that, I want to be in heaven, I am looking forward to it, and yet there are things in my life that are not ready to face Jesus. Is this not how we all feel from time to time? We want Jesus to come again —or do we? We want him to come in glory —or do we? We want the new Jerusalem to come down out of heaven — or do we? We want all wickedness to be punished because we want it to be dealt with and vanquished from the world, and the world made good again. But then we say: but dear me, there's a bit of wickedness in me. What will happen if he comes to deal with *all* wickedness? You see the tension?

So Isaiah goes to prayer, and from the past he turns to the present. They are in exile and God seems silent, he seems cold, he seems distant, and Isaiah realises that the silence of the Father in the present is due to the grief of the Spirit in the past, and one day in the future there will be the anger of the Son. That is the link between these three sections of our study. God seems as far away and as cold and as withdrawn as anyone we have never seen or spoken to. Do you ever feel like that? Do you ever feel that prayer is dead, that God is a long way from you? What has gone wrong?

We know from an earlier chapter what went wrong. Do you remember chapter 59? Your sins have hidden his face from you so that he does not hear. The silence of the Father. And now Isaiah pleads with God the Father. He calls him three times '*our Father*' – that is the basis of prayer. When you begin to pray, you say: our Father. On that basis Isaiah pleads, knowing that they do not deserve it, for three things are needed in order that all the Jews may be saved from the judgement that is coming. He pleads with the Father that all of Israel, the whole of the nation, may be saved from that blood-splashed figure who comes. Here are three tremendous prayers relating to the compassion of God's heart, the co-operation of God's will and the consideration of God's mind.

The appeal to the compassion of God's heart begins: *Look down* . . . . Isaiah knows that if you look at people in trouble you feel for them. Our Lord many a time looked on people and had compassion for them. You cannot have compassion until you have seen a person. That is why the famine appeal funds have discovered that a little picture of a starving child does more to elicit human compassion than any long, wordy appeal. The appeal is to *our Father*. The people have no-one else to look to. Abraham is their earthly father but they cannot turn to him. Jacob is their earthly father but they cannot turn to him. They may be wicked children, rebellious children, they may have abused his love, but he is their Father, and it is to him that they must turn for compassion. Then there was a very naughty prayer:

> *Why, O Lord, do you make us wander from your ways*
> *and harden our hearts so that we do not revere you?*
> 63:17a (NIV)

People still say that sort of thing. They say, 'Why doesn't God make us good?' I have had people ask me when I have been on a panel; students have asked me that when I have had a question time with them. The answer is that God wanted children, not puppets. He wanted children who loved him and who would be good because they loved him. I know that God originally made man very good, but man could choose evil. Yet people often say, 'Well, it's just the way I am made.' So, 'God, why did you make me do this?' is a naughty prayer. We go wrong through our own wilful disobedience not through anything else. O God look down in compassion, look at us. Couldn't you find some compassion in your heart for us? That is a very moving prayer.

The second prayer is not just 'Look down' but '. . . *rend the heavens and come down'* (see 64:1, NIV). It is an appeal to the Lord to do something about all this. Why does he not come and control the wickedness? By the way, you can tell that this is a heartfelt prayer by the number of times the little one letter word *O* occurs. When you are really desperate you say: O God, come and help; O, if you would only . . . . That is a sign of a deep prayer, not just a correct form of address. Then Isaiah, with great boldness, points out to God the reputation he would have among the nations if he comes down. They have never seen a God who helps those who wait for him. He is the only living God. The fear of God would be in people if he came down and did things.

Then Isaiah makes a confession of men's sinful acts against which God's sovereign acts shine out. From halfway through 64:5, Isaiah humbles himself and says we all (i.e. every Israelite there was) sinned. We have all become like one who is unclean. This had gone on for a long time. It is tragic when you meet a man who is in his fifties, sixties, seventies or eighties who realises he is a sinner, because he usually thinks he has been too long in his sins to be saved. 'I have been in my sins a long time, I can't change now.' Young people of course can change quickly, and so to them conversion seems so easy, so simple, but a person in later life who has been a long time in their sins is bound to ask: How can I possibly be saved after such a long time away from God? But you can be. And the glorious news is that right until a dying man's last moment, grace is available to him as it was to a dying thief.

Notice v.6. It is a confession of 'All . . . .' Isaiah includes himself. He sees this figure of Jesus coming towards him in judgement and in anger against sin; he sees the same anger that would come to cleanse the temple and whip the money-changers out of it. It is an anger that appears in the book of Revelation. *They called to the mountains and the rocks, "Fall on us and hide us from the face of him who sits on the throne and from the wrath of the Lamb! For the great day of their wrath has come, and who can stand?"* (Revelation 6:16–17, NIV).

There is a phrase here in v.6 that may be offensive but I want to explain what it means, because it is there in the Hebrew. It is a blunt phrase but it is a realistic one and it states exactly what it means. It says all our righteous deeds have become like a menstrual cloth, something that made a woman unclean, kept her out of the tabernacle and away from worship. Isaiah says that we are all polluted in our garments. Even the best things we have ever done are tainted with sin and self. Even our righteous deeds are spoiled and are not fit to bring into God's presence. It is a most vivid thing to say. But a man is really facing his sin when he realises that it is his good deeds that are tainted, not just his bad ones—that the best thing he has ever done had a little bit of self tainting it; that the finest act of his nature was still the act of a nature that was not the nature of God and not the nature of perfection, and not a nature that loved God with all his heart and soul and mind and strength. This is when you realise that your good deeds when measured by Christ are polluted — the best things you have ever put on are tainted by yourself. This is the realisation and the confession of sin Isaiah makes. We all shrivel like leaves, and our sins sweep us away like the wind. So he calls on the Lord to come.

So he comes to the final prayer. He has pleaded for the compassion of God's heart, then for the co-operation of God's will for him to come down and do something. Now he pleads for the consideration of God's mind. He argues and pleads and reasons. First, he addresses God as 'our Father'. That is the first fact upon which he appeals to God's mind: *we are all your people*. That is his plea. It is as if he is saying then: we are all sinners, but we are all the work of your hands —doesn't that appeal to you Lord? We may have ruined your work but we are your work. We may have marred the image that there is in us, but we are still in your image. You are still our Father even if we are rebellious children. That is a *reasonable* appeal. He continues: *We are the clay, you are the potter.* As a potter takes a lump of shapeless clay and shapes it on the wheel until it becomes a pot, God can shape us. The Lord can remake us. God's beautiful sanctuary is ruined, he could rebuild it. Here is a plea to God to consider.

Let me summarise what we have studied. First, a glimpse of the future and of the anger of Jesus against sin, which will one day be expressed when he tramples out that vintage, brings vindication and puts things right, and there is vengeance upon the evildoer and victory over wickedness. Jesus is coming to do that, but are we ready? From the future, we turn to the past and realise that in spite of all the love that God gave, the law he gave, the leadership that he gave through the wilderness, his people had rebelled and grieved his Spirit and are not ready to meet this figure. So Isaiah turns to prayer to the Father, yet the Father seems silent. Isaiah was only praying for his nation, but what people today want to know is: why can't everybody go to heaven? We have all sinned, why can't we all be saved? God's answer to that is in chapter 65, and next we shall study his answer to this amazing prayer.

29

NEW HEAVENS AND NEW EARTH

Read Isaiah 65

A. SOWING AND REAPING (1-7)
1. REBELLION (1-5)
2. REPAYMENT (6-7)

B. LIFE AND DEATH (8-12)
1. SERVANTS (8-10)
2. SINNERS (11-12)

C. BLESSING AND CURSE (13-16)
1. NATURE (13-14)
2. NAME (15-16)

D. HEAVEN AND EARTH (17-25)
1. STAMINA (17-20)
2. STABILITY (21-25)

One of the main questions I am frequently asked is this: If God is a God of love and of power, why can he not save *everyone* and take *everyone* to heaven? Would it not be a lovely demonstration of his grace if he did? Would it not be a glorious thing if he said: I know you have all sinned, I know none of you deserves heaven but nevertheless I am going to have you all there, and every man or woman who has ever lived will some day be saved? That is a lovely thought — such a lovely thought that many professing Christians have adopted it and even preached it — that one day everybody will be saved and that hell is a non-existent threat, only mentioned in the Bible to try to keep us on the straight and narrow; that in fact God is so loving and so powerful he would never send anybody there! This is answered by chapter 65 and many other passages in the Bible.

Isaiah had the same question, but his was not so much

about the world as his own nation. In this chapter there are four different answers given which complement one another and make up a complete reply. I have divided the chapter into vv. 1–7, 8–12, 13–16 and 17–25, which give the four basic answers. I can sum them all up by saying one thing: God treats people as people, and that is why he cannot save them all. There are many who treat others as though they were objects — things. We may do that and not realise what we are doing, but God would never do that. And God cannot *make* a person be good — that would not be treating people as people. They must be free to refuse to be made good if they are to be real persons. That is the first answer that comes in verses 1–7.

One could call this section 'sowing and reaping' — even though these words do not occur here. The idea is: whatsoever a man sows, that shall he also reap. One of the laws of the universe, one of God's fundamental laws is that this is a universe of justice, a universe in which things are put right, a universe in which right is rewarded and wrong is punished — because God is good. Whatever one is personally responsible for doing, one must pay the consequences of that, whether it be good or evil. Let us see how this principle applies in this case.

In 64:12 Isaiah had asked, *Will you keep silent and punish us beyond measure?* (NIV). Now God replies: *"All day long I have held out my hands to an obstinate people . . . "* (65:2a, NIV). He was ready to be sought by those who did not ask for him. If he seemed far away, it was not his fault — he wanted to be found. This is a fundamental truth about God. The trouble is not that we do not get any response from him but that he does not get any response from us. And God, being good, cannot overlook the sin of those who refuse every overture he makes to them. Here we have at the beginning of this chapter not a picture of a God who has to be sought, a God who is very difficult to find, a God who holds himself a long way away and says you will have to find your way right up here, but a God who is constantly speaking, constantly trying to reach people, a God who spreads out his hands all the day and says come. Just as I used to say to my children, 'Come to Daddy' and after a while I did not even have to say it but could just hold out my hands and they came. This is a picture of God — he holds out his hands all the day long to people and says come to Father, and they do not come. He speaks to his people constantly and says to them that he is willing to be found if they want to seek him. He is ready to answer if you will speak to him. The simple truth is that the majority of the nation of Israel did not really want to find him.

So God had called to them and had been ready to be found. What should a good God do then? The answer is he can do nothing else but repay them for their rebellion, if he is going to treat them as persons. There is nothing more you can do with a person than that, because if you do anything more than that you treat them as a thing and you force them to come — and that is not God and it is not love and it is not God treating a person as a person.

Before we go any further, may I say that this is my burden for the world in which we live. There are hundreds of people living all around us and God has spoken to them and he is holding his hands out to them but they do not want to come, and that is a basic truth. If you want to find this out, do a little house-to-house visitation, or try to get your neighbour along to church. Try to talk to them about God. You will discover that this is the basic problem. It is not on God's side that the fault lies, it is on their side, they do not want to find him. We tell our community: come, we want to tell you about God. We tell them that God lives and that he loves, that we want them to know him, but most do not want it. What more can God do that does not turn them from people into things, that does not leave them free to refuse to come in response to his invitation?

The next thing we learn here is that their rebellion lay not only in their refusal to respond to God's loving overture, but they had developed their own ideas of religion, and they followed their own devices (v. 2, or 'their own imaginations', NIV). If you have worshipped in the Church of England you may know the words from the *Book of Common Prayer* 'We have followed too much the devices and desires of our own hearts . . . .' That is precisely what we do. They did not cease to be religious, but instead of responding to God's call they devised their own religion. This is the biblical view of religion. What is the Bible's answer to other, non-Christian religions? Are they like roads all leading to God? Are they groping after God? Are people coming nearer to God through these religions? The answer is no, these are the devices of man which are the result of refusing God. We now know from archaeology that the earliest religion of man was to worship the high God in heaven. Idolatry was not the first step in religion, it was a later downfall from the high God worship of earliest man. So we know now that man has devised his own religion to defend himself against God. And the proof that this is the right answer is this: when you try to lead a person to the truth in Christ it is their religion that is the biggest barrier. Far from their religion helping them towards the truth it becomes their defence against it. Try and convert an adherent of another religion to the truth in Christ, and tell him that we have the whole truth in Christ for which he has been seeking, and you will usually find it does not work.

Since the majority religion in this country is 'churchianity' you will find that one of the biggest problems in leading a person to Christ here is that their religion is the barrier. 'Oh, I have been christened, I have been confirmed, I have been through the lot,' they say, and that prevents them from coming to Christ.

What had the people Isaiah addressed been doing? They were sacrificing in gardens, which God never told them to do. They were burning incense upon bricks, which was again their own device. They were sitting in tombs and spending the night in secret places. That probably refers to spiritualistic practices through mediums, all of which was forbidden by God. They were eating swine's flesh, and broth of abominable things in their vessels, breaking their own dietary laws. And (v. 5) they had developed an exclusive attitude that said: keep away from me; I am different, I am set apart from you. Have you ever tried to light a bonfire on a wet day and the thing has smouldered away all day and filled the garden and the house with smoke, and your neighbours hanging out their washing have been looking at you and glaring over the garden fence? God says that all this kind of religion which they devise is like a fire that burns all day, like smoke filling his nostrils. It is a vivid picture of something irritating and offensive. Here we have God's verdict on human religion: smoke in his nostrils, a fire that smoulders all the day long. You cannot get it alight and you cannot put it out. That is the trouble with religion. It is like a smouldering thing. It may be alight, yet it is not really a light. Jesus once said that lukewarm people make him sick. *So, because you are lukewarm — neither hot nor cold — I am about to spit you out of my mouth* (Revelation 3:16, NIV). Smouldering, you are neither out nor alight.

God says, *"I will not keep silent but I will pay back in full."* A good God has to repay those who say, I do not want to find God, those who refuse the invitation which is at the moment wide open — to come to him. God would have anybody who came to him this day, any person in the world who will respond to his love with repentance, and accept the salvation that is provided. He will have them on the spot. And the reason why the majority of people do not know God is not his fault, it is that they do not want to come to him. God will repay that. There is a law of retribution and God calls behaviour like that rebellion. Think of family life. If my children absolutely refused to come when I called them and simply went on playing with what they were doing, that would be rebellion, and it does happen from time to time even in the best of families. But it is rebellion pure and simple, and no parent could ignore that in a child, especially when it was continual and there was an absolute refusal to respond to the parent's love.

So we come to the second point that God makes through the prophet. In vv. 8–12, not only does he teach us that there is a process of sowing and reaping, but this must ultimately issue in the distinction between life and death. Sometimes a gardener will debate whether to pull down a tree in the garden, especially if it is blocking the light, or if it is not growing very well, or if it is not producing the fruit it should. But sometimes in the Middle East when a gardener is going around the vineyard and then he looks at a vine and thinks: that vine should come down, it has not been a good one and it is really taking up valuable ground — he is going to chop it down. Then he notices a cluster of grapes in the middle of the vine and he does not chop it down because of that cluster. He says: there is a blessing in the cluster. I'll just wait and get that cluster before I chop it down. In v. 8 God says, *"I will not destroy them all."* He will not chop that nation down completely because there is a cluster in it. The cluster was a small group of people who were in fact seeking him. To me the most amazing thing is that everywhere you go God has a cluster seeking him. You can go to the most dead church and somewhere in it you will find one or two who are seeking God and who really mean business with him. God has his clusters. They called it 'the remnant' in Bible times. God begins to talk about those people as his servants.

This word 'servant' we have seen is a key word in the book of Isaiah. It is used in three ways. First of all, when we came across it in chapters 40 and 41 it meant all the Jews, only it was in the singular — my servant Israel, my servant Jacob. It meant the whole nation. Then, secondly, when we got into chapter 42 and went through to chapter 43 we discovered that the word was now used of one Jew, whom we now know to be Jesus, and once again the word is in the singular. It is *my servant* — one man who was to bear the sins of the many. But now we have come to a third use which refers that word to *some Jews*, and now it is in the plural. It can no longer apply to the whole nation, nor to one Jew, it now applies to a cluster of Jews within the nation, who seek God. They are going to go back to the promised land. When they do, Sharon instead of being a desert will be a fertile pasture. I remember going by bus through the Plain of Sharon. It had been a desert with sand dunes for two thousand years. I saw a herd of black and white Fresian cows up to their knees in green grass, and behind them a row of beehives, white against the hills! A land flowing with milk and honey, that was Sharon. The barren Valley of Achor is on the other side of the hills, in the rain shadow. That valley will be a place for herds to lie down — and you only make herds lie down in green pastures. So what God is saying is this: my servants, this cluster of people who seek me, will go back to the land, which will become fertile, and they will be able to graze every part of it.

But now notice, at the end of v. 10 and the beginning of v. 11, the great distinction before God is so simple. The great division running right through mankind, and right through the nation of Israel, is not between the good and the bad, it is between those who sought God and those who forsook God. That is a very important point. It is between those who responded to his invitation and those who refused it —those who came and those who went. That is what ultimately will divide the human race— not whether they are good or bad, for we are all sinners, but in God's sight his servants are those who seek him, and sinners are those who forsake him and pin their hopes in something or someone else.

Let us look at that something or someone else. The first something in which the others pin their hopes is fortune. I do not know whether you know the Hebrew word for that but you have probably heard it if not used it. It is the word *gad*. When people say 'by gad' they mean by fortune, by luck, by chance. Then the other god that they now had was a god called *destiny* – both of these they had picked up from the surrounding nations. They worshipped fortune and destiny. But the Hebrew word for destiny is *meni* (literally, 'number'). That is precisely the kind of thing people do when they forsake God. They pin their trust in their luck, their number coming up this week. There are people who would gladly spend three hours at a bingo card but say that one hour's Bible study is too long. This is the kind of thing that was happening in Israel. People who just pin their faith in fortune, luck, chance, always filling in their cards for one thing or another, always hoping that their number is coming up. I found in the RAF that even trained pilots who had to be very well educated to manage those machines, who had to have scientific knowledge at their fingertips, used to climb into the cockpit of these aircraft with a rabbit's foot in one pocket and something else in the other. I used to talk to them and say, 'Do you think about death?' because we lost half our pilots in Aden in six months. 'If your number's up your number's up', they said. 'If your number's on that plane that day, you've had it and there's nothing you can do about it' — just sheer fatalism, so they lived by luck, by chance, by fortune, by 'gad', by numbers. There are people today by the thousand living by their lucky numbers. They are not in church, they are not seeking the truth, they do not know any God in whom they can pin their hope for the future, so they are constantly hoping that their number will turn up. That is what the Israelites were doing, and it is to forsake God. When I think of this kind of living I always think of the soldiers gambling for our Lord's clothes at the foot of the cross, and because they were busy with that they never realised that the greatest provision in history was six feet above their heads. Their eyes were glued to those dice and they missed the Son of God. In this I see a picture of those who forsake God and put their trust in fortune and destiny. Says God, *"I will destine you for the sword."*

Did you seek God, or did you forsake him for something or someone else? That is the division, and that is the second answer, and this divides everybody into his servants or sinners in his sight.

The third thing he mentions is that this division must go on to its reward, which will either be blessing or curse. In the next few verses (13–16), we have a tremendous contrast. Everybody cannot possibly share the same destiny if they are responsible for their own attitude to God, and they are. This is drawn in vivid pictures. *'My servants will eat, but you will go hungry.'* God's servants would eat but those who had gone after fortune would be hungry. That contrast is followed by drinking and thirsting, rejoicing and being put to shame, singing from joy and crying out from anguish of heart. Each of these contrasts our Lord Jesus took up and applied to heaven and hell. He taught, for example, that heaven would be like a banquet, and many people are invited to that feast. But they have their excuses and refuse the invitation. So the owner of the house gives an order to the servant to go out and bring in the poor, the crippled, the blind and the lame —and others, so that the master's house would be full. But those who had been invited and refused to come would not eat, they would see themselves shut out.

Our Lord took up the idea of drinking and thirst and he portrayed hell as a very thirsty place, in which a rich man begged for a drop of water on his tongue. Our Lord took up the idea of crying and wailing, he spoke about weeping and wailing and gnashing of teeth. These are serious words. In other words, if we take our Lord's word for it, there is an eternal distinction and there is a separation. God cannot possibly save everybody, because they have refused his invitation and they have rebelled against him. What else can he do?

Not only is the contrast drawn and the nature of the blessing and the curse described here, but there is also something said about the name. The name 'Israel', because the majority of those within the nation rebelled against God, would become accursed, and that is precisely what happened. Through history Israel has been the name of a people who suffer, a people who have got away from God, a people who have kept their religion but lost their God, and this name has become a name of curse. Those who sought God within the nation would be given a new name. People used to bless themselves by the name of Israel (see v. 16) but now if they bless themselves it will be by God, by the name of the God of 'amen', translated 'truth'. That word 'amen' is one of the most wonderful words in the Bible. It means absolutely reliable, certain to take place, surely. If you say 'amen' at the end of a prayer, do you realise what you are saying? I do not want to discourage you from saying it because I love the sound of a grand amen in church. I think it really means that the congregation heard the prayer, and that is encouraging to the preacher. Nevertheless, we must realise what we are doing when we say it. We are saying that it is going to happen. It requires tremendous faith to say that one little word. And God is the God of amen. If he says a thing it is certainly going to take place. He never goes back on his word. He is the God of truth and if he says he will do a thing he will do it. He may wait a time before doing it but he will do it. And people, if they are going to bless themselves in the land, will not bless themselves by Israel — look how they let him down; they will bless themselves by the God of Israel — look how he never let them down — the God of amen, the God of truth.

The final point that God makes here as the reason why he could not save all the Jews is that it is his plan to make a new world, a whole new universe that will be good (see 65:17ff). How could he possibly put in it people who refuse his love? That is the final answer. I find 65:17 to be one of the most thrilling verses in Isaiah. It is something that only the Jews and the Christians know. Nobody else in the world knows what I am going to tell you now. If God had not told us, we would not know either. There is a truth here that science and philosophy will never be able to discover: that God is going to pull this world down and build a new one. That is the truth, and God is the God of truth and amen. I do not know if your heart beats more quickly when you think of that idea. Everything that you see around you is going to be dissolved, pulled down, taken away, and God is going to fashion a new world. In the Bible there is as much about creation at the end as at the beginning. In the beginning God created the heavens and the earth. But then we turn all the pages and we come to the end of the Bible and it says this: *Then I saw a new heaven and a new earth, for the first heaven and the first earth had passed away . . .* (Revelation 21:1a, NIV).

When God makes all things new, we shall be so interested in and fascinated by the new universe in which we live that we will forget about the old. You will forget about the old hills, the new scenery will be so wonderful. The former things will not be remembered. God is going to make a new universe, and I want that to sink into your thoughts and imagination. I find it very difficult to imagine. A scientist has his theories but has no idea that God is going to make a new heaven and earth. Nor does the philosopher, because the idea of a universe vanishing and another one coming in its place is philosophically unacceptable to the human mind and it does not seem logical. But God has said he is going to do it. Therefore those who have this verse, Jews and Christians, know that it is going to happen.

From now until the end of the chapter, God concentrates on what will happen on earth. But there is a problem here: *when* is he referring to? Is he referring in the rest of this chapter to things that will happen after he has created the new heaven and the new earth or before? The answer, as far as I can see, is that for the rest of the chapter he is describing what he will do before the new heaven and the new earth, and what he will do to lead up to that new heaven and new earth. Things are described now which are not true of the present in which we live here, but which could not be true of the new heaven and new earth either. Somewhere must be found a period of time— yet in the future, but before this—in which God can do what he says he will do in the rest of the chapter. The Bible describes such a period. We call it the millennium. Within that period, between the present evil age in which we live and the coming new universe, certain things will happen. Christ will reign in peace and righteousness, but certain other things will happen. These are now described, as a kind of prelude to the new heaven and the new earth.

Let me take one of them. In the time of the psalmist, normal life expectancy was some seventy to eighty years, and now we are pushing it up a bit, and a century is not unusual today. But in the new heaven and the new earth we shall live forever, we shall have eternal life. But in between is a kind of prelude to that, in which people live for hundreds of years, and this is described in the rest of this chapter. No more will babies be born who live just a few days. (That is dying out in this country, it is reduced to a minimum now. But of course a hundred years ago, and even today in some countries, if a woman raises two out of eight children she is doing well.) That will not happen in this era. People will live as long as trees according to this prophecy (and I have seen some trees that are probably five hundred years old). So premature death, which is a major cause of unhappiness, will not exist. Why is this not talking about the new heaven and the new earth? Very simply because there will be neither birth nor death in the new universe, so here we are obviously seeing a prelude to it.

Verse 24: prayer will be a most unusual experience in those days. At the moment in this life I pray and then God answers. But in that period: *'Before they call I will answer . . .'* (Isaiah 65:24a, NIV). I have heard this verse quoted in prayer meetings; but quite frankly let us quote it for the period to which it refers. It is not a promise for this period in which we live. It is a statement as to the kind of vital prayer relationship that will exist in that period. God is going to be so ready to answer prayer that he will answer it before you have asked.

Furthermore, in 65:25 we see again this unique picture of nature under such conditions of stability, safety, peace and security around that there will be no threat at all. Even nature red in tooth and claw will vanish. This is the same period referred to in chapter 11 and in 2:4. So we have this age in which we live our brief lives, in which we hurt one another, in which nature itself threatens our existence; we have the next stage, the prelude to eternity, in which there will be no cause of unhappiness, in which there will be no need for armaments, because nation shall not learn war any more, in which Christ will reign in peace and righteousness; and according to the Bible, after that prelude, in which we see what Christ can do with the old earth and the old heaven, then we see a new creation of a new heaven and a new earth. That is what we are looking forward to. Many people are hoping for such a golden age as this on this earth and the Bible tells us it will come, but only when Christ comes again as King.

Jesus will come and reign and show what he can do with a world like this in its fallen state, and show you what kind of possibility there is when it is ruled in peace, righteousness and justice. But then he is going to smash up this old world and make a new heaven and a new earth that will be absolutely perfect. Such is the vision to which we look forward, about which we sing and for which we long.

30

UNDYING WORM, UNQUENCHABLE FIRE

Read Isaiah 66

A. IGNORED WORD OF GOD (1-6)
1. BUILDING (1-2)
2. SACRIFICING (3-4)
3. LISTENING (5-6)

B. IDEALISED WOMAN OF JERUSALEM (7-14)
1. DELIVERING (7-9)
2. SUCKLING (10-11)
3. NURSING (12-14)

C. INCLUDED WORLD OF GENTILES (15-24)
1. JUDGING (15-17)
2. SURVIVING (18-21)
3. PERISHING (22-24)

We come at last to the final chapter in Isaiah. When you read chapter 66 for the first time it seems a mixture, jumping from one subject to another, but like every part of God's word it hangs together. It is an epilogue to the whole prophecy, bringing together three major themes of Isaiah: God the Heavenly Father and his word to his people through the prophet; Jerusalem, the city that consoled those people through centuries and still does; and the Jews themselves, the children of Israel, the children of God, meant to share with the whole world the blessings they had received — which they never did.

Let us turn to the first thought, bearing in mind that this chapter is addressed to the Jews, probably just during the time when they got back to Jerusalem and were thinking about rebuilding. For as soon as the people of God get Jerusalem the first thing they think about is rebuilding the temple. (This has a strangely contemporary sound about it, as Israel is feverishly discussing the rebuilding of the temple.) When they got the city back following the exile in Babylon, the first thing they thought about was putting the temple up, for that was God's dwelling place. This chapter was written to the Jews as they came back to a Jerusalem that was empty and in ruins.

Let us consider what Isaiah says to the people who are beginning to be concerned about building a temple. It is a perilous time for them. It is so very easy to get wrong notions of God when you are erecting a place of worship. Isaiah's words here are to prevent them from falling into the trap of thinking you can house God. Heaven is his throne, the earth is his footstool. You could not build a house big enough for God! Solomon, when he had finished his temple, knew this. It is always the danger of erecting churches now that you think God is there and nowhere else, that you have to have a building in which to meet him. But God is Creator of all things and cannot be contained like that.

In vv. 3ff., something even more important is made clear: you cannot guarantee the presence of God by putting up a building. The only thing that guarantees God's presence in a building is the right kind of people inside it! This is a prophetic word that we need today. It is not automatic that because a church was erected for the worship of God (whether recently or hundreds of years ago) that you can find God by going in through the front door. God is only present when the right kind of people are there and the right kind of people are these: those who have humble and contrite hearts and who tremble at the word of God. If you have people like that, you have the house of God. For God does not dwell in buildings made of stones and bricks and mortar, he dwells in people who have the right kind of hearts. The body is a temple of the Holy Spirit.

I think that is a word that needs to be said to Israel today. While they discuss the rebuilding of the temple, while they prefabricate the stones, that will not bring his presence, his glory. The only guarantee is people of a humble and contrite spirit and who tremble at his word. It is not the world's ambition to be humble and contrite — that is seen as a sign of weakness. But in God's sight the people whom he looks upon, the people whom he considers, are those who are poor in spirit, and meek, the humble and the broken-hearted. They are contrite because they know that every time they come to the building to worship they have sinned since last they came, and have grieved the Holy Spirit and broken God's word, and if we do not come in a humble and contrite spirit to worship God, the building is not his house and we do not know his presence.

From time to time I have seen people tremble in a pew. I remember sitting behind a young man, and a preacher under great grace preached from the Bible and I saw that young man begin to shake. He was a young man who had done many wrong things and he realised then that he was face to face with God. I remember hearing that man give his testimony just a week or two later in that same wooden hut. And I remember him saying that he reached the point where he threw a knife at his own mother to kill her — but now he was face to face with God and he trembled at God's word. When someone realises that the Bible is not just an ancient book, but that it is living truth, and that what it says about God will always be true, and that we who tremble at his word must have dealings with this God, then they will find him. So if you want to find God do not look round for a building, look round for people who are humble and contrite and who know that they are sinners. When you get inside a building with those people, that building will be the house of God. Even if you met them in somebody's kitchen or out in a field, that would be a holy place.

The second thing is harder to understand. From vv. 3ff., we have a difficult passage which scholars have argued about a great deal. Translators have taken a liberty in putting in some words to convey what they think is the meaning. Here is my rendering of v. 3 as it is in the Hebrew: *He who slaughters an ox kills a man. He who sacrifices a lamb breaks a dog's neck. He who presents a cereal offering offers swine's blood. He who makes a memorial offering of frankincense blesses an idol.* The words 'is like him who' have been put in by some translators, so if you would like to cross them out you are perfectly at liberty to do so. But it leaves a very difficult sentence. In each of these four sentences the first half is something right and good that should be done, and the second half is something wrong and bad which should not have been done. It was right to slaughter an ox. It was right to sacrifice a lamb. It was right to present a grain offering. And it was right to present a memorial offering of frankincense. But it was utterly wrong to kill a man. That is murder. It was wrong to break a dog's neck. It was not an animal that God accepted. It was wrong to offer swine's blood, for the pig was an unclean animal and its blood was no use. And it was wrong to bless an idol.

What is meant by 'he who slaughters an ox kills a man'? It could mean one of three things. I will present them all to you and tell you which I think it means. It could mean that when people are not humble and contrite, even if they make the right sacrifice to God it is as abhorrent as the wrong one. That is the meaning that some translators have adopted when they put in the words 'is like him who'. In other words, you may come to the temple, you may offer a lamb, but because you are not humble and contrite you might as well be breaking a dog's neck. You may slaughter an ox but in God's sight it is as abhorrent as killing a man. In other words, sacrifice without the right attitude of heart is an abomination to God. And in modern terms you may come to church, you may sing the hymns, you may say the prayers, but if your heart is not humble and contrite it is as unacceptable to God as the most savage pagan worship. That is one possible meaning. God does not like outward formal worship, the right ritual, the right liturgy, unless the heart has a right attitude — we know this from the prophets.

A second meaning could be this: that in fact God does not

want any more sacrifices at all, and all the sacrifices they have offered up till now are no longer acceptable, that in fact slaughtering an ox is no longer wanted by God, it is obnoxious to him altogether. The whole principle of sacrifice is finished, just as the first two verses imply that having holy buildings is obsolete. That is a possible meaning but I doubt if it is the meaning here.

The more obvious meaning, and the one to which I incline myself, is this: crossing out those words that have been added, it seems to me that this is a warning about mixing your religion —that it is no good offering the right things in one setting and then going away and offering the wrong things somewhere else, and that in fact it was a word to those who were doing both. You would not think that people could do both and yet they do. In 1 Corinthians 10 and 11 Paul asks Christians how they can come to the Lord's table and eat the bread and the wine there, then go out and eat meat offered to idols. That was mixing their religion. You cannot do both. Idolatry was the religion they were mixing with pure worship. But when we think that covetousness is idolatry, and that many of us have worshipped God and Mammon, we realise that people still mix their religion. It is akin to the idea that if you do the right thing by God on Sunday you can do the wrong thing on Monday.

Now God speaks about the dreadful rebuff that Israel gave to him.

"For when I called, no-one answered,
when I spoke, no-one listened.
They did evil in my sight
and chose what displeases me."

Isaiah 66:4b (NIV)

That is what convinces me that the meaning of this strange v.3 is that the Jews were giving the sacrifices on the Sabbath in a proper way, and during the week going straight off and doing something improper which was evil in God's sight. Let us confess and be humble and contrite enough to admit that we have, to a degree, done exactly this thing and thought that provided we gave God what he wanted on Sunday, we could do what we chose during the week. But that is not so. We have done it with our money. We thought that providing we put in a generous offering we could do what we liked with the rest of our money. Provided that we gave God two services on Sunday we could do what we liked with the rest of our time. But this is mixing religion, it is mixing pure worship and idolatry. For to give yourself the pre-eminence is idolatry and that is the second warning.

Then we come to a third thing that they would restore. When you have got the city back you put up the temple. When you have put up the temple you begin the sacrifices. And when you begin the sacrifices you also start reading and preaching God's word. All these three things happened in the same place in Israel in the temple at Jerusalem.

We have something extraordinary in vv. 5–6. Some people in Israel did tremble at the word of the Lord, and the others ridiculed them and said: you take it too seriously. This is a thing that some Christians are accused of. People say they are taking the word of God too seriously and have religious mania. The people of Israel generally were persecuting, hating and ridiculing those who took the word of God seriously. I have no doubt they called them 'bibliolaters' and all sorts of other names like that. 'Fundamentalists' — I am sure they had their equivalent terms. They would treat them badly and say: you get out of here. They mocked at those who trembled at God's word, and God said that they will be put to shame.

I remember hearing about one parishioner who started attending the church twice on Sunday, and somebody else said, 'What on earth's got into you that you have to go twice on Sunday? Isn't once enough?' They just could not understand that a person could want to do any more than the minimum as a matter of 'duty'. This is religion to the world: as long as it is in a compartment – fine; but when it becomes too much, when it becomes everything to someone – 'mania'! Here, the rest of the people were criticising those who trembled at God's word, took it seriously, and studied it and thought about it when they went home—and lived it. There is a voice now from the temple, a roar from the temple, the voice of the Lord. His enemies are those who criticised those who tremble at his word, and God will deal with them.

You see what all this is about. It is about trying to limit God, either to a little bit of space, a church or a chapel, or to a little bit of time, giving the right sacrifices and then going away and doing what you want, or to give a little bit of your energy and affection, but not trembling, not getting too serious, not getting too deeply into his word. But it is all or nothing with God – he is everywhere in your life or he is nowhere. He must have what he desires on Monday or he does not accept it on Sunday. God must have those who take his word seriously and who tremble at it if necessary, if that word strikes home sharper than any two-edged sword. If he is not Lord of all, he is not Lord at all. That is the message of vv. 1–6. That is one theme of the prophet Isaiah tied up. God demands all your time, all your space, all your energy.

Now the second message is one to make us happy. Speaking to the people of God, Isaiah winds up the theme of Jerusalem. It is interesting just to take the book of Isaiah and study from beginning to end what he says about one city on earth —Jerusalem, the holy city. You will remember how at the beginning it was prosperous and also a sinful city. He described the women of that city and the men of that city. He said that city would crash down, it would be a ruin, desolate, empty. That was how Isaiah began, but he finishes by describing the city in most glorious terms as a happy mother. He says, 'look to her', and from vv. 7–14 he talks about 'her' and 'she', this wonderful city. Now let us look at this city and see what Isaiah now says about it.

First of all, in vv. 7–9 he describes a remarkably quick birth. My sister had such a birth when she had her fourth daughter. When they started laying the table for breakfast in the hospital ward the baby began to come, and she had it before the breakfast was finished being served in the ward! It was a record for the hospital. Mind you, breakfast was not served very quickly, but nevertheless she always reckons the baby came between the porridge and the toast! There is sheer joy in that, obviously. We are given the picture of a woman who brings forth before going into labour. Something is born in a moment, and Isaiah is using this very dramatic figure to describe what happened to Jerusalem when the Jews returned. I want you to imagine this. One day that city was absolutely desolate; it was burned to the ground; the buildings were knocked down; it was a ruin — and if you had come twenty-four hours later you would have found thousands of people living in it. That happened. They were marching back from Babylon and they reached the city. Literally one day there was nobody living in it and the next day it had thousands of people there. So if you had been passing on a journey and then came back you would have wondered what was happening. Not only did that city spring up in a day, but it became a great place in which to rejoice (see vv. 10–11). Working on a farm I noticed how new-born animals lunge for their first breakfast. Perhaps you have seen a baby at a mother's breast lunging for suckling, eager to get at it, eager to take sustenance, eager to rejoice and to feed on what is provided in the mother's body. So this picture of Jerusalem is now of a mother who suckles her infants, who lunge to take from her what she has to give. People come to draw sustenance from this city.

The next picture is of that city prospering, of the baby being carried on the hip. Have you ever seen a baby being carried on the hip? It is seen often in some countries. This is a wonderful picture. One preacher has said that if the meaning of this section (vv. 12–14) had really been realised by Christians the cult of

Mary would never have arisen. For here is God with all the tender feelings of a mother, and those who seek some human woman's intercession, because they think she will be tender, overlook this verse. God is almost taking the place of Jerusalem as the 'mother' of his people: *"As a mother comforts her child, so will I comfort you . . ."* (Isaiah 66:13a, NIV). When Jerusalem is re-established, when her children are drawing consolation from her, *the hand of the LORD will be made known to his servants . . . .* All these words seem to have a striking reality for us now.

Verse 14 finishes with two groups: God's servants and God's enemies. Who are these two groups? Are his enemies the Gentiles, as many Jews thought? No. We must realise that God's enemies are those who are born among his people but who reject his word. The big thing throughout this chapter from beginning to end is the word of the Father, the word of God, and we shall see it right to the end of the chapter. So with the word 'enemies' we pass once again into a sober, serious subject. This chapter is a sandwich with the jam in the middle — the sweet part is in the centre.

Now we return to the children, and something very serious is said. God will look to those who tremble at his word after the temple is rebuilt. Jerusalem will be restored, but are the children fit to live in it? Here we come back to a word which people do not like in connection with God, the word 'fire'. We need to remember again and again that God is fire. Our God is a consuming fire, says the New Testament, not just the Old. This word 'fire' runs right through the history of Israel. God answered by fire in the Sinai desert. He answered by fire when King David prayed. He answered by fire when Elijah challenged the prophets of Baal. Our God is a God of fire, and when he comes will come as fire. What does fire do? Two things: if a thing is good, fire will refine it; if a thing is bad, fire will destroy it. Gold it makes purer, stubble it destroys — and God will come in fire. From vv. 15–24, the word 'fire' is God's last word through Isaiah. We need to look at this word carefully.

Isaiah realises that the children of Israel are not fit to do what God intended them to do. When God called Abraham he said: In you shall all the families of the earth be blessed. God blessed Abraham so that he could bless them. God told him so that he could tell them. He would give things to Abraham so that he could give things to them. This was Israel's missionary calling from the very beginning. They were not chosen to have privileges for themselves; they were not chosen to be an exclusive group; they were chosen to share, and they never did it. Instead of taking their own religion to the world they took the religions of the world to themselves. As we have seen, instead of purifying the idolatry and paganism around them they adopted it. That is the tragedy of Israel's history. They who were to bring light to those who were in gross darkness themselves, because they did not follow their own God but the gods of others. That is the explanation of v. 17. They even ate mice. How could you stoop to such petty paganism as that? Eating mice was a pagan custom of the Canaanite religions. And they were eating swine's flesh. They knew they should never have done that. They were eating other abominable things. I do not quite know what is included but it must have been pretty horrible not to be named. And when God's fire came it would not purify, it would destroy. But, after that, Israel could then begin to go out and do for others what she ought to have done in the beginning. The survivors of this burning would go to many places. Some would go to Spain, to Tarshish, some would go to North Africa, some would go to the Black Sea, some would go to Greece, so the survivors would spread out. When God had come and burned away and destroyed all this, then the people of God would set out to do two things. First, go and tell the world about the glory of God. Can you think of this – a nation of missionaries setting out? At the moment we are conscious of the Jews coming back in, but imagine a day in which they reverse that to go and tell others about God's glory.

Imagine the moment when they go to declare his glory to the nations who have not heard. There it is at the end of 66:19, *"They will proclaim my glory among the nations"* (NIV). That is purpose number one.

Purpose number two (see v. 20) is to gather the remaining Jews, their brothers, from every corner of the world and bring them back to their own land. They will use every available form of transportation: horses, chariots, wagons, mules and camels. Of course he did not include aeroplanes and cars, because who would have understood that language then? This is his way of saying every form of transport will be used to bring back God's people. A wonderful thing this, a kind of universal mission of God's people. I do not know when or how this will be fulfilled. My imagination finds it difficult to see into the future. But I catch something of the wonder of it, and I see that at last Israel herself will do what she was always meant to do and go out on a universal missionary task.

Finally we come to v. 24. What a powerful verse to end the prophecy. Remember that God prepared the nation for this universal mission by fire, by destroying those who were his enemies, those who rebelled against his word. Their corpses will be left as a testimony to the whole world of what happens when people who have the opportunity of fulfilling God's word rebel against it. It is so terrible that when the Jews read the prophecy of Isaiah they refuse to finish with v. 24. What they do is to read v. 23 again after v. 24 so that they can finish with a happy ending. But God finished with this verse and we need to. It is the negative witness of Israel. If they do not positively witness to God's mercy then negatively they will witness to God's justice. One way or another they will be a witness to the whole world, and that is what they have been. If you want a proof of God's love then study the history of his people. If you want a proof of God's judgement and justice then study the history of Israel. Either way they have been his testimony to the nations. When they have been obedient they have been a standing demonstration of his blessing. When they have been disobedient they have been a standing demonstration of his curse. So the survivors of this fire will witness to his glory and the victims of it will witness to his justice.

These words in v. 24, "*. . . their worm will not die, nor will their fire be quenched . . .*" (NIV) are taken up by the Lord Jesus Christ himself, who applies them to hell. We have had in v. 22 the new heavens and the new earth, and that is a wonderful prospect. But let us never forget that alongside the new heavens and the new earth goes the hell described by Jesus for those who have refused the word of God. Lest you think this is Old Testament stuff may I quote a few verses. *God is just: He will pay back trouble to those who trouble you and give relief to you who are troubled, and to us as well. This will happen when the Lord Jesus is revealed from heaven in blazing fire with his powerful angels. He will punish those who do not know God and do not obey the gospel of our Lord Jesus. They will be punished with everlasting destruction and shut out from the presence of the Lord and from the majesty of his power on the day he comes to be glorified in his holy people and to be marvelled at among all those who have believed. This includes you, because you believed our testimony to you* (2 Thessalonians 1:6–10, NIV). That is Paul writing, and he does not write anything more terrible, or more merciful, than Isaiah.

Of course the New Testament does not end with this word, and it is one of the signs that we have been studying an Old Testament book that it finishes with a verse like 66:24. The Old Testament itself finishes with these words: "*. . . or else I will come and strike the land with a curse*" (Malachi 4:5, NIV). For an Old Testament book to end on this note is not surprising, because the people of God again and again rebelled against him and refused his word. Isaiah had known from the very beginning that this is what would happen. When he was called that day, in the temple which later he saw was not needed, God told him that the people would not listen. We have ended this great prophecy, the preaching of this man over forty years. He was called to be a prophet, he was humble and contrite, and he trembled at God's word. He realised that God is holy.